LOCAL GOVERNANCE IN INDUSTRIAL COUNTRIES

Introduction to the Public Sector Governance and Accountability Series

Anwar Shah, Series Editor

A well-functioning public sector that delivers quality public services consistent with citizen preferences and that fosters private market-led growth while managing fiscal resources prudently is considered critical to the World Bank's mission of poverty alleviation and the achievement of the Millennium Development Goals. This important new series aims to advance those objectives by disseminating conceptual guidance and lessons from practices and by facilitating learning from each others' experiences on ideas and practices that promote *responsive* (by matching public services with citizens' preferences), *responsible* (through efficiency and equity in service provision without undue fiscal and social risk), and *accountable* (to citizens for all actions) public governance in developing countries.

This series represents a response to several independent evaluations in recent years that have argued that development practitioners and policy makers dealing with public sector reforms in developing countries and, indeed, anyone with a concern for effective public governance could benefit from a synthesis of newer perspectives on public sector reforms. This series distills current wisdom and presents tools of analysis for improving the efficiency, equity, and efficacy of the public sector. Leading public policy experts and practitioners have contributed to this series.

The first 13 volumes in this series, listed below, are concerned with public sector accountability for prudent fiscal management; efficiency, equity, and integrity in public service provision; safeguards for the protection of the poor, women, minorities, and other disadvantaged groups; ways of strengthening institutional arrangements for voice, choice, and exit; means of ensuring public financial accountability for integrity and results; methods of evaluating public sector programs, fiscal federalism, and local finances; international practices in local governance; and a framework for responsive and accountable governance.

Fiscal Management

Public Services Delivery

Public Expenditure Analysis

Local Governance in Industrial Countries

Local Governance in Developing Countries

Intergovernmental Fiscal Transfers: Principles and Practice

Participatory Budgeting

Budgeting and Budgetary Institutions

Local Budgeting and Financial Management

Tools for Public Sector Evaluations

Accountability for Performance

Macrofederalism and Local Finances

Citizen-Centered Governance

PUBLIC SECTOR
GOVERNANCE AND
ACCOUNTABILITY SERIES

LOCAL GOVERNANCE IN INDUSTRIAL COUNTRIES

Edited by ANWAR SHAH

THE WORLD BANK
Washington, D.C.

ISBN-10: 0-8213-6328-X
ISBN-13: 978-0-8213-6328-7
eISBN-10: 0-8213-6329-8
eISBN-13: 978-0-8213-6329-4
DOI: 10.1596/978-0-8213-6328-7

Library of Congress Cataloging-in-Publication Data
Local governance in industrial countries / edited by Anwar Shah.
    p. cm. – (Public sector governance and accountability series)
Includes bibliographical references and index.
ISBN-13: 978-0-8213-6328-7
ISBN-10: 0-8213-6328-X
    1. Local finance–OECD countries. 2. Local administration–OECD countries. 3. Finance, Public–OECD countries. 4. Public administration–OECD countries. I. Shah, Anwar. II. Series.

HJ9105.L618 2006
336'.0141722-dc22

                                                                          2005057766

Contents

5   Local Government Organization and Finance: Japan   149

6   Local Government Organization and Finance: New Zealand   189

BOXES

FIGURES

TABLES

Foreword

In Western democracies, systems of checks and balances built into government structures have formed the core of good governance and have helped empower citizens for more than two hundred years. The incentives that motivate public servants and policy makers— the rewards and sanctions linked to results that help shape public sector performance—are rooted in a country's accountability frameworks. Sound public sector management and government spending help determine the course of economic development and social equity, especially for the poor and other disadvantaged groups, such as women and the elderly.

Many developing countries, however, continue to suffer from unsatisfactory and often dysfunctional governance systems including rent-seeking and malfeasance, inappropriate allocation of resources, inefficient revenue systems, and weak delivery of vital public services. Such poor governance leads to unwelcome outcomes for access to public services by the poor and other disadvantaged members of the society, such as women, children, and minorities. In dealing with these concerns, the development assistance community in general, and the World Bank in particular, are continuously striving to learn lessons from practices around the world to achieve a better understanding of what works and what does not work in improving public sector governance, especially with respect to combating corruption and making services work for poor people.

This series advances our knowledge by providing tools and lessons from practices in improving efficiency and equity of public services provision and strengthening institutions of accountability in governance. The series highlights frameworks to create incentive environments and pressures for good governance from within and beyond governments. It outlines institutional mechanisms to empower citizens to demand accountability for results from their governments. It provides practical guidance on managing for results and prudent fiscal management. It outlines approaches to dealing with corruption and malfeasance. It provides conceptual and practical guidance on alternative service delivery frameworks for extending the reach and access of public services. The series also covers safeguards for the protection of the poor, women, minorities, and other disadvantaged groups; ways of strengthening institutional arrangements for voice and exit; methods of evaluating public sector programs; frameworks for responsive and accountable governance; and fiscal federalism and local governance.

The *Public Sector Governance and Accountability Series* will be of interest to public officials, development practitioners, students of development, and those interested in public governance in developing countries.

Frannie A. Léautier
Vice President
World Bank Institute

Preface

Globalization and the information revolution are motivating a large and growing number of countries around the globe to reexamine the roles of various levels of government and their partnership with the private sector and civil society. These reforms typically involve shifting responsibilities to local governments and beyond government providers with the objective of strengthening local governance. This movement has generated a large interest in learning from the history of nations as well as from current practices across countries on local government organization and finance. In this context, the experiences of industrial countries, with their diversity of approaches to local governance, can serve as a useful laboratory for developing countries.

This book develops a comparative institutional framework for responsive, responsible, and accountable governance in developing countries. It provides a synthesis of analytical literature on local governance. It traces the historical evolution of local governance and presents a stylized view of alternative models of local governance practiced in various countries. It also presents case studies for eight industrial countries by leading national scholars. The case studies present an in-depth view of local government organization and finance in each country—Canada, France, Germany, Japan, New Zealand, the Nordic Countries, the United Kingdom, and the United States—and highlight features of interest to developing countries.

This book advances the World Bank Institute agenda on knowledge sharing and learning from cross-country experiences in reforming public governance. It is intended to assist policy makers in both developing and industrial countries in making more-informed choices on strengthening local governance and improving social outcomes for their citizens.

Roumeen Islam
Manager, Poverty Reduction and Economic Management
World Bank Institute

Acknowledgments

This book brings together country briefs on local governance prepared for various World Bank Institute learning programs directed by the editor over the past three years. These learning programs were financed by the governments of Canada, Italy, Japan, the Netherlands, and Switzerland. We are grateful to the Canadian International Development Agency, the government of Italy, the Policy and Human Resources Development program of Japan, the Bank-Netherlands Partnership Program, and the Swiss Agency for International Development for financial support for the development and publication of this book. The editor is also grateful to Sana Shaheen Shah of Washington University at St. Louis, who first proposed the idea of such a compilation during her brief internship at the World Bank.

The book has benefited from contributions to World Bank Institute learning events by senior policy makers from Argentina, Australia, Brazil, Canada, Chile, China, India, Indonesia, Kazakhstan, the Kyrgyz Republic, Mexico, Pakistan, Poland, Russia, South Africa, Switzerland, Thailand, and the United States.

The editor is grateful to the leading scholars who contributed chapters and to the reviewers who provided comments. Sandra Gain, Mike Lombardo, Theresa Thompson, and Jan Werner helped during various stages of preparation of this book and provided comments and contributed summaries of individual chapters. Maria Lourdes Penaflor Gosiengfiao provided excellent support for this project.

Contributors

BRIAN DOLLERY is professor of economics and director of the Centre for Local Government at the University of New England, New South Wales, Australia. He has coedited and coauthored a number of books on local government, including *Australian Local Government: Reform and Renewal* (1997), *The Political Economy of Local Government* (2001), *Reshaping Australian Local Government* (2003), and *Australian Local Government Economics* (forthcoming).

DAVID KING is professor of public economics at the University of Stirling in Scotland. He has worked in the field of local government and its finance for many years, and he has written extensively on the subject. His 1984 book *Fiscal Tiers* is one of the defining texts in the field. On two occasions, he has spent a year away from academia advising the U.K. government. He has also advised governments and officials in about 20 other countries, often in the capacity of consultant for the Council of Europe, the Organisation for Economic Co-operation and Development, or the World Bank. His current research is chiefly concerned with a comparison of the macroeconomic performance of centralized and decentralized countries, with a study of needs assessment, and with the application of insights of fiscal federalism to contrast the welfare gains from centralized and decentralized legislation.

JØRGEN LOTZ is an economist graduated from the University of Copenhagen, and he has taught public finance at the economic institute there. He now works as an adviser in the Danish Ministry of Finance. He has chaired the Council of Europe group of experts on local government finances and the Organisation for Economic

Co-operation and Development Working Party 2 on tax policy and statistics. He has worked in the Fiscal Affairs Department of the International Monetary Fund. He has since then served as deputy permanent secretary in the Danish Ministry of Interior, Ministry of Health, and Ministry of Finance.

MELVILLE L. MCMILLAN is a professor in the Department of Economics and a fellow of the Institute of Public Economics at the University of Alberta, Canada. He served as chair of the department from 1987 to 1997. His BA and MSc are from the University of Alberta, and his PhD is from Cornell University. He was on the faculty of the University of Wisconsin at Madison before joining the University of Alberta in 1975. McMillan's research and teaching interests are in public economics and, in particular, urban and local economics, fiscal federalism, and the demand for and supply of public goods and services. These interests were the focus of his research while he was on leave at the Australian National University, Canberra, and the University of York, England. He publishes in these areas and provides policy advice to governments and agencies. McMillan just completed a term on the Editorial Board of the *Canadian Tax Journal.*

NOBUKI MOCHIDA holds a PhD in economics from the University of Tokyo and is currently a professor in the Graduate School of Economics at the University of Tokyo. He was a consultant at the Economics Development Institute of the World Bank. He has also served as an associate professor at the University of Tokyo (1992–95), Tokyo Metropolitan University (1987–92), and Okayama University (1984–87). His major fields of interest are public finance and intergovernmental fiscal relations, and he has written numerous articles in those areas.

RÉMY PRUD'HOMME studied business administration and economics at the University of Paris and Harvard University. He has been a professor of economics at the University of Phnom-Penh, University of Lille, and University of Paris XII (since 1977), where he is now professor emeritus. He was also a visiting professor at the Massachusetts Institute of Technology (1982–83, 1988–89, 1998, 2002). For several years, he worked with the Organisation for Economic Co-operation and Development as deputy director of the Environment Directorate. His main interests are in local public finance, transportation policies, urban and regional policies, and environmental policies. He has been a frequent consultant to a number of governments and international organizations, particularly the World Bank, where he was invited as a visiting research scholar, but also the European Union, the Organisation for

Economic Co-operation and Development, and the Inter-American Development Bank. He served on the boards of the International Institute of Public Finance and the French Economic Association. He has written a number of scholarly books and papers and has contributed about 100 articles to *Le Monde* and *Le Figaro*, the two leading French dailies.

LARRY SCHROEDER is professor of public administration at the Maxwell School of Syracuse University, New York, and a public finance economist whose primary interest is in state and local public finance and financial management. He has conducted research on a variety of state and local government fiscal issues both in the United States and abroad, particularly in developing and transition economies. The research focuses on problems associated with financing the construction and maintenance of public infrastructure in those environments, as well as the broader issues of decentralization, intergovernmental fiscal relations, and effects of institutional arrangements on the provision of public services. He is the coauthor of several books and has written a large number of articles addressing those subjects. Schroeder has consulted with and led policy research projects in numerous countries, especially in South and Southeast Asia but also in Africa and Eastern Europe.

ANWAR SHAH is lead economist and program leader for public sector governance at the World Bank Institute, Washington, D.C. He is also a fellow of the Institute for Public Economics, Alberta, Canada. He has previously served the Canadian Ministry of Finance in Ottawa and the government of the province of Alberta. He has written extensively on public and environmental economics issues and has published books and articles dealing with governance, global environment, fiscal federalism, and fiscal management issues. He has also lectured at leading educational institutions around the globe.

JAN WERNER holds a PhD in economics from the Johann Wolfgang Goethe University in Frankfurt and is lead economist at the Institute of Local Public Finance in Germany. He has previously worked for the European Parliament in Strasbourg, France, and the Lower House of German Parliament in Berlin. In 2005, he was a visiting economist at the Governing Board of the Indirect Tax Authority in Sarajevo, Bosnia and Herzegovina, and was a guest professor at the Université Lumière de Lyon 2 in Lyon, France. Moreover, he was a part-time lecturer at the European Academy for Financial Planning in Bad Homburg, Germany. His research concentrates on local public finance, intergovernmental fiscal relations, subnational regional economics, and political economics.

Abbreviations and Acronyms

ACIR	Advisory Commission on Intergovernmental Relations
BDI	Bundesverband der Deutschen Industrie (Federal Association of German Industry)
BMF	Bundesministerium der Finanzen (Ministry of Finance, Germany)
CIT	corporate income tax
DGD	*dotation globale de decentralization* (decentralization grants)
DGE	*dotation globale d'équipement* (investment grants)
DGF	*dotation globale de fonctionnement* (current expenditure block grants)
EMU	European Monetary Union
EU	European Union
FOCJ	functional, overlapping, and competing jurisdictions
FSS	formula spending share
FCTVA	*fonds de compensation pour la taxe sur la valeur ajoutée*r (value added tax compensation grants)
FY	fiscal year
GDP	gross domestic product
GNP	gross national product
GST	goods and services tax
MIC	Ministry of Internal Affairs and Communications (Japan)
MOF	ministry of finance
MOHA	Ministry of Home Affairs (Japan)
MOI	ministry of interior
NIE	new institutional economics

NPM	new public management
NZBR	New Zealand Business Roundtable
OECD	Organisation for Economic Co-operation and Development
PDI	personal disposable income
PFI	Private Finance Initiative
PILT	payment in lieu of taxes
PIT	personal income tax
RSG	revenue support grant
SNCF	Société Nationale des Chemins de Fer (French national railway agency)
TIF	tax increment financing
TLA	territorial local authority
VAT	value added tax
VCI	Verband der Chemischen Industrie (German Association of Chemical Industry)

A Comparative Institutional Framework for Responsive, Responsible, and Accountable Local Governance

ANWAR SHAH

For forms of government let fools contest;
Whate'er is best administer'd is best.

Alexander Pope

Introduction: Local Government and Local Governance

Local government refers to specific institutions or entities created by national constitutions (Brazil, Denmark, France, India, Italy, Japan, Sweden), by state constitutions (Australia, the United States), by ordinary legislation of a higher level of central government (New Zealand, the United Kingdom, most countries), by provincial or state legislation (Canada, Pakistan), or by executive order (China) to deliver a range of specified services to a relatively small geographically delineated area. *Local governance* is a broader concept and is defined as the formulation and execution of collective action at the local level. Thus, it encompasses the direct and indirect roles of formal institutions of local government and government hierarchies, as well as the roles of informal norms, networks, community organizations, and neighborhood associations in pursuing collective action by defining the framework for citizen-citizen and citizen-state interactions, collective decision making, and delivery of local public services.

Local governance, therefore, includes the diverse objectives of vibrant, living, working, and environmentally preserved self-governing communities. Good local governance is not just about providing a range of local services but also about preserving the life and liberty of local residents; creating space for democratic participation and civic dialogue; supporting market-led, environmentally sustainable local development; and facilitating outcomes that enrich the quality of life of local residents.

Although the concept of local governance is as old as the history of humanity, only recently has it entered the broad discourse in the academic and practice literature. Globalization and the information revolution are forcing a reexamination of citizen-state relations and roles and relationships of various orders of government with entities beyond government—and thereby an enhanced focus on local governance. The concept, however, has yet to be embraced fully by the literature on development economics, because of the long-standing tradition in the development assistance community of focusing on either local governments or community organizations while neglecting the overall institutional environment that facilitates or retards interconnectivity, cooperation, or competition among organizations, groups, norms, and networks that serve the public interest at the local level.

Several writers (Bailey 1999; Dollery and Wallis 2001; Rhodes 1997; Stoker 1999) have recently argued that the presence of a vast network of entities beyond government that are engaged in local services delivery or quality of life issues makes it unrealistic to treat local government as a single entity (see also Goss 2001). Analytical recognition of this broader concept of local governance is critical to developing a framework for local governance that is responsive (doing the right things—delivering services that are consistent with citizens' preferences or are citizen focused); responsible (doing the right thing the right way, or working better but costing less and benchmarking with the best); and accountable (to citizens, through a rights-based approach). Such analysis is important because the role of local government in such a setting contrasts sharply with its traditional role.

This chapter traces the evolution and analytical underpinnings of local governance as background to a better understanding of the case studies of industrial countries in this book. The next section outlines analytical approaches to local governance that can be helpful in understanding the role of governments and comparing and contrasting institutional arrangements. It further develops a model of local governance that integrates various strands of this literature. This model has important implications for evaluating and reforming local governance in both industrial and developing countries. The third section presents stylized models and institutions of local governance as practiced in different parts of the world during past centuries. It compares and contrasts the ancient Indian and Chinese systems of local governance with Nordic, southern European, North American, and Australian models. The last section provides a comparative overview of local government organization and finance in selected industrial countries as an introduction to the in-depth treatment of these countries in the rest of the book.

The Theory: Conceptual Perspectives on Local Governance and Central-Local Relations

Several accepted theories provide a strong rationale for decentralized decision making and a strong role for local governments on the grounds of efficiency, accountability, manageability, and autonomy.

- *Stigler's menu.* Stigler (1957) identifies two principles of jurisdictional design:
  - The closer a representative government is to the people, the better it works.
  - People should have the right to vote for the kind and amount of public services they want.

  These principles suggest that decision making should occur at the lowest level of government consistent with the goal of allocative efficiency. Thus, the optimal size of a jurisdiction varies with specific instances of economies of scale and benefit-cost spillovers.
- *The principle of fiscal equivalency.* A related idea on the design of jurisdictions has emerged from the public choice literature. Olson (1969) argues that if a political jurisdiction and benefit area overlap, the free-rider problem is overcome and the marginal benefit equals the marginal cost of production, thereby ensuring optimal provision of public services. Equating the political jurisdiction with the benefit area is called the *principle of fiscal equivalency* and requires a separate jurisdiction for each public service.
- *The correspondence principle.* A related concept is proposed by Oates (1972): the jurisdiction that determines the level of provision of each

public good should include precisely the set of individuals who consume the good. This principle generally requires a large number of overlapping jurisdictions. Frey and Eichenberger (1995, 1996, 1999) have extended this idea to define the concept of functional, overlapping, and competing jurisdictions (FOCJ). They argue that jurisdictions could be organized along functional lines while overlapping geographically, and that individuals and communities could be free to choose among competing jurisdictions. Individuals and communities express their preferences directly through initiatives and referenda. The jurisdictions have authority over their members and the power to raise taxes to fulfill their tasks. The school communities of the Swiss canton of Zurich and special districts in North America follow the FOCJ concept.

■ *The decentralization theorem.* According to this theorem, which was advanced by Oates, "each public service should be provided by the jurisdiction having control over the minimum geographic area that would internalize benefits and costs of such provision" (Oates 1972, p. 55), because

— local governments understand the concerns of local residents;
— local decision making is responsive to the people for whom the services are intended, thus encouraging fiscal responsibility and efficiency, especially if financing of services is also decentralized;
— unnecessary layers of jurisdiction are eliminated;
— interjurisdictional competition and innovation are enhanced.

An ideal decentralized system ensures a level and combination of public services consistent with voters' preferences while providing incentives for the efficient provision of such services. Some degree of central control or compensatory grants may be warranted in the provision of services when spatial externalities, economies of scale, and administrative and compliance costs are taken into consideration. The practical implications of this theorem, again, require a large number of overlapping jurisdictions.

■ *The subsidiarity principle.* According to this principle, taxing, spending, and regulatory functions should be exercised by lower levels of government unless a convincing case can be made for assigning them to higher levels of government. This principle evolved from the social teaching of the Roman Catholic Church and was first proposed by Pope Leo XIII in 1891. Subsequently, Pope Pius XI highlighted the principle of subsidiarity as a third way between dictatorship and a laissez-faire approach to governance. The Maastricht Treaty adopted it as a guiding principle for the assignment of responsibilities among members of the European Union (EU). This principle is the polar opposite of the *residuality principle* typically applied in a unitary country, where local governments are assigned functions that the central government is unwilling or thinks it is unable to perform.

Implementation Mechanisms

Achieving the optimal number and size of local jurisdictions requires the operation of community formation processes and the redrawing of jurisdictional boundaries.

- *Voting with feet.* According to Tiebout (1956), people consider tax costs and the public services menu offered by a jurisdiction in deciding where to live. Thus, voting with feet leads to the formation of jurisdictions, creating a market analog for public service provision. Oates (1969) argued that if people vote with their feet, fiscal differentials across communities are capitalized into residential property values. This conclusion has been refuted by formal tests of allocative efficiency proposed by Brueckner (1982) and Shah (1988, 1989, 1992). Both tests suggest that optimal provision of public services is not ensured by voting with feet alone but depends also on rational voting behavior.
- *Voting by ballot.* This line of research suggests that collective decision making may not ensure maximization of the electorate's welfare, because citizens and their governmental agents can have different goals.
- *Voluntary associations.* Buchanan (1965) postulates that the provision of public services through voluntary associations of people (clubs) ensures the formation of jurisdictions consistent with the optimal provision of public services.
- *Jurisdictional redesign.* An important process for community formation in modern societies is redrawing the boundaries of existing jurisdictions to create special or multipurpose jurisdictions.

Roles and Responsibilities of Local Governments: Analytical Underpinnings

There are five perspectives on models of government and the roles and responsibilities of local government: (a) traditional fiscal federalism, (b) new public management (NPM), (c) public choice, (d) new institutional economics (NIE), and (e) network forms of local governance. The federalism and the NPM perspectives are concerned primarily with market failures and how to deliver public goods efficiently and equitably. The public choice and NIE perspectives are concerned with government failures. The network forms of governance perspective is concerned with institutional arrangements to overcome both market and government failures.

Local government as a handmaiden of a higher government order: Traditional fiscal federalism perspectives

The fiscal federalism approach treats local government as a subordinate tier in a multitiered system and outlines principles for defining the roles and responsibilities of orders of government (see Shah 1994 for such a framework for the design of fiscal constitutions). Hence, one sees that in most federations, as in the United States and in Canada, local governments are extensions of state governments (*dual federalism*). In a few isolated instances, as in Brazil, they are equal partners with higher-level governments (*cooperative federalism*), and in an exceptional case, Switzerland, they are the main source of sovereignty and have greater constitutional significance than the federal government. Thus, depending on the constitutional and legal status of local governments, state governments in federal countries assume varying degrees of oversight of the provision of local public services. In a unitary state, subnational governments act on behalf of the central government. Therefore, a useful set of guidelines for the assignment of responsibilities for local public services in a unitary state would be the following:

- Policy development and standards of service and performance are determined at the national level.
- Implementation oversight is carried out at the state or provincial level.
- Services are provided by the local or metropolitan/regional governments.

In all countries, the production of services can be public or private, at the discretion of local or regional governments. Responsibilities for public services other than such purely local ones as fire protection could be shared, using these guidelines. The assignment of public services to local or regional governments can be based on considerations such as economies of scale, economies of scope (appropriate bundling of local public services to improve efficiency through information and coordination economies and enhanced accountability through voter participation and cost recovery) and cost-benefit spillovers, proximity to beneficiaries, consumer preferences, and budgetary choices about the composition of spending. The particular level of government to which a service is assigned determines the public or private production of the service in accordance with considerations of efficiency and equity.

In industrial countries, special-purpose agencies or bodies deliver a wide range of metropolitan and regional public services, including education, health, planning, recreation, and environmental protection. Such bodies can include library boards, transit and police commissions, and utilities providing water, gas, and electricity. These agencies deal with public services whose delivery areas transcend political jurisdictions and are better financed by loans, user charges, and earmarked benefit taxes, such as a supplementary mill rate on a property tax base to finance local school boards. If kept to a minimum, such agencies help fully exploit economies of scale in the delivery of services where political boundaries are not consistent with service areas. A proliferation of these agencies can undermine accountability and budgetary flexibility at local levels. Accountability and responsiveness to voters are weakened if members of special-purpose bodies are appointed rather than elected. Budgetary flexibility is diminished if a majority of local expenditures fall outside the control of local councils.

Table 1.1 presents a matrix for and a subjective assessment of how various allocative criteria favor local or metropolitan assignment and whether public or private production is favored for efficiency or equity. The criteria and the assessment presented in this table are arbitrary; practical and institutional considerations should be applied to this analysis, and the reader may well reach different conclusions using the same criteria.

Private sector participation can also take a variety of forms, including contracting through competitive biddings, franchise operations (local government acting as a regulatory agency), grants (usually for recreational and cultural activities), vouchers (redeemable by local government to private providers), volunteers (mostly in fire stations and hospitals), community self-help activities (for crime prevention), and private nonprofit organizations for social services. Thus, a mix of delivery systems is appropriate for local public services. In most developing countries, the financial capacities of local governments are quite limited. Fostering private sector participation in the delivery of local public services thus assumes greater significance. Such participation enhances accountability and choice in the local public sector. Assigning responsibility for the provision of service to a specific level of government does not imply that government should be directly engaged in its production. Limited empirical evidence suggests that private production of some services promotes efficiency and equity.

The fiscal federalism perspectives presented above are helpful, but in practice they have resulted in some major difficulties—especially in developing

TABLE 1.1   Assignment of Local Public Services to Municipal and Regional or Metropolitan Governments

Public service	Allocation criteria for provision							Allocation criteria for public vs. private production		
	Economies of scale	Economies of scope	Benefit-cost spillover	Political proximity	Consumer sovereignty	Economic evaluation of sectoral choices	Composite	Efficiency	Equity	Composite
Firefighting	L	L	L	L	L	M	L	P	G	P
Police protection	L	L	L	L	L	M	L	P	G	G
Refuse collection	L	L	L	L	L	M	L	P	P	P
Neighborhood parks	L	L	L	L	L	M	L	P	G	G
Street maintenance	L	L	L	L	L	M	L	P	P	P
Traffic management	L	M	L	L	L	M	L	P	P	P
Local transit service	L	M	L	L	L	M	L	P	P	P
Local libraries	L	L	L	L	L	M	L	G	G	G
Primary education	L	L	M	M	M	M	M	P	G	P,G
Secondary education	L	L	M	M	L	M	M	P	G	P,G
Public transportation	M	M	M	L,M	M	M	M	P,G	G	P,G
Water supply	M	M	M	L,M	M	M	M	P	G	P,G
Sewage disposal	M	M	M	M	M	M	M	P,G	P,G	P,G
Refuse disposal	M	M	M	M	M	M	M	P	P	P
Public health	M	M	M	M	M	M	M	G	G	G
Hospitals	M	M	M	M	M	M	M	P,G	G	P,G
Electric power	M	M	M	M	M	M	M	P	P	P
Air and water pollution	M	M	M	M	M	M	M	G	G	G
Special police	M	M	M	M	M	M	M	G	P	G
Regional parks	M	M	M	L,M	M	M	M	G	G	G
Regional planning	M	M	M	L,M	M	M	M	G	G	G

Source: Shah 1994.
Note: L = local government, M = regional or metropolitan government, P = private sector, and G = public sector.

countries—because the practice seems to emphasize fiscal federalism's structures and processes as ends rather than as means to an end. These structures and processes were designed as a response to market failures and heterogeneous preferences with little recognition of government failures or the role of entities beyond government. The NPM and the NIE literature (synthesized in the following paragraphs) sheds further light on the origins of these difficulties. This literature highlights the sources of government failures and their implications for the role of local government.

Local government as an independent facilitator of creating public value: New public management perspectives

Two interrelated criteria have emerged from the NPM literature in recent years determining, first, what local governments should do and, second, how they should do it better.

In discussing the first criterion, the literature assumes that citizens are the principals but have multiple roles as governors (owners-authorizers, voters, taxpayers, community members); activists-producers (providers of services, coproducers, self-helpers obliging others to act); and consumers (clients and beneficiaries) (see Moore 1999). In this context, significant emphasis is placed on the government as an agent of the people to serve the public interest and create public value. Moore (1996) defines *public value* as measurable improvements in social outcomes or quality of life. This concept is directly relevant to local and municipal services for which it is feasible to measure such improvements and have some sense of attribution. The concept is useful in evaluating conflicting and perplexing choices in the use of local resources. The concept is also helpful in defining the role of government, especially local governments. It frames the debate between those who argue that the public sector crowds out private sector investments and those who see the public sector as creating an enabling environment for the private sector to succeed, in addition to providing basic municipal and social services.

Moore has argued that, rather than diverting resources from the private sector, local governments use some of the resources that come as free goods—namely, resources of consent, goodwill, Good Samaritan values, community spirit, compliance, and collective public action. This argument suggests that the role of public managers in local governments is to tap these free resources and push the frontiers of improved social outcomes beyond what may be possible with meager local revenues. Thus, public managers create value by mobilizing and facilitating a network of providers beyond local government. Democratic accountability ensures that managerial choices about creating public value are based on broader consensus by local residents (see Goss 2001). Thus, the local public sector continuously strives to respect citizen preferences and to be accountable to them. This environment focused on creating public value encourages innovation and experimentation, bounded by the risk tolerance of a median voter in each community.

The main current of the NPM literature is concerned not with what to do but with how to do it better. It argues for an incentive environment in which managers are given flexibility in the use of resources but held accountable for results. Top-down controls are thus replaced by a bottom-up focus on results. Two NPM models have been implemented in recent years. The first model is focused on making managers manage. In New Zealand, this goal is accomplished through new contractualism, whereby public managers are bound by formal contracts for service delivery but have flexibility in resource allocation and choice of public or private providers. Malaysia attempts to achieve the same through client charters, under which public managers are evaluated for their attainment of specified service standards (Shah 2005).

The second model creates incentives to let managers manage. This is done through the new managerialism approach, as used in Australia and the United States, whereby government performance in service delivery and social outcomes is monitored, but there are no formal contracts, and accountability is guided by informal agreements. In China and the United Kingdom, autonomous agency models are used for performance accountability. Canada uses an alternate service delivery framework: public managers are encouraged to facilitate a network of service providers and to use benchmarking to achieve the most effective use of public monies. The emerging focus on client orientation and results-based accountability is encouraging local governments to innovate in many parts of the world (see Caulfield 2003).

Local government as an institution to advance self-interest: The public choice approach

Bailey (1999) has conceptualized four models of local government:

- A local government that assumes it knows best and acts to maximize the welfare of its residents conforms to the benevolent despot model.
- A local government that provides services consistent with local residents' willingness to pay conforms to the fiscal exchange model.
- A local government that focuses on public service provision to advance social objectives conforms to the fiscal transfer model.

■ If a local government is captured by self-interested bureaucrats and politicians, it conforms to the leviathan model, which is consistent with the public choice perspectives.

In the same tradition, Albert Breton (1995) provides a comprehensive typology of models of government. He distinguishes two broad types of government. The first embodies the doctrine of the common good, and the second acts to preserve the self-interest of the governing elites. The second type can assume either a monolithic or a composite structure. In a monolithic structure, local government is subject to capture by bureaucrats or interest groups. Also, local government may maximize economic rents for dominant interest groups (as in the leviathan model) or may advance compulsion or coercion. If the self-interest model assumes a composite structure, it may encourage Tiebout-type competition among local governments.

The public choice literature endorses the self-interest doctrine of government and argues that various stakeholders involved in policy formulation and implementation are expected to use opportunities and resources to advance their self-interest. This view has important implications for the design of local government institutions. For local governments to serve the interests of people, they must have complete local autonomy in taxing and spending and they must be subject to competition within and beyond government. In the absence of these prerequisites, local governments will be inefficient and unresponsive to citizen preferences (see Boyne 1998). Bailey (1999) advocates strengthening exit and voice mechanisms in local governance to overcome government failures associated with the self-interest doctrine of public choice. He suggests that easing supply-side constraints for public services through wider competition will enhance choice and promote exit options and that direct democracy provisions will strengthen voice (see also Dollery and Wallis 2001). The NIE approach discussed below draws on the implications of opportunistic behavior by government agents for the transaction costs to citizens as principals.

The government as a runaway train: NIE concerns with the institutions of public governance

The NIE provides a framework for analyzing fiscal systems and local empowerment and for comparing mechanisms for local governance. This framework is helpful in designing multiple orders of government and in clarifying local government responsibilities in a broader framework of local governance. According to the NIE framework, various orders of governments (as agents) are created to serve the interests of the citizens as principals. The jurisdictional design should ensure that these agents serve the public interest while minimizing transaction costs for the principals.

The existing institutional framework does not permit such optimization, because the principals have bounded rationality; that is, they make the best choices on the basis of the information at hand but are ill informed about government operations. Enlarging the sphere of their knowledge entails high transaction costs, which citizens are not willing to incur. Those costs include participation and monitoring costs, legislative costs, executive decision-making costs, agency costs or costs incurred to induce compliance by agents with the compact, and uncertainty costs associated with unstable political regimes (see Horn 1997; Shah 2005). Agents (various orders of governments) are better informed about government operations than principals are, but they have an incentive to withhold information and to indulge in opportunistic behaviors or "self-interest seeking with guile" (Williamson 1985, 7). Thus, the principals have only incomplete contracts with their agents. Such an environment fosters commitment problems because the agents may not follow the compact.

The situation is further complicated by three factors—weak or extant countervailing institutions, path dependency, and the interdependency of various actions. Countervailing institutions such as the judiciary, police, parliament, and citizen activist groups are usually weak and unable to restrain rent-seeking by politicians and bureaucrats. Historical and cultural factors and mental models by which people see little benefits and the high costs of activism prevent corrective action. Further empowering local councils to take action on behalf of citizens often leads to loss of agency between voters and councils, because council members may interfere in executive decision making or may get co-opted in such operations while shirking their legislative responsibilities. The NIE framework stresses the need to use various elements of transaction costs in designing jurisdictions for various services and in evaluating choices between competing governance mechanisms.

Local government as a facilitator of network forms of local governance

The NIE provides an evaluation framework for alternative forms and mechanisms of local governance. It specifically provides guidance in dealing with government failures in a hierarchical form of public governance. The framework is also suitable for examining local government involvement in a partnership of multiple organizations. Dollery and Wallis (2001) extend the NIE approach to these issues. They argue that a structure of resource dependency vitiates against collective action in the interest of the common good because of the tragedy of commons associated with common pool resources.

This scenario results in failures in horizontal coordination in a multiorganization partnership.

One possible solution is to introduce a market mechanism of governance whereby a contract management agency enters into binding contracts with all partners. However, this solution is unworkable because the potential number of contingencies may simply be too large to be covered by such contracts. A second approach to overcome horizontal coordination, the so-called hierarchical mechanism of governance, relies on institutional arrangements to clarify roles and responsibilities and to establish mechanisms for consultation, cooperation, and coordination, as is done in some federal systems. Such institutional arrangements entail high transaction costs and are subject to a high degree of failure attributable to the conflicting interests of partners.

In view of the high transaction costs and perceived infeasibility of market and hierarchical mechanisms of governance for partnerships of multiple organizations, a network mechanism of governance has been advanced as a possible mode of governance for such partnerships—the kind to be managed by local governments. The network form of governance relies on trust, loyalty, and reciprocity between partners with no formal institutional safeguards. Networks formed on the basis of shared interests (interest-based networks) can provide a stable form of governance if membership is limited to partners that can make significant resource contributions and if there is a balance of powers among members. Members of such networks interact frequently and see cooperation in one area as contingent on cooperation in other areas. Repeated interaction among members builds trust. Hope-based networks are built on the shared sentiments and emotions of members. Members have shared beliefs in the worth and philosophy of the network goals and have the passion and commitment to achieve those goals. The stability of such networks is highly dependent on the commitment and style of their leadership (Dollery and Wallis 2001, p. 139).

Local government has an opportunity to play a catalytic role in facilitating the roles of both interest-based and hope-based networks in improving social outcomes for local residents. To play such a role, local government must develop a strategic vision of how such partnerships can be formed and sustained. But then the local government would require a new local public management paradigm. Such a paradigm demands local government to separate policy advice from program implementation, assuming a role as a purchaser of public services but not necessarily as a provider of them. Local government may have to outsource services with higher provision costs and subject in-house providers to competitive pressures from outside providers to lower transaction costs for citizens. It also must actively seek the engagement of both interest-based and hope-based networks to supplant local services. It needs to develop the capacity to play a mediating role among various groups.

A synthesis: Toward a framework for responsive, responsible, and accountable local governance

We have reviewed ideas emerging from the literature on political science, economics, public administration, law, federalism, and the NIE with a view to developing an integrated analytical framework for the comparative analysis of local government and local governance institutions.

The dominant concern in this literature is that the incentives and accountability framework faced by various orders of government is not conducive to a focus on service delivery that is consistent with citizen preferences. As a result, corruption, waste, and inefficiencies permeate public governance. Top-down hierarchical controls are ineffective; thus, there is little accountability because citizens are not empowered to hold governments accountable.

Fiscal federalism practices around the world are focused on structures and processes, with little regard for outputs and outcomes. These practices support top-down structures with preeminent federal legislation. The central government is at the apex, exercising direct control and micromanaging the system. Hierarchical controls exercised by various layers of government have an internal rule-based focus with little concern for their mandates. Government competencies are determined on the basis of technical and administrative capacity, with almost no regard for client orientation, bottom-up accountability, and lowering of transaction costs for citizens. Various orders of government indulge in uncooperative zero-sum games for control.

This tug of war leads to large swings in the balance of powers. Shared rule is a source of much confusion and conflict, especially in federal systems. Local governments are typically handmaidens of states or provinces and given straitjacket mandates. They are given only limited home rule in their competencies. In short, local governments in this system of "federalism for the governments, by the governments, and of the governments" get crushed under a regime of intrusive controls by higher levels of governments. Citizens also have limited voice and exit options.

The governance implications of such a system are quite obvious. Various orders of government suffer from agency problems associated with incomplete contracts and undefined property rights, as the assignment of taxing, spending, and regulatory powers remains to be clarified—especially in areas of shared rule. Intergovernmental bargaining leads to high transaction costs for citizens. Universalism and pork-barrel politics result in a tragedy of commons, as various orders of government compete to claim a higher share of common pool resources. Under this system of governance, citizens are treated as agents rather than as principals.

On how to turn this trend around and make governments responsive and accountable to citizens, the dominant themes emphasized in the literature are the subsidiarity principle, the principle of fiscal equivalency, the creation of public value, results-based accountability, and the minimization of transaction costs for citizens, as discussed earlier. These themes are useful but should be integrated into a broader framework of citizen-centered governance, to create an incentive environment in the public sector that is compatible with a public sector focus on service delivery and bottom-up accountability. Such integration is expected to deal with the commitment problem in various levels of government by empowering citizens and by limiting their agents' ability to indulge in opportunistic behavior.

Citizen-centered local governance

Reforming the institutions of local governance requires agreement on basic principles. Three basic principles are advanced to initiate such a discussion:

- *Responsive governance.* This principle aims for governments to do the right things—that is, to deliver services consistent with citizen preferences.
- *Responsible governance.* The government should also do it right—that is, manage its fiscal resources prudently. It should earn the trust of residents by working better and costing less and by managing fiscal and social risks for the community. It should strive to improve the quality and quantity of and access to public services. To do so, it needs to benchmark its performance with the best-performing local government.
- *Accountable governance.* A local government should be accountable to its electorate. It should adhere to appropriate safeguards to ensure that it serves the public interest with integrity. Legal and institutional reforms may be needed to enable local governments to deal with accountability between elections—reforms such as a citizen's charter and a provision for recall of public officials.

A framework of local governance that embodies these principles is called *citizen-centered governance* (see Andrews and Shah 2005). The distinguishing features of citizen-centered governance are the following:

■ Citizen empowerment through a rights-based approach (direct democracy provisions, citizens' charter)
■ Bottom-up accountability for results
■ Evaluation of government performance as the facilitator of a network of providers by citizens as governors, taxpayers, and consumers of public services.

The framework emphasizes reforms that strengthen the role of citizens as the principals and create incentives for government agents to comply with their mandates (see table 1.2).

The commitment problem may be mitigated by creating citizen-centered local governance—by having direct democracy provisions, introducing governing for results in government operations, and reforming the structure of governance, thus shifting decision making closer to the people. Direct democracy provisions require referenda on major issues and large projects and citizens having the right to veto any legislation or government program. A governing for results framework requires government accountability to citizens for its service delivery performance. Hence, citizens have a charter defining their basic rights as well as rights of access to specific standards of public services. Output-based intergovernmental transfers strengthen compliance with such standards and strengthen accountability and citizen empowerment (Shah 2006).

Implications for division of powers within nations: Role reversals for central and local governments

The framework described above has important implications for reforming the structure of government. Top-down mandates on local governance will need to be replaced by bottom-up compacts. Furthermore, the role of local government must be expanded to serve as a catalyst for the formulation, development, and operation of a network of both government providers and entities beyond government. Local government's traditionally acknowledged technical capacity becomes less relevant in this framework. More important are its institutional strengths as a purchaser of services and as a facilitator of alliances, partnerships, associations, clubs, and networks for developing social capital and improving social outcomes. Two distinct options are possible in this regard, and both imply a pivotal role for local governments in the intergovernmental system. The options are (a) local government as the primary agent, subcontracting to local, state, and federal or central government authorities and engaging networks and entities beyond government, and (b) local, state, and national governments as independent agents.

TABLE 1.2 Key Elements of Citizen-Centered Governance

Responsive governance	Responsible governance	Accountable governance
Has subsidiarity and home rule	Follows due process:	Lets the sunshine in:
Has direct democracy provisions	■ The principle of *ultra vires* or general competence or community governance	■ Local government bylaw on citizens' right to know
Has budget priorities consistent with citizens' preferences	■ The procedure bylaw	■ Budgetary proposals and annual performance reports posted on the Internet
Specifies and meets standards and access to local services	■ Local master plans and budgets	■ All decisions, including the costs of concessions, posted on the Internet
Improves social outcomes	■ Zoning bylaws and regulations	■ Value for money performance audits by independent think-tanks
Offers security of life and property	■ Funded mandates	■ Open information and public assessment
Offers shelter and food for all	Is fiscally prudent:	Works to strengthen citizen voice and exit:
Has clean air, safe water, and sanitation	■ Operating budget in balance	■ Citizens' charter
Has a noise-free and preserved environment	■ Golden rule for borrowing	■ Service standards
Offers ease of commute and pothole-free roads	■ New capital projects that specify upkeep costs and how debt is to be repaid	■ Requirements for citizens' voice and choice
Has primary school within walking distance	■ Conservative fiscal rules to ensure sustainable debt levels	■ Sunshine rights
Has acceptable fire and ambulance response times	■ Major capital projects that are subject to referenda	■ Sunset clauses on government programs
Has libraries and Internet access	■ Maintenance of positive net worth	
Has park and recreation programs and facilities	■ Commercially audited financial statements	

(continued)

TABLE 1.2 Key Elements of Citizen-Centered Governance (*continued*)

Responsive governance	Responsible governance	Accountable governance
	Earns trust:	■ Equity- and output-based inter-governmental finance
	■ Professionalism and integrity of staff	■ Citizen-oriented performance (output) budgeting
	■ Safeguards against malfeasance	■ Service delivery outputs and costs
	■ Streamlined processes and e-governance	■ Citizens' report card on service delivery performance
	■ Complaints and feedback acted on	■ Budget, contracts, and performance reports defended at open town hall meetings
	■ Honest and fair tax administration	■ All documents subjected to citizen-friendly requirements
	■ Strict compliance with service standards	■ Open processes for contract bids
	■ Citizen-friendly output budgets and service delivery performance reports	■ Mandatory referenda on large projects
	■ Participatory budgeting and planning	■ Steps taken so that at least 50% of eligible voters vote
	Works better and costs less:	■ Citizens' boards to provide scorecard and feedback on service delivery performance
	■ All tasks subjected to alternative service delivery test—that is, competitive provision involving government providers and entities beyond government	■ Provisions for popular initiatives and recall of public officials
	■ Financing that creates incentives for competition and innovation	■ Bylaw on taxpayer rights
	■ Comparative evaluation of service providers	

- Public sector as a purchaser through performance contracts but not necessarily a provider of services
- Managerial flexibility, but accountability for results
- No lifelong or rotating appointments
- Task specialization
- Budgetary allocation and output-based performance contracts
- Activity-based costing
- Charges for capital use
- Accrual accounting
- Benchmarking with the best
- General administration costs subjected to public scrutiny
- Boundaries that balance benefits and costs of scale and scope economies, externalities, and decision making
- Boundaries consistent with fiscal sustainability

Source: Author.

OPTION A: LOCAL GOVERNMENTS AS PRIMARY AGENTS OF CITIZENS. In this role, a local government serves as (a) a purchaser of local services, (b) a facilitator of networks of government providers and entities beyond government, and (c) a gatekeeper and overseer of state and national governments for the shared rule or responsibilities delegated to them. This role represents a fundamental shift in the division of powers from higher to local governments. It has important constitutional implications. Residual functions would reside with local governments. State governments perform intermunicipal services. The national government is assigned redistributive, security, foreign relations, and interstate functions such as harmonization and consensus on a common framework. The Swiss system bears close affinity to this model.

OPTION B: VARIOUS ORDERS OF GOVERNMENT AS INDEPENDENT AGENTS. An alternative framework for establishing the supremacy of the principals is to clarify the responsibilities and functions of various orders as independent agents. This framework limits shared rule. Finance follows function strictly, and fiscal arrangements are periodically reviewed for fine-tuning. Local governments enjoy home rule, with complete tax and expenditure autonomy. The Brazilian fiscal constitution incorporates some features of this model, albeit with significant deviations.

FEASIBILITY OF OPTIONS. Option A is well grounded in the history of modern governments and is most suited for countries with no history of internal or external conflict in recent times. It is already practiced in Switzerland. War, conquest, and security concerns have led to a reversal of the roles of various orders of governments and to a reduction in local government functions in more recent history. Globalization and the information revolution have already brought pressures for much larger and stronger roles for local governments (see Shah 2001). Although a majority of governments have done some tinkering with their fiscal systems, the radical change recommended here is not in the cards anywhere. This is because the unlikelihood of overcoming path dependency—a tall order for existing institutions and vested interests—makes such reform infeasible. Under such circumstances, option B may be more workable, but here the clarity of responsibilities may not be politically feasible. In general, there is unlikely to be political will to undertake such bold reforms. Piecemeal adaptation of this model will nevertheless be forced on most countries by the effects of globalization and by citizen empowerment, facilitated by the information revolution.

The Practice: Alternative Models of Local Governance and Central-Local Relations

Local governance historically predates the emergence of nation-states. In ancient history, tribes and clans established systems of local governance in most of the world. They established their own codes of conduct and ways of raising revenues and delivering services to the tribe or clan. Tribal and clan elders developed consensus on the roles and responsibilities of various members. Some tribes and clans with better organization and skills then sought to enlarge their spheres of influence through conquest and cooperation with other tribes. In this way, the first Chinese dynasty, the Xia, was established (2070 BC to 1600 BC) (see Zheng and Fan 2003).

A similar situation prevailed in ancient India, where in the third millennium BC (about 2500 BC) a rich civilization was established in the Indus Valley (now Pakistan). This advanced civilization placed great emphasis on autonomy in local governance and enshrined a consensus on division of work for various members of the society. This emphasis led to the creation of a class society in which each member had a defined role: upholder of moral values, soldier, farmer, tradesperson, worker. Each community formed its own consensus on community services and how to accomplish them.

Native American tribes in North America and tribes and clans in Western Europe also enjoyed home rule. Subsequent conquests and wars led to the demise of these harmonious systems of self-rule in local governance and to the emergence of rule by central governments all over the world. This development (roughly around 1000 BC in Western Europe) ultimately led to the creation of unique systems of local governance and central-local relations in most countries. Those systems can nevertheless be classified into the following broad categories for analytical purposes.

The Nordic Model

In the 15th century, Denmark, Norway, and Sweden were ruled by a Danish king. Residents in those countries contributed to the king's coffers but were allowed to run local affairs autonomously (see Werner and Shah 2005). In the absence of central intrusion, the seeds for a locally run, client-oriented welfare state were sown. As a result, local governments assumed most functions of the state, while the central government largely assumed a ceremonial role and foreign relations functions. Local governments, therefore, assumed responsibility not only for local service delivery but also for social protection and social welfare functions. Local governments in Nordic countries serve their residents from cradle to grave. They deliver property-oriented as well as people-oriented services.

In modern times, the central governments in Nordic countries have assumed wider regulatory and oversight functions, but the predominance of local government—more than 30 percent of gross domestic product (GDP) in Denmark—and its autonomy are still preserved because of citizen satisfaction with local government performance. The Nordic model emphasizes small local governments (average jurisdiction of fewer than 10,000 inhabitants) that are primarily self-financing. In Denmark and Sweden, nearly 75 percent—and in Norway, 64 percent—of local expenditures are financed from own-source revenues. Personal income taxes (piggybacking on a national base) are the mainstays of local finance (almost 91 percent of tax revenues), and property taxes contribute a pitiful 7 percent of tax revenues.

The Swiss Model

The origins of the Swiss Confederation are traced to the defensive alliance signed by the cantons of Uri, Schwyz, and Unterwalden in 1291. Prior to that event, the Swiss territories were under the control of independent local governments (cantons). This tradition of local government domination continues in the Swiss system today: local governments enjoy autonomy not only in fiscal matters but also in such areas as immigration, citizenship, language, and foreign economic relations.

This tradition of strong local government is further strengthened through direct democracy provisions in the Swiss constitution, including (a) people's initiatives, (b) referenda, and (c) petitions. The people's initiatives empower citizens to seek a decision on an amendment that they want to make to the constitution. A people's initiative may be formulated as a general proposal or as a precisely formulated text whose wording can no longer be changed by parliament or the government. For such an initiative to be considered, the signatures of 100,000 voters must be collected within 18 months. A popular majority and a majority of all cantons are required for the acceptance of such an initiative.

Through the referenda provision, the people are entitled to pronounce their judgments on matters under consideration by the legislature or the executive or matters on which a decision has already been made. In the latter case, the referendum acts as a veto. Federal laws and international treaties are subject to optional referenda, provided that 50,000 citizens so request within 100 days of the publication of the decree. Under the petition provision, all eligible voters can submit a petition to the government and are entitled to receive a reply. Switzerland consists of 26 cantons and 2,842 communes. Each canton has its own constitution, parliament, government, and courts. The communes are handmaidens of the cantons. They perform some delegated tasks such as population registration and civil defense, but they have autonomous competencies in education and social welfare, energy supply, roads, local planning, and local taxation (see Government of Switzerland 2003).

The French Model

In the French model, the primary role of local governments is to allow citizens at the grassroots levels a sense of political participation in decision making at the national level. The system embodies the thinking of Rousseau and Voltaire on rationality and social cohesion and that of Napoleon on a sense of order and an unbroken chain of command. The national government and its agencies represent the apex of this system, with an unbroken chain of command through regional and departmental prefects to chief executives and mayors of communes at the lowest rung of the system. There is a similar chain of command through line and functional ministries. Therefore, the model is sometimes referred to as the dual supervision model of local governance.

The system permits *cumul des mandats* (concurrent political mandates or the holding of multiple offices or positions concurrently) to provide elected leaders at lower echelons with a voice at higher levels of governments. Public service delivery remains the primary responsibility of the national government, and its agencies may be directly involved in the delivery of local services. The average size of local government jurisdiction is small (covering fewer than 10,000 inhabitants), and local governments have a limited range of autonomous service delivery responsibilities. Local governments use a mix of local revenue instruments and rely significantly on central financing. This model, with its focus on strong central command and dual supervision, proved very popular with colonial rulers from France, Portugal, and Spain, as well as with military dictators, and was widely replicated in developing countries (Humes 1991).

The German Model

The German model emphasizes subsidiarity, cooperation, and administrative efficiency. It entrusts policy-making functions to the federal level and service delivery responsibilities to geographically delineated states and local governments, to which it gives a great deal of autonomy in service delivery.

All purely local services are assigned to local governments. The average local government covers 20,000 inhabitants, and local expenditures constitute about 10 percent of GDP. General revenue sharing serves as a major source of local finances.

The British Model

The British model has elements of the French dual supervision model. It emphasizes a stronger role for centrally appointed field officers and sectoral and functional ministries in the provision of local services. Local governments must coordinate their actions with these officials. Local governments are given substantial autonomy in purely local functions, but they can access only a limited range of revenue instruments. Local governments play a dominant role in such property-oriented services as road maintenance, garbage collection, water, and sewerage and a limited role in such people-oriented services as health, education, and social welfare. Property taxes are the mainstay of local governments. Local governments typically derive two-thirds of their revenues from central transfers. They do not have access to personal income taxes. The role of the chief executive is weak, and local councils play a strong role in local decision making. The average local government is large, covering about 120,000 inhabitants, and local expenditures account for about 12 percent of GDP (see McMillan forthcoming). In former British colonies, the role of field officers was strengthened to provide general supervision and control of local governments on behalf of the central colonial government.

The Indian Model

India had one of the oldest traditions of strong self-governance at the local level. In the pre-Moghul period, local government was in operation more extensively in India than anywhere else in the world. Small villages and towns were regulated by custom and community leadership, with authority normally vested in an elders council headed by a *sarpanch* or *numberdar*. The apex institution was the *panchayat*, with responsibilities for law and order, local services, land management, dispute resolution, administration of justice, provision of basic needs, and revenue collection. These institutions enabled each village and town to function harmoniously.

Subsequent wars and conquest led to a weakening of local governance in India. During the Moghul period, panchayats were required to collect central taxes, but local government autonomy was not disturbed (Wajidi 1990). During the British Raj, with its central focus on command and control and little concern for service delivery, the system of local governance received a major setback. Powers were centralized, and loyalty to the British regime was rewarded with land grants, leading to the creation of a class of feudal aristocrats who dominated the local political scene on behalf of the British government. The central government also appointed roving bureaucrats to run local affairs. Since independence in both India and Pakistan, centralized governance has been maintained, while small steps have been taken to strengthen local autonomy. In India, feudal aristocracy was abolished through land reforms, but in Pakistan, such reforms could not be carried out. As a result, in areas of feudal dominance in Pakistan, local self-governance led to capture by elites.

The Chinese Model

This model places strong emphasis on making provincial and local governments an integral and dependent sphere of national government. This is accomplished in two ways: through democratic centralism, which integrates the local people's congress with the national People's Congress through a system of elections, and through dual subordination of local governments, whereby provincial and local governments are accountable to higher-level governments in general, but the functional departments are also accountable to higher-level functional agencies and departments. The personnel functions are also integrated among various orders of government. Because of its integrative nature, the model permits a large and expansive role for provincial and local governments in service delivery. The average local government jurisdiction is very large. Subprovincial local government expenditure constitutes 51.4 percent of consolidated public expenditures. Subprovincial local governments employ 89 percent of the total government workforce. In China, some clearly central functions such as unemployment insurance, social security, and social safety nets are assigned to provincial and local governments. Local autonomy varies directly with the fiscal capacity of a local government, with richer jurisdictions calling their own tunes while poor jurisdictions follow the pied piper of higher-level governments.

The Japanese Model

The local government system, introduced in Meiji Japan in about 1890, had elements of the French and German models. It emphasized centralized control, as in the French model of local governments, through the Ministry of Interior appointing heads of regional governments (governors of prefectures), who controlled local districts and municipalities. The local government simply implemented policies determined by the central government. In the post–World War II period, direct elections of governors, mayors, and councils were introduced. The practice of agency delegation (German model) was retained, and local governments were expected to perform functions mandated by the central government and its agencies. The Ministry of Home Affairs, which had a supportive role for local governments, was introduced in 1960 (see Muramatsu and Iqbal 2001). Income taxes are the mainstay of local government finance, contributing 60 percent of own-source tax revenues, followed by property taxes (about 30 percent) and sales taxes (about 10 percent of total tax revenues).

The North American Model

In the early period of North American history, local communities functioned as *civic republics* (Kincaid 1967) governed by mutual consent of their members. The framers of the U.S. constitution did not recognize local governments. The Civil War led to the centralization of powers in the United States. Subsequently, the formal institutions of local government were created by states. The judiciary further constrained the role of local government through recognition of *Dillon's rule:* local governments may exercise only those powers explicitly granted to them under state legislation. Subsequently, most states have attempted to grant autonomy to local governments in discharging their specified functions through *home rule* provisions (Bowman and Kearney 1990). Local governments in Canada are faced with similar circumstances as those in the United States. Thus, the North American model recognizes local government as a handmaiden of states and provinces but attempts to grant autonomy (home rule) to local governments in their specific areas of responsibility—predominantly delivery of property-oriented services. Local governments perform an intermediate range of functions. The average jurisdiction of local government in the United States is about 10,000 inhabitants and in Canada, about 6,000. Property taxes are the dominant source of local revenues. Local government expenditures constitute about 7 percent of GDP (see McMillan forthcoming).

The Australian Model

The Australian constitution does not recognize local governments. It is left to the states to decide on a system of local governance in their territories.

Most states have assigned a minimal set of functions to local governments, including engineering services (roads, bridges, sidewalks, and drainage); community services (old age care, child care, fire protection); environmental services (waste management and environmental protection); regulatory services (zoning, dwellings, buildings, restaurants, animals); and cultural services (libraries, art galleries, and museums). Local governments raise only 3 percent of national revenues and are responsible for 6 percent of consolidated public sector expenditures. Property taxes (rates) and user charges are the mainstay (about 70 percent) of revenues, and central and state grants finance about 20 percent of local expenditures. Transportation, community amenities, and recreation and culture command two-thirds of local expenditures. New Zealand bears close resemblance to the Australian model.

A Comparative Overview of Local Government Organization and Finance in Industrial Countries

We have already noted the broad diversity in approaches to local governance in industrial countries. This section provides a few key comparative indicators on local government organization and finance in countries of the Organisation for Economic Co-operation and Development (OECD).

Legal Status of Local Governments

The legal status of local government varies across industrial countries, with local government deriving authority from national constitutions in Denmark, France, Germany, the Netherlands, and Sweden; from state constitutions in Australia, Switzerland, and the United States; from national legislation in New Zealand and the United Kingdom; and from provincial legislation in Canada. It is interesting that there is no clear pattern in the autonomy and range of local services provided by local governments deriving their status from national and state constitutions. However, local governments that are created through legislation are significantly weaker.

Relative Importance of Local Governments

The relative importance of local governments in industrial countries is compared using two indicators: share of consolidated public sector expenditures (figure 1.1) and local expenditures as a percentage of GDP (figure 1.2). On both indicators, Nordic countries are the leaders; the

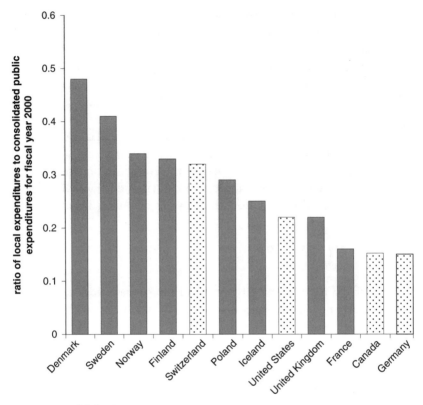

Source: Werner and Shah 2005.
Note: Dotted bars represent federal countries.

FIGURE 1.1 A Comparative Perspective on Local Government Share of Consolidated Public Expenditures, 2000

United Kingdom and United States are in the lower ranges; and Canada, France, and Germany are in the lowest range. Local government in Denmark stands out, claiming about 50 percent of total expenditures, which account for about 30 percent of GDP. Among the industrial countries, New Zealand is an outlier with local expenditures accounting for less than 3 percent of GDP.

Population Size Covered by Local Governments

There are wide variations in the number of municipal governments, with as few as 74 in New Zealand and as many as 35,906 in the United States. Table 1.3 provides the distribution of municipalities by size class for several industrial countries. Similarly, the median size of a municipal government

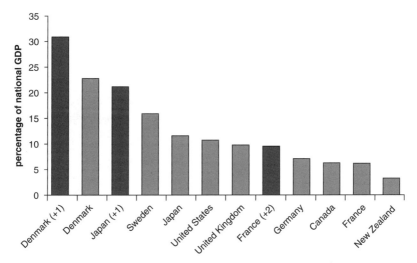

Source: Adapted from Werner forthcoming.
Note: France (+2) includes municipalities, regions, and *départements*; Japan (+1) includes cities and prefectures; Denmark (+1) includes municipalities and counties (*Amtskommuner*).

FIGURE 1.2   Local Expenditures as a Share of National GDP, 2001

jurisdiction in 1998 was smallest in Iceland (1,160 people) and largest in the United Kingdom (about 160,000) (see table 1.4 and Scottish Office 1998). In a large majority of industrial countries, the average municipal government jurisdiction covers fewer than 20,000 people.

Local Spending Responsibilities

There is no uniform model, except that property-oriented services are provided at the local level in almost all countries. In infrastructure, Australian local governments command 27 percent of total expenditures, compared with 62 percent in the United Kingdom and 47 percent and 41 percent in the EU and the OECD, respectively. People-oriented services show more variation. In education, there is no role for local government in Australia, but it takes up more than 60 percent of expenditure share at local levels in Canada, the United Kingdom, and the United States. In the OECD, it averages about 46 percent. In health, local governments have no role in Australia and the United Kingdom but a predominant role in Denmark (about 92 percent); EU and OECD average expenditure shares are 28 percent and 19 percent, respectively. Most industrial countries have significant higher-level intervention in social services and unfunded mandates to local governments in environmental protection.

TABLE 1.3 Size Distribution of Municipal Governments in Industrial Countries According to Year of Latest Census

Number of inhabitants	Canada (2001)[a]	Denmark (2002)	France (1999)	Germany (2001)	Japan (2000)[b]	New Zealand (2002)[c]	Sweden (2003)	United States (2002)[d]
0–499	1,975	0	21,038	3,680	0	0	0	0
500–999	1,023	0	6,763	2,521	0	0	0	18,013
1,000–9,999	1,786	134	7,957	6,097	1,557	14	73	14,057
10,000–49,999	308	125	802	1,348	1,220	40	175	3,125
50,000–99,999	51	12	82	109	224	12	30	461
100,000–499,999	33	3	32	70	206	8	9	219
500,000–999,999	6	1	3	10	11	0	1	22
1,000,000 or more	2	0	2	3	12	0	0	9
Total number of municipalities	5,184	275	36,679	13,838	3,230	74	288	35,906

Source: Statistics Bureau Japan 2000; Statistics Canada 2002; Statistics New Zealand 2005; U.S. Census Bureau 2002; Werner forthcoming.

a. The high number of small Canadian settlements is based on the fact that all First Nation or Native American reserves and bands are affiliated. For example, 1,052 Native American reserves and 5 Nisga'a villages are included in this survey.

b. Japan includes all *shi, machi, mura,* and *gun.* Moreover, the *ku*-area of Tokyo is counted as one *shi* and the population of Okinawa-*ken* is excluded.

c. Besides the 74 territorial authorities, New Zealand also has 1,860 area units, which are very small settlements.

d. United States includes all cities, municipalities, towns, and townships. Moreover, the 2002 census presents only the total number of all local authorities that have fewer than 1,000 inhabitants.

TABLE 1.4 Average Population per Local Authority in OECD Countries

Median population of municipal government[a]	Countries (listed in ascending order of population)
1,000–5,000	Iceland, France, Greece, Switzerland, Luxembourg, Austria, Spain
5,000–10,000	Canada, United States, Italy, Germany, Norway
10,000–15,000	Finland
15,000–20,000	Belgium, Netherlands, Denmark, Australia
30,000–35,000	Sweden, Portugal
35,000–40,000	Japan
40,000–50,000	Ireland, New Zealand
100,000+	United Kingdom

Source: Based on Scottish Office 1998.
a. There were no countries with populations in the 20,000 to 30,000 range.

Overall, local governments in Nordic countries perform the maximal range of local services, encompassing a wide range of people- and property-oriented services. Local governments in southern Europe and in North America fall in a median range and are more focused on property-oriented services. Australian local governments are engaged in the most minimal property-oriented services (primarily "roads and rubbish").

Local Revenues and Revenue Autonomy

Income taxes, property taxes, and fees are major revenue sources for local governments. In Belgium, Denmark, Finland, Germany, Iceland, Japan, Luxembourg, Norway, Sweden, and Switzerland, more than 80 percent of tax revenues are derived from taxes on personal and corporate incomes. In contrast, in Australia, Canada, Ireland, the Netherlands, New Zealand, the United Kingdom, and the United States, property taxes contribute more than 80 percent of local tax revenues. Austria, France, Greece, Italy, Portugal, and Spain rely on a mix of local tax sources, with Spain drawing about 40 percent of tax revenues from sales taxes. For the EU as a whole, income taxes dominate, followed by property taxes, sales taxes, and fees. On average in industrial countries, 50 percent of local revenues come from taxes, 20 percent from user charges, and 30 percent from transfers from higher levels (see McMillan forthcoming). Figure 1.3 illustrates the composition of local operating revenues, and figure 1.4 shows the composition of tax revenues for selected countries.

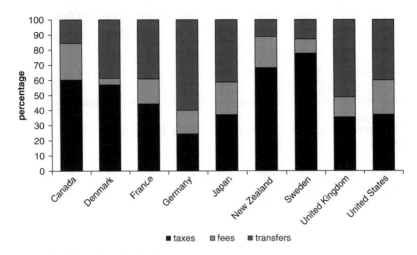

Source: Adapted from Werner forthcoming.
Note: The shared taxes in Germany and Japan are consolidated under transfers. Moreover, local borrowing is excluded from this survey.

FIGURE 1.3 Composition of Operating Revenues for Local Authorities in 2001

Table 1.5 shows that intergovernmental finance is relatively less important in Austria, Canada, Denmark, Finland, New Zealand, and Sweden, whereas in most OECD countries the share of grant-financed local expenditures is quite large (see figure 1.3). This large share of grants indicates that in many OECD countries, local governments typically perform agency functions for higher-level governments and have only a limited range of locally determined responsibilities. General-purpose, formula-based grants using fiscal capacity and need factors dominate in most OECD countries, with the exception of Finland, New Zealand, and the United States. In those three countries, specific-purpose transfers assume greater importance in local finances.

In most countries, airports, parking, water, sewerage, and garbage collection are predominantly financed by fees, whereas social services are primarily financed from general tax revenues and grants. Infrastructure finance relies on a mix of sources that include own-source revenues and reserves, charges, fiscal transfers, borrowing, and public-private partnership arrangements. In most countries, significant help is available from higher-level governments in facilitating access to the credit market for local governments.

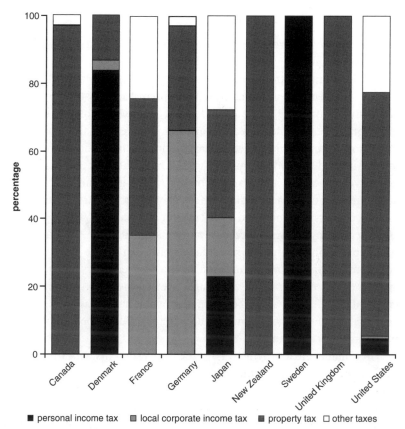

Source: Author's calculation, adapted mainly from Werner forthcoming.
Note: The shared taxes in Germany (personal income tax and value added tax) and in New Zealand (fuel tax for the regional councils) are excluded.

FIGURE 1.4 Composition of Local Tax Revenues, 2001

TABLE 1.5 Intergovernmental Transfers as a Share of Local Government Revenues in OECD Countries in 2000

Transfers as a percentage of total local revenues	Countries (listed in ascending order of the share of transfers)
10–20	Finland, Sweden, Denmark, New Zealand
20–30	Canada, Austria
30–40	France, Japan, Australia, United States
40–50	Ireland, Norway, Belgium, Germany
50–60	Spain
60–70	Greece, Portugal
70–80	Italy, United Kingdom, Netherlands

Source: Statistics bureaus of individual countries; see references.

Facilitating Local Access to Credit

Local access to credit requires well-functioning financial markets and creditworthy local governments. Although those prerequisites are easily met in industrial countries, traditions for assisting local governments by higher-level governments are well established. An interest subsidy to state and local borrowing is available in the United States because the interest income of such bonds is exempt from federal taxation. Needless to say, such a subsidy has many distortionary effects: it favors richer jurisdictions and higher-income individuals, it discriminates against nondebt sources of finance such as reserves and equity, it favors investments by local governments rather than autonomous bodies, and it discourages private sector participation in the form of concessions and build-own-transfer alternatives. Various U.S. states assist borrowing by small local governments through the establishment of municipal bond banks. Municipal bond banks are established as autonomous state agencies that issue tax-exempt securities to investors and apply the proceeds to purchase the collective bond issue of several local governments. By pooling a number of smaller issues and by using the superior credit rating of the state, municipal bond banks reduce the cost of borrowing to smaller communities.

In Canada, most provinces assist local governments with the engineering, financial, and economic analysis of projects. Local governments in Alberta, British Columbia, and Nova Scotia are assisted in their borrowing through provincial finance corporations, which use the higher credit ratings of the province to lower the cost of funds for local governments. Some provinces, notably Manitoba and Quebec, assist in the preparation and marketing of local debt. Canadian provincial governments on occasion provide debt relief to their local governments. In Western Europe and Japan, autonomous agencies run on commercial principles assist local borrowing. Municipality Finance of Finland is owned by the association of local governments and provides debt pooling for municipal governments. Similarly, Kommun Invest of Sweden is owned by the association of local governments but is privately managed to provide credit to local governments. Credit Communal de Belgique is jointly owned by Belgian central and local governments, and deposits are the main source of finance. Dexia in France is privately owned and raises resources entirely through bond issues. The Banco de Crédito Local in Spain is also privately managed and uses bond finance. In Denmark, local governments have collectively established a cooperative municipal bank. In the United Kingdom, the Public Works Loan Board channels central financing to local public works.

An important lesson from industrial countries' experience is that municipal finance corporations operate well when they are run on commercial principles and compete for capital and borrowers. In such an environment, such agencies allow risk pooling, use economies of scale better, and bring to bear their knowledge of local governments and their financing potential to provide access to commercial credit on more favorable terms (see McMillan forthcoming).

Some Conclusions about Local Governance in Industrial Countries

Historical evolution and the current practice of local governance are instructive in drawing lessons for reform of local governance, especially in developing countries. There is great diversity in practice in local governance in industrial countries, but there are also some common strands. The diversity is in the institutional arrangements, which have evolved incrementally over a long period. This evolution has resulted in diverse roles for local governments and diverse relations with central governments across countries. In Nordic countries, local government serves as the primary agent of the people, whereas in Australia, that role is entrusted to state governments, and local government has a minimal role in local affairs.

There is no uniform model for local government size, structure, tiers, and functions across OECD countries. There are, nevertheless, a number of interesting common features. First, most countries recognize that finance must follow function to ensure that local governments are able to meet their responsibilities efficiently and equitably. Second, home rule is considered critical to meeting local expectations and being responsive to local residents. Therefore, local governments must have significant taxing, spending, and regulatory autonomy, and they must have the ability to hire, fire, and set terms of reference for employees without having to defer to higher levels of governments. Only then can local governments innovate in management by introducing performance-based accountability and innovate in service delivery by forging alternative service delivery arrangements through competitive provision, contracting, and outsourcing wherever deemed appropriate. They can also facilitate a broader network of local governance and harness the energies of the whole community to foster better social outcomes. Third and most important, accountability to local residents has been the factor most critical to the success of local governance in industrial countries. This accountability is strengthened through democratic choice, participation, transparency, performance budgeting, citizens' charters of rights, and various legal and financing provisions that support wider voice, choice, and exit options to residents.

Concluding Remarks

We have presented a brief overview of the conceptual and institutional literature on local governance. A synthesis of the conceptual literature suggests that the modern role of a local government is to deal with market failures as well as government failures. This role requires a local government to operate as a purchaser of local services, a facilitator of networks of government providers and entities beyond government, and a gatekeeper and overseer of state and national governments in areas of shared rule. Local government also needs to play a mediator's role among various entities and networks to foster greater synergy and harness the untapped energies of the broader community for improving the quality of life of local residents. Globalization and the information revolution are reinforcing these conceptual perspectives on a catalytic role for local governments.

This view is also grounded in the history of industrial nations. Local government was the primary form of government until wars and conquest led to the transfer of local government responsibilities to central and regional governments. This trend continued unabated until globalization and the information revolution highlighted the weaknesses of centralized rule for improving the quality of life and social outcomes. The new vision of local governance (see table 1.6) presented here argues for a leadership role by local governments in a multicentered, multiorder, or multilevel system. This view is critical to creating and sustaining citizen-centered governance, in which citizens are the ultimate sovereigns and various levels of governments are there to serve as agents in the supply of public governance. In developing countries, such citizen empowerment may be the only way to reform public sector governance when governments are either unwilling or unable to reform themselves.

Acknowledgments

This chapter owes a great deal of intellectual debt to Professors Stephen Bailey, Brian Dollery, Sue Goss, Samuel Humes, Melville McMillan, and Joe Wallis, on whose works this chapter draws quite liberally. I am also grateful to Jan Werner for his contributions.

TABLE 1.6   Role of a Local Government under the New Vision of Local Governance

20th century: Old view	21st century: New view
Is based on residuality and local governments as wards of the state	Is based on subsidiarity and home rule
Is based on principle of *ultra vires*	Is based on community governance
Is focused on government	Is focused on citizen-centered local governance
Is the agent of the central government	Is the primary agent for the citizens and the leader and gatekeeper for shared rule
Is responsive and accountable to higher-level governments	Is responsive and accountable to local voters; assumes leadership role in improving local governance
Is the direct provider of local services	Is the purchaser of local services
Is focused on in-house provision	Is the facilitator of network mechanisms of local governance, coordinator of government providers and entities beyond government, mediator of conflicts, and developer of social capital
Is focused on secrecy	Is focused on letting the sunshine in; practices transparent governance
Has input controls	Recognizes that results matter
Is internally dependent	Is externally focused and competitive; is an ardent practitioner of an alternative service delivery framework
Is closed and slow	Is open, quick, and flexible
Has intolerance for risk	Is innovative; is a risk taker within limits
Depends on central directives	Is autonomous in taxing, spending, regulatory, and administrative decisions
Is rules driven	Has managerial flexibility and accountability for results
Is bureaucratic and technocratic	Is participatory; works to strengthen citizen voice and exit options through direct democracy provisions, citizens' charters, and performance budgeting
Is coercive	Is focused on earning trust, creating space for civic dialogue, serving the citizens, and improving social outcomes
Is fiscally irresponsible	Is fiscally prudent; works better and costs less
Is exclusive with elite capture	Is inclusive and participatory
Overcomes market failures	Overcomes market and government failures
Is boxed in a centralized system	Is connected in a globalized and localized world

Source: Author.

References

Andrews, Matthew, and Anwar Shah. 2005. "Citizen-Centered Governance: A New Approach to Public Sector Reform." In *Public Expenditure Analysis,* ed. Anwar Shah, 153–82. Washington, DC: World Bank.

Bailey, Stephen. 1999. *Local Government Economics: Theory, Policy, and Practice.* Basingstoke, U.K.: Macmillan.

Bowman, Ann, and Richard Kearney. 1990. *State and Local Government.* Boston: Houghton Mifflin.

Boyne, George. 1998. *Public Choice Theory and Local Government.* Basingstoke, U.K.: Macmillan.

Breton, Albert. 1995. *Competitive Governments.* Cambridge, U.K.: Cambridge University Press.

Brueckner, Jan. 1982. "A Test for Allocative Efficiency in the Local Public Sector." *Journal of Public Economics* 19: 311–31.

Buchanan, James. 1965. "An Economic Theory of Clubs." *Economica* 32: 1–14.

Caulfield, Janice. 2003. "Local Government Reform in Comparative Perspective." In *Reshaping Australian Local Government,* ed. Brian Dollery, Neil Marshall, and Andrew Worthington, 11–34. Sydney: University of New South Wales Press.

Dollery, Brian, and Joe Wallis. 2001. *The Political Economy of Local Government.* Cheltenham, U.K.: Edward Elgar.

Frey, Bruno, and Reiner Eichenberger. 1995. "Competition among Jurisdictions: The Idea of FOCJ." In *Competition among Jurisdictions,* ed. Lüder Gerken, 209–29. London: Macmillan.

———. 1996. "FOCJ: Competitive Governments for Europe." *International Review of Law and Economics* 16: 315–27.

———. 1999. *The New Democratic Federalism for Europe: Functional Overlapping and Competing Jurisdictions.* Cheltenham, U.K., and Northampton, MA: Edward Elgar.

Goss, Sue. 2001. *Making Local Governance Work.* New York: Palgrave.

Government of Switzerland. 2003. *The Swiss Confederation—A Brief Guide.* Bern: Bundeskanzlei.

Horn, Murray. 1997. *The Political Economy of Public Administration.* Cambridge, U.K.: Cambridge University Press.

Humes, Samuel, IV. 1991. *Local Governance and National Power.* New York: Harvester/Wheatsheaf.

Kincaid, John. 1967. "Municipal Perspectives in Federalism." Unpublished paper. Cited in Bowman and Kearney (1990).

McMillan, Melville. Forthcoming. "A Local Perspective on Fiscal Federalism: Practices, Experiences, and Lessons from Developed Countries." In *Macrofederalism and Local Finances,* ed. Anwar Shah. Washington, DC: World Bank.

Moore, Mark. 1996. *Creating Public Value.* Cambridge, MA: Harvard University Press.

———. 1999. "The Job Ahead." In *Community, Opportunity, Responsibility, Accountability—Report of the Symposium on the Future of Public Services.* Washington, DC: Office of Public Management.

Muramatsu, Michio, and Farrukh Iqbal. 2001. "Understanding Japanese Intergovernmental Relations: Perspectives, Models, and Salient Characteristics." In *Local*

Government Development in Postwar Japan, ed. Michio Muramatsu and Farrukh Iqbal, 1–28. Oxford, U.K.: Oxford University Press.

Oates, Wallace. 1969. "The Effects of Property Taxes and Local Public Spending on Property Values: An Empirical Study of Tax Capitalization and Tiebout Hypothesis." *Journal of Political Economy* 77: 957–71.

———. 1972. *Fiscal Federalism.* New York: Harcourt Brace Jovanovich.

Olson, Mancur. 1969. "The Principle of Fiscal Equivalence: The Division of Responsibilities among Different Levels of Government." *American Economic Review* 59 (2): 479–87.

Rhodes, R. A. W. 1997. *Understanding Governance: Policy Networks, Governance, Reflexivity, and Accountability.* Buckingham, U.K.: Open University Press.

Scottish Office. 1998. "The Constitutional Status of Local Government in Other Countries." Unpublished report, Central Research Unit, Edinburgh, Scotland.

Shah, Anwar. 1988. "Capitalization and the Theory of Local Public Finance: An Interpretive Essay." *Journal of Economic Surveys* 2 (3): 209–43.

———. 1989. "A Capitalization Approach to Fiscal Incidence at the Local Level." *Land Economics* 65 (4): 359–75.

———. 1992. "Empirical Tests for Allocative Efficiency in the Local Public Sector." *Public Finance Quarterly* 20 (3): 359–77.

———. 1994. *The Reform of Intergovernmental Fiscal Relations in Developing and Emerging Market Economies.* Washington, DC: World Bank.

———. 2001. "Interregional Competition and Federal Cooperation: To Compete or to Cooperate? That's Not the Question." Paper presented at the International Forum on Federalism, Veracruz, Mexico, November 14–17.

———. 2005. "A Framework for Evaluating Alternate Institutional Arrangements for Fiscal Equalization Transfers." Policy Research Working Paper 3785, World Bank, Washington, DC. http://ssrn.com/abstract=873893.

———. 2006. "The Principles and the Practice of Intergovernmental Transfers." In *Intergovernmental Fiscal Transfers: Principles and Practice,* eds. Robin Boadway and Anwar Shah. Washington, DC: World Bank.

Statistics Bureau, Japan. 2000. *2000 Population of Japan.* 1st ed. Tokyo: Ministry of Internal Affairs and Communication.

Statistics Canada. 2002. *Population and Dwelling Counts for Canada and Census Subdivisions (Municipalities), 2001 and 1996 Censuses.* 1st ed. Ottawa: Statistics Canada.

Statistics New Zealand. 2005. *Census of Population and Dwellings: Final Counts 2001— New Zealand by Meshblock.* 1st ed. Auckland, New Zealand: Statistics New Zealand.

Stigler, George. 1957. "The Tenable Range of Functions of Local Government." In *Federal Expenditure Policy for Economic Growth and Stability,* ed. Joint Economic Committee, Subcommittee on Fiscal Policy, U.S. Congress, 213–19. Washington, DC: U.S. Government Printing Office.

Stoker, Gerry, ed. 1999. *The New Management of British Local Governance.* London: Macmillan.

Tiebout, Charles. 1956. "A Pure Theory of Local Expenditures." *Journal of Political Economy* 64 (5): 416–24.

U.S. Census Bureau. 2002. *Government Organization,* Vol. 1, No. 1 of *2002 Census of Government,* Washington, DC: U.S. Department of Commerce.

Wajidi, Muhammad. 1990. "Origin of Local Government in the Indo-Pakistan Subcontinent." *Journal of Political Science* 13 (1–2): 131–39.

Werner, Jan. Forthcoming. *Das deutsche Gemeindefinanzsystem: Reformvorschläge im Kontext der unterschiedlichen Einnahmenautonomie der lokalen Gebietskörperschaften in Europa* [*The Financing of Local Authorities in Germany: Future Fiscal Reforms and Methods of Resolution in the Neighboring European Countries*]. Frankfurt am Main, Germany: Peter Lang.

Werner, Jan, and Anwar Shah. 2005. "Horizontal Fiscal Equalization at the Local Level: The Practice in Denmark, Norway, and Sweden." Unpublished paper, World Bank, Washington, DC.

Williamson, Oliver. 1985. "*The Economic Institutions of Capitalism.*" New York: Free Press.

Zheng, Yingpin and Wei Fan, eds. 2003. *The History and Civilization of China.* Beijing: Central Party Literature Publishing House.

2

Local Government Organization and Finance: *Canada*

MELVILLE L. McMILLAN

There are approximately 4,600 municipal governments in Canada.[1] The most typical forms are cities, towns, and villages and, in the rural areas, counties and rural municipalities, but other forms include some regional and metropolitan municipal governments. The number and average size vary widely across the provinces. For example, two provinces, Quebec and Saskatchewan, account for almost half the total number of municipalities. In addition to these general-purpose municipalities, there are an even larger number of special-purpose local authorities (about 8,000), including boards and commissions that have responsibility for schools, police services, public utilities, conservation areas, local health services, and miscellaneous others. Among these special-purpose bodies, school boards dominate, (a) because they are ubiquitous and their expenditures often almost match those of the municipalities and (b) because their members, like those of municipalities, are directly elected. The role and even presence of other special-purpose bodies vary substantially among the provinces, and the degree of their independence from (or integration with) general-purpose local governments varies, though they are usually minor authorities. Thus, municipalities and school boards are typically considered the major forms of Canadian local government.

Local school boards are responsible for schooling (namely, elementary and secondary education), and municipalities are responsible for a broad (but conventional) range of local services. Municipal services focus on transportation (roadway and public); protection (police, fire, and emergency services); environmental services (water, sewerage, and garbage collection and disposal); recreation and culture; land-use planning and business regulation; local health; and social services. Beyond schooling, local (namely, municipal) government typically plays a very small role in social services such as health or social assistance because the provinces effectively are the suppliers.2 As a share of gross domestic product (GDP), local governments' own revenue (usually 4 to 5 percent) and expenditure (typically 7 to 8 percent) have remained relatively constant since 1970. During that time, however, local governments' share of total government spending has declined from one-fourth to about one-sixth, largely because provincial expenditures have grown primarily in the areas of social expenditures, notably health. Table 2.1 reports the spending by the three levels of government in Canada (plus the municipal–school board division at the local level, when available) and shows the growth in provincial and total government spending since 1965.

The authority of local government in Canada is derived entirely from the provinces. The constitution mentions municipalities only to declare that they are the exclusive jurisdiction of the provinces. As "creatures of the

TABLE 2.1 Canadian Federal, Provincial, and Local Government Expenditures, Selected Years
(as a percentage of gross national expenditure)

Year	Federal	Provincial	Local government[a] Combined	Municipal	School boards	Total government[a]
1965	14.9	11.0	7.8	—	—	26.6
1975	20.8	18.4	8.5	—	—	38.8
1985	24.0	21.5	8.0	—	—	45.9
1988	n.a.	n.a.	8.3	4.54	3.74	n.a.
1995	22.6	23.3	9.0	5.11	4.78	47.7
2000	18.2	20.3	7.3	4.26	3.05	40.5

Source: Adapted from Kitchen (2002, 16) with separate municipal and school board percentages calculated by the author. Local data are separated only into municipal (that is, local general government) and school board data since 1988.
Note: — = not available; n.a. = not applicable.
a. Because of the nonexclusionary accounting for intergovernmental transfers, the individual percentages shown here cannot be added to achieve this total.

provinces" (the status of local governments since 1867), their responsibilities and powers are only those delegated to them by the incorporating province and to which their actions must conform. The provinces have the power to modify those responsibilities and powers, and, indeed, they have the power to create, change, and abolish municipalities at will. The provinces have not been reluctant to reform local government by changing boundaries, responsibilities, powers, and funding. For example, Ontario undertook a major reform of its local government during the 1990s, which included reducing the number of municipalities by 45 percent and amalgamating the six municipalities making up metropolitan Toronto into one megacity. Quebec also recently amalgamated many of its municipalities, and Alberta amalgamated a large number of its school districts. The provinces control their municipalities closely with a host of laws and regulations.

The "provincialization" of schooling, which has crept across the provinces especially during the 1990s, illustrates the authority and intervention of the provinces in local affairs. As recently as 15 to 20 years ago, the conventional arrangement for schooling could be described as a sharing of local and provincial responsibility, in that the province provided (usually) most of the funding (on an equalizing basis) and the local school board generated additional funds (as required) from a local property tax levy. This shared funding arrangement now characterizes only two provinces. Elsewhere, the provinces have assumed full (or essentially full) funding responsibility for schooling and, in doing so, have usually taken over the local school property taxes in the form of a provincial (or provincially set) property tax. Local school boards have been stripped of their taxing powers (or have had them severely restricted); consequently, local voters and taxpayers have been divorced of any discretion in local school finance. Now, in most provinces, only the provincial government decides on the level of school expenditures. Within the bounds of the provincially provided funding, locally elected school boards have discretion in spending to deliver schooling, subject to substantial oversight by the provincial ministries of education. Provincial oversight includes, for example, defining curricula, requirements for common exams, teacher qualifications, and requirements for the schooling of challenged students. The local school boards' loss of (real) tax authority in most provinces renders them more the agents of their provincial governments than local governments themselves. Hence, school boards will not be reported on further in any detail.[3]

The loss of local governments' access to sales and income taxes further illustrates the provincial control. During World War II, the federal and provincial governments came to an agreement giving the federal government full control over (primarily) the personal and corporate income taxes.

The provinces were compensated. However, although the provinces fully regained their tax authority in those areas in 1962, the local governments, some of which had used income and sales taxes before World War II, were excluded from those areas under the World War II agreement and have not had those powers restored. Since 1940, the property tax is essentially the only source of taxation available to Canadian local governments.

The 1990s saw a series of revisions in provincial legislation governing municipalities. This legislation lent itself to relaxing provincial supervision if not to broadening municipal authority. Largely, it conveyed natural person powers to municipalities and afforded authority to act within spheres of jurisdiction rather than just within areas specifically permitted by law.[4] The overall effect of those moves is not clear. The ability to contract (the major role of the natural person power) already existed, and the laws broadening spheres of jurisdiction were often accompanied (and largely offset in many cases) by restrictive regulations. Although the reform of municipal legislation may not have accomplished as much as many municipalities and municipal analysts might have hoped, municipalities have considerable autonomy and, in turn, accountability to their citizens within the scope of the powers granted to them. Councils are elected. All Canadians who are of voting age (18) and residents of the municipality are eligible to vote. Councils manage their own administrations, including the hiring (and firing) of all staff members. As will be discussed later, municipal governments are responsible for determining the level of services and for the financing (setting the taxes, charges, and so forth) that is necessary to fund those services.

A consequence of provincial authority over local government is the considerable interprovincial variation in local government. Although the major features are typically quite parallel, a host of minor (and some not so minor) variations often make generalizations tenuous. Another consequence is that direct relationships between the local and the federal governments are minimal, in part because the provincial governments carefully guard their authority over local government. Regardless, the municipalities (for example, the Federation of Canadian Municipalities) lobby the federal government, which typically results in relatively modest and sporadic federal funding being directed to municipalities. Representative of this support is the federal government's infrastructure program, which was initiated in the late 1990s and is continuing.

The remainder of the chapter focuses on the financial features of Canadian municipal government. Considered first are the responsibilities of municipal government and the associated expenditures. Reviewed second is the revenue side, including own-source revenues, shared revenues, and transfers. The third section focuses on borrowing, notably for infrastructure finance. The fourth section looks at recent developments and potential reforms, and the final sections provide, respectively, an overall assessment and suggested lessons for others.

Municipal Government Responsibilities Associated with Expenditures

Expenditures of municipal governments represented 4.4 percent of gross national product (GNP) in 2001, about 10.5 percent of total government outlays. This percentage is marginally smaller than the 4.5 percent of the GNP it represented in 1988, the first year that independent municipal government data were available.[5] Despite the slightly lower percentage, per capita real (GDP-deflator-adjusted) dollar expenditures by municipal governments increased 15 percent over this period.

The per capita levels and percentage distribution of municipal expenditures for 2001 are shown in table 2.2. The range of per capita municipal expenditures is large—from a low of Cdn$378 in Prince Edward Island to a high of Cdn$1,948 in Ontario.[6] The population-weighted average for Canada is Cdn$1,545. The provinces tend to divide into two groups. For Quebec and the provinces farther west, per capita expenditures are relatively high (above Cdn$1,050), whereas in Atlantic Canada, those expenditures tend to be lower (below Cdn$1,050). Nova Scotia defines the upper end in Atlantic Canada, because its municipal governments, unlike those of other provinces, contribute significantly to schooling (14.2 percent of municipal expenditures). Moreover, Nova Scotia finances more than the norm of social services (at 4.5 percent of municipal expenditures), although that share has dropped dramatically (from 23.3 percent in 1988). Ontario municipalities are the highest spenders, because one-fourth of their outlays go to fund social services. Otherwise, the Ontario outlay would be second to that in Alberta. Among the other provinces, the average share of expenditures going to social services does not exceed 1.5 percent. With respect to expenditures, Ontario has had a tradition of placing somewhat more responsibilities on its municipalities than do the other provinces, but the local government reforms introduced during the 1990s exacerbated that burden. The province assumed full responsibility for funding schools (with new provincial property taxes to contribute to the cost) and, in exchange with the local level, shifted a variety of responsibilities (notably, all social housing costs, the costs of maintaining previously provincial highways, and half of the cost of land

TABLE 2.2 Level and Allocation of Municipal Government Expenditures by Province and for Canada, 2001

Indicator	New-foundland and Labrador	Prince Edward Island	Nova Scotia	New Brunswick	Quebec	Ontario	Manitoba	Saskatchewan	Alberta	British Columbia	Canada	Canada less Ontario
Per capita expenditure (Cdn$)	767	378	1,020	865	1,284	1,948	1,091	1,141	1,581	1,284	1,545	1,296
Percentage of allocation												
General services	16.2	12.9	10.4	11.1	12.2	8.9	13.6	12.4	12.2	10.0	10.4	11.8
Protection	4.7	23.1	21.1	21.0	16.7	13.4	19.7	17.6	14.3	18.8	15.1	16.8
Transportation	28.6	21.5	16.9	20.2	27.2	18.1	23.4	31.7	28.3	16.5	21.4	24.5
Health	0.1	0.1	0.1	0.4	0.2	3.5	2.2	0.6	1.5	1.8	2.2	1.0
Social services	0.2	0.0ᵃ	4.5	0	1.4	24.7	0.3	0.5	1.5	0.2	12.5	1.2
Education	0.1	0	14.2	0.0ᵃ	0.1	0.0ᵃ	0.0ᵃ	0.0ᵃ	0.3	0.0ᵃ	0.3	0.7
Conservation and development	0.7	1.7	0.8	2.4	2.8	1.6	2.4	3.6	3.4	1.4	2.1	2.5
Environment	22.1	12.7	16.8	25.3	12.0	13.3	17.4	15.4	13.9	20.4	14.4	15.5
Recreation and culture	14.5	21.9	10.7	12.6	12.4	8.7	9.4	14.2	13.7	19.5	11.5	14.1
Housing	0.6	0	0.2	0.3	2.9	5.0	0.4	0.4	0.7	0.6	3.2	1.6
Regional planning	1.2	2.3	1.5	2.0	2.5	0.1	2.3	1.7	3.0	2.3	1.3	2.4
Debt charges	11.1	3.7	3.7	4.2	9.4	2.3	8.5	1.7	7.1	6.3	5.0	7.4
Other	0.0ᵃ	0.0ᵃ	0.0ᵃ	0.2	0.0ᵃ	0.2	0.4	0.1	0.0ᵃ	2.2	0.4	0.5
Totalᵇ	100.0	100.0	100.0	100.0	100.0	100.0	100.0	100.0	100.0	100.0	100.0	100.0

Source: Data provided by Statistics Canada, Public Institutions Division. Data are available for earlier years in Statistics Canada (various years).
a. Negligible (less than 0.05 percent).
b. Figures may not add to 100.0 because of rounding.

ambulances) to the municipal governments (for details, see, for example, Kitchen 2002). This reassignment of responsibilities to the municipalities— particularly the added social services component—contrasts with the pre- vailing pattern in Canada and is contrary to best practices recommended by students of fiscal federalism. The level of municipal expenditures and the atypical importance of social service spending make Ontario relatively distinctive among the Canadian provinces. Indeed, one might say that Cana- dian municipal finance is characterized by three (not two) regions: Atlantic Canada, Ontario, and the other provinces.

Table 2.2 highlights the major anomalies in expenditures, including social services in Ontario, education outlays in Nova Scotia, and the low share of protection costs in Newfoundland and Labrador. Otherwise, the patterns are quite homogeneous. The major expenditure areas are protec- tion (predominately fire and policing); transportation (including roads and streets, parking, and public transit); environment (water and sewerage serv- ices, solid waste management, and recycling); and recreation (including parks and playing fields) and culture. Together with general services (munic- ipal administration), these categories account for more than 85 percent of municipal outlays. Debt servicing costs averaged 5 percent in 2001 but ranged from 1.7 to 11.1 percent. Unlike the federal and provincial govern- ments, municipalities cannot borrow for operating purposes; they can bor- row only for capital expenditures.

Because of Ontario's size (38 percent of Canada's population) and unique features, the Canadian average expenditure distribution in table 2.2 may be misleading. That 12.5 percent of Canadian municipal expenditures are directed to social services is almost entirely attributable to Ontario municipalities, which allocate one-fourth of their budgets to that area. As the final column shows, municipalities outside of Ontario devote only 1.2 percent of expenditures to social services. Also, note that the municipal expenditures on housing, while averaging 3.2 percent across Canada, exceed 0.7 percent only in Ontario and Quebec.

Expenditures for capital are an important component of municipal government outlays. In 2000 (the latest year of capital expenditure data), capital outlays accounted for 19.5 percent of municipal expenditures and amounted to Cdn$273 per capita. Municipal governments account for a disproportionate share of government capital expenditures. Although municipal government expenditures represent about 10 percent of total government expenditures, municipal governments account for 35 to 40 percent of total government capital acquisitions. Other local governments add another 5 percent.

Municipal capital expenditures are concentrated on transportation, environment, and recreation and culture, which accounted for 35.9, 27.6, and 14.9 percent, respectively, of the total expenditures in 2000 (see table 2.3). Also relatively important are capital expenditures for general government (8.3 percent) and for protection services (5.9 percent). The first three areas mentioned here represent 78.4 percent of total expenditures, and all five areas represent 92.6 percent of capital spending. This pattern is quite consistent across provinces. For example, transportation, environment, and recreation constitute between 69 and 87 percent of capital expenditures in all but one province.

Intergovernmental transfers are important to capital expenditure finance. Transfers specifically for capital cover 9.4 percent of the outlays, which is a little more than half the 17.3 percent that grants contribute to current outlays.[7] The federal government makes a relatively larger contribution to capital transfers than to transfers for current expenditure purposes (9.5 percent versus 2.0 percent). Intergovernmental transfers contribute most to capital outlays for transportation (14.1 percent), resource conservation and industrial development (13.1 percent), social services (11.3 percent), and

TABLE 2.3 Capital Expenditures of Canadian Municipal Governments, 2000

Indicator	Percentage of total	Percentage funded by grants or transfers
Per capita expenditure (Cdn$)	273	
Distribution of expenditures		
General government	8.3	4.5
Protection	5.9	2.2
Transportation	35.9	14.1
Health	1.0	5.8
Social services	1.0	11.3
Resource conservation and industrial development	2.7	13.1
Environment	27.6	9.0
Recreation and culture	14.9	4.7
Housing	0.7	5.2
Regional planning and development	1.5	1.3
Other	0.4	2.8
Total[a]	100.0	9.4

Source: Data provided by Statistics Canada, Public Institutions Division.
Note: Data are preliminary.
a. Figures may not add to 100.0 because of rounding.

environment (9.0 percent). In the other categories, they finance between 1 and 6 percent of expenditures. However, the relative importance of transfers (among categories and in aggregate) can vary considerably over time as the priorities of the granting governments change.

In summary, with schooling in all provinces but Manitoba and Saskatchewan and social services (assistance) in all provinces but Ontario now essentially a provincial responsibility, local government in Canada has minimal responsibility for what can broadly be considered to be social services. Indeed, municipal government is responsible primarily for services related to property. Although there is provincial variation in responsibilities, there are also substantial parallels.

Municipal Government Revenues

Although the levels of revenues vary among provinces to correspond with expenditures, the sources of municipal revenues are quite consistent. On average, 83 percent of municipal revenues come from own-source revenues—that is, sources such as taxes and charges from which the municipalities themselves determine the amounts to be raised (see table 2.4). The remaining 17 percent of total revenues come from transfers from the provincial and federal governments. Property taxes and property-related taxes, the only significant source of municipal tax revenue, account for half of municipal own-source revenues. Sales of goods and services, about one-fourth of revenues, are the only other major source of own-source revenues.

Own-Source Taxes and Charges

Property and related taxes are the main source (about 63 percent overall) of own-source revenues and represent, across Canada, 52.2 percent of total revenues. Property and related taxes consist of real property taxes and property-related taxes. Real property taxes (taxes on land and improvements) provide, on average, 41.9 percent of total revenues. The difference between the two consists primarily of business taxes, payments in lieu of taxes from other governments and their agencies, lot levies, and special assessments (usually for specific improvements). Business taxes are not collected in British Columbia, Ontario, New Brunswick, and Prince Edward Island. In fact, municipalities in Prince Edward have almost no property-related taxes and rely on the real property tax. Property and related taxes vary considerably in relative importance—from 44.4 percent in Alberta to 73.7 percent in Nova Scotia. Considerably less variation occurs in the actual dollar amounts

TABLE 2.4 Level and Allocation of Municipal Government Revenues by Province and for Canada, 2001

Indicator	New-foundland and Labrador	Prince Edward Island	Nova Scotia	New Brunswick	Quebec	Ontario	Manitoba	Saskatchewan	Alberta	British Columbia	Canada
Per capita revenue (Cdn$)	704	437	1,013	839	1,293	1,914	1,120	1,062	1,739	1,137	1,513
Own-source revenue (percent)											
Property and related taxes	54.3	62.3	73.7	55.1	64.3	48.3	46.7	54.3	44.4	53.0	52.2
(Real property taxes)	(36.3)	(61.2)	(58.0)	(47.7)	(44.2)	(42.2)	(35.3)	(45.4)	(31.6)	(46.3)	(41.9)
Consumption taxes	0.1	0	0	0	0	0	1.4	3.6	0	0.2	0.1
Other taxes	1.0	0.5	0.1	0.5	0.3	1.3	1.1	0.8	1.6	2.4	1.2
Sales of goods and services[a]	16.4	26.9	16.4	25.3	16.5	23.9	23.4	24.3	26.1	29.3	23.0
Investment income	1.9	1.6	3.5	1.0	2.0	4.1	8.0	4.4	10.3	8.5	4.9
Other	0.6	1.5	0.2	0.5	2.3	1.7	0.8	1.0	1.6	0.6	1.6
Total own source[b]	74.3	92.8	94.0	82.4	85.5	79.3	81.5	88.5	84.1	94.2	83.0
Transfers (percent)											
General purpose	6.3	3.3	2.7	12.4	1.9	2.3	7.9	4.6	0.9	1.1	2.4
Specific purpose	19.4	3.9	3.3	5.2	12.6	18.3	10.6	6.9	15.0	4.7	14.6
Federal	2.9	0.3	0.5	1.0	0.2	0.3	1.1	2.	0.5	0.5	0.4
Provincial	16.5	3.6	2.8	4.2	12.4	18	9.5	4.9	14.5	4.3	14.2
Total transfers[a]	25.7	7.2	6.0	17.6	14.5	20.7	18.5	11.5	15.9	5.8	17.0
Total revenue[b]	100.0	100.0	100.0	100.0	100.0	100.0	100.0	100.0	100.0	100.0	100.0

Source: Data provided by Statistics Canada, Public Institutions Division.
a. Includes user fees, charges, and so forth.
b. Figures may not add to 100.0 because of rounding.

per capita that are collected because of interprovincial variation in the composition of municipal revenues.

Table 2.5 provides more detail about municipal own-source revenues. Although property and property-related taxes account for about 63 percent of 2001 own-source revenues, real property taxes alone accounted for 50.5

TABLE 2.5 Canadian Municipal Own-Source Revenue Sources, National Averages, 2001

Source	Percentage of own-source revenue
Property and related taxes	**62.8**
Real property taxes	50.5
Lot levies	2.4
Special assessments	1.8
Grants in lieu of taxes	3.9
Federal government	0.8
Provincial government	1.9
Government enterprises	1.2
Land transfer tax	0.4
Business tax	3.2
Other property and related taxes	0.8
Consumption taxes	**0.2**
General sales tax	0.2
Amusement taxes	n
Other taxes	**1.4**
Licenses and permits	1.4
Other	n
Sales of goods and services	**27.7**
Water	6.6
Rental	2.0
Concession and franchises	0.2
Other	18.9
Investment income	**5.9**
Remitted trading profits	0.5
Interest from own enterprises	0.6
Other interest and investment income	4.8
Other own-source revenue	**1.9**
Other fines and penalties	1.3
Miscellaneous	0.6
Total of major sources[a]	**100.0**

Source: Data provided by Statistics Canada, Public Institutions Division.
Note: n = an amount less than 0.05 percent.
a. Figures may not add to 100.0 because of rounding.

percent. Lot levies and special assessment (for specific improvements or services), grants in lieu of taxes, and business taxes together constitute almost all of the remainder of the property and related taxes. Note that although local governments are not permitted to tax provincial and federal government property, both of those levels of government (except for Prince Edward Island) and their enterprises make payments to the local authorities in lieu of property taxes. The amount is based on their properties in the local jurisdiction and on the property tax that similar private property would generate. The decision on the amount is ultimately that of the provincial or federal government, and in some cases, there are differences of opinion with respect to the adequacy of the grant-in-lieu payment made. As is apparent by its small contribution (0.4 percent), the land transfer tax is little used in Canada. Certain consumption taxes that are fairly common—for example, amusement taxes—generate an almost negligible amount of revenue. Other municipal taxes, notably licenses and permits, also provide only a small amount (1.4 percent) of own-source revenues.

Some further detail on the property tax is warranted. The property tax base includes land, buildings, and structures. In some provinces, machinery and equipment attached to the property are included. Although the assessment of property for tax purposes is based on market value,[8] special consideration is accorded agricultural land, forests, and mining property. In addition, assessments typically favor residential (and especially owner-occupied residential) over commercial and industrial property. The use of differential mill tax rates (that is, rates that differ across classes of property) may add to the variation in the property tax burden among types of properties. Improvements in assessment methods (for example, more frequent assessments, the use of computer-based comparisons) have done much to enhance Canadian property taxation, especially in some provinces (notably Ontario).

Property tax rates are difficult to characterize. Because property values, assessments, and municipal expenditures—as well as other expenditures financed by property taxes—vary widely among municipalities, property tax rates also vary widely. However, it would be reasonable to say that a property tax equivalent to 1 to 2 percent of market value would be typical for residential property.[9] A better representation of the property tax burden is to compare property taxes with GDP or personal income. In 2001, municipal real property taxes in Canada amounted to 1.8 percent of GDP, 2.26 percent of personal income, and 2.96 percent of personal disposable income (PDI). However, consolidated provincial and local property taxes came to 3.1 percent of GDP, 3.9 percent of personal income, and 5.1 percent of PDI. On average in Canada, nonmunicipal property taxes (that is, provincial taxes and, where permitted, school board levies) represent 42 percent of the total property tax bill. Considerable interprovincial variation occurs in real property taxes. Although municipal real property taxes averaged 2.96 percent of PDI in 2001, they ranged from 1.5 to 3.5 percent of PDI across the provinces (see McMillan 2003 for details).

Revenue from the sale of goods and services is the next major municipal source of own-source and total revenue. This source provides 27.7 percent of own-source revenue and 23 percent of total revenues (the latter ranging from 16 to 30 percent across the provinces). Thus, property and related taxes plus revenue from sales account for about 90 percent of own-source revenue and for about 75 percent of total revenue. Water and rental charges are specifically noted, but other sources may include public transit fares, library fees, sewerage and drainage charges, waste collection and disposal charges, and recreational facility fees, among others. The revenues noted here do not necessarily reflect the extent to which municipalities levy user charges. Such charges are widely used by municipal enterprises, notably utility services, and are reflected in this accounting only through the investment income that they yield for the municipality.

Investment income is a modest but still important source of municipal revenue. It accounts for 4.9 percent of total revenue and 5.9 percent of own-source revenue. Investment income is especially important for municipalities in Alberta, British Columbia, and Manitoba. This revenue largely consists of returns from utility ownership.

Own-source revenue averages 83 percent of the total municipal revenues. Although municipal government revenue in most provinces is close to the average, it ranges from about 74 to 94 percent. Newfoundland is at the low end, and Nova Scotia and British Columbia are at the upper end. The remaining revenues come from provincial and federal transfers and, to a very small extent, shared taxes.

Transfers and Shared Taxes

The variation in the reliance on own-source revenue is more obvious when it is considered together with the contribution of intergovernmental transfers. Municipalities in British Columbia and Nova Scotia receive only about 6 percent of their revenue from grants, whereas those in Newfoundland receive about 25 percent.[10] Overall, grants (transfers) provide 17 percent of revenue (see table 2.4). Intergovernmental transfers essentially mean provincial transfers to the municipalities. The federal grants represent no more than 2.9 percent of total revenue in any province and average 0.4 percent of total revenue (or about 2.4 percent of aggregate transfers to municipalities) for all Canada. All federal transfers are designated for specific (expenditure) purposes. Provincial transfers may be general purpose (that is, unconditional) or specific purpose. Overall, specific-purpose provincial grants dominate—14.2 percent compared with 2.4 percent for general-purpose grants—and they dominate in all provinces but New Brunswick, Nova Scotia, and Prince Edward Island.

Federal transfers are small. Even at their peak in the mid-1990s, they never exceeded 1.35 percent of municipal expenditures (Cdn$19 per capita). In 2001, they amounted to 0.42 percent (Cdn$6.50 per capita). Federal transfers are both small and, at least recently, quite variable. Although small, the federal transfers may make important contributions to particular programs. About one-half of the transfers are directed to transportation and housing, although the relative positions of those transfers have been reversed between 1988 and 2001 after a major reduction in housing grants. Until the mid-1990s, housing received considerable federal money, and it accounted for one-sixth of municipal spending on housing, but by 2001, the federal contribution shrank to only 2.3 percent of those outlays. Besides housing, only for resource conservation and industrial development did federal transfers account for more than 1 percent of municipal outlays in any category. Although federal grants for transportation were the largest component of federal transfers to municipalities, they met only 0.6 percent of municipal transportation outlays. At present, the federal contribution is minor in all areas of municipal expenditure. Still, that contribution may be significant to small subprograms that are not recognized at this level of aggregation.

The provincial transfers are much greater in magnitude overall, but they, too, have declined considerably from about 24 to 16 percent of municipal expenditures. Note, however, that the magnitudes and allocation of provincial grants vary considerably among the provinces. Table 2.6 provides information for 2001. Provincial grants amount to only about 5 percent of expenditures in British Columbia and Nova Scotia but about 20 percent in Ontario and Newfoundland. The per capita dollar amounts also vary substantially—from a low of Cdn$40 in Prince Edward Island to Cdn$389 in Ontario. Although the provinces do make unconditional transfers, the conditional (or specific-purpose) grants dominate in all provinces but New Brunswick, and nationally they account for 13.9 percent of the 16.2 percent of municipal expenditures met through provincial transfers. That is, 86 percent of provincial transfers are designated for specific purposes.

The distribution of provincial grants to municipalities is also reported in table 2.6. These grants, too, display considerable variation. The distribution among expenditure categories at the national level actually does not

TABLE 2.6 Provincial and Territorial Specific-Purpose and Unconditional Transfers to Municipalities, Canada and by Province, 2001

Indicator	Canada	Newfoundland and Labrador	Prince Edward Island	Nova Scotia	New Brunswick	Quebec	Ontario	Manitoba	Saskatchewan	Alberta	British Columbia
Distribution of specific-purpose transfers (percent)											
General services	1.6	9.1	3.7	7.8	8.6	2.0	0.7	9.3	5.0	2.8	2.7
Protection	1.0	2.3	2.7	7.9	1.3	1.1	0.8	2.6	4.0	0.4	3.6
Transportation	18.1	6.6	67.1	4.9	26.2	31.5	3.0	38.9	38.2	75.0	12.8
Health	6.0	0.0	0.0	2.1	0.1	1.5	8.3	5.2	0.1	0.1	11.0
Social services	50.9	0.0	0.0	0.8	0.0	10.5	78.5	0.0	3.7	5.1	0.9
Conservation and development	1.7	0.0[a]	13.8	0.3	5.7	3.3	0.8	5.1	10.4	3.7	1.5
Environment	6.4	14.2	0.3	18.7	27.1	18.6	2.1	11.1	15.1	3.0	15.0
Recreation and culture	4.5	22.2	11.9	55.2	26.0	9.1	1.1	17.4	22.3	7.3	7.1
Housing	4.2	1.5	0.0	0.0	2.8	4.0	4.7	3.5	0.0[a]	0.8	2.0
Regional planning	0.5	1.1	0.5	0.0[a]	0.2	1.7	0.0[a]	0.6	0.2	0.3	0.9
Debt charges	4.1	42.7	0.0[a]	1.5	1.8	12.4	0.0	0.0	0.1	1.7	42.0
Other	0.9	0.2	0.0	0.7	0.0	4.2	0.0	6.3	0.9	0.0	0.2
Total[b]	100.0	100.0	100.0	100.0	100.0	100.0	100.0	100.0	100.0	100.0	100.0

(continued)

TABLE 2.6 Provincial and Territorial Specific-Purpose and Unconditional Transfers to Municipalities, Canada and by Province, 2001 *(continued)*

Indicator	Canada	New-foundland and Labrador	Prince Edward Island	Nova Scotia	New Brunswick	Quebec	Ontario	Manitoba	Saskatchewan	Alberta	British Columbia
Provincial and territorial transfers											
Percentage of total expenditure											
Specific purpose	13.9	15.2	4.1	2.8	4.1	12.0	17.7	9.7	4.5	16.0	3.8
Unconditional	2.3	5.8	3.8	2.6	12.1	1.8	2.3	8.1	4.3	1.0	0.9
Total	**16.2**	**21.0**	**7.9**	**5.4**	**16.2**	**13.8**	**20.0**	**17.8**	**8.8**	**17.0**	**4.7**
Per capita (Cdn$)											
Specific purpose	214	116	16	29	35	161	345	106	52	253	49
Unconditional	36	44	14	28	104	24	44	89	49	15	12
Total	**250**	**160**	**30**	**57**	**139**	**185**	**389**	**195**	**101**	**268**	**61**

Source: Data provided by Statistics Canada, Public Institutions Division.
a. Value less than 0.05.
b. Figures may not add to 100.0 because of rounding.

represent the distribution in any province. Throughout Canada, the area of social services receives the largest share, but only because Ontario devotes almost 80 percent of its grants to this purpose. Except for Ontario, municipalities in many provinces have no social service responsibilities, and the others have very little. Transportation is the other large national category for transfers, but although there is somewhat more homogeneity in this case, transfers for transportation still range from 4.9 percent of conditional transfers in Nova Scotia to 75 percent in Alberta. Other large variations can be found among provinces in other categories of spending—for example, health, environment, and debt charges.

The contribution of transfers to municipal spending in the various areas is also of interest. Table 2.7 provides insight into this aspect for all of Canada and for individual provinces. Provincial contributions to outlays have diminished since the mid-1990s, but the pattern among functions is fairly consistent. Grants make relatively large contributions to the expenditures on social services, health, and housing not only nationally but also in many individual provinces. Typically, municipalities have relatively minor responsibilities for such services. Conservation and development also might fit into this group. Transportation stands out in the areas of major municipal spending, with a number of provinces providing transfers that represent significant contributions to spending and other provinces contributing quite small amounts. Environment, as well as recreation and culture, gets support in all provinces, but the amounts vary considerably. Typically, relatively small provincial contributions (1 percent or less) go toward outlays by municipalities for protection. In general, provincial transfers tend to be fairly large relative to expenditures in those areas for which municipalities normally have limited responsibilities but, with the exception of transportation, tend to be smaller in those areas for which municipalities have major responsibilities.

Only the provincial governments provide unconditional grants. These general-purpose grants are small. They represented only 2.4 percent of municipal total revenue in 2001 (see table 2.4). General-purpose grants are modest relative to specific-purpose grants, which account for 14.5 percent of total provincial grants and 14.1 percent of all grants to municipalities. In only one province, New Brunswick, did unconditional transfers exceed specific-purpose transfers in 2001.

General-purpose transfers are intended to provide unconditional financial aid to municipalities to meet necessary expenditures. As a result, they usually equalize to some extent the fiscal abilities of municipal governments.[11] No uniform criteria are used among the provinces for the allocation of unconditional transfers (Kitchen 2002). The range of factors

TABLE 2.7 Provincial and Territorial Specific-Purpose Transfers, Canada (1988, 1995, and 2001) and Provinces (2001)
(*as a percentage of municipal expenditures in specific areas*)

Distribution	Canada 1988	Canada 1995	Canada 2001	Newfoundland and Labrador	Prince Edward Island	Nova Scotia	New Brunswick	Quebec	Ontario	Manitoba	Saskatchewan	Alberta	British Columbia
General services	1.5	2.7	2.1	8.5	1.2	2.1	3.1	2.0	1.3	6.6	1.8	4.7	1.0
Protection	0.7	1.3	0.9	7.3	0.5	1.1	0.3	0.8	1.0	1.3	1.0	0.5	0.7
Transportation	22.5	24.0	11.7	3.5	12.9	0.8	5.3	13.9	2.9	16.2	5.5	42.3	2.9
Health	41.9	44.4	37.6	0.0	0.0	44.6	1.4	80.8	41.7	23.2	0.4	0.8	23.0
Social services	70.2	76.1	56.4	0.0	0.0	0.5	—[a]	91.0	56.1	0.1	31.4	52.1	14.5
Conservation and development	20.9	18.2	11.8	0.2	34.6	1.2	9.6	14.0	8.6	20.7	12.9	17.3	4.2
Environment	10.3	14.4	6.1	9.7	0.1	3.1	4.3	18.5	2.9	6.2	4.5	3.5	2.8
Recreation and culture	7.1	7.8	5.5	23.3	2.3	14.2	8.3	8.7	2.2	17.9	7.1	8.4	1.4
Housing	19.8	39.7	17.9	41.1	—[a]	0.0	33.1	16.7	16.5	80.7	0.1	19.1	13.2
Regional planning	6.4	7.2	5.2	14.1	0.8	0.0[b]	0.5	8.2	4.5	2.6	0.6	1.6	1.6
Debt charges	13.3	11.2	11.4	58.5	0.0[b]	1.1	1.8	15.7	0.0	0.0	0.2	3.7	25.2
Other	12.2	11.4	34.5	107.4	0.0	562.9	0.0	142.3	0.0	146.7	59.3	0.0	0.5
Total specific-purpose expenditure (as % total expenditures)	16.00	20.8	13.9	15.2	4.1	2.8	4.1	12.0	17.7	9.7	4.5	16.0	3.8

Source: Data provided by Statistics Canada, Public Institutions Division.
a. No transfer but zero municipal expenditure for this category.
b. Value less than 0.05.

used is large. Small per capita grants are used in Alberta. However, relatively sophisticated methods based on calculations of expenditure need and revenue-generating capacity are used in New Brunswick to ensure that all municipalities within a class are able to provide an average level of service while imposing no more than the average tax rate, methods that generate relatively large grants (12.4 percent of municipal total revenues). Criteria such as those in New Brunswick follow the spirit of the Canadian federal-provincial equalization system, are used in Nova Scotia, and are a component determining unconditional transfers in Saskatchewan. Quebec equalizes tax bases. Elsewhere, general-purpose grants are determined according to some combination of per capita payments, per municipality payments, payments per kilometer of roadway, and sometimes other factors, with account sometimes taken of the relative tax base. The transfers are from the provincial to the municipal governments, except in Nova Scotia, where the equalization program is intermunicipal, with the province determining the payments to be made by the "better off" municipalities to the "less well off" municipalities.

Limited evidence is available on the effectiveness of the transfer programs to Canadian municipalities. Assessments of unconditional programs are dated. Auld and Eden (1987) and Eden (1987) examined the allocation formulas in various provinces and found, with the exception of the method used in New Brunswick, that most programs do little to reduce fiscal disparities. In an investigation of existing and alternative methods in the Alberta context, McMillan and Norton (1981) concluded that alternative methods typically appeared more effective in promoting fiscal equity. Conditional transfers are linked to specific spending and, thus, go where funds are required to the extent that is reflected in expenditures. The conditions of the specific-purpose grants to Canadian municipalities are probably not atypical of those found elsewhere and are subject to similar criticisms (see, for example, Fisher 1996 and McMillan, forthcoming).

Shared taxes typically play a minor role in Canada. The most substantial and longest-running shared tax arrangement between provincial and municipal governments is that in Manitoba. Manitoba dedicates 2.2 percent of its personal income tax revenues and 1 percent of its corporate income tax revenues to a fund that is distributed to municipalities on a per capita basis. Manitoba has recently introduced a program to share net revenues from provincially operated video lottery terminals. The city of Winnipeg gets 10 percent of that revenue generated within the city. Other municipalities receive 10 percent of the remaining provincial net video lottery revenues—Cdn$5,000 per municipality and the remainder per capita.

British Columbia had a revenue-sharing program with municipalities (from 1978), but it was ended in 1994. British Columbia shares traffic fine revenue with municipalities. This revenue is allocated in proportion to each municipality's share of total municipal policing costs.

A limited form of sharing of provincial fuel tax revenues exists in three provinces. In British Columbia, the province allots 11 cents per liter of the provincial fuel tax collected in the region to the Greater Vancouver Regional Authority for use in funding regional transportation. It also allots 2.5 cents per liter to the Victoria capital region. In Alberta, the province returns to Calgary and Edmonton 5 cents per liter of the provincial fuel tax collected in those cities. In Quebec, Montreal receives 1.5 cents per liter of the provincial fuel tax collected there.

Municipal Government Borrowing

Municipal government debt is essentially limited to long-term borrowing to finance capital investments. Municipalities are not permitted to budget an operating deficit. If an operating deficit should occur, the municipality can secure short-term financing to meet current needs but must budget to repay that debt, usually within the next fiscal year.

Long-term borrowing for financing municipal infrastructure investment is permitted and is common. In all provinces, there is a provincial authority through which or from which municipalities can borrow. These authorities are provincial government agencies in all provinces but British Columbia, which has an authority that is owned and operated by member municipalities. Pooling municipal government debt in a provincial government agency has a number of advantages. For the provinces, it affords a mechanism to monitor municipal debt: because municipalities are under their jurisdiction, they have some implicit, if not explicit, obligation for the repayment of municipal debt.[12] In fact, all the provincial government municipal financing corporations guarantee repayment of the debt that they issue. The pooling of the municipal debt and the provincial guarantee provides lower interest rates than individual local governments would be able to obtain because it reduces risk to the borrower. In addition, the provincial agencies provide advice to municipalities and minimize administration costs. The advantages of the provincial agencies are particularly beneficial to smaller municipalities. Typically, at least large municipalities have the option to go directly to the capital market. Hence, cities such as Edmonton, Saskatoon, and Winnipeg that have selected that option at least occasionally are bond rated.

Ontario is the latest province to create a municipal lending authority. Only in 2002 did the province establish the Ontario Municipal Economic Infrastructure Financing Authority. It was provided with a Cdn$1 billion capital reserve with a further Cdn$120 million rolled in from the Ontario Clean Water Agency. The authority also has the power to borrow for subsequent lending to municipalities for infrastructure investment. All municipalities can apply but must qualify based on financial soundness. The intention is that interest rates on the loans will be subsidized to approximately half the level of market rates. Previously, Ontario municipalities borrowed more or less directly from the capital market. Borrowing, however, had to be approved by a provincial board that determined a municipality's borrowing limit on the basis of repayment capacity, existing debt (and long-term lease) obligations, revenues, and tax base. Only once a request was approved could the municipality proceed to arrange financing.

Subsidies to reduce the need for borrowing or to assist in meeting debt obligations are common. Intergovernmental transfers to assist capital programs have already been noted. In addition, the federal and provincial governments sometimes lend funds for certain programs (for example, environmental or housing programs) at reduced interest rates. Occasionally, the provinces have introduced general interest subsidies on municipal (or local) government debt and sometimes have provided debt relief. Municipal bonds that are exempt from income tax afford an indirect form of interest rate relief to municipal governments that is found in the United States. Bonds of this type were introduced in Canada only as recently as 2003 and then only in Ontario. The Ontario government introduced "opportunity bonds"—the interest from which was free of Ontario (but not federal) personal income tax—as the source of lending capital for the new Ontario Municipal Economic Infrastructure Financing Authority. The lower interest rates that the bonds required because of the Ontario tax-exempt status contributed to the reduced interest cost to the municipalities. The returns on the authority's capital reserve also served to reduce municipal borrowing rates. The provincial tax-exempt infrastructure bonds got less than unanimous acclaim from the economic community and were quickly dispensed with following a change of government in Ontario resulting from the October 2, 2003, provincial election.[13]

Municipal debt is not particularly large in Canada. Local government bonds (municipal and school) and debentures amounted to Cdn$1,167 per capita in 2000. In that year, net debt (financial liabilities in excess of financial assets) amounted to Cdn$324 per capita. If one assumes that municipal debt is held in proportion to the municipal share of local capital spending (about 0.88 during the 1990s), the corresponding municipal amounts would be Cdn$1,027 and Cdn$285. These amounts are 68 percent and 19 percent, respectively, of municipal annual revenues. Although total local bond and debenture debt declined slightly between 1996 (its peak year) and 2000 (the latest data), local net debt has fallen sharply since 1994 from Cdn$786 to Cdn$324 per capita. Also, although local net debt relative to local government revenues has been declining steadily for the past 25 years, the drop in the 1995 to 2000 period from 30.6 to 12.7 percent has been dramatic. Clearly, local (and obviously municipal) governments have been accumulating financial assets and reducing net debt, perhaps in anticipation of a renewal of needed capital spending.

Recent Developments

The preceding data reported on Canadian municipal governments as of 2001. A number of notable developments have occurred recently in municipal finance, and those may motivate further changes. Consideration is given first to national trends since 1988 (the first year that municipal data are available separate from aggregated local government data). Provided next is a subnational perspective. The infrastructure situation is examined. Finally, note is made of potential new developments.

A National Perspective

In the first half of the 1990s, the provincial and federal governments were struggling with large deficits. They made substantial efforts to get their fiscal affairs in order and, after the mid-1990s, had achieved surpluses or, for the provinces collectively, at least small deficits if not surpluses. Part of the deficit reduction program was a substantial reduction in intergovernmental transfers by both the federal and provincial governments—moves that some have characterized as a period of "fend-for-yourself federalism" (Tindal and Tindal 2003, 195). Municipalities bore much of the brunt of the cuts in transfers. Table 2.8 demonstrates this reduction. Total transfers to municipalities accounted for 22.36 percent of municipal expenditures in 1988 and 25.47 percent in 1995 but only 16.64 percent by 2001. The bulk of the reduction came from a one-third cut in provincial grants after 1995, but the federal government's reductions also contributed.[14]

Despite the cut in grants, municipalities managed to keep municipal expenditures abreast—but only abreast—of national output, incomes, and other subnational (provincial and school board) expenditures over

TABLE 2.8 Canadian Municipal Fiscal Variables in Selected Years

Variable	1988	1995	2001
Intergovernmental transfers (as % municipal government expenditures)			
Federal	0.70	1.35	0.42
Provincial	21.66	24.12	16.22
Total	22.36	25.47	16.64
Municipal government expenditures (as % GDP)			
Program expenditures	4.11	4.71	4.19
Total expenditures	4.54	5.11	4.40
Municipal expenditures (as % consolidated provincial and local government expenditures)	16.10	16.80	16.30
Constant dollar per capita municipal expenditures (Cdn$)	1,262	1,452	1,453
Debt charges (as % municipal expenditures)	9.50	7.80	5.00
Municipal own-source revenue (as % PDI)	5.27	5.89	5.87
Real property taxes (as % total municipal government revenue)	32.20	33.80	41.90
Municipal real property taxes (as % GDP)	1.42	1.71	1.80
Municipal real property taxes (as % PDI)	2.21	2.67	2.96

Source: McMillan 2003.

the 1988–2001 period. As reported in table 2.8, municipal total expenditure as a percentage of GDP was 4.54 percent in 1988 and 4.40 percent in 2001. In addition, municipal program spending also barely changed, moving from 4.11 to only 4.19 percent of GDP in the same period.[15] Finally, municipal program expenditures as a percentage of consolidated provincial and local (subnational) program expenditures also showed no trend, starting at 16.1 percent and ending at 16.3 percent.[16] Despite the loss of transfers equivalent to almost 9 percent of their expenditures, municipalities managed to maintain their expenditure shares over this 14-year period. In fact, real (inflation-adjusted) municipal total expenditures per capita rose about 15 percent from Cdn$1,262 to Cdn$1,453.[17] In part, municipalities were assisted by the falling costs of debt service (from 9.5 percent in 1988 and 7.8 percent in 1995 to 5.0 percent in 2001), but ultimately, the necessary funds had to come from own-source revenues.

The required increase in own-source revenues came primarily from increased real property taxes. Real property taxes rose from 32.2 to 41.9 percent of total revenue—a change of 9.7 percentage points, representing a 30.1 percent increase in the real property tax share, most of which occurred in the last six years. Meanwhile, property-related taxes grew little over the period and declined from 16.2 to 10.3 percent of total revenue. Sales, fees, and charges increased from 20 to 23 percent, the only other major category to show an increase. Thus, there was a contribution from sales, fees, and charges, but the real burden of making up the difference has fallen on the real property tax.

Between 1988 and 2001, real property taxes increased sharply. As a percentage of GDP, real property taxes increased 26.8 percent (from 1.42 to 1.80 percent), and as a percentage of PDI, they increased 33.9 percent (from 2.21 to 2.96 percent). The constant (1992) dollar per capita tax rose from Cdn\$418 to Cdn\$544, or by 30.1 percent. These changes represent substantial increases in what is often regarded as a less popular tax.

One can arrive at a number of observations and tentative conclusions with respect to events of the 1988 to 2001 period. The municipalities managed to maintain their expenditures relative to GDP, PDI, and total subnational government spending. Real dollar per capita expenditures even rose by about 15 percent. Any new downloaded expenditure responsibilities do not show up as higher relative aggregate expenditures, an observation that does not deny their existence. However, for the most part, downloads may have been small, accommodated by reductions elsewhere, or both, but they were troublesome nonetheless. Capital spending may have suffered, and deteriorating infrastructure may be temporarily masking the problems.

A Subnational Perspective

Because municipal affairs are provincial policy, national data may obscure as much as they reveal. Hence, it is also useful to consider a more provincial or, at least, subnational perspective. A province-by-province review cannot be done here, but it is useful to focus to some extent on Ontario, which has followed a rather different approach not only with its municipalities but also in its most recent reforms.

Subnational data indicate that Ontario differs from the other provinces. It has a relatively large municipal sector (25.5 percent of consolidated provincial local expenditures compared with 14.2 percent in the other provinces) and, unlike elsewhere, that sector has actually grown (from 22 percent) particularly after reforms introduced in 1997 (see table 2.9). There is evidence of real responsibility downloading in Ontario.

TABLE 2.9 A Subnational Perspective on Selected Canadian Municipal Fiscal Variables, 1988 and 2001

Variable	1988	2001
Municipal program expenditure (as % consolidated provincial and local government program expenditure)		
Ontario	22.00	25.50
Other provinces	15.70	14.20
Municipal own-source revenue (as % PDI)		
Ontario	5.01	6.62
Other provinces	5.46	5.34
Municipal real property taxes (as % PDI)		
Ontario	2.14	3.52
Other provinces	2.25	2.57

Source: McMillan 2003.

As elsewhere, Ontario municipalities have become more reliant on their own-source revenues. However, the burden of own-source revenue as a percentage of PDI increased 1.61 percentage points (to 6.62 percent) in Ontario, while the average burden of own-source revenue elsewhere actually declined marginally from 5.46 to 5.34 percent. The municipal real property tax burden (as a share of PDI) has increased in all provinces to meet rising own-source revenue requirements, but especially so in Ontario, where it rose from 2.14 to 3.52 percent between 1988 and 2001 compared with an average increase from 2.25 to 2.57 percent in the other provinces.[18] Again, the sharp and significant change in Ontario occurred after the 1997 reforms.

An interesting difference also appears in Quebec. Provincial data indicate that Quebec was the only province not to reduce transfers to its municipalities. Between 1988 and 2001, total transfers to Quebec municipalities increased from 8.0 to 14.0 percent of municipal expenditures. Also unique, as a municipal contribution to the province's fiscal restraint effort, the Quebec government required an annual contribution of Cdn$356 million by its municipalities for three years (1998–2000) to a Local Activities Special Financing Fund. That Cdn$356 million annual contribution was equivalent to about 30 percent of transfers then in place.

Changes in social service financing in Nova Scotia also deserve comment. During the last half of the 1990s, social service outlays fell from one-fourth of municipal expenditures in 1995 to 4.5 percent in 2001 as the province assumed greater responsibility for social services. Because provincial transfers funded about three-fourths of municipal social service outlays, transfers to the municipalities declined as well, and the drop in transfers for social services accounted for 74 percent of the reduction in the total grants to municipalities over that period. Thus, the substantial fall in grants as a percentage of municipal expenditures (from 24.8 to 5.9 percent between 1988 and 2001) results partly from a provincial-municipal reallocation of responsibilities. A better comparison is that, had the 2001 social service arrangements been in place in 1995, transfers would have represented about 15 percent of municipal expenditures. A decline in the contribution of transfers from 15 to 5.9 percent is still substantial but more modest than the simple numbers suggest.

The pressure to maintain services in the face of declining grants during an economic slump posed problems for municipalities throughout the country during much of the 1990s. The result was fiscal pressure, especially from the revenue side. In general, though, the municipal governments seem to be coping relatively well. However, the burdens put on Ontario municipal governments and their taxpayers appear extraordinary, which suggests that the municipal fiscal squeeze might be a problem primarily related to Ontario.

Infrastructure Concerns

Many, including Federation of Canadian Municipalities (1999) and Vander Ploeg (2003), have expressed concern about the quality of municipal infrastructure in Canada and the ability of municipalities to meet future infrastructure needs. A widely expressed opinion is that Canada has an infrastructure deficit; that is, municipalities have not kept up with capital requirements and have capital in need of repair and replacement. In addition, analysts and others also are concerned about the abilities of municipalities not only to overcome that deficit but also to extend the municipal capital stock as required.[19]

Few detailed studies of capital needs have been conducted. Recently, however, the Union des Muncipalités du Québec and Conference Board of Canada (2003) conducted an intensive study of municipal infrastructure in Quebec. That report concluded that an infrastructure problem exists in Quebec municipalities. The average age of municipal capital (increasing since the 1970s) is high, the existing capital stock has deteriorated, and new investments have been inadequate. The cost to catch up will be high, and the cost of additional new capital will increase that cost. The report held that municipalities will be unable to fund the required expenditures from their traditional revenue sources (notably the property tax). Consequently, federal and provincial aid is being requested—largely for shares of tax revenues— to assist the municipalities in meeting the necessary infrastructure renewal. Some analysts suggest that the Quebec situation is likely typical of that in other provinces. Vander Ploeg (2003) estimates that the six large cities in western Canada have an infrastructure deficit amounting to Cdn$176 per capita.

Capital expenditures by municipal government (and local government in total), as measured by real per capita capital acquisition, have been relatively stable throughout the 1990s. At the local government level (for which a long data series is available), new capital acquisition has continued to decline (from the 1960s to now) relative to capital consumption allowances (though it still exceeds them).[20] Declines such as these have been widely observed elsewhere. Since 1999, capital outlays by local governments have increased markedly. Real dollar outlays in 2002 were about 30 percent higher than in 1998. This resurgence in local—and thus municipal—capital expenditures may reflect the improvement in the economy and in incomes, the reduced cost burden of servicing debts, relatively low interest rates, and recognition of infrastructure needs.

Future Directions

A notable development in Canadian municipal finance resulted from the emergence of Canada's recent prime minister, Paul Martin, as a champion of a "new deal" for municipalities. He initiated this cause during his campaign for leadership of the Liberal Party, and it was mostly associated with a sharing of federal fuel tax revenues. Toward that initiative, the federal budget of 2004 provided municipalities full (versus the partial 57 percent) relief from the federal goods and services tax (GST). This measure was estimated to provide municipalities Cdn$580 million in sales tax relief in its first year. The 2005 federal budget announced the New Deal for Cities and Communities program, which is to provide Cdn$5 billion in funds for municipalities over the next five years, starting with Cdn$600 million in 2005–6. The Cdn$600 million translates into about Cdn$18.75 per capita today or about 1.2 percent of 2001 municipal expenditures. Immediate potential funding from the new deal plus the added savings from the GST is equivalent to about 2.4 percent of 2001 municipal expenditures—clearly a healthy increase from recent levels of federal government transfers. As planned, the new deal could be expected to amount to 3 percent of municipal expenditure after five years. However, although under way, how this program will evolve is uncertain because the federal government changed with the January 2006 election. Meanwhile, the provinces (with the exception of Alberta, which is now again flush with natural resource revenues) have shown little interest in restoring grants to their municipalities.

A number of studies have examined the municipal fiscal situation and options for enhancing municipalities' fiscal situation (see, for example, Canadian Tax Foundation 2002a, 2002b, 2002c; Kitchen 2000, 2003; Kitchen and Slack 2003; McMillan 2003; TD Bank Financial Group 2002; and Vander Ploeg 2001, 2002a, 2002b). Potential is often seen for restoring and reforming transfers, both conditional and unconditional, but given the experience of the past decade, analysts and municipalities look askance at this avenue. Forms of revenue sharing with provincial governments are sometimes proposed, especially by municipalities, although it is unclear why these programs would be any more secure than the conventional transfer programs that were cut so substantially. Witness the demise of the revenue-sharing program in British Columbia. Much more attention is paid now than previously to expanding sources of own-source revenue to give municipalities more control of their funding.

Before new sources are considered, there is a possibility that the property tax might serve adequately for municipalities if it were solely a municipal tax. Currently, in most provinces, the property tax is both a municipal and a provincial tax. The property tax emerged as a provincial tax when the provinces took over the full financing of schools (effectively in all but two provinces), and in so doing, they also replaced the local school property taxes with a provincial property tax. Provincial property taxes are substantial. They amount to 70 percent of the municipal property taxes and add (in 2001) a property tax burden of 2.1 percent of PDI to the municipal tax burden of 2.96 percent. Although local property taxes may not have been ideally suited for school finance, they had a long historical connection with school funding and, more recently, represented the only local tax available to local governments including school boards. Provincial governments have the full range of tax options available to them and, thus, could end the provincial property tax and shift that burden to other provincial taxes. This strategy would leave the property tax as solely a municipal tax in most provinces, a situation that might provide municipal governments more ability to use it for financing municipal services. Despite municipal calls for abandonment of provincial property taxes, no new moves in this direction are being proposed.

A variety of new municipal taxes have been suggested. Following examples in the United States, where municipal sales taxes account for about 10 percent of local general-purpose (municipal) government revenue, the idea of a municipal general sales tax is often put forward. Although the tax is common in the United States, problems arise in that (a) sales tax bases are quite uneven and (b) consumer mobility and business location decisions result in fiscal spillovers and economic distortions (Sjoquist, Wallace, and Edwards 2004). Municipal vehicle fuel taxes have also been proposed. They have problems similar to those of municipal general sales taxes. Sales and fuel taxes might be better suited for revenue-sharing programs to prevent the problems associated with local taxes of this type. Revenue sharing, however, puts control back in the hands of the provincial governments with which the municipal governments are sharing revenue. Given the importance of transportation as a municipal expenditure responsibility, it is odd that municipal governments in Canada have no transportation-related revenue. A local vehicle registration fee has been suggested to meet that objective while avoiding the border problems associated with fuel taxes and retaining local control. Local income taxes (also common in the United States) are another possibility.[21] Although local income taxes, like local property taxes, are less susceptible to problems associated with taxpayer mobility (Oates and Schwab 2004), they have typically received less attention in the discussion. Note that the administrative and compliance costs of all these taxes can be minimized by piggybacking the municipal tax on existing provincial (or, if need be, federal) taxes. Note, too, that regardless of the source of greater own-source revenue, as municipal governments come to rely more on own-source revenue, there may be a greater need to pay attention to equalization grants if fiscal disparities expand.

Some municipalities have taken the initiative toward reforming municipal finance. For example, the city of Winnipeg proposed a fiscal makeover it called the "New Deal Initiative."[22] The proposed changes would have reduced the general property tax from 39 percent to one-fourth of city revenues (primarily by reducing residential property taxes), raised user fees and charges, introduced a municipal general sales tax of 1 percent and a municipal fuel tax of Cdn$0.05 per liter, introduced liquor and hotel taxes, and resulted in the city getting a share (revenue from a 0.5 percent rate) of the provincial sales tax and Cdn$0.05 per liter of the federal fuel tax. Although the city's former mayor, Glen Murray, promoted this initiative forcefully and adroitly, it is not yet clear how successful the overall venture will be, especially since he has left office. The proposal suffered a setback when the Manitoba government announced that it would not cooperate in permitting a 1 percent city sales tax or share revenue from 0.5 percent of the provincial sales tax rate with the city. The provincial government expressed willingness, however, to discuss municipal fuel, liquor, and hotel taxes.

An Overall Assessment of Municipal Government Finances

A brief overview will clarify the assessment in this section. Municipal government represents about 10 percent of total government expenditure. Local expenditures are made, with few exceptions, to provide services benefiting local residents (notably, fire and police protection, roads and public transport, water and waste management, and recreation and cultural services). Municipal government relies on own-source revenues for more than 80 percent of revenues. Own-source revenues essentially consist of property and property-related taxes as well as user charges and fees. Transfers, which are almost entirely provincial, now account for 17 percent of total revenue (down from 23 percent in 1988). Those transfers are predominantly conditional. The reduction in transfers has resulted in a heavier municipal property tax burden that together with provincial property taxes (and local school taxes where they exist), pushed property tax burdens back to peak levels of the 1960s. Ontario is unique in the level of property taxes, the increase in those taxes after 1997, and the social service responsibilities its municipalities bear. Municipal tax increases during the 1990s may have been restrained by deferred capital expenditures that contributed to an emerging infrastructure deficit. In this context, it is not surprising that municipal finance has surfaced on the public policy agenda.

Criteria for this assessment come from the work on fiscal federalism. In that work, the assignment of both expenditure responsibilities and revenue-raising and taxing powers is a central issue. Decentralization, or subsidiarity, is a tenet of fiscal federalism.[23] The principle is that responsibility for services should be assigned to the lowest level of government capable of providing the service effectively. For local government, the focus is on achieving effective local government by realizing autonomy, responsiveness, accountability, and a strong benefit-cost link for local services.[24]

Expenditure Responsibilities

Judged by the criteria of fiscal federalism and practicality of performance, the services provided by Canadian municipalities typically are well suited to local government. Protection (fire, police), transportation, environment (water, sewerage, solid waste), recreation and culture, general services, debt charges, conservation and development, and regional planning—which together account for more than 80 percent of municipal spending nationally and more than 90 percent in most provinces—are services that essentially provide local benefits (in other words, limited benefits spill over jurisdictional boundaries) for which tastes vary and for which local management and a local scale of operations are efficient. These services suit well the duties of a government that is limited to user charges and property taxes. An important and interesting feature of local government in Canada over the past 20 years has been the expanding provincialization of school finance, which has effectively made schooling entirely a provincial responsibility (despite the local school boards).

Social expenditures by municipalities—those for health, social services, education, and housing—are minor in most provinces. In eight provinces, they total 4 percent or less of total outlays. Although municipal support for schooling makes Nova Scotia stand out, the striking anomaly is Ontario, where social spending represents one-third of municipal expenditures. Local governments are not well suited to financing redistributive services. Consequently, social services in particular and social spending in general have been progressively reduced (most recently in Nova Scotia) or essentially eliminated (in eight provinces) as a municipal responsibility. Ontario makes concessions by means of transfers, but those transfers offset only a little more than half the costs. Ontario's reforms of the 1990s aggravated the situation because, although they were initially proposed to be revenue neutral, the numbers did not work out. Ontario is the most obvious case of a province downloading service responsibilities. Elsewhere, this downloading has taken the form of shifting onto municipal governments added responsibility for raising revenue from their own sources.

Revenue-Raising Authority

Tax assignment becomes an issue in governments with a multitiered structure. Taxes on immobile tax bases (notably property) as well as fees and charges on service beneficiaries are well suited to municipal government. Because efficient resource allocation is seen to be the major municipal objective, a close link between local public benefits and local public levies is strongly recommended; that is, the benefit principle should prevail. As Bird (1993) has noted, "The essential economic role of local government is to provide local residents with those public services for which they are willing to pay" (111). In addition, the levies to be imposed on local citizens as required to finance local services should be determined by citizens' local government. Benefit-related finance and local determination of local levies are fundamental criteria of local public finance. Furthermore, revenue sources ideally should be adequate, predictable, fair, visible, not exportable, and easily administered.

The revenue structure of Canadian municipalities conforms rather well to the model outlined. Own-source revenues account for 83 percent of revenues (more than 90 percent in most provinces) and are almost entirely locally determined.[25] Half of total revenues come from property and related taxes, and one-quarter from user charges. Lot levies and special assessments (about 4 percent of own-source revenues) fit the benefit criteria well. More debatable is the business tax (about 3 percent of own-source revenues). Business taxes, plus high property taxes on nonresidential property, raise questions about tax shifting and exporting (Kitchen 2002; Kitchen and Slack 1993). Further reliance on user charges is often advocated, especially for environmental and recreational services. Yet higher service charges have not figured predominantly in the municipal response to the decade's fiscal stresses. Instead, greater real property taxes have carried the load.

Municipalities have not had revenue sources that correspond well to their major expenditure area, transportation. In particular, there is no mechanism through which municipalities can allocate costs directly to vehicles and their users. Fuel taxes and license fees are the realm of the provincial and federal governments. Tolls have been limited to a few specific projects and to public transit.

The adequacy and appropriateness of the property tax can be questioned when municipalities are being asked or expected to meet more social expenditures without compensating transfers. Ontario is the obvious concern. There, social expenditures are now 33.2 percent of municipal budgets, at least half again as much as in 1988. Elsewhere, social expenditures have risen, if at all, only marginally. However, municipalities in other provinces may be concerned that the perceived need for social spending at the municipal level has increased in the face of provincial and federal cutbacks.

The assumption of full financial responsibility for schooling by more provinces (for example, Alberta, British Columbia, and Ontario) has been a feature of recent local-provincial finance. The paralleling feature is the failure of those provinces to fund schooling from traditional provincial revenue sources and their strategy, instead, to convert the local school property tax into a provincial property tax. The school property tax, which does not relate well to school benefits or taxpayers' ability to pay, made sense when a local contribution to schooling was required and the only sufficient local tax base was property. Elimination of provincial property taxes for schooling (at least on residential property) might enhance municipalities' abilities to fund spending from traditional revenue sources.

A potential concern is that municipalities are forced to rely too much on the property taxes when, if given the choice, they would balance property taxes with other forms of taxation. The issue is what alternative forms of taxation are appropriate. Ideally, taxes assigned to local governments (a) should maintain the local benefit-cost link and not spill over to tax those not benefiting from the local expenditures that they finance and (b) should keep tax-induced economic distortions to a minimum. Meeting those criteria may, especially in multijurisdictional regions, significantly limit the range of attractive options.

Typically, municipal capital spending is partly debt financed. Probably wisely, because of the implicit obligation, all provinces monitor municipal debt and borrowing closely. All provinces now have agencies that assist municipalities in securing capital financing. Agencies such as these are to be recommended. While they provide a convenient means to monitor municipal borrowing, they also provide substantial benefits to municipalities, especially the smaller ones, by lending advice and expertise, by reducing administrative costs, and by reducing interest costs through debt pooling as well as through borrowing with the guarantee of the province. Although the provincial municipal infrastructure finance agencies are helpful, another likely useful approach is to permit (at least larger) municipalities the option of going to the capital markets directly.

The restriction against municipal borrowing for operating purposes is not unusual in other countries. Given the nature of municipal expenditures and revenue sources, this restriction is not unreasonable. Although in most cases it may not be needed, it likely prevents some troublesome situations.

Intergovernmental Transfers

Objective and independent assignments of expenditure and revenue-raising responsibilities ensure neither an efficient nor an equitable fiscal system. One potential problem is a mismatch of fiscal capacity and expenditure responsibilities resulting in a fiscal gap that calls for some reshuffling of responsibilities or revenue sources or for unconditional gap-reducing intergovernmental transfers, or for all three. Even if no fiscal gap occurs at the municipal level overall, there may still be "rich" and "poor" municipalities creating legitimate demands for unconditional equalization grants. Interjurisdictional spillovers of benefits, taxes, or both call for grants to correct distortions and to improve fairness. The best design for such grants is specific to the spillover activity. Specific-purpose, or conditional, grants are a means by which different tiers of government share responsibilities for services that do not fit neatly into any single level. Schooling has been one such responsibility. Conditional transfers are also one way by which one level of government essentially contracts with another level to perform specific services. In addition, political reasons motivate intergovernmental grants. Raw political power may be one motivation, but a more positive view is that some grants are a means to motivate cooperation and contributions while stretching the grantor's budget. Hence, grants may exist for various reasons. Because grant programs often appear to be designed to meet more than a single objective, assessment is complicated.

Unconditional grants to municipalities are provided only by the provincial governments and, typically, in relatively modest amounts. For Canada as a whole, unconditional assistance averages 2.4 percent of municipal revenues, with the largest relative contributions being made to Manitoba (7.9 percent) and New Brunswick (12.4 percent). Such funds normally come from provincial general revenues, but in Manitoba, monies come from a well-established revenue-sharing program. Those grants are distributed by formulas on some form of equalizing basis. Often, the available funds are inadequate to meet the equalization requirements implied by the distribution mechanisms. Typically, some funds are allocated to every municipality; hence, the unconditional transfers may be motivated partly by fiscal gap-closing objectives. Given the modest magnitude of unconditional funding, most provinces must see the municipal fiscal gap and fiscal equalization problems as minor. One might wonder about this apparent position, especially when municipalities must increasingly rely on own-source funds. The levels and distribution criteria for unconditional funding could benefit from a careful review.

Conditional transfers in most provinces are mostly for transportation, environmental (water and sewerage) services, and recreation and culture. The externality element in transportation is obvious, but for the other categories, it is more obtuse. Even if funding is not explicitly designated for capital projects (or for debt service costs), it is predominantly associated with them. Emphasis on assistance to capital projects raises questions about the potential misallocations between capital and operating costs that have been evident in some situations.

A striking feature of the existing conditional transfers is the variation in their relative contribution to municipal spending for a particular purpose. For example, transfers for transportation meet 2.9 percent of expenditures in Ontario but 42 percent in Alberta. However, spillovers are usually not easily determined, and priorities can vary. Of interest is that transfers for policing, a service likely involving significant externalities, make only very small contributions to those costs, yet transfers for recreation, likely providing local benefits, cover a far higher share of that service's costs.

Ontario's loading of significant social expenditures onto municipalities is exceptional. This unusual arrangement could be quite workable as a responsibility-sharing arrangement given the appropriate transfer programs—that is, generous conditional social transfers and effective equalization. Ontario's social transfers still leave the municipalities to meet half that cost, which amounts to about 16 percent of their total expenditures, a level that still far exceeds the municipal social expenditure outlay in any other province.

Federal transfers to municipalities are small (0.4 of 2001 municipal expenditures in Canada), and they are directed mostly to social housing and transportation. With recent reductions, the federal contribution to expenditures in any of the main areas has become increasingly minor, the largest in 2001 being to housing where federal transfers provided 2.33 percent (down from 16 percent in 1995).[26] Federal transfers may contribute in important ways to various subprograms, but the overall contribution has been small and declining.

The analyst would expect federal transfers in areas involving national externalities or in areas of federal jurisdiction benefiting from municipal input and cooperation. Efforts to alleviate poverty—such as social housing, immigrant settlement, and assistance for urban Aboriginal groups—seem logical. Although housing has been identified as a component of the federal urban strategy, the levels planned will not notably enhance the federal role. The fiscal priority of the recent and announced federal strategy has, interestingly, been infrastructure (see, for example, OECD 2002 and Prime Minister's Caucus Task Force on Urban Issues 2002). Beyond federal visibility from input into municipal projects that afford broad local public benefit (as opposed to small social projects benefiting narrow groups of disadvantaged people), the national interest in and benefit from many of these investments is difficult to imagine. With a form of federal sharing of Canada's fuel tax with municipalities having been initiated, it will be interesting to see what level of funding will be provided in the longer term and how those funds will be distributed, especially under a new federal government.

Lessons for Developing and Other Countries

Canadian local government offers a variety of lessons, not all positive, for countries considering refining or reforming their local governments.[27] On the responsibility side, the expenditure responsibilities of municipal government are well suited for the local level of government. The bulk of the services and the vast majority of the expenditures that are required serve local citizens and do so largely through services to property. Some of those services are provided through municipal public enterprises that operate as businesses and yield returns to their municipalities. With few exceptions, Canadian municipalities are not involved in services whose objective is largely redistributive (that is, social services). Ontario is the exception; the magnitude of Ontario's social spending done by the municipalities is exceptionally large, and half of that is financed from municipal sources. The Ontario reforms that augmented the local social service burden were contrary to widespread recommendations, which is not to say that local governments cannot perform social service functions well. The Scandinavian countries provide a good example of success, but that success requires a broader range of taxes than Canadian municipalities levy, and it also requires a strong equalization system. Alternatively, a well-designed system of grants that enables upper-level governments to contract with local governments for those services is needed. Schooling is the major social responsibility associated with local government in Canada. Interestingly, schooling is still considered a local responsibility, although the provincial governments have taken over essentially all the funding in 8 of the 10 provinces. Oddly, in doing so, the provinces have retained a provincial (or provincially determined) property tax to help fund provincial education expenditures when the school property tax is actually a remnant of local school finance and the provinces have superior taxes with which to fund schooling. Although municipal government is well structured, schooling in Canada is barely a local function today, and most students of fiscal federalism would consider its finance hardly exemplary.

The services of municipal governments provide local benefits, and under the benefit principle, local residents are expected to pay for them. Municipal governments rely on own-source revenues to fund 85 to 90 percent of their expenditures. Given the nature of the services provided and the local nature of the revenue raising, the property tax works quite effectively as the major source of municipal revenue, along with charges and fees on users. Criticisms of the property tax abound (for example, its assessments, its excessive burden on business, and its regressive nature), but a superior alternative is difficult to identify. Furthermore, accountability to local voters is high as local councils determine the rates and fees to meet the expenditures their citizens request and are prepared to finance. Note, too, that the federal and provincial governments make payments in lieu of taxes to contribute to the cost of local services in the municipalities in which they have property.

The recent reduction in transfers to the municipalities has increased their reliance on own-source revenues. This move has raised the question of how willing local taxpayers are to provide adequate municipal services from existing revenue sources. Because the combined municipal and provincial (more than 40 percent of the total) property tax rates are quite high by historical standards, the question arises as to whether the property tax would be more acceptable and adequate for municipal purposes if there were no provincial property tax. Moving the provinces out of the property tax field seems an obvious recommendation. In this environment, analysts and municipal authorities are looking at alternative tax sources—notably, sales taxes, fuel taxes, income taxes, and vehicle registration fees—but they are not uniformly suitable, and only the provinces can confer those taxing powers.

The dramatic cut in transfers to municipalities demonstrates a major problem that transfers pose for municipal governments; that is, they are not reliable. Transfers may be rationalized by economic factors, but they are determined by politics and the circumstances of the grantor. Hence, the amount and the allocation of grants among programs can change substantially over time. Although circumstances may vary among provinces, the considerable inconsistency in the support afforded certain functions suggests (it would take considerable investigation to verify) a rather ad hoc determination of specific-purpose grants. Whether provincial-municipal grant systems would work as effectively if much of the funding were made unconditional must be a reasonable consideration. Unconditional funding is typically modest (in both share and amount) and, in most cases, likely has a fairly small effect on reducing fiscal disparities among municipalities. Unconditional funding of the design found in New Brunswick (in other words, a design that considers the difference between fiscal needs and fiscal capacities and that is adequately funded) is the most effective approach to achieving equalization. The fact that equalization is funded by the provinces everywhere but in Nova Scotia can be seen as a positive aspect of unconditional funding. Intermunicipal transfers foster discontent and animosity among municipalities. Manitoba provides the only example of successful and long-lived unconditional funding through revenue or tax sharing. Overall, the Canadian municipal transfer system has its share of deficiencies. Definitely on the positive side, however, is the transparency of the system. The distribution of the grants is determined to a large extent by known criteria, and the after-the-fact distribution is public information.

All provinces monitor municipal finances and, in particular, supervise municipal borrowing. This oversight can be helpful to municipalities and provincial governments alike. Municipalities can borrow only to fund capital expenditures (not operating outlays). In each province, there is now a municipal finance authority that assists municipalities in obtaining infrastructure finance. Nine of those authorities are provincial government entities that can offer an advantage relative to municipally organized agencies. The advantages of debt pooling and provincial guarantees (along with the supervision that existed anyway) lower the cost and difficulty of borrowing, especially for small municipalities. However, to keep those municipal finance authorities competitive, policy makers may find it useful to permit municipalities to pursue capital on their own in the capital market.

Overall, Canadian municipal government works well. The services it provides are local, the financing is largely from those who benefit, and the expenditures and tax levels are determined locally by locally elected councils whose members are accountable to the electorate and are responsible for managing the local civil service. Intergovernmental transfers are not always well designed for correcting for spillovers and for reducing fiscal disparities among municipalities, but they are a transparent, if not especially reliable, source of municipal revenue.

Notes

1. Valuable general references on Canadian local government are Kitchen (2002) and Tindal and Tindal (2003).
2. Ontario is somewhat of an exception in that local governments there carry a much larger responsibility for social services and assistance than in the other provinces.
3. Besides the provinces, Canada has three northern territories. Because of their small populations (0.32 percent of the national population) and unique circumstances, they are not considered in this analysis.
4. Natural person powers are those available to individuals and corporations. They include powers to enter into contracts, buy and sell products, hire employees, borrow, invest, and establish companies. These powers had not been provided generally to municipalities; rather, municipalities had only specific powers under specific legislation. See Garcea and LeSage (2005), especially 61–62.
5. Before 1988, data were available only for local government, that is, the combination of (the comparably sized) general-purpose local authorities (municipalities) and local school authorities (school boards). The data suggest that, since 1965, the relative magnitude of local government has been relatively stable.
6. In 2005, the average rate of exchange for the Canadian dollar was US$0.825.
7. The transfers specifically tied to capital outlays probably understate the de facto contribution, because numerous other grants are associated with capital expenditures.
8. Market value is the standard for assessing property. For property types for which numerous market transactions are available (such as houses, apartments, business buildings), market value comparisons can be readily achieved, especially with computer-assisted assessment. A number of property types are sold rarely if at all (for example, railroads, pipelines, electricity generating plants), and for those, alternative

assessment methods must be used. Often, in those cases, value is based on inflation-adjusted cost minus depreciation.

9. For some insight into property tax rates for residential and business properties in different provinces, see Bish (2003) and Kitchen (2002).

10. Transfers in Prince Edward Island also are relatively small, 7.2 percent of total revenue, but municipal expenditures there are low.

11. Equalization played a particularly important role in the assistance that the provinces provided to school boards when the boards had access to and relied heavily on local tax sources. With the provincialization of school finances in most provinces, uniform provincial funding has taken over that role.

12. In Ontario, no municipality has defaulted on its debt since the 1930s. Although information for other provinces is not at hand, the Ontario experience is likely not atypical.

13. Note, too, that, unlike in the United States, nonbusiness property taxes are not deductible from provincial or federal personal income taxes—another form of indirect subsidy to municipal government.

14. There have also been numerous complaints of provincial governments downloading or off-loading responsibilities onto municipal governments without compensation, but (outside of Ontario) these complaints and their effects have not been well documented.

15. Program expenditures are expenditures minus debt servicing costs (that is, expenditures made directly on services or programs for the community).

16. Note that as a result of the slow growth in GDP during the economic funk of the early and mid-1990s, these values in 1995 are larger because of the adverse effect on the denominator of the ratio. Fortunately, both 1988 and 2001 are in periods of relatively comparable economic prosperity.

17. Nominal dollars are adjusted using the GDP price index. There is no price index for municipal government expenditure; however, the GDP index not only seems more appropriate than the consumer price index but also approximates the index for (total) government current expenditures.

18. The total (provincial and local) property tax burden (relative to PDI) also increased between 1988 and 2001. In Ontario, it rose from 4.70 to 6.05 percent, and the average increase in the other provinces was from 3.71 to 4.46 percent. Ontario has a particularly high provincial property tax, matched only by the local school taxes in Saskatchewan.

19. Concern for public infrastructure is not limited to the municipal level. Concern is also often expressed about infrastructure for which provincial and federal governments are responsible.

20. Recall that during the 1990s municipal capital expenditures represented 88 percent of local capital outlays.

21. Local payroll taxes are a variant along this line.

22. For information, see the city of Winnipeg's Web site (http://www.winnipeg.ca/cao/) and the Web site of the Canadian Broadcasting Corporation in Manitoba (http://www.cbc.ca/manitoba/).

23. Most public finance textbooks have a chapter on fiscal federalism, and the original work of Oates (1972) is valuable. References directed more toward local government include Bird (1993) and McMillan (2002, forthcoming).

24. A variation on these objectives is a focus on decentralized decision making, local autonomy, effective provision of services, interjurisdictional and interpersonal equity, and adequate resources.
25. The leading exceptions are federal and provincial government payments in lieu of property taxes, which are included under own-source property and related taxes. Even so, they reasonably parallel local taxes.
26. Of interest is the fact that, despite the fluctuations in federal funding, the consolidated federal, provincial, and local expenditures for housing held quite stable at close to 1 percent of consolidated expenditures throughout the 1988–2001 period.
27. For a more comprehensive assessment of the lessons about local government that are provided by industrial countries, see McMillan (2002, 2004, forthcoming).

References

Auld, D. A. L., and Lorraine Eden. 1987. "A Comparative Evaluation of Provincial-Local Equalization." *Canadian Public Policy* 8 (4): 515–28.

Bird, Richard M. 1993. "Threading the Fiscal Labyrinth: Some Issues in Fiscal Decentralization." *National Tax Journal* 46 (June): 207–27.

Bish, Robert L. 2003. *Property Taxes and Business Property in British Columbia*. Victoria, BC: Public Administration and Economics Department, University of Victoria.

Canadian Tax Foundation. 2002a. "Municipal Finance and Governance Reform Symposium, Part One." *Canadian Tax Journal* 50 (1): 145–210.

———. 2002b. "Municipal Finance and Governance Reform Symposium, Part Two." *Canadian Tax Journal* 50 (2): 550–605.

———. 2002c. "Municipal Finance and Governance Reform Symposium, Part Three." *Canadian Tax Journal* 50 (3): 968–1018.

Eden, Lorraine. 1987. "Provincial-Municipal Equalization in the Maritime Provinces." *Canadian Public Administration* 30 (4): 585–600.

Federation of Canadian Municipalities. 1999. *Quality of Life Infrastructure Program Proposal: Federal Budget Submission to Finance Minister Paul Martin*. Ottawa: Federation of Canadian Municipalities.

Fisher, Ronald C. 1996. *State and Local Public Finance*. Boston: Richard D. Irwin.

Garcea, Joseph, and Edward LeSage, eds. 2005. *Municipal Reform in Canada: Reconfiguration, Re-Empowerment, and Rebalancing*. Don Mills, ON: Oxford University Press.

Kitchen, Harry M. 2000. "Municipal Finance in a New Fiscal Environment." Commentary 147. Toronto: C. D. Howe Foundation.

———. 2002. "Municipal Revenue and Expenditure Issues in Canada." Tax Paper 107, Canadian Tax Foundation, Toronto.

———. 2003. "Financing Cities and Fiscal Sustainability." In *Paying for Cities: The Search for Sustainable Revenues*, ed. Paul Boothe, 19–36. Edmonton: Institute of Public Economics, University of Alberta.

Kitchen, Harry M., and Enid Slack. 1993. "Business Property Taxation." Government and Competitiveness Project Discussion Paper 93–24. Kingston, ON: Queen's University, School of Policy Studies.

———. 2003. "Special Study: New Financing Options for Municipal Governments." *Canadian Tax Journal* 61 (6): 2215–75.

McMillan, Melville L. 2002. "Designing Local Governments for Performance." The World Bank, Washington, DC. (unpublished)

———. 2003. "Municipal Relations with the Federal and Provincial Governments: A Fiscal Perspective." Paper presented at the Municipal-Provincial-Federal Relations Conference, Institute for Intergovernmental Relations, Queen's University, Kingston, ON, May 9–10.

———. 2004. "Financial Relationships between Regional and Municipal Authorities: Insights from the Examination of Five OECD Countries." IIGR Working Paper 2004(3), Institute of Intergovernmental Relations, Queen's University, Kingston, ON. http://www.iigr.ca/iigr.php/site/publication_detail?publication=349.

———. Forthcoming. "Local Perspectives on Fiscal Federalism." In *Macrofederalism and Local Finances*, ed. Anwar Shah. Washington, DC. The World Bank.

McMillan, Melville L., and Deryk G. Norton. 1981. "The Distribution of Unconditional Grants to Alberta Municipalities: Existing and Alternative Methods." *Canadian Tax Journal* 29 (March–April): 171–83.

Oates, Wallace E. 1972. *Fiscal Federalism.* New York: Harcourt, Brace, Jovanovich.

Oates, Wallace E., and Robert M. Schwab. 2004. "What Should Local Governments Tax: Income or Property?" In *City Taxes, City Spending: Essays in Honor of Dick Netzer*, ed. Amy Ellen Schwartz, 7–29. Northampton, MA: Edward Elgar.

OECD (Organisation for Economic Co-operation and Development). 2002. *OECD Territorial Reviews: Canada.* Paris: OECD.

Prime Minister's Caucus Task Force on Urban Issues. 2002. *Final Report: Canada's Urban Strategy—A Blueprint for Action.* Judy Sgro, chair. http://www.judysgro.com.

Sjoquist, David L., Sally Wallace, and Barbara Edwards. 2004. "What a Tangled Web: Local Property, Income, and Sales Taxes." In *City Taxes, City Spending: Essays in Honor of Dick Netzer*, ed. Amy Ellen Schwartz, 42–70. Northampton, MA: Edward Elgar.

Statistics Canada. Various years. *Public Sector Statistics.* Catalogue 68-213-XIE. Ottawa: Statistics Canada.

TD Bank Financial Group. 2002. *A Choice between Investing in Canada's Cities or Disinvesting in Canada's Future.* TD Economics Special Report. Toronto: TD Bank Financial Group.

Tindal, C. Richard, and Susan Nobes Tindal. 2003. *Local Government in Canada*, 6th ed. Scarborough, ON: Nelson.

Union des Muncipalités du Québec and Conference Board of Canada. 2003. *The Fiscal Situation of Quebec's Municipalities: Summary Report.* Ottawa: Conference Board of Canada.

Vander Ploeg, Casey. 2001. *Dollars and Sense: Big City Finances in the West, 1990–2000.* Calgary, AB: Canada West Foundation.

———. 2002a. *Big City Revenue Sources: A Canada-U.S. Comparison of Municipal Tax Tools and Revenue Levers.* Calgary, AB: Canada West Foundation.

———. 2002b. *Framing a Fiscal Fix-Up: Options for Strengthening the Finances of Western Canada's Big Cities.* Calgary, AB: Canada West Foundation.

———. 2003. *A Capital Question: Infrastructure in Western Canada's Big Six.* Calgary, AB: Canada West Foundation.

3

Local Government Organization and Finance: *France*

RÉMY PRUD'HOMME

Currently, at least four levels of government operate in France: the central government, regions, *départements,* and *communes.* One could add two other semi- or quasi-levels of government: the European Union (EU) and groupings of communes. These institutions also have taxing, spending, borrowing, and regulatory powers. However, groupings of communes, as their name indicates, do not have directly elected councils and can be seen as creatures of communes. Similarly, the EU can be said to be a creature of member governments. The powerful decision-making body in the EU is the council of ministers of member countries, which meets periodically in Brussels, not the directly elected European Parliament (which has only a consultative voice) nor the permanent European Commission. This paper will focus on the role, function, and financing of the three subnational governments in France: regions, départements, and communes.

Jurisdictions

Communes and départements date back to the French Revolution. The list and maps of communes and départements have not changed much since 1790. There are nearly 37,000 communes, and they were patterned after prerevolutionary Catholic parishes. Close to 100 départements were created at the time of the French Revolution to replace former Old Regime provinces. Paris is at the same time a commune and a département. A vocabulary ambiguity exists for both terms *communes* and *départements:* they represent not only geographic areas but also the local governments that administer them. In this chapter, we will mostly use these words to designate the local governments, although in some cases (which will be clearly indicated by the context), they might also designate the areas.

Although not much has changed with respect to communes and départements, substantial changes have occurred with respect to population. Massive rural-to-urban migration and subsequent suburban developments led to a dramatic decline of the population within some communes (in fact, some communes no longer have a permanent residing population), and combined with France's total population increase, those redistributions led to equally dramatic increases in the population of other communes. The same is true of départements. The net result is that immense disparities exist between the population size or density of communes and départements, as shown in table 3.1.

Regions are much more recent in France. They appeared in the 1960s as administrative jurisdictions, with partly elected, partly appointed consultative bodies; gained authority; and became full-fledged subnational governments in 1982. Now, France has 22 metropolitan regions (including Corsica) plus 4 overseas regions. They are extremely diverse in size and population.

Because communes are many and small, there is an obvious need for them to combine. For many decades, the central government has tried to encourage mergers of communes but with little success. In the 1960s, it created *communautés urbaines,* a form of metropolitan government in which the communes of an urban agglomeration jointly (a) manage a number of urban public services and (b) levy taxes. This structure was made compulsory for four large agglomerations (Lyon, Strasbourg, Bordeaux, Lille)[1] and optional for others, but only nine additional agglomerations agreed to create communautés urbaines. At present, the 14 communautés urbaines regroup 355 communes and 6.2 million inhabitants.

A more popular—and much softer—form of communal cooperation consists of *syndicates,* created either for one specific function such as garbage collection or water supply or for several functions. There are about 15,000 single-purpose and 3,000 multipurpose syndicates, financed by negotiated contributions from member communes. In the area of urban transportation, about 150 organizing authorities have been created; they benefit from a special and important tax.

TABLE 3.1 Area and Population Size of French Départements,
Communes, and Regions, 2002

Indicator	Communes	Départements	Regions
Number			
European territory	36,570	96	22
Overseas territory	214	4	4
Area size (European territory only) (km²)			
Average	15	5,700	24,700
Median	11	5,900	25,700
Standard error	15	1,900	11,200
Minimum	..	105	8,300
Maximum	758	10,000	45,300
Dispersion coefficient	1.00	0.34	0.45
Population size (European territory only)			
Average	1,600	610,000	2,660,000
Median	200	503,000	2,080,000
Standard error	13.9	466,000	2,240,000
Minimum	—	74,000	260,000
Maximum	2,130,000[a]	2,560,000	10,950,000
Dispersion coefficient	8.7	0.76	0.84

Source: Ministère de l'Intérieur, Direction Générale des Collectivités Locales, 2006a, chapter 1. Calculations by Bernard-Henri Nicot, SIRIUS, Université de Paris XII.
Note: .. = negligible; — = not available. Calculations exclude overseas communes, départements, and regions.
a. Paris, which is at the same time a commune and a département.

In recent years, the central government (through specific subsidies) has encouraged communes to create *communautés d'agglomérations* in urban areas and *communautés de communes* in rural areas. These forms involve the pooling of tax resources and responsibilities. Today there are more than 150 communautés d'agglomérations regrouping nearly 3,000 communes and 20 million inhabitants and more than 2,000 communautés de communes regrouping 28,000 communes and 25 million inhabitants.

Economic Weight

How important are local governments in France? Table 3.2 presents a quantitative approach to this question based on national accounts data for 2002. Several important points emerge. First, subnational government income and expenditures represent about 10 percent of gross domestic product (GDP) in France. Second, in expenditure terms, the weight of local governments is about

TABLE 3.2   Income and Expenditures of French Local Governments, 2004

Source	Amount (€ billion)	Percentage of GDP	Percentage of central government
Total expenditures	179	9.0	47.7
Intermediate consumption	38	3.0	173.5
Wages	51	2.8	45.9
Interest on debt	3	0.2	7.4
Services and transfers	46	2.8	23.6
Investment	36	2.2	495.0
Total income	177	10.7	55.0
Taxes	88	4.6	29.6
Other (including transfers)	88	5.3	348
Balance	−2	−0.1	4

Source: Ministère de l'Intérieur, Direction Générale des Collectivités Locales, 2006a, chapter 2. The source uses national accounting data.

half that of the central government.[2] Third, local taxes cover about half of local government expenditures and represent, therefore, about 5 percent of GDP. Fourth, as a consequence, transfers from the central government to local governments account for about 5 percent of GDP and cover the other half of local government resources. Fifth, local governments invest about five times as much as the central government. Finally, local governments balance their accounts, and their indebtedness (as measured by interest paid on debt) is small relative to central government indebtedness.

What is the relative importance of communes, départements, and regions? Table 3.3 provides an answer for 2003 in terms of expenditures (but data on income tell the same story).

TABLE 3.3   Expenditures of Communes, Groupings of Communes, Départements, and Regions, 2003

Level of government	Amount (€ billion)	Percentage of total
Communes	122.7	66.5
Groupings of communes	*44.3*	*24.0*
Départements	46.0	24.9
Regions	15.8	8.6
Total, local governments	**184.5**	**100.0**

Source: Ministère de l'Intérieur, Direction Générale des Collectivités Locales, 2006a, table 3.1. The source uses public finance accounting concepts.
Note: The values for *groupings of communes* are included in those for *communes,* hence the italics.

It appears that expenditures are largely dominated by communes, which account for two-thirds of total local governments' expenditures. Départements account for about one-fourth, and regions, though their importance is increasing fastest, represent less than one-tenth of the total. The role of groupings of communes, as entities formally (although not politically) independent of communes, is large and increasing rapidly.

Governance

Communal (also called *municipal*) councils are elected every six years. People vote for party lists, and the list that comes in first benefits from a premium that gives it a majority in the council. The council elects one of its members—the leader of the winning list—as its chair, or mayor. Consequently, no postelection negotiations take place to form a council majority, and there is also no possibility of a conflict between the mayor and the council. A mayor can run for mayorship as many times as he or she wants. Two consecutive mandates (12 years) are quite frequent, three mandates (18 years) are not uncommon, and some mayors have even stayed in office for four (and, in exceptional cases, five) mandates. Mayors are well known and usually command respect and popularity. (People typically say, "All politicians are bad, except for my mayor.") In that sense, communes are indeed a pillar of democracy in France.

Communal groupings, by contrast, have a weak legitimacy. Their governing boards are not elected but, instead, are appointed by the (elected) mayors of the constituting communes—even when those groupings have the power to levy taxes.

For electoral purposes, départements are divided into 20 to 30 jurisdictions, and each jurisdiction sends one member to the council for six years. Every three years, half the seats are up for reelection. The council elects one chairperson from among its members. Every three years, depending on possible changes in the council majority, a new chair can be elected to rule out potential conflicts between a council chair and a council majority. Here again, there are no limits on the reelection of council members or chairpeople.

The electoral system for regions is now similar to that of communes. Elections are held every six years, by party lists, with a premium to the winning list, which ensures a clear majority in the regional council. The council elects the leader of the winning list as chair.

Communes and départements have always enjoyed a fair degree of formal autonomy. They have had elected councils, their own taxes, borrowing powers, and municipal or départemental employees.[3] The central government never had the power to remove a council chair who was not of its liking. Nevertheless, traditionally the central government imposed many constraints and exerted many controls over communes and départements. This power was supported by the spatial organization of the central government, which was—and still is—patterned after the departmental structure. In every département (that is, in the geographic area corresponding to every département governing body), there is a representative of the Ministry of the Interior, a prefect (who is appointed by the central government), and a representative of each of the central government ministries (appointed by the relevant ministry).

Communes and départements were free to set their own tax rates, though minimum and maximum limits were imposed and there was a fixed link between the rates imposed on the various local taxes. For a long time, even in the post–World War II period, communes and départements needed central government authorization to increase the fees charged on various services that they provided. Similarly, authorization was needed to borrow. An entity controlled by the central government, Caisse des Dépôts et Consignations, had a de facto monopoly on lending to subnational governments. Central government ministries granted subsidies on a project-by-project basis, which made it practically impossible for a mayor to develop a particular infrastructure investment without the agreement and support of the central government. For a long time, communes and départements were treated like children who required supervision and guidance. In a département, the prefect had more power than the elected council chair; the département budget was actually prepared by the prefect staff, and in many cases, the prefect chaired council meetings, even in the presence of the elected council chair.

This multifaceted control or tutelage of subnational governments defined centralization in France as much as or more than the relatively large ratios of central-to-local taxes and responsibilities. The history of decentralization in France, which occurred over the 1970–1990 period, is largely the history of the gradual relaxation and abandonment of these controls much more than the history of the shift of central-to-local taxes and responsibilities. Now, French subnational governments enjoy an extremely high degree of autonomy. They do pretty much what they want with their taxes, their expenditures, their debt, their regulations, and their employees. Constraints and mandates are minimal. In that sense, today's France can be considered a relatively decentralized country.

Local Government Expenditure Responsibilities

The responsibilities of each type of government are not always clearly and formally defined. In some areas, they are. It, for example, is clearly stated that municipal roads must be maintained by communes and vocational training must be provided by regions. But in many other areas, nothing prevents any government from intervening. For instance, a commune, département, or region can equally decide to subsidize an orchestra. In addition, particularly for investments, several levels of government (including the central government) can get together to finance a particular project.

Welfare

The actual delivery of welfare transfers is in the hands of départements. But most of those transfers are decided by the central government; the central government then gives to départements the subsidies that are calculated to meet that need. (Départements complain that those subsidies do not cover the cost of the mandated expenditures.) In fact, the mandated expenditures define a national minimal payment, but départements can be—and often are—more generous and give more. In addition, communes also can give money to people in need and can provide services for them.

Education

All four levels of government are very much involved in education. The basic division of labor is that local governments are responsible for developing and maintaining the physical stock of capital (namely, the school buildings) whereas the central government is responsible for labor (namely, for recruiting, monitoring, promoting—and paying—teachers) and for curriculum development. Communes are responsible for primary school buildings, départements are responsible for junior high school buildings (called *collèges*), and regions are responsible for senior high school buildings (*lycées*). Local governments are also increasingly involved in additional education expenditures, such as art schools or school cafeterias. In a labor-intensive activity such as education, the allocation of responsibilities for the bulk of education expenditures remains centralized, which goes a long way toward explaining the relatively low level of subnational government expenditure in France. Recruitment and wages are uniform throughout the territory. This uniformity does not mean that there are no geographic disparities in school quality: the more senior and often the best teachers tend to congregate in schools located in the most pleasant areas. But these disparities are not as great as those found in countries where education is funded subnationally.

Vocational Training

Vocational training is one of the few public services for which the responsibility is not shared. It rests solely with regions.

Transportation

Transportation, by contrast, is the business of all levels of government. The central government is responsible for national roads, for most regulation, for the supervision and heavy subsidization of rail transportation, for canals (through a national agency), and for harbors. Regions are responsible for some major roads; in addition, many road investments have been cofinanced by regions and the state (and often also départements). A recent development is the involvement of regions in rail transportation. That involvement started in the mid-1990s as an experiment in six regions and has been extended to all regions. Regional passenger rail transport is now negotiated regionally between each region and the regional branch of the Société Nationale des Chemins de Fer (SNCF), the French national railway agency. Subsidies to SNCF are beginning to be, and will become, an important share of regional expenditures. Départements are responsible for departmental roads and for the organization (and subsidization) of bus transportation, including school bus transportation. The central government is currently moving roads from the national category to the departmental category. Finally, communes are responsible for communal roads, including streets, and for urban public transportation.

In most cases, urban transportation is clearly a metropolitan issue and function. Because there are so many communes in France, practically all urban areas include a relatively large number of communes. Worth mentioning is a special institution that has been created to carry out the responsibilities of communes for public transportation. For every urban area, in the perimeter relevant for metropolitan transportation, communes get together to create an organizing authority. This grouping is in principle voluntary, although it is usually inspired by the prefect of the département involved. It is facilitated by a specific transport tax (*versement transport*), which is based on wages, earmarked for public transportation and managed by the organizing authority. The board of this authority is composed of representatives of the mayors of the constituting communes. The organizing authority defines bus lines or tram lines, subsidizes them heavily (above 50 percent in most cases), and usually contracts out the service to a private enterprise.[4] Organizing authorities are usually a creation of communes, but in certain cases, a département may also be a member. Organizing authorities receive subsidies, particularly investment subsidies, from the central government.

Economic Development

Economic development is a mixed bag that includes the development of industrial estates, or investment subsidies to (and capital participation in) enterprises, often designed to redirect development to specific areas. Governments of all levels are involved in promoting economic development.

Urban Planning

Communes are responsible for preparing master plans (that is, sketching out the desirable future economic, social, and geographic development of an urban area) and land-use maps that allocate different zones to different uses (and forbid certain uses in certain zones).

Water, Sanitation, Garbage Collection

Environmental services such as the collection and disposal of garbage or the provision of water are the responsibilities of communes. As in the case of urban public transportation, communes can and do get together to provide these services. They create ad hoc groupings, or syndicates, of varying perimeters to benefit from economies of scale. In many cases, the service is contracted out to a private enterprise.

Culture, Sports, and Leisure

All levels of governments are involved in the providing or subsidizing of culture, for example, in the form of public theater, music conservatories, museums, and concert halls. Usually, the communes provide sports facilities and parks.

Safety

Fire protection is mainly the responsibility of départements, but the central government intervenes in the case of forest fires, as well as floods. Communes are responsible for regulating road traffic and are beginning to intervene in the area of public security (that is, they can create nonarmed surveillance bodies). However, the central government is solely responsible for police.

A Caveat with Respect to Allocation of Responsibilities

Can data on expenditures of local governments give a more quantitative picture of this allocation of responsibilities? Unfortunately not. Data on expenditures by type, for each level of government, are shown in table 3.4. However, we were unable to identify a meaningful breakdown of expenditures by function. We

TABLE 3.4 Expenditures by Type, Communes, Départements, and Regions, 2003
(€ billion)

Type of expenditure	Communes	Départements	Regions	Total
Wages	30.0	5.3	0.5	35.7
Transfers	8.2	11.3	6.2	25.7
Interest	3.2	0.7	0.3	4.2
Investments	43.3	16.1	7.8	67.3
Other	38.0	12.6	1.0	51.5
Total	**122.7**	**46.0**	**15.8**	**184.4**

Source: Ministère de l'Intérieur, Direction Générale des Collectivités Locales, 2006a, table 3.1.
Note: These data are not commensurate with the national accounts data of table 3.2; they include neither expenditures of groupings of communes nor expenditures of certain quasi-local government institutions.

TABLE 3.5 Expenditures by Function, Communes, Départements, and Regions, 2003
(€ billion)

Type of expenditure	Communes	Départements	Regions	Total
Education	14.7	3.5	3.4	21.6
Vocational training	n.a.	n.a.	2.4	2.4
Welfare	11.2	17.7	n.a.	28.9
Transportation	n.a.	5.7	4.4	10.1
Economic development	2.5	4.0	1.0	7.5
Culture, sports, and leisure	22.0	n.a.	n.a.	22.0
Other	72.3	15.1	4.7	92.1
Total	**122.7**	**46.0**	**15.9**	**184.6**

Source: For départements and regions, Ministère de l'Intérieur, Direction Générale des Collectivités Locales, 2006a, table 3.7; for communes, Ministère de l'Intérieur, Direction Générale des Collectivités Locales, 2006b.
Note: n.a. = not applicable. Data on debt reimbursement have been excluded. Percentages obtained for communes larger than 10,000 inhabitants have been applied to the total expenditures of all communes.

compiled table 3.5 from various Ministry of Finance and Ministry of Interior sources, but it is not clear that the categories used for communes are similar to those used for départements and regions.

In table 3.5, the excessive size of the share of "other" suggests that reporting and cost accounting are imperfect. It is hard to believe that general administration (which is not allocated to specific functions, as it should be) accounts for half the expenditures of local governments. Nevertheless, the ranking of functions by importance of expenditures shown in table 3.5—welfare; economic development; education; transportation; culture, sports, and leisure; and vocational training—appears quite plausible.

Local Government Own-Source Taxes and Charges

French local governments collect about 5 percent of GDP in taxes. There are about a dozen local taxes. Table 3.6 presents local tax proceeds by type of tax and level of government. Before discussing in turn the most important of these local taxes, we must consider a few general issues.

■ *Shared tax* bases. As is apparent from table 3.6, for several taxes (particularly those with the highest yield), two or three different levels of

T A B L E 3 . 6 Local Taxes, by Type and Level of Government, 2004 (€ *billion*)

Type of tax	Communes and groupings	Départements	Regions	Total
Housing tax	8.6	3.9	n.a.	12.5
Property tax	10.7	4.6	1.2	16.5
Land tax	0.9	..	..	0.9
Business tax	14.8	6.9	2.0	23.6
Garbage tax	3.9	n.a.	n.a.	3.9
Transport tax	4.8	n.a.	n.a.	4.8
Property registration tax	n.a.	4.3	n.a.	4.3
Vehicle license tax	n.a.	0.1	n.a.	0.1
Electricity tax	0.9	0.4	n.a.	1.3
Additional property registration tax	1.8	n.a.	n.a.	1.9
Vehicle registration tax	n.a.	n.a.	1.4	1.4
Urban development tax	0.4	0.1	0.1	0.6
Other	0.6	..	..	0.4
Total	**47.3**	**20.5**	**4.8**	**72.5**

Source: Ministère de l'Intérieur, Direction Générale des Collectivités Locales, 2006a, table 5.1.
Note: .. = negligible; n.a. = not applicable. Numbers may not sum to total because of rounding.

government have access to the same tax bases. There are no "shared taxes" in the usual sense of taxes shared between the central government and subnational governments, a practice common not only in Latin America but also in Germany. What are shared here are not tax proceeds but tax bases. Consider, for instance, the property tax (*taxe sur le foncier bâti*) to be paid on a particular building. Let us assume that the tax base is €100. The communal council will decide on a rate of 10 percent, the département council on a rate of 5 percent, and the regional council on a rate of 1 percent. In principle, we do have three different taxes, and the rate of each tax has been voted on by a legitimate elected council. The commune will raise €10, the département €5, and the region €1. The owner of the building receives a tax bill that indicates this breakdown clearly. In practice, however, few taxpayers study their tax bill in detail, and the owner is likely to notice only the €16 he or she pays as property tax. This approach does not induce accountability. Départements and, even more so, regions are tempted to increase their tax rates, hoping that the communes will shoulder the blame. Symmetrically, communes and, even more so, départements and regions, are discouraged from lowering tax rates because they know that they will not get political credit for it, particularly if other governments increase their tax rates at the same time.

■ *Tax assessment and collection.* Local tax assessment and collection are not done by local governments themselves but, instead, by the central government on their behalf. The central Ministry of Finance assesses tax bases, and local governments determine tax rates. The central government collects the money and hands it over to local governments—minus a 4 percent fee for the service rendered.[5] This practice does not diminish the "localness" of the taxes involved: what constitutes this localness is the political decision embodied in rate setting. Assessment and collection are quasi-technical functions that could even, in theory at least, be contracted out to private enterprises that are properly monitored. This system of assessment and collection being done by the central government has several major advantages. One is that it protects taxpayers from—and local officials from the temptation of—local arbitrariness or favoritism in tax assessment and collection. Another advantage is that economies of scale are involved. Indeed, in the case of the numerous very small communes, local tax assessment and collection would not only be costly but also impossible in practice. A third advantage is that tax assessment is uniform throughout the territory. It is done by the same institution, with standardized procedures. Local tax bases are therefore known in a comparable fashion for all local governments, which makes it possible to devise transfer systems that are based, at least in part, on tax bases and that are designed to reduce tax base disparities—a major goal of transfer systems.

■ *Central government interference.* Broadly speaking, local government councils enjoy great freedom in tax matters. They cannot invent and create taxes of their own, but they can—and do—decide on tax rates. This freedom, however, is not unlimited. A given commune cannot decide overnight to quadruple the rate of its business tax. At least for the main taxes, there are some constraints on maximum tax rates: they cannot exceed two or two and one-half times the average national tax rate. There is also a compulsory link between tax rate increases on business tax (paid by enterprises) and tax rate increases on housing and property taxes (paid by households—and voters). The former cannot be higher than the latter, a limit that prevents local government from increasing only those taxes paid by nonvoting enterprises. In a number of cases, the central government intervenes to reduce the tax burden of taxpayers without decreasing the tax proceeds of local governments. For instance, in the name of economic development and employment, the central government sets a limit on the business tax paid by an enterprise as a proportion of its value added in the same accounting period: it cannot be more than 4 percent. If the product of the tax rate by the tax base turns out to represent 5 percent of the value added of the enterprise, then the enterprise pays only 4 percent of this value added. The difference, 1 percent, is paid by the central government to the local government. As a result, the central government has become a major—indeed the main—local tax payer. Whether this 1 percent should be treated as a local tax or as a subsidy is a matter for discussion.

Let us now consider the five local taxes that account for more than €3 billion: business tax, property and garbage tax, housing tax, transport tax, and property registration tax. Together, they represent more than 85 percent of local government tax income.

Business Tax

Business tax (*taxe professionnelle*) has long been the most important local tax in France, and it still is, despite recent cuts in its tax base. It is paid by all enterprises or, more precisely, by all establishments in the jurisdiction in which they are located. In other words, an enterprise with 20 branches or factories or warehouses will pay 20 different business taxes. The tax base used to be a mix of capital and wages.[6] In 1999, wages were eliminated from the calculation of the tax base. A central government subsidy compensated for the resulting reduction in the tax base and tax proceeds. As mentioned above, the upper limit to the amount of business tax that a particular enterprise (or, rather, establishment) can be made to pay is 4 percent of its value added.

Business tax is an important tax in France. It is the fifth heaviest French tax, after value added tax, personal income tax, corporate income tax, and fuels tax. It represents 1.4 percent of GDP and a much larger share of the value added by private enterprises (because GDP includes a nonprivate enterprises component). No wonder it has been—and still is—heavily criticized in France.

The main criticism is that the tax is unfair, in the sense that it does not treat all enterprises equally; critics "demonstrate" this unfairness by showing that taxes paid per worker, or per euro of value added, differ from one sector to another. By this reasoning, any business tax is unfair. For any conceivable tax base, it will always be possible to find one or several criteria (tax per unit of capital, tax per euro of profit, and so forth) for which there will be intersectoral or interenterprise disparities in taxes paid. A more serious criticism, valid for any business tax in any country but particularly worrisome in a country with small jurisdictions (such as the French communes), is that a major part of the tax burden is exported out of the tax jurisdiction. A detailed study (Prud'homme 2000) conducted on a sample of communes suggested export leakages of about 80 percent. The political cost of increasing tax rates in a particular commune is low because the burden of the tax will be borne mainly by people who do not live and vote in the commune. Accountability suffers.

In contrast, business tax has several advantages. It is a high-yield local tax and the foundation of local governments' fiscal autonomy. Because it taxes production factors, it induces rather than punishes efficiency. It has proven to be a useful incentive for siting of unpleasant facilities such as garbage incinerators or power plants. Communes—and their voters—do not like such facilities, but they like the business tax that comes with them. This incentive facilitates negotiations and siting decisions. For many years, business tax had another virtue: it had an equalizing effect. Businesses, particularly industrial establishments, were usually located in industrial communes inhabited by relatively low-income industrial workers. Communes with low property tax bases per capita happened to be communes with high business tax bases per capita. With deindustrialization and the development of service activities not necessarily located in low-income areas, this disparity-reducing feature lost much of its importance. But it has not disappeared: poor communes in terms of household income are not necessarily poor communes in terms of tax bases.

As with all taxes on enterprises, the burden of the tax is borne in part by the central government—or, more precisely, by central government taxpayers. Tax payments are deductible from corporate income, and a reduction in corporate income means a reduction in corporate income tax, the rate of which is about 35 percent.

Communal groupings have an effect on business tax. Communautés urbaines have the power to levy it in addition to what is levied by member communes. An enterprise located in a communauté urbaine will therefore pay business tax four times, at the rate decided by each entity: the commune, the communauté urbaine, the département, and the region. In principle, the communal rate is lower than what it would be in the absence of communauté urbaine; in practice, it is probably not much lower. The other groupings (communautés d'agglomérations and communautés de communes) have the option of choosing a uniform rate for their business tax, and central government subsidies encourage them to do so. This approach has the advantage of eliminating tax competition within the grouping. Tax competition is not necessarily bad, but it has to be accompanied by benefit competition, which is not the case in an urban agglomeration, where the benefits of public services provided by any commune are often available to all agglomeration inhabitants and enterprises. More than 1,000 groupings, representing 38 million inhabitants (63 percent of total population), have opted for the groupingwide uniform business tax rate. However, differences remain (a) between the business tax rates of different groupings and (b) between the communes of a given grouping for the rates of other taxes.

Property Tax and Garbage Tax

The property tax, or *taxe sur le foncier bâti* (literally, tax on built-up land), is based on the value of property. Technically, the tax base is the rental value of the property, but there is presumably a fixed relationship between sales values and rental values, so this criterion does not matter much. Assessment is done by the central government Ministry of Finance, with the help of a cadastre (also managed by the central government), and takes into account characteristics such as the size, comfort, and location of each property. The views of local committees are also taken into account. Unfortunately, reassessments are rare and unpopular because owners of underassessed buildings strongly oppose them, and the few courageous ministers of

Finance who have attempted to undertake reassessments paid a high political price for doing so. As a result, it is widely believed that the ratio of assessed value to market value varies significantly from one property to another (no serious studies have been conducted to confirm this belief, however). Industrial and commercial properties are assessed and taxed just like residential properties and at similar rates. Communes, départements, and regions each decide on the tax rate they will apply, and the Ministry of Finance does the rest (that is, collects the tax from property owners and sends the proceeds to each commune, département, and region).

The garbage tax, or *taxe d'enlèvement des ordures ménagères,* has exactly the same base as the property tax and can be seen as an addition or a surcharge to it. It is called *garbage tax* because its proceeds are earmarked for garbage collection and disposal. It is imposed only by communes, and not even by all communes, because some prefer instead to charge fees that are based on the amount of garbage collected—fees that are not recorded as taxes.

Housing Tax

The housing tax, or *taxe d'habitation,* is also a form of property tax and is also based on the rental value of the housing structure. It is paid by the dweller, not by the owner, on both rented and owner-occupied houses, which implies that, unlike the property tax, it is not paid on nonresidential structures. Tax rates are decided by communes and départements because the region does not benefit from this tax. The housing tax is politically important because it is paid by some 25 million households, including many households that do not pay personal income tax.[7] Communes can and do decide that low-income households are tax exempt. Overall, the burden of the housing tax is not negligible: it represents exactly 1 percent of a household's pretax income.

It has been argued that the housing tax is regressive relative to income because the ratio of housing value to income is supposed to decline when income increases. But it has also been argued that such a decline is not well established, particularly in a country where many relatively low-income people live in subsidized houses of low rental or market value. In any case, housing tax exemptions, which are common and important, reduce significantly the potential regressiveness of the housing tax.

Transport Tax

As mentioned previously, about 150 transport "organizing authorities" created in all important urban areas have the power to levy a tax, *versement transport.* The tax is paid by all enterprises with more than 10 employees and is based on wages. (Though a wage tax, it is called a transport tax because the proceeds are earmarked for public transportation.) The rate is chosen by the organizing authority and is usually between 0.75 and 2.0 percent. The tax represents about 0.3 percent of GDP.

Property Registration Tax

Départements (and only départements) also levy a property registration tax, or *droits d'enregistrement.* The base of the tax consists of all sales of buildings in the jurisdiction.

Evolution of Taxes

How have local taxes evolved in recent years? Relative to GDP, they have declined, as shown in table 3.7, which gives data for 1998 and 2003.

Table 3.7 distinguishes between local taxes effectively paid by local taxpayers and the share of local taxes contributed by the central government as a result of tax rebates or exemptions determined by the central government (the latter could alternatively be classified as subsidies). The decline in taxes paid by taxpayers cannot be explained by a decline in tax rates. Available data suggest that, for most taxes, tax rates have increased rather than decreased. The decline also cannot be explained by an elasticity of local tax bases to GDP lower than one; the elasticity of the business tax base to GDP has for years been greater than one, and the same is true of housing rental value. There is no reason to think that reduced efficiency in tax collection could explain this decline. The main cause is to be found in central government decisions to eliminate

TABLE 3.7   Local Taxes as a Percentage of GDP, 1996 and 2002 *(percent)*

Payer	1998	2004	Change
Local taxpayers	3.9	3.2	−18
Central government	0.9	1.4	+55
Total	4.8	4.6	−4

Source: Calculated from Ministère de l'Intérieur, Direction Générale des Collectivités Locales, 2006a, table 5.6, and INSEE 2006.
Note: Local taxes are taxes for which the rate is decided by local governments; however, a substantial part is paid by the central government, which compensates local governments for the tax burden ceilings that it imposes.

some local taxes, such as the yearly vehicle license tax (which was a départe-ment tax), and to downsize the base of certain taxes, particularly the busi-ness tax. Local governments received additional subsidies instead, which implies some increases in national taxation. These changes were politically rather uncontroversial. National taxes were considered less distortive and less painful than local taxes. Politically, this consideration counted more than the implied loss in local fiscal autonomy, which was realized and deplored.

Central-Local Fiscal Transfers

As in most other countries, the transfers, grants, and subsidies from the central government to local governments are a very important part of local government resources and a sizable part of central government expendi-tures. Precise numbers vary with the definition of local governments used (whether it includes utilities or not) and with the treatment of central gov-ernment contributions to local taxes (whether they are counted as local taxes or as transfers). In 2004, in France, such transfers represented about half of local government income and about 16 percent of central government expenditures. How this money is allocated is obviously of prime impor-tance. Four general points are noteworthy.

First, all transfers are automatic and formula driven. There are no dis-cretionary subsidies to local governments. It is true that the allocation rules and formulas could be changed in a way that would increase the transfers received by a particular government, together with all the other local governments that have similar characteristics. Otherwise, however, no minister, not even the president of the republic, can favor a particular local government.

Second, nearly all transfers are block grants that are provided with no strings attached. Local governments can do what they want with the sub-sidies they receive, even if and when those grants are calculated in refer-ence to well-defined uses. A few specific transfers, granted by particular ministries, are exceptions to this rule, but they account for only 2 percent of total transfers. This arrangement is a great change from the situation that prevailed 30 years ago, when most subsidies were earmarked for a specific use or project. Official documents (followed by many analysts) continue to distinguish between operating subsidies and investment sub-sidies. This distinction is a mere accounting curiosity with no practical meaning.[8] For a given local government, subsidies are as good as own-source taxes.

Third, allocation procedures are extremely complicated, and few people, if any, understand them fully.[9] There are about 20 different subsidies. None has been introduced from scratch, with a well-thought-out design. All have been introduced to replace a former subsidy or to compensate for a tax that has been either eliminated or modified by the central government. Each had to take into consideration the previous situation to avoid introducing major changes that would have been politically unacceptable. Each formula, therefore, embodies features of a distant past. But the central government usually took advantage of each change to introduce additional objectives—for instance, increased fairness—in the allocation formula. This approach produced complex formulas that were designed to change over the course of time. The actual outcome of each of these formulas is hard to predict, and their combined outcome is practically impossible to predict. The simple question about the extent to which the transfer system reduces per capita disparities in tax bases and how much of this reduction (if any) can be attributed to each subsidy remains largely unanswered.

Fourth, the system constantly changes. Because it changes by the addition of new features rather than by the substitution of new features for old features, this quest for improvement is one of the causes of the complexity of the system. The data and description that follow relate to 2002, but in 2003, a new system (or more precisely, the first phase of a new system) was introduced. That new system makes the description here obsolete, but only in part, because, as mentioned, a particular year's system incorporates many features of the preceding year's system.

Table 3.8 shows the main types of subsidies in 2004 and singles out the most important ones. Some additional explanations of general subsidies, decentralization subsidies, and compensating subsidies are needed to understand the category of block grants.

General Subsidies

In particular, further explanations for three general subsidies will be helpful. These are DGF (*dotation globale de fonctionnement,* or current expenditure block grants), FCTVA (*fonds de compensation pour la taxe sur la valeur ajoutée,* or value added tax compensation grants), and DGE (*dotation globale d'équipement,* or investment grants).

DGF

About 10 transfers can be categorized as general subsidies. By far the most important is the current expenditures block grant, or DGF. Parliament

TABLE 3.8 Central-to-Local Government Transfers, 2004

Type of transfer	Amount of transfer (€ billion)	Percentage of total transfers	Percentage of total block grants
Block grants	59.1	98	
General subsidies	43.3		73
DGF	36.8		
FCTVA	3.8		
DGE	0.9		
Other	1.8		
Decentralization subsidies	3.9		7
DGD	0.8		
Vocational training	1.9		
Education	0.9		
Other	0.3		
Compensating subsidies	11.9		20
Specific subsidies	1.1	2	
Total	60.2	100	100

Source: Ministère de l'Intérieur, Direction Générale des Collectivités Locales, 2006a, chapter 6.
Note: DGD = dotation globale de decentralization; DGE = dotation globale d'équipement; DGF = dotation globale de fonctionnement; FCTVA = fonds de compensation pour la taxe sur la valeur ajoutéer.

determines the total amount and the allocation criteria annually, guided by general principles that it enacted in the past. These principles can be overruled, but unless there is a consensus to support that action, it is done at a high political cost.

The total amount of the block grant is determined in relation to what it was for the previous year, using the following formula:

$$B_n = B_{n-1}(1+r)(1+t/2)$$

where B_n is the block grant for year n, B_{n-1} is the grant for the preceding year $n-1$, r is the inflation rate in year n, and t is the GDP growth rate during year $n-1$.

Local governments as a whole are guaranteed to have a block grant at least equal to that of the previous year in real terms and to see it increase at half the GDP growth rate. The block grant is then divided between communes and départements, pro rata their share during the previous year—that is, 72.5 percent for communes and 27.5 percent for départements. From 2004, regions also have a share of DGF.

The communal block grant is then divided into two parts: a "standard" part (81 percent) and a "policy" part (19 percent). The standard part (*dotation forfaitaire*) reflects the situation in 1993. Every year, each commune gets what it obtained in 1993 on a per capita basis, multiplied by a coefficient that is the same for all communes. In 1993, the grants were determined mainly on the basis of four criteria: (a) tax bases, (b) expenditures needs, (c) tax effort, and (d) past grants. Tax bases played an important role in the calculations: communes with low tax bases would, all other things being equal, obtain more. The problem created by the multiplicity of tax bases was solved with the notion of "tax potential" (*potentiel fiscal*) defined as follows:

$$B_i = \Sigma_k B_{i,k} \times T_k$$

where $B_{i,k}$ is the tax base of commune i for tax k, T_k is the average tax rate for tax k for all communes of France, and B_i is the tax potential of commune i. In simpler terms, the fiscal potential of a commune is what the commune would collect if it were to apply the average national tax rate for each of its taxes.

Needs of the commune also played an important role, in several ways. The commune size in population terms was taken into account, with (generally) larger communes getting more, on a per capita basis, than smaller communes to reflect the idea that needs increase with commune size. Some special categories of communes, such as city center communes and resort communes, were also favored. Finally, criteria such as the length of the communal road network, the number of school-age children, and the share of low-income houses were also taken into account.

The tax effort of a commune, defined as the ratio of taxes collected to taxes that would be collected if average tax rates were applied, had also been introduced (in 1985) and played a role, though a relatively minor one. Finally, the past situation of the commune played a role. The global grant had been introduced as a replacement for particular local taxes that were eliminated in a distant past (1969), and new allocation criteria were supposed to replace only gradually previous communal income. Even in the 1993 situation, there was an echo of this distant time.

The policy part (*dotation d'aménagement*) of the communal block grant is used to further specific goals. The bulk of it goes to sponsor communal groupings, which the central government considers desirable. Communes that form communautés d'agglomérations or communautés de communes get more transfers than those that do not. This incentive is not foreign to the rapid development of communal groupings in recent years. The rest goes to "needy" communes in urban areas (*dotation de solidarité urbaine*) or in rural areas (*dotation de solidarité rurale*). The criteria used to define these communes and to allocate the grant are complex, but it is interesting to note that they refer to socioeconomic characteristics (income, share of low-income housing, and so forth) rather than to fiscal and financial characteristics (tax bases).

FCTVA

Another important general subsidy is the value added compensation grant, or FCTVA. Consider a given investment (for instance, the purchase of a computer or the construction of a building) of €100 that is undertaken by a private enterprise and by a local government. Both will pay a price that includes a value added tax (VAT) of about €20. The private enterprise will use the computer or the building to produce goods or services that will be sold at a price that will include a VAT of, let us say, €50. The enterprise will deduct the €20 paid on its investment and will send the tax authorities a check of only €30. The local government will also use the computer or the building to produce goods or services that are usually not sold and have no VAT attached. The local government cannot deduct the €20 already paid. The VAT system, therefore, discriminates against local governments. To eliminate or correct this distortion, the central government reimburses the local governments for the VAT they paid on their investments. The amount involved is not negligible and represents more than 5 percent of total local government taxes.

DGE

There is also an investment grant, or DGE, for communes and départements. For communes, it is first allocated to the département level (pro rata communal tax bases—tax potential, population, length of communal roads, number of communes) and then allocated by each prefect assisted by a committee of mayors to communes as a function of their investments. Richer communes (that is, communes with a tax potential above a certain threshold) are excluded.

Decentralization Subsidies

A second group of subsidies, *decentralization subsidies,* were introduced in the 1980s when some expenditures responsibilities were shifted from the central government to subnational governments. Estimates were made of the cost savings this shift implied for the central government, and equivalent transfers to the various local governments were then decided. Some of these subsidies are specific and well identified, such as subsidies to cover the cost of vocational training (a responsibility transferred to regions) or the cost of construction and maintenance of school buildings (transferred to départements and regions); others are global. The decentralization process continues. Currently, the responsibility for relationships with SNCF for regional passenger transport—and the heavy subsidies to rail transport they imply—are being shifted to regions. This change is accompanied by another specific decentralization subsidy. As can be expected, when local governments obtain a new responsibility (that they demanded), they complain that the decentralization subsidy that comes with it does not cover the additional cost. They are usually right.

Compensating Subsidies

As mentioned above, the central government tends to intervene in local taxation and to grant deductions and allowances of all sorts. Local governments, which are usually happy with these interventions because they reduce the taxes paid by their electorate, systematically protest that the central government cannot be generous with someone else's money, and they ask for compensation. They usually get it. Local governments thus have the best of both worlds: the same revenues for their coffers and lower taxes for their taxpayers.

The most recent (and important, in monetary terms) example is the elimination of the wages component from the base of the business tax. The business tax base used to consist of capital (about two-thirds of the base) and wages (one-third). In 1999, the central government decided to eliminate the wages component so that it could reduce labor costs in France. This decision implied, all other things being equal, a decline of one-third of revenues generated by the most important local tax in France. The central government immediately pledged to compensate local governments for this enormous revenue loss, thus creating a new subsidy that now amounts to €8 billion.[10]

The subsidy system is therefore extremely complex, and its outcomes are haphazard. Most of the changes introduced in recent years were designed to give more to some local governments without, at the same time, giving less to any governments and without increasing total subsidies. DGF does have a redistributive effect in the sense that it reduces disparities in tax bases. However, it is uncertain whether most of the other subsidies have the same effect. FCTVA, for instance, is allocated pro rata investments, and there are reasons to expect investments per capita to be higher in jurisdictions with a high tax base. Similarly, the subsidy that compensates the elimination of the wage component of the business tax base benefits primarily those local governments that had enterprises with high wage bills: they are unlikely to be the poorest local governments, in terms of either income of inhabitants or tax bases. Overall, the system is likely to be redistributive. The Gini coefficient measuring the inequality of local government income after transfers have been made is lower than the one measuring the inequality of local government income (or tax bases) before transfers have been made. But a similar result would be achieved by an equal per capita transfer.

Current Reform

In 2003, it was decided to simplify the system just described. A number of the grants and subsidies formerly classified as decentralization or compensating subsidies were shifted to the DGF. In the 2004 budget, the importance of DGF practically doubled to €36.7 billion. Regions, as well as communes and départements, will benefit from it. Most of the new DGF will be used to give each local government (a) the grants it received before, increased by less than the nominal increase of GDP, and (b) a redistributive grant, mostly based on the tax bases or fiscal potential of each subnational government.

Local Government Borrowing

Local governments in France do not borrow much and, consequently, are not much in debt, particularly when compared with the central government. This fact is illustrated in table 3.9, which presents national accounts data with a broad but meaningful definition of *local governments*.

When the central government budget is heavily unbalanced, with expenditures greater than revenues by more than 15 percent, local governments' budgets (taken together) are basically balanced. The data given in

TABLE 3.9   Borrowing and Indebtedness, Central and Local Governments, 2004

National accounts data	Central government	Local governments
Revenues (€ billion)	322	177
Expenditures (€ billion)	374	179
Balance (€ billion)	−52	−2
Balance in relation to revenues (%)	−16	−1
Indebtedness (€ billion)	840	112
Indebtedness in relation to revenues (%)	260	63
Indebtedness in relation to GDP (%)	51	7

Source: Ministère de l'Intérieur, Direction Générale des Collectivités Locales, 2006a, tables 2.1 and 7.7. The source uses national accounts concepts.

table 3.9 for 2004 are representative of the past decades. Central government accounts have always been in deficit. Local government accounts have been in deficit or in surplus, but always by only a small margin.

Consequently, the debt of the central government is heavy, relative to its revenues, and is increasing, whereas the debt of local governments is modest and declining. Local government debt represents only two-thirds of local governments' yearly income and one-seventh of the combined public debt of the country. It is not, at least for the moment, a serious macroeconomic issue.

Net numbers do not give a full picture of the scene, however, and table 3.10, which presents gross numbers, is a useful complement. It suggests that, for a given year, new loans account for nearly 10 percent of total revenues, even though reimbursements represent a flow of a similar order of magnitude (actually slightly lower in 2003, the year for which these data are available). It also shows the magnitude of interest payments relative to total expenditures: slightly more than 2 percent.

All types of local governments borrow in roughly similar proportions relative to their incomes, as shown in table 3.11. Regions are slightly more in debt than communes or départements, which reflects the fact that investments are a larger part of their expenditures.

Who lends to local governments? The answer to this question is given in table 3.12. First, it appears that bonds floated on the market play only a minor role. They account for only 2 to 4 percent of total debt for communes and départements. The share is much higher (about 18 percent) for regions, but overall, it remains modest.

TABLE 3.10   Local Governments' Borrowing-Related Flows, 2003

Indicator	Local governments
Resources (€ billion)	189
Resources through borrowing (€ billion)	19
Expenditures (€ billion)	184
Expenditures in the form of reimbursements (€ billion)	17
Interest paid (€ billion)	4
Net borrowing (€ billion)	+2
Interest in relation to expenditures (%)	2.2
Borrowing in relation to resources (%)	10.0
Reimbursements in relation to expenditures (%)	9.2
Net borrowing in relation to resources (%)	1.0

Source: Ministère de l'Intérieur, Direction Générale des Collectivités Locales, 2006a, table 3.1. The source uses public finance accounts concepts.

TABLE 3.11 Indebtedness of Local Governments, by Type, 2004

Type of government	Indebtedness (€ billion)	Percentage of total resources	Percentage of GDP
Communes	49.6	39	3.0
Départements	18.7	41	1.1
Regions	8.4	54	0.5
Total	76.7	40.5[a]	4.7

Source: Ministère de l'Intérieur, Direction Générale des Collectivités Locales, 2006a, tables 3.1 and 7.1. The source uses public finance accounts concepts, which are different from the national accounts concepts used in table 3.9.
a. This number indicates the indebtedness of all local governments relative to the resources of all levels of government.

TABLE 3.12 Local Government Debt, by Lenders and Levels of Government
(percent)

Type of debt	Communes	Départements	Regions
Bonds floated on the market	1.3	3.6	17.7
Public and quasi-public institutions[a]	34.8	17.2	20.1
Private banks	63.9	79.2	62.2
Dexia	*38.5*	*41.2*	*30.3*
Total	100.0	100.0	100.0

Source: Author's calculations.
Note: Data are 1996 for communes and 2000 for départements and regions. The values for *Dexia* are included in those for *private banks,* hence the italics.
a. Caisse des Dépôts et Consignation, Caisses d'Épargne, and Crédit Foncier.

Second, most (60 to 80 percent) of the loans to local governments are made by private banks. Third, the private bank picture is dominated by Dexia (about 40 percent of total lending). Dexia started in the 1980s, under the name of Crédit Local de France, as a subsidiary of the powerful and publicly owned Caisse des Dépôts et Consignations, which had a long history of dealing with local governments, but in a semimonopolistic position. Crédit Local de France was later privatized. It then merged with Crédit Communal de Belgique (the Belgian bank for local governments), to create Dexia. When the quasi-monopoly it enjoyed in France was broken and when competition for lending to local governments became open, many people thought that Dexia's share of the market would decline. It did not, and Dexia expanded into other areas, such as public finance initiatives and international lending. Dexia's experience would tend to suggest that lending to local governments is a fairly specialized type of banking, requiring specific expertise that is not necessarily available in the ordinary banking sector.

How does one explain the relative moderation of local governments in borrowing? It does not result from central government–imposed constraints. Local governments are practically free to borrow from whomever they want, to float bonds on the market, to obtain loans from French and foreign banks, as they please or as they can. This situation is in sharp contrast to the one that prevailed in the 1970s and early 1980s. Then, local governments could borrow only from state-owned institutions such as Caisse des Dépôts et Consignations or Caisses d'Épargne and only for amounts decided by the Ministry of Finance. Originally, loans were granted only on a project- by-project basis. However, those loans were made at concessionary rates, significantly below market rates. All of these constraints were progressively relaxed.

In addition, moderation does not result from the market discipline associated with a bond market and facilitated by the influence of rating agencies. This U.S.-type model, which was much favored by the World Bank for its client countries, does not function in France, at least not at present. The international rating agencies (plus a couple of French ones) do operate in France, and they have rated some regions and départements, as well as a few large cities. But the share of the bond market is too small for this model to function, at least for the time being.

The constraints on borrowing are financial and political. Banks would be reluctant to lend to overindebted local governments. They know what ratios of interests to revenues are socially and politically sustainable, and they refuse to make loans that would lead to significantly higher ratios. But local governments themselves are prudent. They realize that loan financing is costly. They fear that their political image would be affected by excessive indebtedness. Debt-to-revenues or interest-to-revenues ratios are part of the public debate, and they are available on the Internet. The long tenure of municipal governments (at least 6 years, usually 12 years, and in many cases, longer) encourages borrowing responsibility.

Would the central government bail out a failing local government? In principle, it would not; in practice, it would to a certain extent. In one case, a relatively large commune (Angoulême) nearly went bankrupt in the 1980s. The mayor fled to Argentina. The Ministry of Finance, the lending banks, and the local politicians got together and reached an agreement that implied (a) a serious loss for the banks, (b) very high tax rates for local taxpayers, and (c) some central government subsidies. This agreement was not clearly stated, but banks learned that irresponsible loans to local governments could be very costly, and politicians learned that excessive indebtedness could lead to lasting high taxes and a damaging image.

A related interesting feature is that local governments' financial balances are not held by private banks but by the Treasury. Each local government has an account with the Treasury. The Treasury credits that account with (a) the taxes that are collected, as mentioned above (not when they are actually collected, but every month for one-twelfth of the total amount) and (b) the subsidies granted to the local government. In addition, on order from the local government, the Treasury debits the account of all expenditures.

Local Government Administration

Traditionally, a local mandate (as council member, mayor, chairperson) was considered an honor and was not a paid position. That tradition was at a time when the job did not take too much time (and when such mandates were often held by people who did not need money). The situation has changed. Being a mayor, for instance, is a full-time job, even in a relatively small commune. Locally elected officials are now paid, but their compensation is decided by the central government and is not very high. Wages are a function of the jurisdiction size. The mayor of a 40,000-person commune, for instance, earns about €27,000 per year. The mayors of Paris, Marseille, and Lyons (the three largest communes) get about twice as much. In addition, mayors can be—and often are—members of Parliament. Remunerations for département and region council members range between €20,000 and €30,000, but these functions are not full time.

Staff members, numbering about 1.5 million, are civil servants. They are recruited on the basis of competitive exams and, once recruited, cannot be fired. This has benefits as well as costs. On the one hand, it protects local government employees from political arbitrariness and ensures a much welcome continuity in the operation of local government administration. On the other hand, the practice can make it difficult for politicians to introduce new policies. How is this potential conflict solved?

First, in many cases, local civil servants will be loyal to the newly elected politician and will do their best to follow his or her directives. Second, particularly in large communes and in départements and regions, a new mayor or chairperson will bring with him or her a private office of his or her choosing and political persuasion. This private office might consist of 10 to 15 people, usually not only technically well qualified but also politically reliable, whose task will be to oversee the permanent staff, to help make delicate and important decisions, and more generally to make sure that the mayor's or chairperson's directives prevail. When the mayor or chairperson quits, so does the entire private office. Third, the mayor or the chairperson can put aside key staff members who do not want (or with whom he or she does not want) to cooperate. They will keep their salary but will be constantly short-circuited and deprived of any real responsibility. Some might be happy to be paid to do nothing, but most will look for another position in a politically more friendly local government. This situation is often the case with the secretary-general of a commune, the most senior civil servant, who has often worked closely with the previous mayor on topics that were partly technical and partly political.

There are complex links between the central civil service and the local civil service. The two are distinct but similar. Under some conditions, members of one body can be lent to the other, which means that they keep the option of going back to their original body. However, in the 1980s, when regions were created, the regions recruited a number of people from the national civil service, often for senior positions, by offering substantial bonuses in addition to the standard civil service wages.

An additional element of flexibility is worth mentioning. Local governments, particularly communes, do create and control a number of satellites such as development agencies, garbage collection companies, and public transport agencies. These satellites are formally private enterprises, even if their capital is 100 percent controlled by the commune and their board chaired by the mayor. The boards can staff the enterprises with whomever they want and can pay them at market rates.

Conclusion

It is difficult to pass judgment on the efficiency and accountability of the system of local government just described, particularly because it has changed so much in the past decades and because it continues to change. A few tentative points can nevertheless be made.

First, the new tasks allocated to local governments in recent years seem to be reasonably well undertaken, in ways equal to or better than before, when they were in the hands of the central government. School buildings are better maintained by regions and départements than they were by the Ministry of Education, but regions and départements spend more money on the task than the Ministry of Education did. Reportedly, the départements spend welfare money better than the central government did. Regions are most probably better equipped than the central government to discuss with the railroad company what regional passenger lines should be subsidized and for how much (the central government was unable to do it anyway). In those areas, the decentralization of responsibilities is generally considered successful.

Second, accountability mechanisms exist now, but they are relatively weak. One such mechanism is the desire of politicians to be reelected and the fact that they can be reelected. This mechanism, however, functions much better at the commune level than at the département or region level. People know (or think they know) whether their mayor is good or bad, and they take his or her performance into account at election time as much as or more than that mayor's party affiliation. However, at the level of the region or the département, people usually vote as they would in a national election, for the party of their liking.

Another accountability mechanism is the relatively large share of local taxes in local government resources, including the fact that two of these taxes, the housing tax and (to a lesser extent) the property tax, are paid by most voters. Unfortunately, several factors weaken this standard and effective mechanism. It does not work for the business tax, which is exported out of the jurisdiction where it is levied. The fact that several levels of governments levy the same taxes dilutes responsibility in the eyes of taxpayers-voters. The rapid development of groupings of communes, which are not led by directly elected people, is also eroding accountability. Finally, the ratio of taxes to subsidies has dangerously declined in recent years.

Third, there are at present no macroeconomic problems associated with increased decentralization. Local governments have not misused the freedom they were given, either in tax or in borrowing matters. They have behaved very responsibly.

Fourth, in France as in most countries, decentralization has been driven by political considerations more than by economic efficiency considerations. New institutions have been created, at least in part, to distribute more widely power—and income—to politicians and their clients. These actions have an economic cost. To merely function, any institution, be it a government or an enterprise, has fixed costs. Part of the money spent is spent to cover those fixed costs, not to produce public goods and services. In the past years, most départements and regions constructed costly départements and region "buildings" or "houses," which are examples of such fixed costs. The multiplication of governments increases fixed costs, not to mention the coordination costs it implies. The lack of cost accounting makes it difficult to examine this issue in depth, but one must fear that too large a share of local public expenditures goes into mere administration. The problem is exacerbated by the coexistence of regions and départements. Many people believe that there are too many levels of government. Eliminating one of these levels would reduce fixed costs, but paradoxically, for that very reason, such a step is strongly opposed politically and would be next to impossible to implement.

Developing countries can learn several things from the French experience. One is that the standard measures of decentralization (local expenditures in relation to total public expenditures, local taxes in relation to total taxes) are much too crude to be meaningful. Changing them is unlikely to achieve much. The key parameters of features of a local government organization and finance system are often details of the election system or the subsidy system.

Second, changes in the degree, nature, and significance of a decentralization system should be gradual. It took France 30 years to move from a highly centralized system to a fairly decentralized one. The idea that a decentralization reform can be conducted in a few years, or by a single law, is not very realistic and might be counterproductive.

A third lesson is that no system is ideal and definitive. Reforming and improving the system of multilevel government are constantly on the agenda in France—and in most other countries. The reason is that a multilevel system targets too many goals at the same time: redistribute political power, improve economic efficiency, reduce interjurisdiction and interpersonal disparities, facilitate macroeconomic management, and so forth. A weakness in one of these objectives is spotted. Changes are made to improve matters on this score. But these changes are likely to worsen matters with respect to another—also perfectly legitimate—objective. These new weaknesses will, in turn, call for additional changes. This process must be accepted. The system should not be frozen but should remain reasonably flexible and able to accommodate changes easily. Constitutions, in particular, should not attempt to define a detailed system permanently.

A fourth lesson is that the number of jurisdictions and their distribution on a map are not major issues. The very large number of communes in France (37,000) is often presented as a serious shortcoming. It is not. It does present problems, but the communes have found solutions in the form of groupings of various types. If France were starting from scratch, it would not create the present map of 37,000 communes. But because this map has existed for more than two centuries, the costs of redesigning a completely new (and better) map outweigh the benefits. In this area, outcomes are path dependent.

Fifth among the lessons is that strong local autonomy does not imply complete local independence. There are no local governments worth the name without a high degree of autonomy. But strong local autonomy does not mean that local governments could or should be completely separated from the central government. Local taxes in France are administered, assessed, and collected by the central government; this arrangement does not seriously affect local autonomy and probably improves the efficiency of local tax collection. Another example is the wages of local government officials. In some countries, in the name of local autonomy, locally elected councils decide as they please on the level of wages of the mayor. This practice has resulted in some politicians in relatively small (and usually very poor) municipalities or provinces voting themselves salaries much higher than the salary of the chair of the U.S. Federal Reserve Board. In France, such salaries are determined by a central government law, and nobody sees it as an infringement of local autonomy.

A final lesson might be that, in decentralization, the better can be the enemy of the good. Four levels of government (five if one were to count groupings as a level of government and six if one were to consider the European Union) is a lot, even in a relatively rich country such as France. For each level of government, there are justifications and benefits. But there are costs, too. In France, they barely balance each other. But in a poorer country, it is doubtful that they would balance at all. In a poorer country, the costs of the marginal level of government would outweigh its benefits.

Notes

1. It was also made compulsory for Le Creusot, a much smaller agglomeration.
2. In France, social security, which includes medical insurance, pensions, unemployment allowances, and maternity allowances and which is about equal to central government revenues, is not considered part of central government revenues.
3. The case of Paris was a noteworthy exception: from 1871 to 1976, the mayor was appointed, not elected.
4. Authorities such as these institutions do not facilitate accounting. Frequently, this transport tax is omitted from the list of "local taxes," although it is undoubtedly a local tax. Also, because the expenditures of organizing authorities do not appear in communal accounts, they are often omitted from "commune expenditures."
5. The Ministry of Finance also guarantees local governments against taxpayers' default and claims that the fee charged is also in part an insurance policy premium.
6. For small enterprises in the service sector—for example, a lawyer—this mix can include turnover. Incidentally, this tax base provides data on the stock of capital (and on wages paid) at the commune, département, or region level, which is very useful for the analysis of geographic development.
7. More than half of French households do not pay personal income tax.
8. The surplus on the operating budget is used to finance the investment budget. Consequently, a subsidy to the operating budget will make it possible to increase the internal transfer to the investment budget and, therefore, to investments. Conversely,

a subsidy to the investment budget makes it possible to reduce this internal transfer and, therefore, to increase operating expenditures.

9. It is reported that the longstanding chair of a powerful local finance committee is about the only person who has a good command of the system; some people claim that the commune of which he is the mayor is rather well treated by the system. However, cautious analysts note that correlation is not causality.

10. In practice, these kinds of changes are not made overnight; they are planned to be gradual, with sliding formulas extending over many years.

References

INSEE (Institut National de la Statistique et des Études Économiques). 2006. *Tableaux de l'économie française 2005–2006*. Paris: INSEE. http://www.insee.fr.

Ministère de l'Intérieur, Direction Générale des Collectivités Locales. 2006a. *Les collectivités locales en chiffres 2006*. Paris: Ministère de l'Intérieur. http://www.dgcl.interieur.gouv.fr.

———. 2006b. *Les finances des communes de plus de 10,000 habitants 2003*. Paris: Ministère de l'Intérieur. http://www.dgcl.interieur.gouv.fr.

Prud'homme, Rémy. 2000. "'Taxe professionelle' as an Exportable Local Tax." *Environment and Planning C: Government and Policy* 18: 545–53.

4

Local Government Organization and Finance: *Germany*

JAN WERNER

Germany is a federal state with a three-level administrative struc-ture. In addition to the federal government, whose ministries are based both in Germany's capital, Berlin, and in its former capi-tal, Bonn, there are 16 federal states (*Bundesländer*),[1] plus a number of regional administrative bodies.

Within the regional administrative bodies, a further distinction is made between the regional planning associations (*regionale Planungsverbände*),[2] the 323 rural districts (*Landkreise*), the 116 incorporated cities (*kreisfreie Städte*), and the municipalities, which form part of the rural districts. The towns and municipalities, which after numerous territorial reforms in the respective federal states between 1970 and 1977 have become notably compact in terms of their inhabitant structures,[3] are the smallest local units in Germany. At the end of 2000, there were 13,897 municipalities in Germany, which in terms of their inhabitant numbers can be subdi-vided as shown in table 4.1.

In Germany, tax revenues are distributed among the individual regional administrative bodies, using both their own assigned revenues[4] and shared revenues. Hence, for example, tax receipts from real property tax are available to the municipalities in full, and they also receive a fixed percentage of the tax receipts from value

117

TABLE 4.1 Numbers of Inhabitants in Germany's Municipalities, 2000

Number of inhabitants	Number of municipalities
Fewer than 100	226
100–499	3,454
500–999	2,521
1,000–4,999	4,809
5,000–9,999	1,288
10,000–49,999	1,348
50,000–99,999	109
100,000–199,999	43
200,000–499,999	27
500,000 and up	12

Source: Statistisches Bundesamt 2002, p. 56.

added tax (VAT) and personal income tax (PIT). The distribution of the most important tax revenues is shown in table 4.2.

The political accountability for the expenditure is not clearly defined in Germany. For example, the level and criteria of social welfare are fixed by the central government, but disbursement of grants and examination of social

TABLE 4.2 Share of Tax Revenues Assigned to the Central Government, Federal States, and Municipalities

Tax	Share of tax revenues in 2003			Revenues in 2001 (€billion)
	Central government share (%)	Federal state share (%)	Municipal share (%)	
Consumption tax[a]	100.0	—	—	60.750
Inheritance tax	—	100.0	—	3.069
Property tax	—	—	100.0	9.076
Personal income tax	42.5	42.5	15.0	141.396
Value added tax	51.4	46.5	2.1	138.935
Corporate income tax	50.0	50.0	—	– 0.426
Interest rebate	44.0	44.0	12.0	29.846
Trade tax[b]	14.8	7.7	77.5	24.533

Source: Werner 2003, p. 83.
Note: — = not applicable.
a. Tax on mineral oil, electricity, tobacco, spirits, coffee, and sparkling wine.
b. The breakdown refers to the 2001 tax year. The municipal share of the "German Unity" fund and the municipal share of the reformed fiscal equalization system were allocated to the central government.

TABLE 4.3 Distribution of Accountability for Some Areas of Expenditure

Area of expenditure	Central government	Federal states	Rural districts	Municipalities
Foreign policy	X			
Currency policy	X			
Defense policy	X			
Social welfare	X			
Roads, railways, and inland water transportation	X	X	X	X
Education		X		
Police		X		
Construction supervision			X	
Maintenance and new building of school facilities			X	
Public transportation			X	
Maintenance and new building of public hospitals			X	
Kindergarten				X
Fire department				X
Theaters and museums				X
Parks and sports facilities				X
Waste management				(X)
Electricity supply				(X)
Water supply				(X)

Source: Author.
Note: (X) means that most municipalities have arranged special-purpose associations for this task. These associations are owned and politically controlled by the municipalities. A minority of municipalities have sold their special-purpose associations to private companies, but they have concluded long-term arrangements with the private companies.

neediness are the responsibility of the local authorities. Moreover, the central government delegates a huge number of administrative duties—mainly in the area of social security—to the federal states and local authorities and bears the expenses of those delegations. Table 4.3 shows the distribution of the accountability for some areas of expenditure among different tiers of government.[5]

Historical Development

When the Federal Republic of Germany was established in 1949, municipalities were granted self-government under the country's constitution,[6] but they were not granted revenue-generating autonomy. The central government received revenues from VAT, its most important source of taxes, and the federal

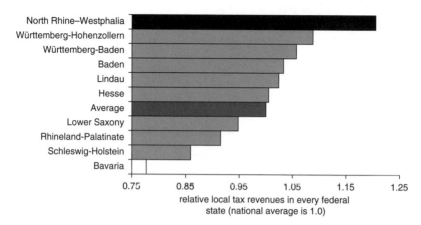

Source: Werner forthcoming.

FIGURE 4.1 Local Tax Revenues in Every Federal State, 1949, Based on Number of Inhabitants

states received revenues from PIT, corporate income tax (CIT), and trade tax. The municipalities were considered part of the federal states, and under the state laws, they were able to receive a share of trade tax and local excise duties.[7]

In 1949, local tax revenues already differed between municipalities. Industrial cities in the federal state of North Rhine-Westphalia received huge tax yields from trade tax, while small, rural townships in the south—mainly in the federal state of Bavaria—received only tiny tax revenues. Figure 4.1, in which tax revenues are measured against the size of the population, gives a survey of the situation in every federal state.

The reform of Germany's finances in 1955 replaced the previous arrangement of tax revenue distribution in Germany's constitution; from then on, a third of personal and corporate income taxes were allocated to the federal government. At the same time, a fiscal equalization system was created among Germany's federal states to compensate for any additional financial burden arising for the states.

In the course of the financial reform of 1956, municipalities were explicitly referred to in Germany's constitution. The revenues derived from trade tax and property tax were assigned to those municipalities.

Since the financial reform of 1969, municipalities have obtained a fixed portion of PIT, including the tax on wages and the assessed tax on income earned. As a compensation for this local amount of PIT, the federal government and states were each granted a 50 percent entitlement to trade tax revenues by means of a share that municipalities had to hand over to the states and the central government ("trade tax handover rate"). All in all, local authorities have benefited from the tradeoff between a fixed portion of PIT against a portion of (local) trade tax. Because of the financial reform of 1969, municipalities were no longer exclusively dependent on the economic situation of local firms. Moreover, the local tax structure was more diversified, and local mayors had an incentive to attract individuals subject to PIT. Before this major financial reform, a local authority was able to raise its tax revenues only by focusing on industrial companies. Since 1969, townships have had positive motivation to offer a good package of public goods to their inhabitants because they benefit not only from corporate taxes but also from taxes on individuals.

On January 1, 1980, payroll tax was abolished in the Federal Republic of Germany as one of the three assessment bases of trade tax. The consequent revenue losses to municipalities were compensated for by a reduction in the trade tax handover rate and an increase in the share of revenues municipalities receive from PIT from 14 percent to 15 percent.

Local tax revenues were still differentially distributed in fiscal year 1980, but the gap between industrial and rural municipalities was reduced when compared with the situation in 1949. Furthermore, local tax disparities exist largely between the economically strong, southern part of Germany (Baden-Württemberg, Hesse, Bavaria) and the economically weak, northern coastline (Lower Saxony, Schleswig-Holstein). From January 1, 1994, onward, municipalities were given a share of 12 percent of interest income tax in compensation because the interest income tax reduced the municipalities' share of PIT. In 1998, trading capital tax, another component of trade tax, was abolished in the western states of Germany,[8] and the municipalities were given a 2.2 percent share of VAT revenues to compensate for the shortfall.

As a result of the reunification of Germany in 1990, local tax disparities increased again, and tax yields shifted from a north-south inequality to an east-west inequality. The five, newly formed federal states (Saxony-Anhalt, Mecklenburg-Western Pomerania, Thuringia, Saxony, and Brandenburg) in particular possess relatively low tax revenues when compared with the national per capita average, whereas municipalities in the formerly rural and economically weak federal state of Bavaria received 10 percent more in 1999 than the national average. Figure 4.2 presents the local tax revenues in all 13 federal states.[9]

After Germany's fiscal equalization system was reformed by the so-called Solidarity Pact II (Spahn and Werner forthcoming; Werner and Shah forthcoming), current discussion on federalism is now focused on the municipalities' finances, and there are numerous proposals for reform in this context. This chapter will therefore explain the revenue structure of the

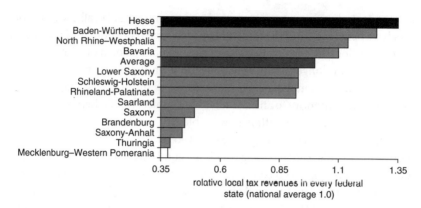

Source: Based on data from Torgler and Werner 2004, p. 25.

FIGURE 4.2 Local Tax Revenues in Every Federal State, 1999, Based on Number of Inhabitants

German cities, towns, and municipalities and will give an outline of the most important local taxes, namely, trade tax and real property tax.

Financial Situation of the Local Administrative Bodies: Problems and Reform Proposals Presented So Far

Germany's 13,897 municipalities constitute the third level of Germany's fiscal federalism, the central government and the 16 federal states being the first two levels. This section outlines the income structure and taxation powers of Germany's municipalities. It then classifies the different reform proposals and presents my own suggestion for reform.

Revenue Structure of Germany's Municipalities

Although the two parts of Germany were reunited more than a decade ago, there are still enormous inequalities between the territory of the former Federal Republic of Germany (the western states) and that of the former German Democratic Republic (the eastern states) in many aspects of everyday life. In addition to quite different unemployment rates—in February 2005, the unemployment rate in the western states was 10.4 percent compared with 20.7 percent in the eastern states—there are also enormous differences as far as income and private wealth are concerned. In 2003, while every household in the western states had average assets of €149,000, households in the eastern states had, on average, assets of only €60,000 (BMA 2005a, xxv). In terms of income levels, the relationship is similar. In 2003, the gross annual income of a salaried German employee in the western states was €28,747, whereas in the eastern states people received a comparable gross income of only €21,950 annually (see BMA 2005b, 101).

Because of these economic disparities, the income structures of the municipalities in the western and eastern states are quite different. In 2001, municipalities in the western states had revenues of €105.1 billion, which can be subdivided as shown in figure 4.3 (shared taxes are also consolidated under *taxes*). Municipalities in the eastern states had revenues of €19.9 billion in 2001, which consisted of the revenue items in figure 4.4.

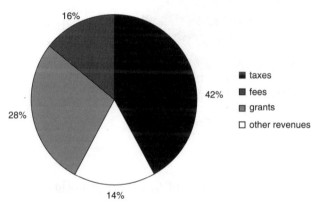

Source: BMF 2002, p. 1.

FIGURE 4.3 Revenues of Germany's Municipalities in Western States, 2001

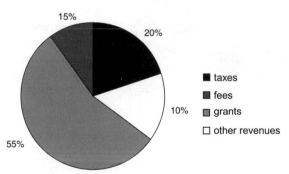

Source: BMF 2002, p. 1.

FIGURE 4.4 Revenues of Germany's Municipalities in Eastern States, 2001

For the municipalities in the western states, tax revenues are the biggest revenue item, whereas the municipalities in the eastern states are mainly funded by grants. The biggest source of tax revenue for the municipalities in Germany's western states is their fixed share of PIT and trade tax. In contrast, for the municipalities in the eastern states, trade tax and real property tax constitute the biggest revenue items. Figures 4.5 and 4.6 show the respective structure of the tax revenues in 2001.

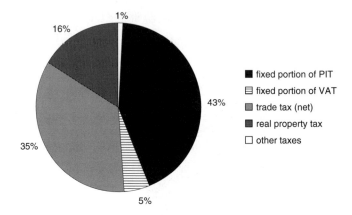

Source: BMF 2002, p. 7.

FIGURE 4.5 Tax Revenues of Germany's Municipalities in Western States, 2001

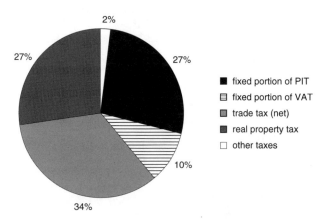

Source: BMF 2002, p. 7.

FIGURE 4.6 Tax Revenues of Germany's Municipalities in Eastern States, 2001

Taxation Powers of the Municipalities

In addition to their fixed share of PIT and VAT, municipalities in Germany are entitled to stipulate municipal assessment rates within the real property tax and trade tax, which ensures at least some basic elements of fiscal autonomy.

Trade tax

All German businesses are subject to trade tax; however, freelance work is exempt. Originally, trade tax had three tax assessment bases: payroll, trading capital, and trading profit. Two of these tax bases have been abolished: payroll tax as of January 1, 1980, and trading capital tax as of January 1, 1998. In compensation for the abolition of payroll tax, the municipalities received a higher share of PIT, and in compensation for the loss of trading capital tax, they were allocated a proportion of VAT.

Trade tax is determined by deducting a tax-exempt amount from trading profits and then multiplying the resulting amount by a tax assessment figure, which is usually 5 percent and is fixed by a federal law. This interim result, known as the *tax assessment amount,* is then multiplied by the respective municipal tax rate. Over the past several years, the municipal tax rates, which municipalities are allowed to determine independently, have seen the trends shown in figure 4.7.

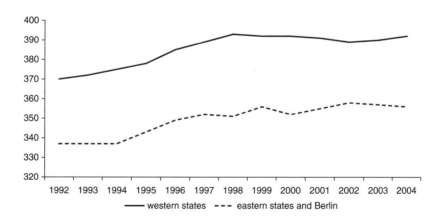

Source: BMF 2002, p. 14; Werner forthcoming.

FIGURE 4.7 Development of the Average Local Trade Tax Rates, 1992–2004

In fiscal year 2002, the cities of Kempten (337 percent), Rüsselsheim (340 percent), and Fulda (340 percent) had the lowest local trade tax rates among the 191 cities that have more than 50,000 inhabitants. The highest local rates were levied in the city of Bottrop (490 percent) and in metropolitan Munich (490 percent) and Frankfurt am Main (490 percent).

Only in densely populated areas between the core cities and the surrounding municipalities does a small level of tax competition exist. For example, in the area around Frankfurt am Main, Eschborn (300 percent), Bad Vilbel (300 percent), and Rüsselsheim (340 percent) have been successful in reducing the tax revenues of the city of Frankfurt. The same situation can be illustrated near Hamburg with the city of Winsen (280 percent). Only the small Nordic township of Norderfriedrichskoog can afford to levy a zero tax rate for trade tax and real property tax purposes. However, this small township is truly an exception.[10] Hence, we can conclude that there is no strong tax competition at the local level in Germany.

Real property tax

Under the German real property tax system, the value of property—irrespective of the economic profit it generates—is taxed. Properties used for agriculture or forestry are subject to real property tax A, and all other properties are subject to real property tax B. Publicly owned real property is not taxed. Under the real property tax system, like the trade tax system, the value of property is multiplied by a tax assessment figure (0.6 percent for real property tax A and 0.35 percent for real property tax B)[11] which is determined by the central government. The resulting tax assessment amount is then multiplied by the municipal tax rate.

Although the tax assessment figure of real property tax B is lower than that of real property tax A, the tax revenues from real property tax B are significantly higher, because municipalities usually set a higher local tax rate for real property tax B. During the past several years, municipalities have raised their rates for real property tax B considerably (figure 4.8). However, in an international comparison, taxation of real property by German municipalities is notably moderate (slightly more than €110 in the western states and less than €80 in the eastern states)[12] (figure 4.9).

Other municipal taxes in Germany

There are a number of other municipal taxes in Germany, which can be considered petty taxes. These petty taxes include alcohol tax, entertainment tax, dog license tax, pub license tax, hunting license tax, fishing license tax, and second home tax.

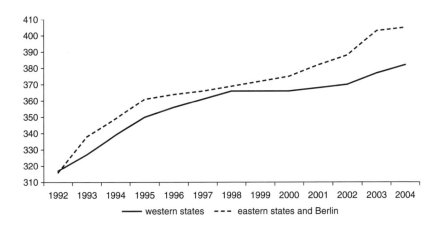

Source: BMF 2002, p. 18; Werner forthcoming.

FIGURE 4.8 Development of the Average Local Rate of Real Property Tax B, 1992–2004

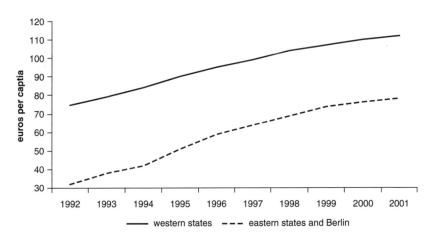

Source: Based on data from BMF 2002, pp. 9–10; Werner forthcoming.

FIGURE 4.9 Tax Burden Inflicted by the Real Property Tax, 1992–2001

According to the municipal laws governing these taxes, municipalities are free to decide whether to levy the taxes and at what rate. Receipts from petty taxes amounted to €628 million in 2001.

Proposals for Reform of Germany's Municipal Finances

The financial situation of Germany's municipalities has deteriorated considerably in recent years, partly because of the dramatic drop in trade tax revenues in 2001 and 2002. These revenues declined not only because of the weak economic situation but also as a result of the increase in the share of trade tax that municipalities must hand over to the states and to the central government. This trade tax handover rate is set by the central government.[13] Germany's municipalities responded to the dire municipal budget situation by cutting their spending on fixed-asset investments, as figure 4.10 shows.

The following sections outline two main suggestions for reforming municipal finances, followed by my own reform proposal.

BDI and VCI proposal: Municipal income and profit tax

Together with the German Association of Chemical Industry (Verband der Chemischen Industrie, or VCI), the Federal Association of German Industry (Bundesverband der Deutschen Industrie, or BDI) has submitted a proposal for a municipal income and profit tax.[14] The proposal of the two associations was elaborated by a group called the Research Group for the Reform of the Trade Tax, led by Wolfgang Ritter.

The proposal does not envisage municipalities levying their own tax, but it would entitle them to impose proportional and uniform surcharges on

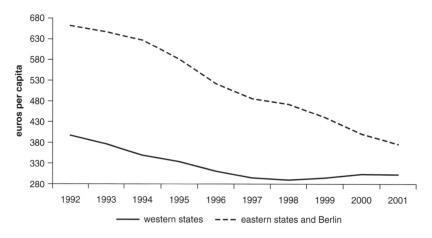

Source: BMF 2002, p. 21.

FIGURE 4.10 Development of Fixed-Asset Investments by Municipalities, 1992–2001

PIT and CIT. This concept is meant to minimize the administrative burden while simultaneously extending the municipal tax obligation from the business community to all taxpayers (BDI and VCI 2001, 18). The BDI and VCI model envisages the abolition of trade tax, the trade tax handover rate, and the 15 percent municipal share of PIT. Dividends would be exempt from the surcharges, thus preventing double taxation because they are already subject to CIT and PIT.[15]

The abolition of trade tax would constitute a financial relief for both the central government and the federal states because trade tax could no longer be offset against the PIT liability or deducted from the CIT liability. This relief would more than compensate for the shortfall caused by the abolition of the trade tax share that the municipalities must hand over to the states and central government.

In addition, the BDI and VCI model proposed a change in the tax rates for 2005:

- The entry level of PIT levied by the central government was lowered to 11.5 percent, and the maximum PIT rate was decreased to 32.2 percent.
- At the same time, the CIT rate was raised to 28.6 percent.

The implementation of those measures is meant to boost the financial and political scope for municipalities when they impose surcharges on PIT and CIT to ensure that nobody is left with a higher tax burden because of the fiscal reform.

Putting the outlined BDI and VCI model into practice requires a constitutional change, and Germany's Constitutional Law would have to be changed in accordance with all political players. Article 106, section 5, of the constitution would have to be changed in the sense that municipalities would no longer receive a proportion of PIT but would levy a surcharge on the tax. Article 106, section 6, of the constitution would then have to be changed so that municipalities could themselves determine the rate of the PIT and CIT surcharges.

The BDI and VCI model has the massive disadvantage that, once this kind of municipal fiscal reform has been successfully implemented, municipalities would no longer have an incentive to encourage companies to settle in their area. Rather, the tax burden would be shifted from the business community to the residential community, and municipalities would concentrate in particular on taxing the approximately 30 million people required to pay PIT—with the exception of the low income generated by the moderate surcharge on CIT.[16] Although the supporters of a municipal rate on PIT and CIT have partly conceded that this problem exists, their suggested solutions, such as the right to impose a surcharge on trade income, which would be paid for by the business community instead of the residential community, are impractical and would cancel out one of the benefits of the BDI and VCI model, namely, simplification of the German tax law (Fuest and Huber 2001, 18).

Another issue that needs to be considered is that eliminating trade tax while simultaneously introducing a municipal surcharge on PIT and CIT might lead to enormous taxation differences within densely populated areas between the core cities and surrounding municipalities. The profitable belt of municipalities surrounding Germany's major cities would be boosted at the expense of the densely populated areas. In their simulation calculations[17] for municipalities in the Saarland, Fuest and Huber (2001) concluded that the state capital of Saarbrücken would have to levy a municipal surcharge of 21.0 percent, whereas the administrative district of St. Wendel would be able to generate the same tax revenues with a municipal surcharge of just 8.4 percent (Fuest and Huber 2001, 37). Whether these types of fiscal disparities will be tolerated both socially and politically in Germany in the long run is doubtful. Up to this point, the goal of Germany's constitution, which is intended to create the same living conditions for everyone, has been the highest maxim; consequently, heavy tax competition as is practiced in Switzerland, for example, has been ruled out. Yet in spite of all the economic differences[18] and problems, one should not belittle the success of the Swiss fiscal federalism but, rather, look at it in the context of the positive influence of direct democracy (Feld and Savioz 1997, 529; Freitag and Vatter 2000, 598).

Jarass and Obermair proposal: A municipal business tax

The model of the Bavarian Convention of Municipal Authorities, which was developed jointly by Lorenz Jarass and Gustav Obermair and which, in a slightly modified manner, has been favored by several other leading municipal associations[19] since March 2003, moves in a completely different direction.

In contrast to the BDI and VCI proposal, the Jarass and Obermair proposal does not eliminate trade tax but instead develops it further as a municipal business tax and thus revitalizes trade tax (Bavarian Convention of Municipal Authorities 2003, 5). The Jarass and Obermair model for trade tax reform is based on the notion of a municipal tax on value added,[20] but under the municipal business tax in the Jarass and Obermair proposal, wages[21] would not be included in the tax assessment base. Jarass and Obermair suggest that the tax base consist of the following components (Jarass and Obermair 2003,

159): (a) profits, (b) all net-paid debt interest, and (c) a yet-to-be-defined percentage[22] of paid rents and leases for real estate and licensed products.

Employers' associations have rejected this proposal, which by fully including debt interest and by partially including rents and leases consists of two components that are not related to earnings. They see a further weakening of medium-size companies because of this asset taxation.

In addition to increasing the tax assessment base, the municipal business tax is designed to extend the tax obligation from the businesses that are currently taxable to self-employed people as well as agricultural and forestry businesses (Jarass 2003, 12). Because the tax obligation would thus be extended and the tax assessment base would be broadened, financial scope would exist to lower the municipal business tax rates and increase the amounts exempt from taxation. The exempt amount for a sole proprietorship, currently around €24,500, would be increased to €40,000, though trading partnerships would be excluded from this increase. However, for the purpose of offsetting debt interest against tax, partnerships would receive a special exempt amount of €10,000 (€20,000 for sole proprietorships).

The model further envisages the abolition of trade tax on affiliations[23] and some special regulations for financial companies.

The model may become tricky when it comes to cross-border trade, because, in many business sectors, it is difficult to fiscally trace the extent to which a value enhancement is generated in a specific business location. The problem of the municipal rates and the resulting lack of tax competition among the municipalities has not yet been coherently explained in the Jarass and Obermair model either. Despite protests from various lobbies, however, it is sensible to tax self-employed people, because both bakers, in their capacity as businesspeople, and lawyers use the municipal infrastructure to their advantage; hence, both professions should bear equally the costs of establishing and maintaining that infrastructure.

A further proposal: The three-pillar model

Most models for reforming municipal finances in Germany do not take into account certain important areas. For example, although a variety of models have been proposed that would modernize or replace trade tax, those models do not take into account real property tax.

Both the BDI and VCI model, which would shift the tax burden from local companies to the residential community, and the model developed by Jarass and Obermair, whose assessment base rests to a large extent on components that are not earnings related, show structural flaws. On the one hand, the BDI and VCI model aggravates the problem of the city and its surrounding area; on the other hand, Jarass and Obermair's model burdens companies with a tax on assets, whose assessment base is difficult to define in administrative terms. Despite this criticism, however, both models have a number of positive aspects, which have influenced the three-pillar model.

To be able to rest on a solid financial foundation even during fluctuations in the business cycle, municipalities need three reliable tax sources that they are able to influence directly with their own tax rates to guarantee municipal self-government and financial autonomy: (a) municipal real property tax, (b) municipal PIT, and (c) municipal CIT.

Until now, the German tax burden on property and real estate assets has been more than moderate. In an international comparison, the current real property tax rates (both A and B) are much lower than if, for example, set against the North American and Canadian property taxes; the British council tax; and the Danish *grundskyld, daekningsafgigt,* and *frigorelseafgift,* as well as the French *taxe sur le foncier bâti* and the *taxe sur le foncier no bâti.* The valuation of real property assets in Germany is also outdated. Leaving the assessment to municipalities and providing the following general guidelines through federal legislation could solve the problem of valuing such assets relatively easily:

1. Three benchmark indicators could be used to determine the tax assessment base for real property: (a) maximum ground space, (b) maximum floor space, and (c) size of the property.[24] All three figures, which are fixed in every municipal building plan, the land registry office, or both, would be multiplied. Thus, it would be irrelevant whether the respective property actually had buildings on it or whether building was restricted to a minimum when the building permission was granted.
2. Municipalities would divide individual building sections into special building zones, to which they allocate individual building zone factors. Municipal parliaments themselves would decide on not only how high this building zone factor should be but also how big the zone should be.
3. Municipal parliaments would also set the municipal real property tax rates, with all zones being subject to the same municipal assessment rate.
4. All properties—private property, commercial property, property for agricultural and forestry use, and public property—would be subject to municipal real property tax. However, for public properties, the zone factor would be 1.0.
5. The central government would not impose a uniform tax assessment rate, thus eliminating the current distortion among the tax rates of up to 375 percentage points.

Hence, municipal real property tax would be calculated in the following manner:

Ground space ×	Floor space ×	Size of property ×	Zone factor ×	Municipal tax rate	= Tax liability
(measured in decimal number)	(measured in decimal number)	(measured in square meters)	(measured in decimal number)	(measured in € per square meters)	(measured in €)

Municipal real property tax, the first pillar of the three-pillar model, would deliberately create tax incentives for making the best possible use of property; hence, greater investment in construction on vacant properties would occur. Moreover, the tax promotes higher density in urban development.

Municipal PIT, the second pillar of the model, includes the positive aspects of the BDI and VCI model. Municipalities are given the right to impose a further tax surcharge on PIT and simultaneously give up their entitlement to a fixed percentage of PIT revenues. The municipal right to impose a surcharge would increase tax competition among local administrative bodies and, at the same time, make inhabitants contribute directly to the cost of maintaining and building municipal infrastructure. For taxpayers, in particular, this approach is much more transparent because they no longer contribute to the financing of communal facilities (kindergartens, club subsidies, municipal roads, public swimming pools, and social and cultural facilities) in an indirect fashion by means of a fixed percentage of PIT but, rather, by means of the more noticeable municipal surcharge.

However, the upper limit of the municipal surcharge should not be tied to the number of inhabitants, as in Croatia (Loncarevic 2002, 36), and the autonomy of setting the PIT rate should not be linked to other local tax rates, as in France (Guihéry and Werner 2005). Therefore, a nationwide upper and lower limit for the local surcharge on PIT is necessary.[25] On the one hand, this restriction will prevent a municipal "race to the bottom," and on the other hand, there will be no enormous municipal tax rate divergence between municipalities. However, the three-pillar model does not solve the disparities between cities and their surrounding areas. Rather, a feasible fiscal equalization system at the municipal level has to even out these tax disparities. In particular, the negative experience with tax competition in Switzerland should be an incentive to ensure that tax disparities between municipalities are not too large to ensure that there is sufficient acceptance of the three-pillar model, particularly among leading municipal associations.

The third pillar of a workable municipal fiscal system is municipal CIT. This tax is a modernized version of trade tax, which rests on two components: the profit component and the minimum component.

Under the local CIT system, businesses as well as self-employed people and agricultural and forestry businesses would be subject to taxation because all those professional groups benefit from the municipal infrastructure. All taxpayers would be taxed according to their declared taxable profits. However, all taxpayers would be allowed a tax-exempt amount, and this amount would be twice as high for trading partnerships as it would be for public limited companies. The exempt amount would be sufficient to exclude very small businesses from taxation. The higher amount for trading partnerships would strengthen these partnerships because the current possibility of offsetting debt interest would be eliminated, hence facilitating administration. The principle of business location would continue to apply; however, municipal CIT would prohibit any kind of affiliation.

If a business or a freelancer does not report a profit, then the minimum component of tax would apply. This component is intended to ensure minimum taxation. Many other countries have a minimum tax, and this concept has been introduced successfully, for example, in Switzerland.[26] The assessment base should be the number of employees and the turnover, with very small businesses of up to three employees being exempt from the minimum component.

Although the profit component should be taxed through a municipal rate determined by the municipalities themselves, the minimum component would have to be fixed centrally by the federal legislators. In addition, the tax burden inflicted by the minimum component would have to be extremely moderate and use interest on equity as fixed by the rates of interest on long-term treasury bonds as a guideline.

The regulations applying to the profit component do not require further complication by inclusion of a uniform nationwide tax assessment figure, and any involvement of the central government and the federal states—as in the case of the percentage of trade tax that the municipalities have to hand over to the central government and the states—should be avoided. Germany's towns and municipalities, in particular, have largely had to pay the price for recent reforms[27] and were allocated new tasks while the connectivity principle was disregarded. For this reason, a reform of municipal finances also will have to ensure that the flow of funds is shifted in favor of municipalities.

Local Financial Equalization between the Federal States and Municipalities

In every federal state in Germany, a local equalization system (*kommunaler Finanzausgleich*) exists. These systems differ vastly. Every state must transfer a portion of its tax revenues[28] to local authorities under an arrangement called *obligatory tax sharing* (*obligatorischer Steuerverbund*). On the one hand, federal states must distribute part of their tax revenues to cities, rural districts, and municipalities.[29] On the other hand, federal states can fix the volume of their obligatory tax sharing independently. The percentage shared ranges between 11.54 percent in Bavaria and 26.66 percent in Mecklenburg-Western Pomerania.

In addition to this obligatory tax sharing, there exists an arrangement known as *facultative tax sharing* (*freiwilliger Steuerverbund*) under which the states are able to give local authorities a share of further revenues such as grants from the equalization system among the federal states, grants from the central government because of economic weakness, or proceeds from the motor vehicle tax. Table 4.4 describes the situation in 2001 in 13 of the 16 federal states; no equalization system existed in the three city-states, Hamburg, Berlin, and Bremen, that year.

Illustration: The Equalization System in Hesse

This section, which describes the equalization system in the federal state of Hesse, is intended to provide an idea of the volume and distribution of the local equalization system in Germany. Hesse, which is one of the "donor states" (Werner and Xue 2004, 64) in the context of the equalization system among the federal states, distributed €2.552 billion to its local authorities in fiscal year 2005. Table 4.5 illustrates the complete amount of vertical grants to Hessian municipalities, rural districts, and incorporated cities.

This amount is divided among 421 municipalities, 21 rural districts, and 5 incorporated cities. Table 4.6 shows the breakdown among the three types of local authorities—municipalities, rural districts, and incorporated cities—and summarizes the classification between conditional and unconditional grants in fiscal year 2005.

The calculation formula for unconditional, general grants (*Schlüsselzuweisungen*) is quite similar to the equalization system among the federal states (for a detailed illustration, see Spahn and Werner forthcoming). A financial strength indicator has to be calculated for every

TABLE 4.4 Local Financial Equalization between Federal States and Municipalities, 2001
(*as a percentage of total revenue*)

Federal state	Obligatory tax sharing	Trade tax	Motor vehicle tax	Conveyance duty	Wealth tax	Fiscal equalization among federal states	Vertical grants for deficit coverage	Vertical grants for special requirements
Baden-Württemberg	23.000	23.000	23.390	55.000	0	23.000	0	0
Bavaria	11.540	11.540	65.000	38.000	0	11.540	0	0
Brandenburg	25.000	25.000	25.000	25.000	25.000	25.000	25.00	25.000
Hesse	23.000	23.000	23.000	23.000	23.000	23.000	0	0
Lower Saxony	17.010	0	17.010	17.010	17.010	17.010	17.01	17.010
Mecklenburg–Western Pomerania	26.990	0	26.990	26.990	26.990	26.990	26.99	26.990
North Rhine–Westphalia	23.000	0	0	13.430	0	0	0	0
Rhineland-Palatinate	21.000	0	21.000	21.000	21.000	21.000	21.00	21.000
Saarland	20.000	0	20.000	20.000	20.000	20.000	20.00	20.000
Saxony	25.799	25.799	25.799	25.799	25.799	25.799	0	25.799
Saxony-Anhalt	24.000	23.000	23.000	23.000	23.000	23.000	23.00	26.300
Schleswig-Holstein	19.780	19.780	19.780	19.780	19.780	19.780	19.78	19.780
Thuringia	23.000	23.000	23.000	23.000	23.000	23.000	23.00	40.000

Source: Werner 2003, p. 108.

TABLE 4.5 Calculation of the Vertical Grants from Hesse to the Local Authorities, 2005
(€ billion)

Revenue source	Distribution
Portion of PIT, CIT, VAT, and the trade tax	11.613
Wealth tax[a]	0.010
Conveyance duty	0.313
Motor vehicle tax	0.645
Total tax revenues	12.581
Less payment under the equalization system among the federal states	− 1.750
Total remaining revenues	10.831
Obligatory tax sharing (23% in Hesse)	2.491
Grants from Hesse to municipalities around the city of Frankfurt for the public transportation system	0.002
Grants from Hesse to all municipalities	0.092
Transfer to the local authorities because of municipal hospitals	0.059
Total value of the local equalization system in Hesse	2.552

Source: Author's calculations based on data from the budget plan of the state of Hesse for fiscal year 2005.
a. Wealth tax has not been levied since 1997. However, some revenue is still being collected from previous years.

TABLE 4.6 Distribution of the Vertical Grants among Municipalities, Rural Districts, and Incorporated Cities, as well as Classification between Conditional and Unconditional Grants, 2005
(€ billion)

Type of grant	Distribution
Unconditional general grants *(Schlüsselzuweisungen)*	**1.342**
Municipalities	0.6135
Rural districts *(Landkreise)*	0.4595
Incorporated cities *(Kreisfreie Städte)*	0.269
Grants to a public charitable society supporting the municipalities *(Landeswohlfahrtsbund)*	**0.064**
Special-purpose grants	**0.663**
Unconditional grants for capital investment	**0.103**
For general use	0.0515
For school buildings	0.0515
Conditional grants for capital investment	**0.380**
For local hospitals	0.247
For local infrastructure	0.133
Total	**2.552**

Source: Author's calculations based on data from the budget plan of the state of Hesse for fiscal year 2005.

municipality and is composed of a city-specific total sum of local taxes (trade tax, property tax, and a fixed portion of PIT and VAT).

The financial strength indicator is compared with a local needs indicator, which is based on the number of local inhabitants, unemployed people, and pupils. The local needs indicator includes more social features than does the indicator of equalization among the federal states (*Länderfinanzausgleich*), which is based only on population.

If the financial requirements of a municipality are higher than its financial strength, then the city will receive equalization funds from the state of Hesse through an unconditional, general grant (for a detailed illustration, see Broer 2001).

Local Government Borrowing

In the past few decades, the financial situation of the three levels of government has changed considerably. Although the 11 federal states of the Federal Republic of Germany had their highest amount of public debt at the beginning of the 1950s, the central government had accumulated its highest amount of public debt shortly before Germany's reunification.

In the course of Germany's reunification, the federal government devised a number of "shadow budgets"[30] to finance the burden of German reunification. Consequently, the financial situation of the federal government became less constrained during the past few years, whereas the federal states incurred enormous amounts of public debt during the first decade after reunification.

Local authorities do not suffer from a strong burden of interest payments like the central government, but since the German reunification, the debt of eastern local authorities especially has risen rapidly (similar observations can be made between the western and eastern federal states; for the bailout issue in the equalization system among the federal states, see Spahn and Werner forthcoming). Table 4.7 shows the development of the ratio between interest payments and total revenues in all tiers of government.

Compared with the central government and states, creditors of local governments are quite clear and unilateral. More than 90 percent of local borrowing is financed directly by the banking sector; however, municipal bonds do not play a major role in Germany. Moreover, the majority of the direct loans originate from public savings banks and their state clearinghouse banks, the *Landessparkassen*.

TABLE 4.7 Development of the Ratio between Interest Payments and Total Revenues, 1991–99
(*percent*)

Tier of government	1991	1992	1993	1994	1996	1998	1999
Central government	11.4	11.3	11.7	12.0	13.5	14.0	18.9
Western states	8.2	8.3	8.3	8.3	8.0	8.0	7.9
Eastern states	0.2	0.4	2.0	3.1	4.5	8.1	8.0
Western authorities	4.5	4.3	4.4	4.3	4.2	3.9	3.7
Eastern authorities	0.4	1.0	1.8	2.3	3.1	3.4	3.4

Source: Rehm 2001, p. 21.

Another feature of the link between public savings banks and local authorities has to be considered: local authorities both own public savings banks and simultaneously guarantee the credit rating of those banks (*Gewährträgerhaftung*). Savings banks administer the accounts of local authorities and usually offer them borrowing conditions that are below those of private banks. Hence, a situation may arise in which a local mayor—as a member of the executive board of a public savings bank—has to decide about his or her own municipal loan. Table 4.8 gives a brief description of the local debt structure from 1950 to 1999.

Because of the Maastricht Treaty, a higher interest rate applies to debt management. In Germany, the main limitation concerning federal borrowing is contained in article 115 of its federal constitution: "Revenue from borrowing shall not exceed the total expenditure for investment

TABLE 4.8 Local Debt Structure
(€ *billion*)

Year	Bonds	Direct loans from financial institutions	Social security system	Other loans
1950	0.000	0.205	0.000	0.051
1955	0.036	1.641	0.235	0.424
1970	0.359	16.527	0.503	3.201
1990	0.077	101.880	1.858	1.307
1995	0.716	96.599	1.715	1.373
1999	1.015	98.864	0.177	1.976

Source: Author's calculations based on data from the German Federal Bank.

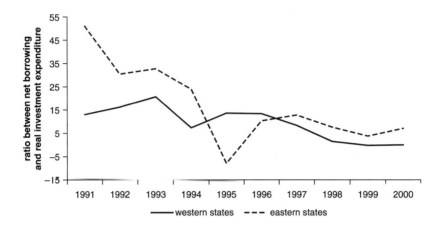

Source: Färber 2002, p. 139.

FIGURE 4.11 Development of the Ratio between Net Borrowing and Real Investment Expenditure, 1991–2000

provided for in the budget estimates; exceptions shall only be permissible to avert a disturbance of macroeconomic equilibrium. Details shall be the subject of federal legislation."

Local borrowing differs from central government and state borrowing for several reasons. Nearly two-thirds of public investment in Germany takes place at the local level. The relationship between net borrowing and the total amount of real investment expenditure is described in figure 4.11.

As in the case of the local equalization system, the federal states are able to fix local borrowing limits independently; therefore, the set of laws controlling local borrowing limits differs from state to state. Generally, local borrowing is permitted only to fund investment expenditure, and local mayors are allowed to use borrowing only if all other sources of revenues (taxes and fees) have been used. Furthermore, local authorities must submit their budgets to the federal Ministry of Finance or its respective regional agencies. In the extreme case of financial incompetence of a local mayor, the ministry declines the allowance of local budgets, and the mayor has to present a revised budget. Theoretically, the ministry is also able to assume complete control of the local budget. Those strict rules are quite reasonable because, in the case of a local bailout, the federal state must balance the local debt completely; therefore, a municipality cannot become bankrupt.

Local Government Administration

More than 4.7 million people work for the public sector in Germany, which means that the ratio between public servants and the total population is 1 to 13. These public servants consist generally of 2.3 million employees; 1.7 million clerks (such as police officers, teachers, tax clerks, and judges); and more than 600,000 blue-collar workers.

The average monthly gross income of a clerk amounted to €3,200 in June 2003, whereas an employee received €2,750 per month, and a blue-collar worker earned an average gross wage of €2,240 per month. The salary arrangement is fixed by federal law and differs only between the western states and eastern states in Germany. Therefore, local authorities cannot start a "salary competition" among one another to attract the best staff members. On the one hand, local authorities are absolutely free to hire new staff members—as long as they can do so within their budgets. On the other hand, because of the rigid dismissal protection laws, local authorities cannot fire an incapable public servant.

Local Tax Administration

The German tax administration is an extremely tangled web. Generally, the central government operates a number of special agencies with particularly detailed areas of responsibilities. Furthermore, the central government alone is responsible for customs, duties, and criminal investigation, whereas the federal states deal with tax administration. The central government bears the expenses of tax administration and pays the federal states for this work. Local authorities administer only the small petty taxes described earlier. Additionally, local authorities send the final trade tax and real property tax assessments to their local taxpayers, but the complete tax calculation is done at the regional tax office.

In contrast to the central government, local authorities do not pay an amount to the federal states for tax administration. This circumstance—combined with the fact that the federal states are not involved in tax yields from real property tax—could explain why the federal states and the central government try to avoid a revaluation of private and commercial property: the extra tax yield belongs to the municipalities, and the two other players of the fiscal federalism have to pay the costs of the revaluation. Figures 4.12 and 4.13 describe the structure of the tax administration of the central government and the federal states.

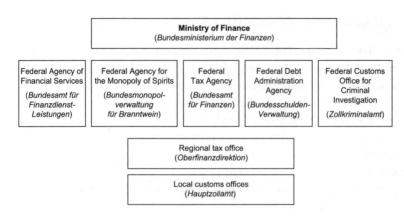

Source: Author.

FIGURE 4.12 Structure of the Tax Administration of the Central Government

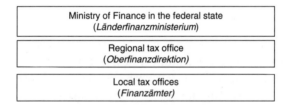

Source: Author.

FIGURE 4.13 Structure of the Tax Administration in the Federal States

Conclusion and Policy Implications

During the past few years, Germany's fiscal federalism has undergone a process of perpetual reform. On the one hand, relative tax revenues have decreased because of economic development in Germany. On the other hand, tax receipts that have existed up to now (the CIT is a good example in this context) will shortly be phased out because of changes in the system. In addition, other incidents such as the judgment by the Constitutional Court in Karlsruhe[31] require a constant renewal of Germany's fiscal federalism.

Although the court's orders have already led to the implementation of some initial reforms in the fiscal equalization system among Germany's states after the Solidarity Pact II, there is still no workable solution when it comes to the problem of Germany's municipal finances. Unfortunately the reform commission set up by the Ministry of Finance was not able to conclude with a unanimous decision, because the BDI and VCI proposal and the Jarass and Obermair proposal were so different from each other in their conceptual orientations. The three-pillar model, which encompasses the advantages of the models presented up to now and largely minimizes their disadvantages, could be considered a compromise between these two proposals.

In Europe, three conceptions of local public finance exist. The Anglo-Saxon countries and France fund their local authorities basically with vertical grants and taxes on property. In contrast, a group of countries—most notably Switzerland, Belgium, Croatia, and the Scandinavian countries—give huge tax autonomy to their local authorities; therefore, a local surcharge on personal income tax is common. A third way to finance local authorities was chosen by Austria, Germany, and Poland, each of which developed a local tax system with its own revenues and tax sharing. Figure 4.14 summarizes the main differences among the three conceptions.

One of the biggest advantages of Germany's local public finance system is the feature of tax sharing, because local authorities receive a stable revenue base and municipalities do not depend on a local business tax or trade tax. Furthermore, tax sharing has an advantage over vertical grants, because central governments commonly use grants to punish or reward local authorities. But the only institution that should have the duty and the authority to punish or reward the local government is the voters. If the voters' function is extinguished, then the healthy effect of the political yardstick competition cannot occur.[32]

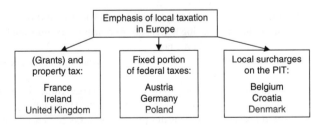

Source: Author.

FIGURE 4.14 Conceptions of Local Public Finance in Europe

Another advantage of Germany's local public finance system is that it prevents tax exporting. Except for second home tax, every local tax has more or less a benefit-tax link to the respective local authority. The benefit-tax link could be boosted enormously, however, if the fixed portion of PIT was abolished and municipalities received the right to impose a further tax surcharge on PIT. Even though the municipal right to impose a tax surcharge increases tax competition among local administrative bodies, it also makes inhabitants contribute directly to the costs of the municipal infrastructure. For inhabitants, in particular, this arrangement is much more transparent because they no longer contribute to the financing of communal facilities in an indirect fashion.

As mentioned before, political accountability for expenditure is not clearly defined in Germany. Moreover, Germany's local public finance system suffers from tremendous complexity, and all things considered, the German fiscal federalism was and is in an extreme state of flux.

Notes

1. Three of the 16 federal states are city-states (Berlin, Bremen, and Hamburg). These three federal states do not separate their municipal budgets from their respective federal budgets and, thus, have only a federal budget. Similar budget structures can be found in Austria for the municipality of Vienna and the federal state of Vienna, as well as in Denmark, with its capital Copenhagen and the city of Frederiksberg, which possess a city status and an *Amtskommuner* status.
2. The metropolitan regions of Stuttgart, Hanover, and Frankfurt are called *regional planning associations.*
3. In France, there were 36,679 municipalities in 1999, of which about 32,000 municipalities had fewer than 2,000 inhabitants. Yet Germany is far from creating a realigned municipal structure, which Denmark did when it reformed its territories in 1970.
4. According to article 106 of Germany's constitution.
5. Cities combine the accountabilities of a rural district and a municipality in one administration unit.
6. Version of May 23, 1949, article 28, section 2.
7. Most of these taxes can be considered petty taxes. These petty taxes include the alcohol tax, entertainment tax, dog license tax, pub license tax, hunting license tax, fishing license tax, and second home tax.
8. In the new federal eastern states of Germany, the trading capital tax was never imposed.
9. The three city states of Berlin, Bremen, and Hamburg were excluded because they do not separate their municipal budgets from their respective federal budgets.
10. Since 2004, a zero tax rate for trade is not possible because the central government has fixed a minimum tax rate of 200 percent.
11. The tax assessment figure is 0.6 percent for real property tax A and 0.35 percent for real property tax B.

12. In Croatia, Denmark, France, and the United Kingdom, real property is taxed at a much higher level than in Germany.

13. In 2000, the share of the trade tax that the municipalities had to hand over to the states and the central government was approximately €5.52 billion, and in 2001 it was approximately €5.51 billion. At the same time, the municipalities' trade tax receipts fell by €2.5 billion.

14. As early as 1968, the Scientific Advisory Council at the Ministry of Finance (Bundesministerium der Finanzen, or BMF) had looked at, reviewed, and approved a municipal income tax with the right to levy a proportional surcharge. In its 1982 report on reforming the municipal taxes, the Scientific Advisory Council at the BMF looked at this possibility again and did not come up with a satisfactory solution with respect to distribution and the problem of the municipal surcharge rates. For this reason, it rejected the introduction of such a tax (see BMF 1982, 115, 123).

15. At corporation level, dividend income is taxed by a municipal profit tax, in addition to the corporate income tax, and it is also taxed at shareholder level because, according to the so-called semi-income taxation system, PIT is payable and, hence, the municipal income tax is payable (see Fuest and Huber 2001, 31).

16. In particular, the corporate income tax has seen a significantly negative development in terms of its fiscal yield after the change from a system of total income taxation to a system of semi-income taxation.

17. The calculations were based on the tax receipts of 1999.

18. The differences in the 1999 average per capita income of the two neighboring Swiss cantons of Jura (€21,839) and the city of Basle (€53,602) are more than indicative of the economic differences.

19. These associations include the German Convention of Municipal Authorities; the German Convention of Administrative Districts; and the German Confederation of Cities, Towns, and Municipalities.

20. The idea of a tax on value added has often been floated in financial science (see BMF 1982, 135; SVR 1995, clause 346). The tax on value added ought not to be confused with the conventional value added tax, or VAT, which is basically a tax on the sale of products and services. The goal of the tax on value added is to impose a levy on the total amount of all the additional values a business itself has generated over a period of time. It consists of (a) the net output minus all previous investments, (b) indirect taxes, (c) the depreciation of assets, and (d) all governmental subsidies.

21. In Scherf's (2002, 605) plan for a municipal tax on value added eligible for inclusion, he does actually want to tax wages.

22. Up to now, Jarass has talked only of an appropriate share and has not fixed any concrete percentage rates.

23. Affiliation allows companies with premises in different municipalities to balance their internal yields and losses between the premises. Therefore, a municipality with a strong local firm might not receive any tax yield from the trade tax because of the company balance losses from other national premises or from foreign premises. However, this kind of tax balance weakens the local tax-benefit link and, fortunately, was restricted by new federal laws dated May 16, 2003, and December 23, 2003.

24. Indicator c is measured in square meters, whereas the two indicators a and b are measured in decimal numbers and calculated in relation to the total size of the

property. For example, if a property has a size of 400 square meters and the building on this property has two floors, with the ground space of 240 square meters, the respective benchmark indicators are a = 0.6 , b = 2.0, and c = 400.

25. The practical implementation in Denmark, where the combined tax rate of the central government, the municipalities, and the administrative districts is restricted to 59 percent all together, is a relevant example.
26. The Swiss minimum tax also applies to companies that do not intend to make a profit yet do benefit from public services. The minimum tax, which uses turnover, real estate assets, and invested capital as its assessment bases, applies only if the yields from the minimum tax are higher than those from other corporate taxes. It is charged in 14 of the 26 Swiss cantons. The cantons of Nidwalden, Schaffhausen, and Aargau impose a minimum tax along with the profit tax and capital gains tax if the tax revenues they receive from the public limited companies and the cooperatives fall below a certain amount, hence ensuring that minimum taxation takes place.
27. In particular, the explanations given by Fehr and Tröger (2003, 750) clearly show that when fiscal reforms take place, municipalities pay the price for compromise proposals between the central government and the federal states.
28. As described already, the federal states do not have their own revenues but, rather, share the revenues from the PIT, corporate income tax, and VAT.
29. According to article 107, section 1 of the German constitution.
30. From 1990 to 1994, the shadow budgets were the "German Unity" fund and the loan processing fund; from 1994 to 1998, they relied on federal railway assets; from 1995 to 1998, they relied on creating the inherited debt repayment fund and the "hard coal" equalization fund; and from 1996, they relied on creating the compensation fund.
31. The states of Baden-Württemberg, Bavaria, and Hesse have successfully filed a lawsuit at Germany's Constitutional Court in Karlsruhe. For this reason, on June 23, 2001, the states and the central government agreed on a reform of the fiscal equalization system, which came into force in 2005 and will last until 2019 (see Torgler and Werner 2005; Werner and Shah forthcoming).
32. Moreover, Torgler and Werner (2005) have analyzed how fiscal autonomy affects tax morale in Germany. Strong evidence has been found that higher fiscal autonomy leads to higher tax morale, controlling in a multivariate analysis for additional factors (see Torgler and Werner 2005).

References

Bavarian Convention of Municipal Authorities. 2003. *Reform der Gewerbesteuer— Anforderungen und Auswirkungen*. Munich, Germany: Bavarian Convention of Municipal Authorities.

BDI (Bundesverband der Deutschen Industrie) and VCI (Verband der Chemischen Industrie). 2001. *Verfassungskonforme Reform der Gewerbesteuer, Konzept einer kommunalen Einkommen- und Gewinnsteuer*. Cologne, Germany: BDI.

BMA (Bundesministerium für Arbeit und Sozialordnung). 2005a. *Lebenslagen in Deutschland: Der zweite Armuts- und Reichtumsbericht der Bundesregierung*. Berlin: BMA.

————. 2005b. *Lebenslagen in Deutschland: Der zweite Armuts- und Reichtumsbericht der Bundesregierung-Daten und Fakten*. Berlin: BMA.

BMF (Bundesministerium der Finanzen). 1982. *Gutachten zur Reform der Gemeindesteuern in der Bundesrepublik Deutschland*. Schriftenreihe Heft 31. Bonn: BMF.

————. 2002. *Eckdaten zur Entwicklung und zur Struktur der Kommunalfinanzen*. Berlin: BMF.

Broer, Michael. 2001. *Der kommunale Finanzausgleich in Hessen: Historische Darstellung und ökonomische Analyse unter besonderer Berücksichtigung der Schlüsselzuweisungen*. Frankfurt am Main, Germany: Lang.

Färber, Giessela. 2002. "Local Government Borrowing in Germany." In *Local Public Finance in Europe: Balancing the Budget and Controlling Debt*, ed. Bernard Dafflon, 135–64. Cheltenham, U.K: Edward Elgar.

Fehr, Hans, and Michael Tröger. 2003. "Wer finanziert den Fonds 'Deutsche Einheit'? Die Gemeindefinanzen im Zeichen der Bund-Länder-Finanzbeziehungen." *Jahrbücher für Nationalökonomie und Statistik* 223 (6): 743–51.

Feld, Lars P., and Marcel R. Savioz. 1997. "Direct Democracy Matters for Economic Performance: An Empirical Investigation." *Kyklos* 50 (4): 507–38.

Freitag, Markus, and Adrian Vatter. 2000. "Direkte Demokratie, Konkordanz und Wirtschaftsleistung: Ein Vergleich der Schweizer Kantone." *Schweizerische Zeitschrift für Volkswirtschaft und Statistik* 136 (4): 579–604.

Fuest, Clemens, and Bernd Huber. 2001. *Zur Reform der Gewerbesteuer: Gutachten erstellt im Auftrag des Ministeriums für Wirtschaft im Saarland*. Munich, Germany: Ministry of Finance of Bavaria.

Guihéry, Laurent, and Jan Werner. 2005. "Les finances publiques en Allemagne—Quelles réformes?" *Revue de l'OFCE* 94 (1): 111–37.

Jarass, Lorenz. 2003. "Gewerbesteuer vernünftig reformieren." *ifo Schnelldienst* 56 (9): 11–14.

Jarass, Lorenz, and Gustav M. Obermair. 2003. "Von der Gewerbesteuer zur Kommunalen Betriebssteuer." *Wirtschaftdienst* 83 (3): 157–63.

Loncarevic, Branka. 2002. "Kroatien-Recht-Steuerrecht." In *Kroatien*, ed. Bundesanstalt für Außenwirtschaft, 22–48. Cologne, Germany: Bundesanstalt für Außenwirtschaft.

Rehm, Hannes. 2001. *Management der Öffentlichen Schuld: Befund, Probleme, Perspektiven*. Stuttgart, Germany: Deutscher Sparkassenverlag.

Scherf, Wolfgang. 2002. "Ersatz der Gewerbesteuer durch eine anrechenbare Wertschöpfungsteuer." *Wirtschaftsdienst* 82 (10): 603–8.

Spahn, Paul Bernd, and Jan Werner. Forthcoming. "Germany at the Junction between Solidarity and Subsidiarity." In *Subsidiarity and Solidarity: The Role of Intergovernmental Relations in Maintaining an Effective State*, 57–85. Cheltenham, U.K.: Edward Elgar.

Statistisches Bundesamt. 2002. *Statistisches Jahrbuch 2002*. Wiesbaden, Germany: Statistisches Bundesamt.

SVR (Sachverständigenrat zur Begutachtung der gesamtwirtschaftlichen Entwicklung). 1995. *Jahresgutachten 1995/96—im Standortwettbewerb*. Wiesbaden, Germany: SVR.

Torgler, Benno, and Jan Werner. 2004. "Fiscal Autonomy and Tax Morale: Evidence from Germany." Paper presented at the annual congress of the Verein für Socialpolitik, Dresden, Germany, September 28–October 1.

———. 2005. "Tax Morale and Fiscal Autonomy: Evidence from Germany." *Public Finance and Management* 5 (4): 423–52.

Werner, Jan. 2003. "El Federalismo Fiscal Aleman: En Estado de Fluctuación." *Zergak— Gaceta Tributaria del Pais Vasco* 25 (3): 81–113.

———.Forthcoming. *Das deutsche Gemeindefinanzsystem: Reformvorschläge im Kontext der unterschiedlichen Einnahmenautonomie der lokalen Gebietskörperschaften in Europa.* Frankfurt am Main, Germany: Peter Lang.

Werner, Jan, and Anwar Shah. Forthcoming. "Fiscal Equalization and Subnational Governments: Lessons from the German Experience." In *Macrofederalism and Local Finances,* ed. Anwar Shah. Washington, DC: World Bank.

Werner, Jan, and Xue Wue. 2004. 德 国 联 邦 州 之 间 的 财 力 均 衡 ["Equalization among the German Federal States."] 财政研究 [*Public Finance Review*] 5 (7): 63–5.

5

Local Government Organization and Finance: *Japan*

NOBUKI MOCHIDA

Japan is a homogeneous unitary state with a two-tier system of local government. The local government system consists of 47 prefectures and about 3,200 municipalities under prefecture-level governments. Since the late 1940s, Japan's local autonomy has been guaranteed by the postwar constitution. The Japanese system can be characterized using aggregate public finance data. On the expenditure side, local government expenditure accounts for a large proportion: more than 70 percent of general government expenditure, which considerably exceeds the ratio found in average Organisation for Economic Co-operation and Development (OECD) countries. However, large local expenditures are not accompanied by local control on the revenue side.

Indeed, fiscal decentralization is one of the most important subjects that Japan faces at the beginning of the 21st century. The resolution to promote decentralization was passed by both houses in 1993, and the Decentralization Promotion Law was enacted under the Liberal Democratic Party, Socialist Party, and *Sakigake* coalition government in 1995. The Committee for the Promotion of Decentralization released recommendations five times, and at last the omnibus law of decentralization was enacted in 1999. In fiscal year 2002, the government launched an ambitious reform of the

149

three main components of local government financial resources—earmarked grants, local taxes, and the local allocation tax—the so-called "Trinity Reform." In recent years, the government has promoted municipal mergers to strengthen administrative capacity. The number of municipalities is estimated to be reduced from 3,229 in fiscal year 1999 to 1,822 in fiscal year 2006.

An Overview of Japan's Local Government

A brief history of Japan's central-local relationship is relevant here (Muramatsu and Iqbal 2001). This section also will describe briefly the concept of controlled decentralization.

Centralized System

In about 1890, a highly centralized system was created in Meiji, Japan, which was based on the German model. Gradually, political parties mobilized the residents, using local councils to enhance local democracy and to express local interests to the central government in the 1920s. However, wartime mobilization completely recentralized the country. After World War II, the American occupational reform introduced direct elections at the prefecture and municipal levels, making those levels completely self-governing. The Ministry of Interior was abolished, and many direct democratic methods, such as recall and initiative, were adopted. However, the U.S.-dispatched mission of Dr. Carl Shoup (General Headquarters Supreme Commander for Allied Power 1949)—a proposal to clearly separate the functions of governments in a layer-cake model and give priority to municipalities—was not implemented. Instead, after the occupation period, Japan recentralized many government functions (including police and education) from the local government, reintroduced many control mechanisms, and adopted what Akizuki (2001) called the "controlled decentralization" approach.

On the administrative side, these vertical controls consisted of agency delegation functions, personnel exchange, and a newly established Ministry of Home Affairs (MOHA). Under the agency delegation function, the central government delegated the carrying out of major programs to prefecture and municipal chief executives, who could, in principle, be removed by the central government authorities for noncompliance.

MOHA was set up in 1960 as a successor to the prewar Ministry of Interior, although MOHA's character was not quite the same as that of the prewar ministry. The newer ministry possessed several administrative and financial instruments to control the behavior of local governments. In 2001,

MOHA was merged with the Ministry of Posts and Telecommunications to become the Ministry of Internal Affairs and Communications (MIC).

Under the personnel exchange system, selected senior positions in prefecture administration are filled by central government dispatches (Akizuki 2001). Personnel exchanges are functional instruments that proved to be effective in implementing national plans and, perhaps, to be useful in building local capacity.

Fiscally, the central government controls local budgets, local tax rates and bases, local borrowing, and large fiscal transfers (Mochida 2001). In Japan, national legislation determines local tax bases and rates. However, localities do have some flexibility to introduce additional taxes, with MIC's approval, and to vary their tax rates within ranges specified by the Local Tax Law.

MOHA (now MIC) also controlled local borrowing. Under the current approval system for bond offering, local governments have to obtain permission to issue long-term bonds from MIC. In Japan, fiscal transfers from the central government to the localities account for about one-third of central government revenue. Of that total transfer, half is the local allocation tax, an equalization transfer program. The money is distributed on the basis of a set of complicated formulas that are designed to equalize the standards of public services while taking into account the difference in revenue capacity.

Controlled Decentralization

Japan's postwar experience is unique in that it has not seen decentralization and centralization as being antagonistic but, rather, as coexistent. The controlled decentralization concept put forward by Akizuki is useful here (Akizuki 2001). As the central government's distrust of local government has been alleviated, the relationship between the two sides has shifted from a controlling-controlled relationship to an equal partnership. Although Akizuki points to personnel exchange between the central and local levels as a good example of this shift, another example is the "agency-delegated functions" that were clearly detailed in article 150 of the Local Government Law.

The agency-delegated functions noted in article 150 refer to a system that effectively obliged leaders of local governments to act as agents of the central government, even if they were popularly elected. The agency-delegated function restricted deliberations by city councils. If a popularly elected leader were to defy a government order, he or she would be dismissed. However, in 1992, criticism of this system, which had evolved along with efforts to improve local administrative capacity, led to abolishing the central government's authority to remove leaders from office. After long debate, agency-delegated functions covering 561 items were abolished in 2001 in accordance with recommendations of the Committee for the Promotion of Decentralization. The central government's agency-delegated function system, which covered 40 percent of municipal duties and 80 percent of prefectural duties, was thus eliminated, and 60 percent of the relevant duties became autonomous duties of local governments.

A further example of the shift toward equal partnership between central and local government is the change in the role of the ministry-level unit that oversees administration (Akizuki 2001). The prewar Ministry of Interior (*Naimusho*), which had tremendous power covering all areas of domestic affairs, was broken up and replaced by the scaled-down Ministry of Home Affairs, or MOHA (*Jichisho*), in 1960. In 2001, MOHA was merged with the Ministry of Posts and Telecommunications to become the Ministry of Internal Affairs and Communications, or MIC engages in fiscal supervision of local bodies as a central government ministry while at the same time representing the interests of local governments within central government departments. In this way, MIC functions on two levels. Incentives for MIC and local governments to cooperate with one another are easy to understand.

First, in all problems related to local governments—such as reduction of the local allocation tax—MIC protects the interests of local governments and engages in tough fights with other central government ministries (especially the Ministry of Finance) that want to get their hands on local government finances. Local governments, of course, want to maintain this mechanism. And, from MIC's perspective, if it loses the support of local governments—which forms the main foundation of its authority—it cannot survive as a significant player in the central bureaucracy. The main source of the ministry's power in the central government is its position as a representative of local government. Regardless of its position as a fiscal supervisor of local governments and regardless of various forms of friction that occur between the ministry and local governments (an example being the "fiscal war" during Ryokichi Minobe's term as governor of Tokyo), the relationship between MIC and local governments has become more and more interdependent with the passage of time.

Expenditure Responsibilities

The concept of vertical fiscal imbalance and the process by which the central government delegates expenditure responsibilities are key to understanding Japan's governmental expenditures.

Vertical Fiscal Imbalance

The so-called vertical fiscal gap is a concept that is fundamental to understanding the intergovernmental relationship in all countries. Although local governments play a large part in expenditure responsibilities, the central government has a higher position in terms of allocation of tax bases (see table 5.1).

Concentration of tax bases in the central government peaked in Japan during World War II. After the war, efforts to reinforce and strengthen local tax were implemented, inspired by a report submitted by a mission team headed by Professor Carl Shoup of Columbia University (General Headquarters Supreme Commander for Allied Power 1949). Furthermore, local tax grew at an almost parallel rate to national tax through the period of rapid economic growth. However, no signs indicated that the relative relationship between local tax and expenditure would improve. Since 1970, the final expenses of local governments have exceeded those of the central government because local governments' investments in education, welfare, and public works have overlapped those of the central government. A mismatch has emerged: expenditure has been decentralized to local governments whereas tax bases are concentrated in the central government.

Looking at final expenses, the current shares of the central government and local governments are 43 percent and 57 percent, respectively, so local governments have a higher share (table 5.1). However, in terms of allocation of tax revenue, the positions are switched (60 percent and 40 percent), with

TABLE 5.1 Basic Statistics Pertaining to Local Tax, 1910–2000

Year	National tax: local tax	National tax: local tax (after adjustment through intergovernmental transfer)	Local tax as a percentage of local revenue
1910	—	—	47.0
1930	64.2: 35.8	57.7: 42.3	30.3
1940	84.5: 15.5	77.6: 22.4	20.6
1950	69.6: 30.4	56.0: 44.0	34.6
1960	68.0: 32.0	54.0: 46.0	35.6
1970	67.5: 32.5	50.8: 49.2	35.4
1980	64.1: 35.9	46.0: 54.0	34.0
1990	65.2: 34.8	47.0: 53.0	41.6
2000	59.7: 40.3	43.0: 57.0	35.4

Source: Based on MIC 2005c; Mochida 1993.
Note: — = not available.

the central government having the top share. Local tax makes up 35 percent of local revenue. This situation led the Committee for the Promotion of Decentralization, which is an advisory committee for the prime minister, to make reducing the gap between expenditure and tax revenue an objective within its basic strategy for decentralization.

In terms of tax revenues and public expenditures, a comparison of Japan's local governments with those Group of Seven countries having unitary arrangements reveals that Japan's dependence on transfers may be as large as in Italy, more than in France, but less than in the United Kingdom (OECD 2000). The ratio of independent revenue sources to total revenue is less than 15 percent in 65 percent of all municipalities in Japan (Mochida 2004).

Delegation of Expenditure Responsibilities

Local government accounts for a very large portion (more than 70 percent) of general government expenditure, which considerably exceeds the ratio found in average OECD countries. Table 5.2 summarizes local government expenditure by function. Judging from the net total of expenditure, two expenditures, public works and education, are high. Public works expenditures are 17.8 percent of net total expenditure. Most public works expenditures are property related: urban development, local roads, and housing. Social welfare and general affairs expenditures are lower but are still fairly high. In general affairs, diplomacy, defense, the judiciary, and criminal law are the responsibilities of the central government; fire and police account for 9.8 percent of net total local government expenditure. In recent years, although specific areas within the "other economic affairs" category—such as agriculture, forestry and fishery expenses and civil engineering work expenses—have declined, public debt payments have been increasing.

Unlike in countries with the dual federalism system, in Japan the function of the central government and the local government is not separated clearly; various levels of Japanese governments have overlapping and shared responsibilities. Consequently, policy and standards of main functions such as education, medical treatment, and public works are planned within the central government; oversight of implementation is carried out by prefectures; and services are implemented or provided by the local governments.

Japan's system, therefore, can be characterized as a combination of centralized tax assignment with delegated expenditure responsibility. Put another way, Japan's fiscal system resembles cooperative-administrative federalism (Shah 1994). In my view, compared with other federal arrangements,

TABLE 5.2 Local Government Expenditure by Function, 2003

Type of expenditure	Prefecture		Municipality		Net total	
	¥ billion	Percentage of total	¥ billion	Percentage of total	¥ billion	Percentage of total
General affairs[a]	3,214	6.6	6,436	12.9	9,039	9.8
Social security and welfare[b]	3,966	8.1	11,930	24.0	14,540	15.7
Health and hygiene	1,550	3.2	4,506	9.1	5,896	6.4
Education	11,644	23.8	5,634	11.3	17,201	18.6
Public works	8,289	16.9	8,438	16.9	16,439	17.8
Other economic affairs[c]	6,763	13.8	3,524	7.1	9,534	10.3
Debt service	6,688	13.7	6,601	13.3	13,191	14.2
Others	6,803	13.9	2,715	5.4	6,741	7.2
Total	48,917	100.0	49,784	100.0	92,581	100.0

Source: Based on MIC 2005c.
a. Includes assembly, police, and fire fighting.
b. Includes elderly welfare and child welfare.
c. Includes commerce and industry expenses as well as agriculture, forestry, and fishery expenses.

the influence of Japan's central government may be moderately strong as in Germany, stronger than in Canada and Switzerland, but less strong than in Australia.

Tax Assignment between Central and Local Governments

Table 5.3 summarizes local revenue components. Local taxes account for 31 percent of revenues for prefectures and 33.7 percent of revenues for municipalities. An interesting note is that the median is 23 percent for prefectures and 18 percent for municipalities, indicating that the distribution of local taxes is skewed toward the upper end. Local governments have borrowed heavily. The local allocation tax is an unconditional grant from a defined pool; fees and charges are negligible. The local transfer tax is a variant of the local tax: it is collected by the central government for administrative purposes.

A characteristic of Japan's local tax is that it shares tax bases with the national income tax and consumption tax (see figure 5.1). Of the total local tax revenue, the percentage of municipal tax, 57 percent, is slightly higher

TABLE 5.3 Total Annual Revenue of Local Government, Fiscal Year 2003

	Prefecture		Municipality		Total	
Source of revenue	¥ billion	Percentage of total	¥ billion	Percentage of total	¥ billion	Percentage of total
Local tax	15,426	31.0	17,239	33.7	32,665	34.4
Local transfer tax	174	0.3	519	1.0	694	0.7
Local allocation tax	9,978	20.0	8,090	15.8	18,069	19.0
Specific-purpose grant	7,842	15.7	5,218	10.2	13,060	13.8
Local borrowing	7,652	15.4	6,205	12.1	13,789	14.5
Others	8,739	17.6	13,924	27.2	16,610	17.6
Total	49,811	100.0	51,195	100.0	94,887	100.0

Source: Based on MIC 2005c.

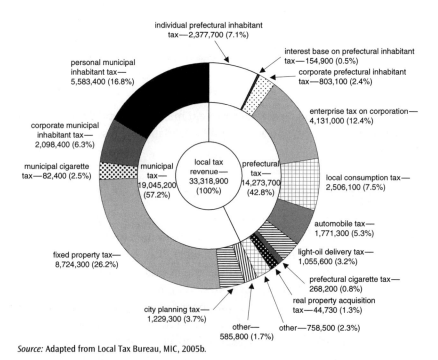

Source: Adapted from Local Tax Bureau, MIC, 2005b.

FIGURE 5.1 Composition of Local Tax, Planned Amounts for Fiscal Year 2005 Local Finances

than the percentage of prefectural tax, 43 percent. The enterprise tax and prefectural inhabitant tax make up large parts of the prefectural tax. The next largest is the local consumption tax. The enterprise tax is a tax on business that is levied on individuals or corporations engaged in business, using income or added value as the tax base. Prefectural inhabitant tax is similar to municipal inhabitant tax in that it is levied on individuals and corporations in the district; both are called inhabitant tax. The tax base of the local consumption tax is the national consumption tax (a value added tax).

The fixed property tax makes up the majority of municipal tax. This tax and the municipal inhabitant tax together account for nearly 90 percent of the total municipal tax. The former is a property tax levied on the owners of fixed property (land, buildings, and depreciable property), with appropriate land price used as the tax base.

Main Local Taxes

The main local taxes comprise property tax, inhabitant tax, general sales tax, and tax on business. Each is described in more detail in the following sections.

Property tax

In Japan, 38.16 million people, or roughly 30 percent of the population, pay fixed property tax to a municipality. The tax is levied on the land, buildings, or depreciable property they own. The land and buildings—comprising 177.94 million lots of land and 60.66 million buildings—are regularly reassessed every three years. With a standard tax rate of 1.4 percent and tax revenue of ¥8.679 trillion (fiscal year 2003), property tax stands as the number one municipal tax.

Of note is the tireless addition of improvements to the fixed property tax to adapt it to socioeconomic conditions in Japan. Specifically, the fixed property tax faced a major challenge: rising land prices and the increasing tax burden that accompanied them.

During the period of rapid economic growth, it was necessary to correct differences among municipalities in assessed ratio, because the assessed value of property was low compared with the market price. Consequently, in 1964, the method for assessing fixed property was standardized throughout the country. Integrated assessment was conducted using (a) acquisition cost coupled with rebuilding value for buildings, (b) sample value for purchase and sale for land, and (c) percentage depreciation for depreciable property.

In 1973, when an economic boom was sparked by the Plan for Remodeling the Japanese Archipelago, a daring measure was taken whereby the assessed value and the amount of the tax base, which had been separate since 1964, would be brought into line with each other in three years. A special measure was introduced that halved the assessed value of small-scale residential sites to alleviate burden.

Although land prices rose dramatically during the "bubble economy" of the late 1980s, the assessed value of local governments was left unchanged. A lively debate emerged about whether the low fixed property tax was inviting land speculation. Because of that issue, the assessed value of the fixed property tax was raised nationwide to 70 percent of posted price (known as the *70 percent assessment*) in the reform of 1994. The government introduced complicated adjustment measures to alleviate the amount of burden that emerged as a result of the 70 percent assessment.

Because this reform invited a rapid increase in land valuation, two adjustments were initiated: (a) a special tax base (an expansion of the assessment exception for small-scale residential sites from one-fourth to one-sixth) and (b) a tax burden adjustment measure (control of tax increase to 15 percent over a three-year period, even if assessed value were to increase by 300 percent). These adjustments lessened the tax burden.

Inhabitant tax

Inhabitant tax is a fundamental local tax on personal income for both municipalities and prefectures. In 2005, tax revenue from individual prefectural inhabitant tax was ¥2.378 trillion, and tax revenue from personal municipal inhabitant tax was ¥5.583 trillion. Taken together, these inhabitant taxes make up approximately 24 percent of local tax revenue.

The current personal inhabitant tax comprises three elements: (a) an income base (tax rates of 5, 10, and 13 percent) that is levied on the previous fiscal year's income (using the national income tax calculation); (b) a per capita base in which each household bears a uniform rate (¥1,000 per year for the prefectural tax and ¥3,000 per year for the municipal tax); and (c) tax on interest, dividends, and income from capital gains (uniform tax rate of 5 percent). Note that, in the interest of spreading local inhabitants' burden of expenses for public services as widely as possible, the minimum amount of taxable income is set lower than that of the national income tax. In the case of a salaried worker in a household comprising a married couple with two children, the minimum amount of taxable income is ¥2.7 million compared with a ¥3.25 million minimum amount in national tax.

Each month, a taxpayer pays income tax and personal inhabitant tax to his or her employer through tax withholding at the source. The employer then delivers the personal inhabitant tax to the municipality in which the employee resides.

The Japanese government is currently attempting to reform the personal inhabitant tax. From the standpoint of "benefit principle and low regional disparity," a report by the Government Tax Commission (MIC 2005b) proposes an inhabitant tax levied at a proportional tax rate of 10 percent, with no change to the burden of the overall income tax that combines personal inhabitant tax and the national income tax. Currently, annual revenue from the personal inhabitant tax is ¥7.9 trillion, and annual revenue from the national income tax is ¥14.3 trillion. If the inhabitant tax—a gradually progressive structure made up of three grades (5, 10, and 13 percent)—is abolished and a proportional tax with a uniform rate of 10 percent is created, then annual revenue from the local income tax will be ¥10.9 trillion, and annual revenue from the national income tax will be ¥11.3 trillion. Thus, if a proportional tax rate of 10 percent is realized, then annual income tax revenue of ¥3 trillion will be transferred from national tax to local tax.

General sales tax

It is interesting to note that in terms of assignment of the value added tax, Japan's experience diverges slightly from traditional fiscal federalism theory. Japan introduced a multistage value added tax in April 1989. At the same time, Japan established a consumption transfer tax (*shohijoyozei*) that transfers a set percentage (20 percent) of the national consumption tax to prefectures on the basis of objective standards such as population and number of employees. Later, a new coalition government made up of three parties (the Liberal Democratic Party, the Social Democratic Party of Japan, and the New Party Sakigake) abolished the consumption transfer tax in the tax reform of 1994 and established a new local consumption tax at the prefecture level in its place, which has been implemented since April 1997.

The local consumption tax is complicated, combining both the origin principle and the destination principle. An outline of the local consumption tax is as follows: (a) all prefectures levy the tax; (b) the taxpayers are businesspeople; (c) the tax base is the national consumption tax; (d) the tax rate is 25 percent (which amounts to 1 percent of consumption, since the national consumption tax is 4 percent of consumption); (e) although under normal circumstances self-assessment and payment will be made to the prefectures, in the interim, self-assessment and payment will be made to the central government (tax offices); (f) each prefecture will adjust the amount of local consumption tax paid to it with the other prefectures to ensure that it is proportionally distributed to final consumption statistics; and finally, (g) each prefecture will transfer one-half of the monetary amount to municipalities within it according to population and number of employees.

In this way, under Japan's local consumption tax, local governments in the places of origin have authority to tax. However, with the system that is in place, local consumption tax is collected by the central government, and tax revenue is then later returned to local governments in the place of final consumption through an adjustment system.

In the short time since the birth of the local consumption tax, tax revenue has already reached ¥2.506 trillion per year (fiscal year 2005). As a result, the tax now ranks number two behind the enterprise tax on corporations in terms of revenue. Advantages of the tax are that it has little regional disparity and relatively low interregional mobility. The variation coefficients of prefectural tax and the postadjustment local consumption tax are 0.28 and 0.09, respectively. Thus, the latter has a much lower level of disparity. However, this adjustment criterion has several problems (see Mochida 2004).

Tax on business

Until fiscal year 2004, the prefectural enterprise tax (*jigyozei*) was levied on corporations using the same tax base (net income) that the national corporate income tax used. The enterprise tax is a fundamental tax that makes up approximately 30 percent of prefectural tax income. The standard tax rate was a gradual progressive tax rate (5 to 9.6 percent) matched to business income.

The enterprise tax borne by large-scale corporations (capital of ¥100 million or more; approximately 33,000 corporations of all 2.47 million corporations) was reformed into a pro forma tax in 2004 to stabilize tax revenue and to clarify the tax as a benefit tax (corporations that receive local public services pay the tax regardless of whether they receive a profit).

More specifically, MOHA, the predecessor of MIC, had issued a reform proposal that put forward the idea that "value added (profit + gross pay + paid interest + rent) has the greatest advantages as tax bases." This idea was presented in the midterm report of the Government Tax Commission (issued in July 2000) as policy (see MIC 2005b). Then, a pro forma tax having a value added share of one-fourth was established in the fiscal year 2003 tax reform that targeted corporations with capital exceeding ¥100 million. Application of this tax began in fiscal year 2004.

The enterprise tax borne by incorporated enterprises having capital exceeding ¥100 million comprises three elements: (a) an income component that is imposed at a lower rate (3.8 percent) compared with that of the former enterprise tax (7.2 percent); (b) a 0.48 percent tax on corporations' value added (payment of remuneration, net paid interest, net paid rent, total of profit); and (c) an assets component of 0.2 percent against the capital of a corporation. One-fourth of the tax base is the pro forma tax, with the remaining three-fourths being the same as for the former enterprise tax. As was the case with the former enterprise tax, the prefectures have the ability to raise the tax rate up to a maximum of 20 percent in excess of the standard tax rate. For manufacturing industries that are engaged in business activities covering a multiple number of prefectures, tax revenue is proportionally appropriated to each region by the number of employees (for corporations having capital exceeding ¥100 million, the number of factory employees is counted at a rate that is one and one-half times the actual number).

Although the reformed enterprise tax is expected to bring in stable tax revenue, the business world has expressed a number of concerns. The tax burden of pro forma tax is heavier on new incorporated enterprises that generally have little profit. Moreover, because the tax base has been switched from net income to external standards in the form of capital and added value, the risk of economic fluctuation will shift from local governments to incorporated enterprises.

Overlapping Tax Bases

Here we examine Japan's experience—both the successes and the failures—with respect to local tax systems. One characteristic in Japan's tax system is frequent overlapping of the tax bases of national tax and local tax. About 50 years ago, the Shoup report (General Headquarters Supreme Commander for Allied Power 1949) envisioned an ideal tax system that clearly separated tax revenue into a national tax, a prefectural tax, and a municipal tax. However, Japan's postwar economy and society did not implement that recommended tax system as it was proposed; instead, it established a tax system that modified the approach.

In Japan, only local governments collect automobile-related taxes and fixed property taxes (fixed property tax and city planning tax), and only the central government collects inheritance and gift taxes. However, personal income taxation is conducted by both the central government (income tax) and local governments (inhabitant tax and income component); the tax bases for these taxes are shared by the national tax and local tax. Similarly, both the central government (tax on business) and local governments (inhabitant tax, corporate income tax component for inhabitant tax, and enterprise tax) engage in taxation on corporate income, and overlapping tax bases are also apparent here. Of interest is that the central government's consumption tax and local governments' local consumption tax also share tax bases in broad-based consumption tax, with the ratio of national tax to local tax standing at 8:2. Although overlapping tax bases between central and local government are rare in unitary countries, Japan is an exception (Policy Research Institute, Ministry of Finance 2002).

A problem with the overlapping tax base system is that the taxpayer has difficulty determining how much he or she is paying to the central government and how much to the local government. In addition to the national tax on business, incorporated enterprises pay the enterprise tax, inhabitant tax on corporations, and fixed property tax. Most likely, few taxpayers know which local governments are receiving the local consumption tax they pay. A further problem is that, because tax sources overlap, lower national tax revenue also has an effect on local tax. As a part of the permanent tax reduction enacted by the Obuchi cabinet in 1999, fixed-rate tax reductions were implemented for the income tax (20 percent of the tax amount) and personal inhabitant tax (15 percent of the tax amount), and the personal inhabitant tax was lowered by ¥1.1 trillion on an average fiscal year basis.

Nevertheless, the system of overlapping tax bases also brings the following advantages. In the case of the national and local consumption taxes, administrative cost falls because the national tax office can collect both taxes. Furthermore, by sharing the same elastic tax base (income), the local governments can make up for inelasticity in the tax revenue of fixed property-related taxes and can cover expanding costs for personal services such as education and welfare. Thus, local tax with overlapping tax bases will probably continue in Japan.

Dispersion of Bases to Income, Consumption, and Property

Another characteristic of Japan's local tax system is that the tax bases are dispersed (fiscal year 2005) roughly evenly to personal income taxation (24.5 percent), corporate income taxation (22.2 percent), consumption taxation (21.1 percent), and property taxation (32.3 percent). This kind of dispersed system contrasts with concentrated tax systems in which specific tax items have greater weight. Both the business tax of France and the council tax of the United Kingdom are fixed property-type local taxes. And Northern European countries such as Denmark and Sweden have local income taxes.

Thus, the systems of these countries are built around a single local tax (Mochida and Lotz 1999).

An advantage of a dispersed tax system is that it can alleviate the regional disparity and risk of tax revenue variation for specific tax items (Policy Research Institute, Ministry of Finance 2002). Although corporate income tax (inhabitant tax on corporations and enterprise tax) tends to be unevenly distributed in large urban areas, the degree to which local taxes are unevenly distributed as a whole is alleviated by tax items such as the personal inhabitant tax and local consumption tax, which are more equitably distributed (see table 5.4). In the same way, the corporate income tax tends to vary greatly in response to business cycles; however, the variability of local tax as a whole is alleviated by stable tax revenue from the local consumption tax and fixed property tax (Mochida 2001; OECD 2005).

Furthermore, distribution of tax sources has the benefits of easing the regressive nature of specific tax items and making the tax burden as a whole proportional (Boadway, Hobson, and Mochida 2001). In Japan, the gradual regressiveness of the indirect consumption tax and fixed property tax for residences is canceled out by the progressiveness of the inhabitant tax. In other words, residence-based taxes generally have an income-proportional burden structure.

However, Japan's local tax system—with its dispersed tax bases and many tax items—is far from visible to taxpayers. In Denmark and the United Kingdom, where tax bases are concentrated, the payments balance of local budgets is brought into equilibrium by adjusting the tax rate

TABLE 5.4 Regional Uneven Distribution and Variability of Local Tax

Local tax	Degree of regional uneven distribution (2002)	Tax revenue variability (1985–2002)
Personal inhabitant tax	0.27	0.09
Inhabitant tax on corporations	0.40	0.21
Enterprise tax	0.49	0.26
Local consumption tax	0.16	0.07
Fixed property tax	0.19	0.13
Total	0.22	0.05

Source: Adapted from OECD 2005, table 5.4.
Note: Degree of regional uneven distribution is measured using the variation coefficient of per capita local tax revenue. Variability of tax revenue is measured using the variation coefficient of the ratio of local tax to gross domestic product from 1985 to 2000.

(Mochida and Lotz 1999). Flexibility to set local tax rates plays an important role as a bridge between the quality of local public services and residents' assessment of these services. Because Japan's tax bases are dispersed, problems emerge when deciding which tax item's rate will be used to balance revenue and expenditure. Furthermore, corporations, being without voting rights, are vulnerable to bearing tax burden increases.

Uniformity of Tax Rates

A third characteristic of Japan's tax system is that although flexibility to set tax rates in Japan is by no means inferior to that in other countries, not all local governments fully apply their authority. According to an OECD survey (OECD 1999), 94 percent of municipal taxes and 83 percent of prefectural taxes have overlapping national-local tax bases and are classified as taxes for which the local government body has the authority to set tax rates. The discretionary self-taxing power of local governments in Japan is high compared with that in Austria, Belgium, Germany, Italy, and Spain (OECD 2005). In fact, the degree of this self-taxing power is nearly on par with the Northern European countries. For some tax items—such as the local consumption tax and cigarette tax—a legally fixed tax rate is established, and local governments do not have the authority to set their own rates. However, the majority of local taxes are taxes for which standard tax rates and maximum tax rates are established by law and for which local governments have the authority to set tax rates within a limited range. Nonetheless, except with respect to the inhabitant and enterprise taxes on corporations, the actual practice of moving tax rates above or below the standard tax rates has not taken root in individual local governments, as was anticipated by the Local Tax Law. The personal inhabitant tax, local consumption tax, and fixed property tax are levied in a manner that is essentially very close to tax sharing. The tax rates of these local taxes are nearly uniform throughout the country (Mochida 2004).

The self-taxing power of local governments was strengthened through a supralegal tax measure (*hoteigai-mokutekizei*) that was introduced in local tax reform in fiscal year 2000. As part of this reform, the central government must allow the establishment of a new local tax if three conditions are satisfied: (a) the tax rate is not excessively high, (b) it does not obstruct the distribution of goods, and (c) it is not contrary to national economic policy. Using this reform, many prefectures and municipalities have introduced supralegal taxes that include industrial waste taxes, hotel accommodation taxes, and recreational fishing taxes. However, some problems with these taxes have been identified.

Because the tax burden shifts to nonresidents, the tax policy of local governments lacks discipline, and tax revenue is low considering the high costs of tax collection. Also, because few opportunities arise to introduce supralegal taxes into rural areas, regional disparities are emerging.

Nonetheless, uniformity in tax rates has the benefit of creating fair burden among taxpayers across the country to finance public expenditure. To the extent that the differences in tax rates correspond to differences in the local services level, the differentials conform to the principle of benefit taxation. However, if the gaps that emerge between people simply because they live in different areas are not rectified, then fiscal equity cannot be guaranteed. Japan has succeeded in bringing competitive conditions into line by correcting gaps in tax rates that have emerged from nondiscretionary causes (for example, special fiscal demand, uneven distribution of tax sources, and disasters and climatic conditions).

Specific-Purpose Grants

Although grants are used for many purposes, they are largely classified into two groups—unconditional grants and conditional grants—depending on whether the local government has discretion in how they are used. In Japan, the local allocation tax serves as an unconditional grant. The local allocation tax is intended to rectify imbalances in regional revenue sources and to ensure the delivery of standard public services. In contrast, national treasury grants serve as conditional grants. They can be described as specific revenue resources that are provided by the central government for specific public expenditures.

National Government Disbursement

An important issue concerns political influence in the distribution of specific-purpose grants. As is well known, in developing countries and economies in transition, the allocation of grants is occasionally determined through personal networks. In more developed countries, politics influence distribution in other ways. Two contrasting examples are local governments in France, which are issued grants in accordance with objective allocation standards set by bureaucratic institutions, and local governments in Italy, which take grants from the government through the political might of politicians. According to Steven Reed, the operation of Japan's grant system is closer to the French example than the Italian example (Reed 2001). Although abundant anecdotes tell of powerful politicians in Japan who

apply pressure on grant allocation to ensure benefit for their own constituency, the truth is that the existence of pork-barrel politics has not been
organizationally or systematically proven.

In Japan, funds that are issued from the national treasury to local
governments for specific uses are called *national government disbursements*.
Articles 10 to 10–4 of the Local Finance Law, which is the basic law pertaining
to local finances, list the following four types of national government disbursements through which the government is obligated to bear a specified
share of public services incurred by local governments:

- Expenditures for duties that local governments must implement in areas
  in which the central government and the local government have a relationship of mutual interest pursuant to laws requiring that the central
  government positively bear such expenditures. Such expenditures may
  include compulsory education expenditures, public financial assistance
  expenditures, health care facilities expenditures, expenditures for health
  care for elderly people, children's allowances, and agricultural committee
  expenditures.
- Public works expenditures for road projects, forest road projects, and
  urban planning projects that are stipulated by law and that must be
  implemented according to comprehensive plans to conform to national
  standards.
- Expenditures for disaster relief projects and so forth that are stipulated in
  laws and for which it is difficult to procure financial resources with local
  taxes and the local allocation tax.
- National treasury payments for agency-like tasks to cover expenditures
  when local governments are made to perform duties that are the responsibility of the central government on behalf of the central government.
  Such duties could include elections for Diet members and registration of
  aliens.

As is shown in figure 5.2, national government disbursements to local
governments reached a total of ¥20.4 trillion in 2004. In both prefectures
and municipalities, disbursements are largest for public works projects. Such
disbursements include not only expenditures related to civil engineering
(roads, ports and harbors, and so forth) but also grants for construction
expenditures pertaining to elementary and junior high school buildings and
to welfare facilities for elderly people. The central government simply guides
the implementation of measures for these projects through laws and budgets; the central government has little involvement with them, and local

Total of ¥20.4 trillion								
Social security 11.7						Education and science promotion 2.9	Public works 4.8	Other 1.0
Medical care for the elderly 3.6	National health insurance 2.5	Public financial assistance 1.7	Nursing care insurance 1.7	Child care 0.6	Other 1.6	Share of compulsory education expenditures 2.5		

Source: Data from MIC 2005b.

FIGURE 5.2 Breakdown of National Government Disbursements, Fiscal Year 2004

governments maintain discretion. Although these grants tend to be targets for reductions because public works projects are covered by government bonds, it is difficult to tie them to transfers of tax revenue sources to local governments.

The next largest disbursements are grants for medical care for the elderly. These grants are followed by those for compulsory education expenditures, national health insurance, public financial assistance, and nursing care insurance. The central government legally requires the local governments to execute such duties and mandates specific standards. Local governments are allowed almost no discretion. Even if grants are cut and tax resources are transferred to local governments, the local governments still have no discretion with respect to duties, and burden is simply transferred locally.

Extensive Use of Regulation

In recent years, more and more people have been paying close attention to reform of national treasury grants and obligatory shares. This trend was launched when the Committee for the Promotion of Decentralization, which was established in 1995 as an advisory committee for the prime minister, recommended a reduction in national government disbursements in its final report (see MIC 2005b). Using that report, the Japanese government formulated a policy (approved by the cabinet) calling for abolition of some ¥4 trillion in grants by fiscal year 2006.

Why is reform of national treasury grants and obligatory shares on the current political agenda in Japan? One reason is that control of local governments through grants hinders the autonomy and flexibility of those local governments. The central government not only specifies the use of grants and obligatory shares (in education, health care, and so forth) but also legally obligates local governments to implement such duties and sets specific standards. For example, under national standards for road improvement in mountainous regions, a project does not receive a grant unless the road has two lanes. Also, the number of teachers is calculated using 40 as the number of schoolchildren or students in a single class. In addition, the brands of materials used in public works projects are specified.

The central government's involvement in kindergartens and nursery schools illustrates the difficulty. Although kindergartens and nursery schools have common functions, kindergartens are under the jurisdiction of the Ministry of Education, Culture, Sports, Science, and Technology, whereas nursery schools are under the Ministry of Health, Labor, and Welfare. As a result, while a comparatively large number of kindergartens have capacity to spare, children sometimes must wait to get into nursery schools. The desire of local governments to use these facilities more effectively by bringing them together is not being realized. The process of petition, hearings, and preparation of complicated documents before local governments can actually receive national treasury grants takes both time and money. In the case of small grants, the cost of applying for the grant and of preparing reports on circumstances and policies as well as other documents can exceed the grant itself.

Economic Stabilization and Redistribution of Income

Although intergovernmental transfer is also being used in Japan as a means for economic stabilization and interregional distribution of income, the results of this strategy reveal a problem (OECD 2005). Grants and obligatory shares related to public works have the largest share at ¥4.8 trillion. In addition, for independent local public works, the costs of repaying principal and interests have been introduced into the local allocation tax. This kind of generous support has a number of objectives. For example, public works projects were used as an economic stimulus measure during the difficult economic times of the early 1990s. Also, rectification of income disparities among regions has been an important element when determining allocation of public investment. In truth, although rates of return of public investments in high-income prefectures are high, per capita public investment in low-income prefectures is double that of high-income prefectures. Nonetheless, high levels of public investment did not lead to self-sustaining regional economic development and, instead, resulted in increased dependence by local economies on public works projects. Stimulus measures using public investment through intergovernmental transfer exceeded rectification of spillover effect by a large margin.

This kind of generous support for public investment reduces the incentive to conserve costs in public works projects. Lack of competition in public procurement is a serious problem. And the possibility of wide-ranging bid rigging at the local government level cannot be denied. In addition, many local governments enact policies that give priority to local enterprises when engaging in public procurement. It was estimated that improvements in public procurement in fiscal year 2000 resulted in a 15 percent cost savings (OECD 2000). In fiscal year 2000, the Act for Promoting Proper Tendering and Contracting for Public Works was enacted for the purpose of improving transparency and fairness in bidding. In later years, however, bid rigging in connection with waterworks projects was discovered.

Fiscal Equalization System

Japan's experience in intergovernmental fiscal transfer is significant for another reason. During Japan's period of rapid economic growth (in the 1950s and 1960s), disparities between large urban areas and rural villages widened, and this disparity led to major migration from the latter to the former. This situation closely resembles the serious problem of regional disparities emerging in line with economic development that is seen in developing countries and economies in transition today.

A point that should be remembered here is that even when economic growth in Japan was accelerating at full speed, the fruits of this growth were distributed fairly to all corners of the country through the local allocation tax system. In Japan, public investments (roads, ports and harbors, housing, mines, forestation, and flood control) have more weight in the government sector than in other developed countries. And in terms of regional distribution, this public capital has been supplied relatively generously to local governments in rural areas that were left behind during the country's rapid growth. The financial resources that supported this funding came from intergovernmental fiscal transfer in the form of the local allocation tax and so forth. In other words, the local allocation tax helped create employment through public works projects in regions that were left behind by economic growth. This support solidified the constituencies of Japan's ruling party—the Liberal Democratic Party—in rural areas, which in turn contributed to economic growth that occurred in line with political stability.

Formula Driven Transfer: Local Allocation Tax

The local allocation tax plays a key role as the fiscal equalization transfer system in Japan. Revenue from the local allocation tax accounts for 21 percent of local revenues, on average. Box 5.1 demonstrates the computation of the local allocation tax in detail (Mochida 1998). This tax is derived from a revenue pool that is based on fixed portions of five national taxes and is allocated according to a formula that is based on differences in basic needs and basic fiscal capacities. The total size of equalization is a fixed portion of the national taxes on individual income, corporate income, and value added, as well as the alcohol and tobacco taxes. The local allocation tax is paid annually to local governments whose basic financial needs exceed basic financial revenues. Those rich localities whose revenue exceeds need are neither eligible for the grants nor obligated to contribute money for fiscal adjustment. Using this formula, the national government can transfer funds that will fill the gap between each region's fiscal need and fiscal capacity to ensure that an authority with a reasonable tax effort will be able to provide a reasonable level of public services.

Effect of Fiscal Equalization

It is worth noting the extent to which the Japanese equalization system reduces territorial fiscal inequalities. Comparing per capita local tax revenue and per capita revenue from general fiscal sources (namely, local taxes and local allocation tax) at the prefecture level in 2003, one notes that the disparity in the financial resources among rich and poor districts is considerably reduced by the local allocation tax. In table 5.5, for example, the per capita local tax of Aichi prefecture, which ranks behind Tokyo in terms of fiscal capacity, is about ¥143,500, whereas that of the prefecture with the lowest fiscal capacity, Okinawa, is about ¥67,800 (fiscal year 2003). However, the figure for general revenue resources after distribution of the allocation tax in Okinawa is about ¥210,500, compared with about ¥158,100 in Aichi. In other words, the weaker a local government's fiscal capacity, the more local allocation tax it can receive. In this way, rank in the size of general revenue resources is reversed.

Fiscal equalization systems have played a role in rectifying disparities in fiscal capacity that arise in line with economic growth. The equalization effect can be measured using a value that results after dividing the difference between the Gini coefficient of the per capita local tax and the Gini coefficient of general revenue resources by the Gini coefficient of the per capita local tax. During the 1960s, when regional gaps caused by economic growth

BOX 5.1 Components Formula of Local Allocation Tax

The local allocation tax has continued to the present with some minor alterations. Since 1954, the framework of the local allocation tax has been founded on the former distribution tax, enforced between 1940 and 1949, while retaining the formula used in the equalization grant for the distribution of funds to localities. In the local allocation tax system, the total amount to be distributed to local authorities is a fraction of yields from major national taxes (see equation 5.1):

$$TT = 0.32 \times (NT_y + NT_a) + 0.358 \times NT_c + 0.295 \times NT_v + 0.25 \times NT_t \quad (5.1)$$

where TT denotes total financial pool of transfer, NT_y is the total yield of personal income tax, NT_c is that of corporate income tax, NT_a is that of alcohol tax, NT_v is 80 percent of value added tax revenue, and NT_t is total yield of the tobacco tax. These prescribed percentages of five major national taxes are apportioned among local bodies in proportion to the difference between fiscal need and revenue, expressed by equation 5.2:

$$LAT_i = N_i - C_i \quad (5.2)$$

where LAT_i denotes local allocation tax to ith region, N_i is basic financial need of ith region, and C_i is the basic financial capacity of ith region. It is annually paid to local governments whose basic financial needs exceed their basic financial revenues. Rich localities with revenue that exceeds need are neither eligible for the grants nor required to contribute money for fiscal adjustment, as is the case in some countries.

Before the calculation of basic financial needs, public services for each prefecture and municipality are divided into particular service items (*gyôsei-kômoku*). In the prefectures, there are 24 service items, such as police, roads and bridges, and primary school; for each municipality, there are 24 service items, such as city planning, parks, and garbage collection. Basic financial needs of ith local authority are calculated as shown in equation 5.3:

$$N_i = \Sigma_k (I_{ik} \times U_{ik} \times M_{ik}) \quad (5.3)$$

where I_{ik} is a measurement unit for service K of ith region, U_{ik} is unit cost for service K of ith region, and M_{ik} is a modification coefficient for service K of ith region. For each local body, according to the formula mentioned above, basic financial needs for each service item are calculated as the number of measurement units by multiplying the unit cost, adjusted by modification coefficients. The total basic need in each locality is the sum of the amounts needed for all service items combined.

The first step is to select measurement units. A measurement unit reflects the number or size of the beneficiaries of a particular expenditure. For

(Box continues on the following page.)

example, a measurement unit for education is number of teachers, that of police is number of police officers, and that of roads is length of roads.

The second step is to determine a unit cost. Unit cost is a kind of net standard cost per measurement unit for each service item. Assuming a certain local body with standard conditions and scale, the unit cost for each service item is calculated on the basis of the following equation 5.4 (in a prefecture, only one fictitious local body with a population of 1.7 million and a land area of 6,500 square kilometers is assumed as a "standard local body"; in a municipality, population is 100,000 and land area is 160 square kilometers):

$$U = (C_g - R_s) \div S \tag{5.4}$$

where U is unit cost, C_g is gross standard cost, R_s is special revenue, and S is a figure of measurement unit.

The third step is to determine modification coefficients. The unit cost, however, is uniform throughout the country, and no consideration is given to either the unique services or the special circumstances of localities. So an exceedingly complex adjustment is made of the unit cost applicable to such services and localities by means of detailed modifiers determined in accordance with their differences. Modification coefficients are currently classified according to eight categories.

The basic financial revenue of each locality is expressed as a combined total of two types of revenue: (a) 80 percent in the case of prefectures and 75 percent in municipalities of the sum of the yields of all regular local taxes, assuming that each is levied at the uniform rate or standard rate prescribed in the local tax law, and (b) the sum of revenues from local transfer taxes. This revenue is expressed in equation 5.5:

$$C_i = G \times (B_{ij} \times t_j) + LTT_i \tag{5.5}$$

where G is 0.75 (for a municipality) and 0.80 (for a prefecture), B_{ij} is ith region's jth tax base, t_j is the standard tax rate on the jth tax base, and LTT_i is revenue from the local transfer tax of particular region i. There are two reasons for adopting such prescribed percentages. First, it is impossible to measure completely the basic financial needs of all local governments with a uniform formula. Second, it is necessary to retain incentives for local governments to collect their own taxes. At the same time, all revenues allotted from the local transfer tax are included, because the tax is collected by the national government and has no relation to tax collection efforts at the local level.

The funds available for transfer calculated in advance, however, do not necessarily cover the sum of the entitlement—that is, the aggregate amount of the deficiencies of local governments with basic financial needs that exceed their basic revenues. The method currently used is to increase the size of the fund by borrowing from the Fiscal Investment and Loan Program (see Mochida 2001).

Source: Based on Mochida 2001, 109–11.

TABLE 5.5 Fiscal Adjustment Effect of the Local Allocation Tax, 2003

Prefecture	Local tax (¥)	Local allocation tax (¥)	General revenue resources (¥)
Tokyo	325,772	0	325,772
Aichi	143,512	14,575	158,087
Shizuoka	119,819	50,826	170,645
Fukui	119,398	168,706	288,104
Osaka	114,529	35,463	149,993
Tochigi	112,560	85,673	198,233
Mie	112,451	96,574	209,024
Ishikawa	107,217	128,170	235,387
Ibaragi	107,213	73,436	180,649
Yamanashi	105,607	160,711	266,318
Shiga	104,482	104,728	209,210
Miyagi	104,412	84,269	188,681
Toyama	104,160	139,991	244,151
Gunma	103,489	80,459	183,948
Kanagawa	102,406	18,893	121,299
Nagano	101,941	116,727	218,668
Tokushima	101,520	178,082	279,603
Fukushima	99,634	120,295	219,929
Gifu	99,598	98,265	197,864
Kagawa	99,397	121,268	220,665
Niigata	98,870	128,467	227,338
Hiroshima	97,927	81,409	179,336
Kyoto	97,138	76,330	173,467
Hokkaido	96,740	129,278	226,018
Okayama	95,137	106,169	201,307
Fukuoka	93,600	58,474	152,075
Yamaguchi	93,189	133,680	226,869
Saga	92,631	168,358	260,989
Chiba	92,630	38,174	130,804
Saitama	90,718	37,582	128,300
Hyogo	90,027	71,601	161,629
Aomori	88,851	163,347	252,198
Iwate	87,880	179,920	267,799
Tottori	87,785	218,352	306,137
Shimane	87,608	253,507	341,115
Yamagata	85,903	162,057	247,960
Ehime	84,076	130,432	214,508
Oita	83,778	163,324	247,102
Akita	83,079	192,508	275,587

(*continued*)

TABLE 5.5 Fiscal Adjustment Effect of the Local Allocation Tax, 2003
(continued)

Prefecture	Local tax (¥)	Local allocation tax (¥)	General revenue resources (¥)
Wakayama	81,142	166,008	247,151
Kumamoto	81,111	130,813	211,924
Kochi	78,640	221,602	300,242
Nara	78,536	112,506	191,042
Kagoshima	70,265	169,058	247,323
Miyazaki	77,887	171,568	249,455
Nagasaki	70,931	161,247	232,178
Okinawa	67,760	142,741	210,501

Source: MIC 2005a.

widened, the local allocation tax reduced fiscal capacity gaps by as much as 70 percent (Mochida 2004). However, because gaps requiring rectification closed during the "lost decade" that began in the 1990s, the effect of the allocation tax's fiscal equalization function declined. This decline does not suggest that the local allocation tax is no longer needed. Although Japan's central government obligates local governments to perform many duties, it does not provide these local governments with sufficient revenue sources. The function that the local allocation tax has in implementing national minimums in local governments is essential, even when the economy is stagnant and regional gaps are closing.

Eliminating Different Net Fiscal Benefits

Probably, the strongest case for equalization transfer has been based on the premise of "horizontal equity among the citizens" (Buchanan 1950). Equity requires that equalization should be full, which appears to be the logic in Japan's local allocation tax. In the absence of a corrective device, decentralization will entail that people with a given income receive different net fiscal benefits in two different regions. This differential would violate horizontal fiscal equity and would induce inefficient allocation of the labor force. The benchmark case commonly used is one in which residence-based taxes are roughly proportional to income, and the benefits of public spending are roughly equal per capita (Boadway and Hobson 1993). Local budgets will no longer be distributionally neutral, and fiscal equity will be violated if average per capita incomes differ across jurisdictions. In this case, the appropriate response is to equalize per capita residence-based taxes. These results are the same with respect to both fiscal equity and fiscal efficiency.

Studying at the institutional context, Boadway, Hobson, and Mochida (2001) concluded that the system of equalization transfers in Japan is consistent with the application of equalization principles. They arrived at this conclusion because the mix of residence- and source-based taxes at the local government level set against the mix of expenditure functions at the local government are broadly consistent with the case for equalization. The examinations in their paper have shown that, on the tax side, the so-called benchmark case does apply to Japan. In other words, as a whole, residence-based taxes are roughly proportional to income, except for families with the lowest income. This result is not surprising given that the progressivity of the inhabitant tax (personal income tax) is offset against the regressivity of indirect and residential property taxes.

On the expenditure side, the estimation stated by Boadway, Hobson, and Mochida (2001) made it clear that the incidence of the two major types of publicly provided private goods should be viewed as slightly progressive. They reasonably concluded that local budgets, apart from the contribution of source-based taxes and pure public goods, tend to be redistributive. It would not be too misleading to characterize total local residential taxes as being proportional to income and local expenditure as being distributed on a slightly progressive base. This progressivity leads to a call for full or more than full equalization of residence-based tax capacity in Japan.

Key Challenges Facing Japan's Fiscal Equalization

The system design and role of intergovernmental fiscal transfer is dependent on the stage of historical development and the political atmosphere in each country. A "one size fits all" approach is not appropriate. However, it is also true that common characteristics can be seen among good examples. This section brings together Japan's experiences—including its failures—in implementing intergovernmental fiscal transfer.

First, Japan's experience shows that the funding pool for fiscal equalization should be stable so that local governments can prepare their budgets appropriately. However, the funding pool for intergovernmental transfers must be combined with some degree of flexibility to ensure that nothing prevents macroeconomic stabilization. A way of resolving these conflicting demands is to fix the funding pool to a certain percentage of national revenue and to review this rate through regular negotiations (Litvack, Ahmad, and Bird 1998).

In internal revenue sharing in the Philippines, 40 percent of internal revenue is secured as a pool for fiscal transfer, whereas in general allocation in Indonesia, 25 percent of national revenue is secured for this same purpose. However, in actual operations, government discretion continues to influence these funding pools.

In Japan, approximately 32 percent of five national taxes (income tax on individuals, corporate income tax, value added tax, liquor tax, and cigarette tax) are secured by law as a funding pool for the local allocation tax. A benefit of this method is that abundant resources are provided to the local allocation tax system during periods of rapid economic growth. However, the tax's funding pool is sensitive to economic fluctuations and thus tends to expand or contract. Unfortunately, the income tax on individuals and corporate income tax, which are part of the funding pool of the local allocation tax, and the inhabitant tax and enterprise tax, which are important taxes for local governments, have overlapping tax bases. All of these taxes have a truly correlative relationship with economic fluctuations. This situation has caused major shortages in financial resources during the "lost decade" that began in the 1990s.

Although rules for eliminating the gap between the funding pool and entitlements are established in law, those rules do not always function effectively. Article 6, paragraph 3-2, of the Local Allocation Tax Law (Law 211 of 1950) addresses a situation in which a shortage in financial resources in local fiscal planning comes to roughly 10 percent or more of the normal allocation tax amount, and this condition has continued for two years and is predicted to continue for another year or longer. The law stipulates that, in such cases, the tax-sharing ratio will be raised. In actuality, the tax-sharing ratio has been gradually raised since 1954 when it was 20 percent. In 1966, the shares of three national taxes were raised to 32 percent to deal with financial resource shortages in local governments. Furthermore, in 1989, the value added tax and cigarette tax were added to the funding pool. However, though the situation described in article 6 of the Local Allocation Tax Law has continued in actuality for eight consecutive years since 1996, the tax-sharing ratio has not been raised. (The rate of financial resource shortage was 99.3 percent in 2002, which means that the allocation tax funding pool for an approximately one-year period was insufficient.)

Second, Japan's experience shows that the fiscal equalization system should ideally determine entitlement after considering both standard fiscal need and latent fiscal capacity (Bird and Vaillancourt 1998). Developing countries face absolute shortages in basic services that include education, sanitation, welfare, sewerages, and roads. No matter the region, a system that considers both need and capacity is essential when providing adequate financial resources for the supply of services that meet national standards. A problem with this method is that, because of limited data, it is being managed with general indicators such as population, area, and type of local government body.

Japan's postwar experience offers examples of both success and failure with respect to this point. During the 1950s and 1960s, Japan was an economically poor country. Depending on where one lived, there were significant gaps in schools and other educational facilities, as well as in roads, hospitals, waterworks, and medical care for elderly people. The Japanese public strongly desired public services that conformed to uniform standards. The local allocation tax thus secured financial sources that made it possible for local governments anywhere in the country to supply standard public services by combining the allocation tax with local taxes.

However, once a minimum level for education, health care, and medical care was achieved, the definition of the level of standard fiscal need became ambiguous. Here, the fact that the local allocation tax becomes asymmetric in adjusting for the business cycle is a problem (Mochida 2004; OECD 2005). The local allocation tax funding pool—namely, a set percentage of the national tax—expands when the economy is growing. Hence, when the Japanese economy was strong, people were tempted to think that this windfall tax revenue was more generous than the minimum standards of local public services. However, when the economy was in decline, the falling allocation tax became problematic. As a result, for a large part of the shortages in the allocation tax funding pool, borrowing by the special account for the local allocation tax and repayment of the capital and interest on this borrowing were compensated for with local bonds (temporary special fiscal local bonds) that were disposed of with future allocation tax. In other words, adjustment of the allocation tax to the business cycle is asymmetric. To break from this vicious cycle, the Japanese government is currently reviewing the "standard fiscal need" that is calculated in local fiscal plans. Inevitably, independent local public works whose settlement amount greatly exceeds planned size will be scaled back.

Third, Japan has found that the mechanisms of the fiscal equalization system should be neutral and should not distort the autonomous fiscal management of local governments. Furthermore, they should give local governments motivation to engage in sound fiscal management. Fiscal transfer that covers gaps between actual expenditure and actual revenue is not desired because it leads to moral hazards in local governments. Here, Japan's experience shows both good and bad examples. The calculation formula for the local allocation tax contains a number of attractive features that are intended to control moral hazards. Because it is calculated based on standard tax revenue, local allocation tax entitlements are not affected, even if the actual tax rate changes. And the local allocation tax does not grow, even if the local tax rate is lowered. Furthermore, 25 percent of the estimated tax revenue amount (reservation ratio) is excluded from the fiscal equalization system. As a result, local governments are given some incentive to expand their tax base. Nevertheless, some believe that because the implicit marginal tax rate is 75 percent, the reservation rate is too low to help local governments escape from the poverty trap.

However, the local allocation tax hinders local governments' incentive to provide efficient services in a number of areas. The main problem areas are as follows:

■ The expenditures of repaying capital and interest on local bonds are included in the standard fiscal need of the local allocation tax through the modification coefficient for debt services (that is, through calculation of investment expense by converting population, area, and so forth as well as amount of local bonds issued into measurement units). Because of the modification coefficient for debt services, local governments are becoming more and more dependent on local bonds. For example, in comprehensive regional improvement projects, 75 percent of financial resources are procured through local bonds, and 55 percent of the expense of repaying the capital and interest on these bonds is included in the local allocation tax in the next fiscal year. This situation occurs because the local allocation tax system is used as part of the country's fiscal policy. Of ¥130 trillion in outstanding local bonds, an estimated ¥47.4 trillion, or 36 percent, are repaid by the central government through the local allocation tax (Mochida 2004). The modification coefficient's inclusion rate (into the public bond allocation tax) was reduced to prevent softening of local governments' budgets, a move that started with new projects in fiscal year 2002; however, this step is not sufficient.

■ Local allocation tax premiums to small local governments (called *modification coefficients for local government size*) are intended to take into account reasons for cost increases that occur in line with small-scale waste. However, these large premiums are criticized for obstructing efforts toward administrative reform and mergers. Consequently, the modification coefficients for local government size were scaled back in fiscal year 2002: first, the special measure for municipalities having populations of fewer than 4,000 people was abolished, and second, the sampling range for calculating modification coefficients for local government size was narrowed from all municipalities to the most efficient two-thirds.

■ Because the implicit marginal tax rate is 75 percent, neoclassical economists criticize the local allocation tax as harming local governments' incentive to expand the local economy. Consequently, the government raised the reservation rate of the prefectures from 20 to 25 percent in 2002. However, some have commented that this criticism does not have sufficient factual evidence (Horiba, Mochida, and Fukae 2003). In other words, it is systematically impossible for local governments to arbitrarily take allocation tax from the central government by intentionally lowering the effective tax rate on fixed property; therefore, local governments create no moral hazard.

Local Bond and Borrowing

In many countries, local borrowing is an important source for financing long-term development projects such as roads, bridges, and waterworks. Local borrowing for such projects is justified on the grounds that the benefits of these projects often last decades; thus, future taxpayers should bear the cost of these projects.

Outstanding Local Debt

Figure 5.3 shows the ratio of outstanding local debt to gross domestic product (GDP) and the weight of local bonds in revenue for the past 55 years. From the time immediately following World War II until 1974, local taxes and the local allocation tax were sufficient to cover expanding expenditures. Although local bonds were issued to develop the infrastructure demanded by economic growth (roads, bridges, ports, and harbors), outstanding debt against GDP ratio fell to 5 percent or less during this 20-year period.

Local finances reached a major turning point with the oil crisis of 1974–75. The oil crisis and continuing austerity measures in its wake led to stagflation. The gap between expenditure and revenue widened, which led to a dramatic increase in the relative level of outstanding local debt to between 15 and 20 percent. This period marked the start of local bonds being used to cover fiscal deficits and the beginning of borrowing by the local allocation tax special account from the Trust Fund Bureau as a mainstay of local finance policy.

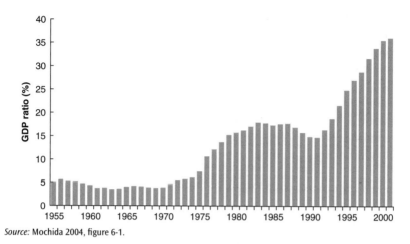

Source: Mochida 2004, figure 6-1.

FIGURE 5.3 Local Debt Outstanding to GDP Ratio, 1955–2000

During the bubble economy of the late 1980s, the trend toward rising outstanding debt stopped, and debt that had been incurred through the local allocation tax special account, which could be described as an adverse legacy of the oil crisis, was repaid. However, entering the 1990s, the percentage of outstanding local debt against GDP once again reached a new high—from 14 to 36 percent—and shows no signs of falling. A level of 30 percent or more is high not only when considering Japan's history but also when comparing with levels in European and North American countries.

Debt Expenditure Ratio and Financial Rehabilitation Plan

Although the following revenue sources are ranked as exceptions to no-loan policies, they are listed in article 5 of the Local Finance Law as being undertakings for which local bonds can be issued: (a) revenue source for expenditures pertaining to transportation, gas, and water supply, and to other services undertaken by local public enterprises; (b) revenue source for investments and loans; (c) revenue source necessary for refunding local debts; (d) revenue source for expenditures pertaining to temporary measures, recovery works, and relief measures in times of disaster; and (e) revenue source pertaining to expenditures for construction works and procurement of land by governments whose local tax rate is above the standard tax rate.

During the half-century between the 1950s and 2005, prefectures have had to obtain the central government's approval to issue bonds, and municipalities have had to get approval from prefectural governments. This setup is intended to prevent not only excessive local government debt but also the concentration of funds to affluent local governments. Although free bond issuance in which approval is not required legally exists in principle under article 226 of the Local Government Law, article 250 of the same law stipulates that the system requiring approval by the central government or prefectural governments should remain in place "for the time being."

The Comprehensive Decentralization Law of 2000, as part of an effort to strengthen the autonomy and self-responsibility of local governments, calls for the abolition of the approval system for local bonds in fiscal year 2006 and a shift to a prior consultation system. Under the new system, the issuance of local bonds will be determined not on the basis of authoritative approval but, rather, in accordance with consultations with the minister of internal affairs and communications as well as others. Local bonds that receive the consent of the minister and others will continue to have guaranteed public fund allocations and inclusion of principal and interest repayment in local fiscal plans. However, local governments will be permitted to issue bonds simply by reporting this fact to their local councils beforehand, even if they do not receive the consent of the minister and others. In other words, a difference in the degree of central government responsibility to provide implicit government guarantee will emerge between local bonds issued under the current approval system and local bonds issued after the shift to the consultation system.

Regardless, MIC will continue to carefully supervise the financial situation of local governments to ensure that local governments do not default on their debts. The debt expenditure ratio used when granting permission to issue local bonds (*Kisaiseigen-hiritu*) will be used as a judgmental criterion in supervision of that process. The debt expenditure ratio used when granting permission to issue local bonds is the average ratio of interest payment costs for public bonds (excluding those disposed of with the local allocation tax) against general revenue sources over the previous three years. The equation defining this determination follows:

$$\text{Debt expenditure ratio} = \frac{A - (B + C + E)}{D - (C + E)}$$

where A denotes public bond cost; B represents revenue earmarked for public bonds; C is the bond repayment cost included in basic financial needs as disaster recovery expenditure in calculation of the ordinary local allocation tax; D denotes general-purpose resources (that is, mainly ordinary taxes, the local allocation tax, and the local transfer tax); and E represents bond repayment cost included in basic financial needs through public works modification in calculation of the ordinary local allocation tax.

If a local government's debt expenditure ratio exceeds 15 percent, it will be required to formulate a plan to rectify public bond burden and will be obliged to lower its debt expenditure ratio to 13 percent within seven years by securing revenue and cutting expenditure for each fiscal year. Furthermore, if this ratio exceeds 20 percent, the range within which the local government can issue bonds will be significantly limited. In general, 15 percent is seen as the "warning line" and functions as the upper limit for absorbing public bond cost.

In the event that a local government's fiscal deficit exceeds a certain level, it will be designated as a *local government under a financial rehabilitation plan* and will engage in fiscal rehabilitation under central government management. The equation defining this determination follows:

$$\frac{\text{Net}}{\text{revenue}} = \frac{\text{Revenue} - \text{Expenditure} - \text{Revenue sources to be carried over}}{\text{Local tax} + \text{Local transfer tax} + \text{Local allocation tax}}.$$

In the event that the net revenue and expenditure ratio of a local government exceeds a deficit of –5 percent (prefectural government) or –20 percent (municipal government), its issuance of bonds will be restricted. This restriction will be lifted if the MIC approves the financial rehabilitation plan that the local government submits at that time. However, local governments running deficits will be designated as a *local government under a financial rehabilitation plan* and will be placed under the direct control of the central government. Although short-term financing and a special local allocation tax are provided to local governments under financial rehabilitation plans, these governments are forced to reduce excessive personnel, cut salaries, raise their collection of usage and handling fees, and take other measures under the jurisdiction of the central government. Although a fiscal crisis occurred amid an economic downturn that followed the Korean War (during which 70 percent of prefectures and 40 percent of municipalities ran deficits), the fiscal rehabilitation system ended that crisis in 1959 with no defaults on local bonds. The most recent example of a local government under a financial rehabilitation plan is Akaike town in Fukuoka prefecture.

Implicit Government Guarantee

Until now, the implicit government guarantee (that is, the local bond approval system, local bond plans that include public funds, the debt expenditure ratio used when granting permission to issue local bonds, and the local government under the financial rehabilitation plan system), which protects local governments from bankruptcy, has played a major role in Japan, whereas market discipline has had a limited role. Local bonds that are supported by the implicit government guarantee have been used for a long time because social and economic conditions made them necessary.

The first reason they have been necessary is the integrated intergovernmental relationship in which functions of the central government and local governments overlap. In Japan, the central government requires local governments to implement public services and sets the standards for such services through law, regardless of the financial strength or weakness of the local government. The implicit government guarantee thus ensures that local governments that issue few local bonds and that have low name recognition will not be shut out of the market. A framework will be required through which weak municipal governments can receive financing (a) without individual assessment of credit risk by investors and financial institutions and (b) irrespective of their size or fiscal capacity, provided that they swiftly attempt to meet national standards required by the national government.

A second reason worth considering is that although public investments make up 8 percent of the GDP, which is high by international standards, local governments implement 80 percent of such investments. In cases where countercyclical fiscal policy is implemented, public investments cannot be pursued without conformity and cooperation with local government (Hayashi 1998; Mihaljek 1997). Means are in place by which the central government controls and guides all areas of local fiscal policy—for example, the Local Tax Law, which can change tax laws throughout the country through a single law; local public finance programs, which seek conformity in macrolevel economic policies for local governments; and local bond plans that ensure fund allowances for local bonds. While scaling back public investment and grants, the central government has asked local governments to implement independent local public works to boost the economy. Local governments have responded in kind by procuring revenue sources through local bonds with allocation tax measures.

However, the implicit government guarantee had many side effects. From the end of World War II until today, most local governments in Japan have not been concerned about market discipline through the issuance of local bonds, because issuance conditions were basically uniform for all local governments, regardless of liquidity or creditworthiness. For example, the issuance conditions for publicly advertised bonds were the same for all local governments that issue such bonds (including the Tokyo metropolitan area) until fiscal year 2000. These conditions existed because there were no disparities in the creditworthiness of local bonds as a result of the implicit government guarantee and because local bonds were considered equal to national bonds. A number of positive analyses have been performed on factors behind determination of local bond value in the secondary market. Using data from December 2001, Mochida (2004) discovered that although the major factor behind value gaps is difference in liquidity, credit risk cannot be completely discounted. Furthermore, because private sector funds made up only 40 percent of the total amount of local bond funds, the public sector had a strong influence on determination of issuance conditions for publicly advertised bonds and private placement bonds. Thus, a paradox emerged whereby the more implicit the government guarantee became, the weaker the supervision of local governments by investors and taxpayers became.

Fiscal Rules and Market Discipline

Because the approval system for bond issues will soon be abolished, the importance of related supervisory mechanisms—fiscal rules and market discipline—will grow. One mechanism described earlier, which designates certain governments as *local government under a financial rehabilitation plan* can be humiliating for local governments, and thus, this system can be interpreted as a mechanism for enforcing execution of fiscal rules. Furthermore, in its assessment of Japan for fiscal year 2005, the OECD (2005) recommended that short-term financing and the special local allocation tax to local governments under financial rehabilitation plans be abolished to prevent moral hazards.

Fiscal rules will need to be made even stricter, because despite the rapid accumulation of local bonds, existing fiscal rules pertaining to repayment of principal and interest do not always have binding authority. The primary reason for this lack of binding authority is that portions that are repaid through the local allocation tax are deducted from the debt expenditure ratio. Since the latter half of the 1980s, between 30 and 100 percent of the cost of repaying principal and interest (determined according to the type of local bond and the fiscal capacity of the issuing local government) has been included in the basic financial needs of the local allocation tax. Of ¥130.9 trillion in outstanding local bonds, the local allocation tax's burden for repayment of principal and interest has reached ¥47.4 trillion. In today's Japan, residents who benefit from the issuance of local bonds do not bear the debt that arises from such bonds. Thus, local governments have no incentive to engage in balanced budgets, which in turn nurtures fiscal crises at the local level. Accordingly, it will be necessary to abolish public works modification and to more comprehensively define the cost of repaying principal and interest.

Another reason fiscal rules need to be made even stricter is that fiscal rules—whether anchored in the debt expenditure ratio used when granting permission to issue local bonds or anchored in the actual balance—are determined according to flow-based accounting indices, and thus, they have little binding authority against outstanding debt. Because outstanding debt is directly tied to the capacity of local governments to service debts, it is a fundamental factor in measuring credit risk. Mochida (2004) provides a correlation coefficient matrix for 28 local governments that issued publicly advertised bonds in fiscal year 2001. Mochida shows no significant correlation between the debt expenditure ratio used when granting permission to issue local bonds and the period of time within which debt repayment is possible. For supervision by rules as well as market credibility to be ensured, stock-based balance sheets that reflect actual fiscal conditions and consolidated financial statements that include the third sector should be prepared.

A final reason for making fiscal rules stricter is that the concept of net revenue, which is the basis for dropping local governments to *local government under financial rehabilitation plan* status, is too generous. Local governments have the flexibility to manipulate their net revenue by issuing more public bonds or by liquidating funds. Thus, to measure net cash flow for individual fiscal years, local governments should be excluding local bonds and liquidated funds from revenue when calculating net revenue. In its assessment of Japan for fiscal year 2005, the OECD (2005) recommended that the net revenue rule be changed to a rule for balanced operating revenue and expenditure.

Until now, funds for local bonds depended on public funds. A look at sources shows that though the share of private sector funds is approximately 40 percent, the total share of the Trust Fund Bureau—which must secure targets for investment of funds that will flow in passively—and of the Japan Finance Corporation for Municipal Enterprises reached 60 percent. The share of public funds was rapidly curtailed in line with reform of the central government's investment and loan program in 2000; thus, local governments must now diversify fundraising means and expand fundraising routes (especially publicly advertised bonds) from the private sector.

However, a number of prerequisites must be satisfied if market discipline is to function effectively (Ter-Minassian and Craig 1997). First, sufficient information must be disclosed on the comprehensive amount of debt of the borrower and on the borrower's capacity to service debts. Some 80 to 90 percent of local governments at the prefectural and government-designated city level supply balance sheets and account sheets showing the fiscal conditions of local governments and administrative costs to institutional investors. However, the fact that assets are not measured at their fair value and the fact that few balance sheets include the so-called third sector present a problem.

The second prerequisite is that portfolio regulations not be placed on financial institutions (for example, quotas on issuance of national bonds and local bonds). In Japan, bidding systems and methods for forming syndicates are already gaining ground in the selection of financial institutions that underwrite not only publicly advertised bonds but also private placement bonds.

The third prerequisite is a credible commitment from the central government not to bail out local governments that default on their debts. In Japan, the central government does not assume the expense of repaying principal and interest of local governments that fall into *local government under a financial rehabilitation plan* status. However, because of the effect of borrowing in the local allocation tax special account and local allocation tax measures for repayment of principal and interest, the amount of burden that local governments principally recognize they must repay is less than half of their outstanding local loans. Because no bankruptcy laws for local governments exist in Japan, it is unclear whether the central government's commitment to maintain a no-bailout policy will have sufficient credibility in the event that difficulties in repayment occur.

The final prerequisite is that borrowers be able to engage in quick policy making that matches market signals (such as worsening bond ratings) before they become unable to take on new loans. Local government leaders have short terms of office, which leads to a tendency for shortsightedness. Often, local governments in Japan do not quickly respond to market signals (such as worsening bond ratings) and issue more local bonds despite financial institutions' withdrawal from syndicates or refusal to underwrite bonds, among other measures. As the above discussion demonstrates, the conditions under which uniform dependence on market discipline functions are not completely in place in all instances. Consequently, efforts must be made to expand revenue source routes and to fund routes from the private sector on the premise that the autonomous revenue sources of local governments will be reinforced.

References

Akizuki, Kengo. 2001. "Partnership in Controlled Decentralization: Local Governments and the Ministry of Home Affairs." In *Local Government Development in Post-War Japan*, ed. Michio Muramatsu, Farrukh Iqbal, and Ikuo Kume, 63–84. Oxford, U.K.: Oxford University Press.

Bird, Richard M., and François Vaillancourt, eds. 1998. *Fiscal Decentralization in Developing Countries*. Cambridge, U.K.: Cambridge University Press.

Boadway, Robin, and Paul Hobson. 1993. "Intergovernmental Fiscal Relations in Canada." Canadian Tax Paper 96, Canadian Tax Foundation, Toronto.

Boadway, Robin W., Paul A. Hobson, and Nobuki Mochida. 2001. "Fiscal Equalization in Japan: Assessment and Recommendations." *Journal of Economics* (University of Tokyo) 66 (4): 24–57.

Buchanan, James M. 1950. "Federalism and Fiscal Equity," *American Economic Review* 40: 583–99.

General Headquarters Supreme Commander for Allied Power. 1949. *Report on Japanese Taxation by the Shoup Mission*. Tokyo: General Headquarters Supreme Commander for Allied Power.

Hayashi, Takehisa.1998. "Macroeconomic Policy and Local Finance." [In Japanese.] *Local Finance* (May): 4–12.

Horiba, Isao, Nobuki Mochida, and Keishi Fukae. 2003. "Moral Hazard Effect of Local Allocation Tax on Property Tax." [In Japanese.] *Aoyamagakuin Journal of Economics* 54 (4): 27–58.

Litvack, Jennie, Junaid Ahmad, and Richard Bird. 1998. *Rethinking Decentralization in Developing Countries*. Washington, DC: World Bank.

Local Tax Bureau, MIC (Ministry of Internal Affairs and Communication). 2005. *Report on Local Taxes*. [In Japanese.] Tokyo: MIC.

MIC (Ministry of Internal Affairs and Communication). 2005a. *Annual Report of Local Finance*. [In Japanese.] Tokyo: MIC.

———. 2005b. "Materials on the Local Tax System." [In Japanese.] Unpublished document. Tokyo: MIC.

———. 2005c. "White Paper on Local Public Finance." [In Japanese.] MIC, Tokyo.

Mihaljek, Dubravko. 1997. "Japan." In *Fiscal Federalism in Theory and Practice,* ed. Teresa Ter-Minassian, 285–323. Washington, DC: International Monetary Fund.

Mochida, Nobuki. 1993. *Toshizaisei no Kenkyu*. [*Public Finance of Japanese Cities*.] Tokyo: University of Tokyo Press.

———. 1998. "An Equalization Transfer Scheme in Japan." In *Welfare State, Public Investment and Growth,* ed. Toshihiro Ihori and Hirofumi Shibata, 269–93. Tokyo: Springer-Verlag.

———. 2001. "Taxes and Transfers in Japan's Local Finances." In *Local Government Development in Post-War Japan,* ed. Michio Muramatsu, Farrukh Iqbal, and Ikuo Kume, 85–111. Oxford, U.K.: Oxford University Press.

———. 2004. *Fiscal Decentralization and State-Local Finance: Fundamental Perspectives*. [In Japanese.] Tokyo: University of Tokyo Press.

Mochida, Nobuki, and Jørgen Lotz. 1999. "Fiscal Federalism in Practice: The Nordic Countries and Japan." *Journal of Economics* (University of Tokyo) 64 (4): 55–86.

Muramatsu, Michio, and Farrukh Iqbal. 2001. "Understanding Japanese Intergovernmental Relations: Perspectives, Models, and Salient Characteristics." In *Local
Government Development in Post-War Japan,* ed. Michio Muramatsu, Farrukh Iqbal,
and Ikuo Kume, 1–28. Oxford, U.K.: Oxford University Press.

OECD (Organisation for Economic Co-operation and Development). 1999. "Taxing
Powers of State and Local Government." OECD Tax Policy Studies 1, OECD, Paris.

———. 2000. *Economic Surveys: Japan.* Paris: OECD.

———. 2005. *Economic Surveys: Japan.* Paris: OECD.

Policy Research Institute, Ministry of Finance. 2002. *Comparative Study of Local Finance
System* (in Japanese). Tokyo: Policy Research Institute.

Reed, Steven. 2001. "Impersonal Mechanisms and Personal Networks in the Distribution
of Central Grants to Local Governments in Japan." In *Local Government Development in Post-War Japan,* ed. Michio Muramatsu, Farrukh Iqbal, and Ikuo Kume,
112–31. Oxford, U.K.: Oxford University Press.

Shah, Anwar. 1994. "The Reform of Intergovernmental Fiscal Relations in Developing
and Emerging Market Economies." Policy and Research Series 23, World Bank,
Washington, DC.

Ter-Minassian, Teresa, and Jon Craig. 1997. "Control of Subnational Government Borrowing." In *Fiscal Federalism in Theory and Practice,* ed. Teresa Ter-Minassian,
156–74. Washington, DC: International Monetary Fund.

6

Local Government Organization and Finance: *New Zealand*

BRIAN DOLLERY

Overview of the Current Local Government System

New Zealand local government originated with the passage of the Municipal Corporations Ordinance through the Legislative Council in 1842. This legislation provided the legal basis for establishing a borough in any district with a population exceeding 2,000 people; the resulting borough would be governed by an elected council with the power to raise revenues through rates and with an obligation to provide fire services, jails, roads, sewers, and water (Bush 1995). However, constitutional difficulties led the British imperial government to disallow the ordinance in 1843. That original legislation was later replaced by similar legislation in the form of the 1845 Public Roads and Works Ordinance. Nevertheless, "local government as we understand it today proceeded in fits and starts until the passage of the Municipal Corporations Act 1867, which provided for a uniform urban territorial authority structure, although its application was not mandatory" (Palmer and Palmer 2004, p. 247).

Further development of municipal governance in New Zealand was hampered by the tensions that existed between the provincial system and a centralist tradition until the abolition of the provinces and the introduction of the Municipal Corporations Act 1876, as well as the subsequent passage of the Counties Act 1876. This legislation brought all existing local authorities under uniform legal standards and provided for the creation of new municipal entities. Accordingly, "from 1876 onwards, local bodies multiplied, with many *ad hoc* authorities being added, such as harbour boards, rabbit boards, and water boards" (Palmer and Palmer 2004, p. 247).

In constitutional terms, New Zealand is characterized by a centralized unitary system of government, with all power vested in the national government. Local government is thus entirely a statutory creature of the central government, having no formal constitutional standing and depending for its existence on legislation that can be changed at any time by the will of the national parliament. The current statutory basis for local government in New Zealand is the Local Government Act 2002, in conjunction with the Local Government (Rating) Act 2002 and the Local Election Act 2001, which were enacted as the culmination of extensive local government reform in collaboration with the national municipal representative body, known as Local Government New Zealand. This legislation has heralded a new dawn for local governance in New Zealand.

The Local Government Act 2002 provides the legal framework that specifies the purposes of local authorities, enumerates the powers of municipal entities and the manner in which these powers can be discharged, seeks to enhance the accountability of councils, and enables local government to play a broader role than did previous legislation. A critical element of the act is that it provides New Zealand municipal authorities with a power of general competence for the first time in their history. Although this power of general competence is not yet a "pure" authority, it nevertheless implies that "under a power of general competence, local government can do anything that is not expressly forbidden by law or given exclusively to another organization" (Palmer and Palmer 2004, p. 250). Accordingly, a municipal authority can undertake any activity or business and enter into any transaction; it has full powers, rights, and privileges to carry out its role, subject to the provisions of the Local Government Act 2002, as well as other enactments and laws. Territorial authorities and regional councils must exercise their powers primarily for the benefit of their own spatial regions.

At present, New Zealand local government comprises 12 regional councils and 74 territorial local authorities (TLAs) that are subdivided into 16 city councils and 58 district councils (Local Government New Zealand, 2004a).[1] At a more detailed level, local authorities can be classified into four discrete categories: TLAs, regional councils, community boards, and ad hoc bodies. TLAs together comprise 16 city municipalities with populations in excess of 50,000 residents and 58 district councils that deliver various conventional local government services. Twelve regional councils, with average populations of some 303,735 people each, perform a largely regulatory role. There are 159 community boards affiliated with TLAs that form a link between these authorities and the local community. Ad hoc bodies consist of 24 licensing trusts, which variously administer alcohol outlets and a motley array of seven specialist organizations such as Infrastructure Auckland and the Otago Museum Trust Board.

In general, "in New Zealand, local government provides waste management, water, local roads, land management, parks, libraries, and other local infrastructure and public goods" (Kerr, Aitken, and Grimes 2004, p. 1). It does not provide either education or health services. New Zealand local government thus has a rather narrow "services to property" focus that is similar to Australian local government rather than the much broader "services to people" emphasis of American, British, and Canadian local authorities. At a more detailed level, it is possible to identify some 60 separate functions performed by local government in New Zealand. For analytical convenience, Bush (2003, p. 163) has grouped these functions into six main categories.

- *Control of nuisances.* In this role, municipal authorities oversee a broad range of activities, including animal and plant pests, litter, noise, pollution, refuse, and sewerage.
- *Regulation of specific activities.* Numerous issues require local government regulation, including alcohol distribution, traffic control, dangerous materials, swimming pools, and waterways.
- *Planning.* This complex and often controversial function is administered under the Resource Management Act 1991 and deals with the management of the natural and physical environment through the planning process.
- *Community improvement.* Territorial bodies are charged with improving the communities they represent through economic development (such as land subdivision and tourism promotion); entertainment and recreation (such as libraries and parks); and the funding of selected community projects and centers, roads and sidewalks, and urban renewal schemes.
- *Social welfare.* To a limited degree, TLAs are involved in some social welfare programs such as child care centers and public housing for elderly people.
- *Public utilities.* Most TLAs operate various utilities (such as airports, electricity companies, and water services) and trading organizations (such as business ventures involved in alcohol trading and gambling).

In addition to these six primary functions, local government also has responsibilities in relation to the 1840 Waitangi Treaty between the British Crown and various Maori chieftains, especially in relation to the exercise of traditional Maori rights with respect to natural resource use and the administration of the Resource Management Act 1991 (Hayward 2003). Although recent legislative change has sought to address Maori representation in local government and to enhance Maori representation in local environmental decision making, the role of Waitangi Treaty principles in local government remains unclear. Indeed, it has been argued that "the relationship between Maori and local government is fascinating, frustrating, challenging, and increasingly important for both parties" (Hayward 2003, p. xi).

The financial operations of local government in New Zealand are closely prescribed by legislation, especially in terms of revenue-raising activities. In 2001, on average, property taxes or rates accounted for 57 percent of total income; various user charges, including fines and petrol taxes, contributed almost 20 percent; intergovernmental grants and subsidies from the national government, largely directed at road construction and maintenance, amounted to about 10 percent; sundry commercial ventures yielded approximately 9 percent; and the remaining income derived from interest and investment dividends (Bush 2003). These sources of revenue have three noteworthy features. First, these average figures conceal a substantial variation between individual TLAs, particularly large urban centers such as Auckland City, which often may have relatively large utilities and trading operations. Second, by international standards, reliance on intergovernmental grants is low; New Zealand local government is financially self-sufficient to a comparatively high degree. Finally, although rate income on property is conceptually straightforward as a means of taxing property, its application and calculation in New Zealand are exceptionally complicated. Graham Bush has described these complications as follows:

> The bottom line for ratepayers can comprise as many as four different types of true rates (cents in the dollar), two uniform annual charges, and an impost for water and sewerage facilities supplied. The rates themselves are normally calculated differentially, whereby different rates in the dollar are applied to similarly valued properties of different classification (for example, residential and commercial). (Bush 2003, p. 164)

In contrast, expenditure unsurprisingly reflects the nature of New Zealand local government and its primary functions. For the average TLA, about

52 percent of outlays covered service provision, approximately 23 percent of the typical budget was directed at staff employment, about 20 percent was spent on asset depreciation, and approximately 4 percent was expended on redemption and interest on loans.

Borrowing as a source of funding is permitted under the enabling legislation as a way to finance capital projects on the presumption that it is reasonable to amortize infrastructure over its lifetime. By contrast, New Zealand municipalities are not allowed to use borrowing as a means to fund current activities.

Bush has described local government in New Zealand as "rational, lean, generally uniform, and its basic features are easy to grasp." In essence, "except for community boards, each unit is a separate legal entity known as a corporation, and as such is invested with certain legal rights" (Bush 2003, p. 161). Individual municipalities are governed by elected councilors under the leadership of a popularly elected mayor (or appointed chairperson in the case of regional councils and community boards). Actual elections are conducted using the traditional "first-past-the-post" method or alternatively by means of the preferential single-transferable-vote method. Local government elections are held on the second Saturday in October every third year (Statistics New Zealand 2002). In general, national party politics and party platforms play a limited role in New Zealand local government elections.

Although the legal powers of a municipality are formally vested in an elected council, the employees of TLAs nevertheless enjoy considerable de facto authority, especially the chief executive officer (Dollery 2003). This official appoints and manages paid staff members in terms of the Employment Relations Act 2000.

Under the Local Government Act 2002, a new era of local government began in New Zealand. One important component of the new legislative regime stresses accountability and performance by individual local government bodies. This emphasis has had substantial implications for the operations of councils. For instance, accountability criteria now require municipal bodies first to prepare and publicize an annual plan that is subject to extensive public consultation and then to report on the fulfillment of the plan shortly after the close of the fiscal year. Moreover, the construction of long-term plans is also obligatory. Similarly, councils are now able to use a variety of different mechanisms to deliver their services, and more than two-thirds of services previously delivered "in house" are now handled through self-contained and self-governing local authority trading enterprises or are contracted out to private firms.

Local Government Expenditure Responsibilities

The major responsibilities of the 12 regional councils in New Zealand fall under the Resource Management Act 1991 and the Soil Conservation and Rivers Control Act 1941. These responsibilities embrace control of noxious plants and pests, harbor regulation and marine pollution control, regional dimensions of civil defense, aspects of regional transport planning, and regional transportation carriers. Additional responsibilities have fallen on some regional bodies, including activities formerly accomplished by land drainage boards. By contrast, the 74 TLAs (comprising 16 city councils and 58 district councils) are much more focused on traditional "services to property" functions that are characteristic of both Australian and New Zealand local governments. Their expenditure responsibilities not only center on land management, libraries, local roads, parks, waste management, water, and other local infrastructure and public goods but also include civil defense, health inspection, liquor licensing, and pensioner housing. Community boards are largely advisory bodies, whereas ad hoc organizations are special-purpose bodies.

A significant difficulty facing scholars researching New Zealand local government resides in securing the requisite data. The reason for this unfortunate problem is that the (then) Department of Statistics annual authoritative report titled *Local Authority Statistics* ceased publication after fiscal year 1987/88. Since that time, researchers have had access to fewer data, and the data they do obtain are fragmented and less reliable.

Nevertheless, a detailed breakdown of actual expenditures by individual local government council is provided in *Local Government New Zealand Measures Reports—2004* (Local Government New Zealand 2004b), which was derived from the NZLG Database (2004 version) on the basis of reporting by all local government authorities in New Zealand for the following expenditure categories: total operating expenditure, capital expenditure, roads, waste management and refuse, wastewater, water supply and treatment, economic development, flood control and drainage, council staff numbers, and chief executives' salaries.[2]

If we single out functional categories from these data and aggregate the 2004 data for all 74 TLAs, then we can get some idea of the relative burden imposed by the different expenditure categories. This information is provided in table 6.1. It should be stressed that because the six expenditure categories available from *Local Government New Zealand Measures*

TABLE 6.1 Aggregate Expenditure by Functional Responsibility, 2004

Functional category	Aggregate expenditure (NZ$)
Road maintenance and construction	959,514,000
Wastewater	335,516,000
Water supply and treatment	311,297,000
Waste management and refuse	194,881,000
Economic development	130,250,000
Flood control and drainage	30,753,000
Total operating expenditure	**3,890,934,000**
Capital expenditure	**17,426,898,000**

Source: Adapted from Local Government New Zealand 2004b.

Reports—2004 (Local Government New Zealand 2004b) do not encompass all of the expenditure categories, (a) we cannot calculate percentages and (b) the categories in table 6.1 do not exhaust all total operating expenditures.

Table 6.1 ranks the major expenditure functions in descending order and indicates that the category of road maintenance and construction represents the most important expenditure responsibility of those categories listed. However, the aggregated data in table 6.1 mask massive differences among TLAs. For instance, Kaikoura District Council spends only NZ$926,000 on roads per year, whereas the Auckland City Council outlays NZ$153,459,000 in the same category. Similar differences also occur for all other expenditure categories in table 6.1. The extraordinary diversity in size among New Zealand TLAs echoes Australian local government, which possesses the same characteristic, also to a marked degree (see, for instance, Worthington and Dollery 2001).

Given data constraints, a second feasible way to assess the expenditure responsibilities of New Zealand local government that would enable us to observe trends is to examine actual expenditure in terms of the major sources of outlays. Table 6.2 provides aggregate data for the 174 TLAs in question for the period from 1999 to 2003.

At least two interesting features are evident in the data in table 6.2. First, for the entire period 1999–2003, the aggregate municipal authorities in New Zealand experienced an operating surplus. Second, the various categories constituted a surprisingly constant proportion of total expenditure over the period in question.

TABLE 6.2 Aggregate Local Authorities Financial Statistics: Actual
Expenditure, 1999–2003

(NZ$ thousand)

Year	Purchases of goods and services, grants and donations, and all other expenditure	Employee costs	Interest paid	Depreciation	Total expenditure excluding nonoperating and extraordinary items[a]	Operating result (surplus or deficit)[a]
1999	1,754.3	849.1	165.6	697.3	3,466.4	+160.0
2000	1,808.1	830.9	153.9	715.7	3,508.5	+241.2
2001	1,891.9	839.7	146.1	730.5	3,608.2	+230.7
2002	2,002.7	880.0	143.1	765.5	3,791.3	+ 356.5
2003	2,043.7[b]	944.9[b]	149.8[b]	832.9[b]	3,971.2[b]	+ 258.8[b]

Source: Adapted from Statistics New Zealand 2004.
a. Because of rounding, individual figures may not always add up to the stated totals.
b. Figures for 2003 are provisional.

Local Government Own-Source Taxes and Charges

Revenue-raising activities of local authorities in New Zealand are tightly pre-scribed by law. In general, six sources of revenue are available. In terms of their historical monetary yield, they can be listed in the following order: rates on property, sales of goods and services, grants and subsidies (from central government), license fees and fines, petroleum taxation, and interest and dividends on investments (Bush 1995).

Rates on property represent by far the most important single source of revenue for local government in New Zealand, accounting for almost 60 percent of total revenue. A property rate represents a local tax on land and property. It has several distinct advantages over other forms of local taxa-tion. The incidence of rates cannot easily be transferred; it is highly visible (unlike a local sales tax); it is relatively cheap to collect because property is easy to identify, define, and measure; it promotes local autonomy and accountability; and it can generate sufficient income (Bailey 1999).

The legal basis for rating property in New Zealand is provided by the Local Government (Rating) Act 2002. According to Palmer and Palmer, the act has three main purposes:

> Provide local authorities with flexible powers to set, assess, and collect rates to fund local government activities;
>
> Ensure rates are set in accordance with decisions that are made in a transpar-ent and consultative manner;

Provide processes and information to enable ratepayers to identify and understand their liability for rates. (Palmer and Palmer 2004, p. 164)

As indicated previously, the New Zealand rating system is extremely complex because municipal councils can choose from among various different methodologies for striking a rate. For example, rates can be levied on the capital value of the land or, alternatively, on the annual land value (and not the property value of the land in question). It is also possible to impose rates on a differential basis, thereby enabling TLAs to vary the effect of the base chosen by levying uniform annual charges and, thus, to determine a desired spread of the overall burden of rates between, say, businesses and residents. In actual terms, 50 TLAs use land value, 23 TLAs use capital value, and a single TLA imposes annual rental value (Kerr, Aitken, and Grimes 2004).

Local government in New Zealand enjoys the ability to impose targeted rates for special purposes such as additional specified infrastructure. The Local Government (Rating) Act 2002 exempts various categories of land from rates, including land used for charitable, educational, and religious purposes, as well as Crown land and national parks.

Kerr, Aitken, and Grimes (2004) provide an interesting macroeconomic perspective on rates in the aggregate New Zealand economy. They contend that the total value of property in New Zealand in 2002, representing NZ$336 billion, amounts to a comparatively broad tax base relative to the cost of local government services. If it is assumed that the real rate of return on property is 5 percent per year, then that rate would generate an annual income of some NZ$17 billion and would constitute approximately 14 percent of national income. Total local government expenditure in 2002 was NZ$976 million out of NZ$33 billion total public sector outlays, or about 3 percent of total public sector expenditure. Thus, "local government expenditure was 5.7 percent of the implied services from property, so even if all local authority expenditure was financed from property taxes the implied tax rate would be very low—less than half the rate of GST (value added tax) and approximately one-seventh of the top personal tax rate" (Kerr, Aitken, and Grimes 2004, p. 17).

Despite the strong advantages of rates as a method of financing local government, the yield generated by a given property tax rate (or a given tax base) will generate different magnitudes of income for different councils because different local government jurisdictions vary with respect to the value of land and property, and hence, the rate base is different. Consequently, the problem of horizontal fiscal imbalance emerges in local government systems (such as the New Zealand municipal system), which rely heavily on rates without significant central government financial intervention.

Although little research effort has been directed at the problem of horizontal fiscal imbalance among municipal councils in New Zealand, Kerr, Aitken, and Grimes (2004) have investigated this question empirically. They found that there are some potentially serious consequences to the heavy reliance in New Zealand local government on local tax bases to finance local goods and services. Kerr, Aitken, and Grimes (2004) argue that, because the taxable capacity of different TLAs varies substantially across different municipal jurisdictions, relatively poor councils have lower per capita tax bases. Accordingly, "in comparison to a nationally funded system where expenditure might be roughly equalized per capita," such as the state and territory local government grant commissions in Australia, "the level of services TLAs can afford varies greatly," so "neighboring TLAs can experience very different tax bases and hence cost of services, meaning that firms that are very close geographically might face very different rates and services." Although "some of this variance could be an efficient response to different local conditions," the variance seems, nevertheless, "likely to be greater than optimal" (Kerr, Aitken, and Grimes 2004, p. 39).

A smaller but nonetheless significant source of income, comprising almost 20 percent of total revenue, derives from the sale of goods and services, either through local authority trading enterprises, such as airports, electricity companies, and water services, or through sundry business ventures involved in alcohol trading, gambling, and other business. In essence, these activities are financed on the basis of the user pays principle.

Shared Taxes

Local government in New Zealand is empowered only to tax ratable property and thus cannot levy any other tax. Moreover, the national exchequer does not engage in tax sharing with local government. A partial exception to this rule may be found in the taxation of petroleum, about which Bush (1995, p. 249) has made the following salient observations:

> The petrol tax, levied through areas at a maximum rate of $0.00.66 litre (petrol) and $0.00.33 (diesel), is distributed according to the proportion that any one TLA's rates and charges bear to the whole area. Its use is discretionary, but its yield is now derisory, amounting for most local bodies to between 0.5 and 1 percent of income, and many no longer itemise it separately in the balance sheet. The regional petrol tax, which was introduced in mid-1992 and terminated at the end of 1995, was collectable in the five main urban regions and applied to support public transport: for 1995–96 the Auckland Regional Council budgeted the tax to provide 15 percent of its $50 million support of trains, ferries and buses.

Intergovernmental Fiscal Transfers

In the overall assessment of New Zealand local authorities below, the degree of vertical fiscal imbalance between the central government and municipal councils in New Zealand is exceptionally low by international standards, and local government is self-funded to a remarkable degree. This finding is true even in comparison with Australia, whose local government sector performs largely identical functions (Dollery 2002). Accordingly, and unlike the elaborate Australian state and territory local government grants commissions, New Zealand does not require an extensive system of intergovernmental grants to correct for vertical fiscal imbalance.

The data contained in table 6.3 demonstrate that over the period from 1999 to 2003, grants and subsidies from the central government represented a fraction over 10 percent of total local government income and remained stable throughout the period at that level. Most of these funds are limited to public transportation and to road maintenance and construction. As a useful rule of thumb, the magnitude of central government finance accruing to any single TLA is essentially a function of the dominance of roads in a given TLA. Moreover, most funds allocated to public transportation are directed at assisting bus and train services in Auckland and Wellington (Bush 1995).

TABLE 6.3   Local Authorities' Quarterly Financial Statistics (Actual Revenue)
(*NZ$ thousand*)

				Investment income			
Year	Sales of goods and services and all other income	Rates, petrol tax, license fees and fines	Government grants and subsidies	Interest revenue	Dividends, donations, insurance claims, and bad debts	Total investment income	Total revenue excluding non-operating and extraordinary items[a]
1999	687.5	2,176.0	390.6	153.1	219.2	372.3	3,626.4
2000	712.4	2,304.3	398.7	147.3	187.0	334.3	3,749.7
2001	730.5	2,416.7	398.6	143.2	150.0	293.2	3,838.9
2002	769.7	2,518.2	440.0	126.5	293.4	419.9	4,147.8
2003	812.1[b]	2,646.1[b]	471.4[b]	153.6[b]	146.8[b]	300.5[b]	4,230.0[b]

Source: Adapted from Statistics New Zealand 2004.
a. Because of rounding, individual figures may not always add up to the stated totals.
b. Figures for 2003 are provisional.

Several other minor grants and subsidies exist. For instance, under the Rates Rebate Act 1973, councils have received a refund of revenue forgone from the central government for property rates rebates to specified low-income groups. Some rental housing and senior citizen accommodations still draw a subsidy from the national exchequer. Moreover, given local government's responsibilities under the Resource Management Act 1991 and the Soil Conservation and Rivers Control Act 1941, control of pests and noxious weeds also attracts small subsidies. Occasional community development projects receive central government grants.

Local Government Borrowing

Borrowing to finance current ordinary activity is by law not permitted for local government authorities in New Zealand, with the sole exception of securing part of the forthcoming fiscal year's anticipated income in advance. However, it is customary to fund long-term infrastructure projects by means of loans in accordance with the standard principle of local public finance allowing the cost of a capital asset to be amortized over the life of the asset. The financial behavior of individual municipal authorities, including local government borrowing, is closely scrutinized by the central government auditor-general, who has imposed extensive reporting requirements and who can conduct special investigations if grounds exist for believing monies have been wasted or due process overlooked (Palmer and Palmer 2004).

The *Local Government New Zealand Measures Reports—2004* (Local Government New Zealand 2004b) shows that total gross public debt held by all New Zealand TLAs stood at NZ\$2,366,362,000 as of June 30, 2003. This debt amounts to an average figure of approximately NZ\$31,977,865 per municipality, which conceals massive differences among individual councils, ranging from the Chatham Islands Council, which owes nothing, to the Mackenzie District Council, which owes NZ\$4,000, to the Christchurch City Council, which has a total gross debt of NZ\$366,441,000.[3]

In an assessment of borrowing by local authorities over the long term, Bush (1995, p. 251) arrived at the following conclusion:

> To assess local government borrowing and debt purely according to raw figures is seriously flawed. What is meaningful is not the hundreds of millions of dollars normally borrowed each year or the total indebtedness of several billion dollars, but what proportion of income is consumed by interest and capital repayment, the solidity of the assets created, and the ratio of debts to assets. From these standpoints local body borrowing appears prudent and even conservative.

Empirical evidence supports this conclusion. For instance, in 1994, the ratio of debt to total income from all sources was calculated, and only 14 local authorities lay above the cutoff point of 0.5 (Bush 1995).

Local Government Administration

Local government management in New Zealand is controlled by legislation under which municipal authorities are obliged to conduct their affairs in an open and proper manner, to separate regulatory functions from nonregulatory activities, and to ensure that their operations are directed to their constituents (Caulfield 2003). Enabling legislation obliges councils to set clear objectives, to prepare strategic plans, and to monitor and measure performance. TLAs are allowed to privatize and corporatize their trading activities and to run their operations along standard business lines. Moreover, municipalities are permitted to use competitive tendering processes so that service delivery can be undertaken either by in-house cost centers or by private for-profit contractors.

The statutory powers of a municipal council are legally vested in an elected council whose members are typically remunerated through a combination of a daily meeting allowance and an annual salary that is set by the Higher Salaries Commission. Elected councils are empowered to appoint a chief executive officer as a general manager on a fixed-term contract. Subject to council approval, the general manager is entitled to appoint, manage, and dismiss both permanent and temporary staff members in terms of the conditions of the Employment Relations Act 2000. A council must also put in place an equal opportunity program.

Beginning with the Local Government Act 1989, and given further impetus with the promulgation of the Local Government Act 2002, a new era of local government began in New Zealand. From the perspective of local government administration, these reform measures stimulated a move from "governing" to "governance," which provided chief executive officers with much greater latitude through an emphasis on "letting managers manage," an emphasis that is a continuing source of tension between elected representatives and chief executive officers (Drage 2002). The new statutory basis for local government lays down regulatory stipulations covering heightened accountability and performance requirements for individual councils, with significant implications for their management. Thus, accountability criteria now require local authorities to prepare and publicize an annual plan, provide for extensive public consultation, and then report on the achievement of the plan shortly after the close of the fiscal year (June 30) each year. In addition, the preparation of long-term plans is also obligatory. As indicated above, municipal councils can now use a variety of mechanisms to deliver their services, and more than two-thirds of services previously delivered in house are either handled through self-contained and self-governing local authority trading enterprises or contracted out to private firms.

Robert Howell (1995) conducted an interesting study on the effect of the new legislation on the management of New Zealand local government. After an analysis of 10 local authorities, Howell (1995, p. 82) summarized his findings as follows:

> If governance is defined as an information gathering and decision making process whereby the purpose of the organization is defined, the strategies and rules for attaining that purpose are determined, and authority given for the use of resources for the implementation of those strategies, then on the evidence of the ten authorities surveyed, it cannot be said that New Zealand local authorities are well governed. In no authority was there a clear statement of the role of elected members versus management, and in the evidence from policy manuals, delegation registers, and agendas, councillors appeared preoccupied with operational details. In part, this was due to the inadequacy of the notion of "policy," but also because there are too many councillors, leading to too many committees. The definition of a business unit needs to be standardised, and the governance and management responsibilities of those units should be given further consideration.

In defense of current arrangements, it should immediately be noted that the Howell (1995) study predated the Local Government Act 2002 and attendant legislation. However, it did take place well after the landmark Local Government Act 1989.

Overall Assessment of Local Government Finances

Perhaps the best way of providing an overall assessment of local government funding in New Zealand is by placing it in the context of the finance of other Organisation for Economic Co-operation and Development (OECD) local government systems. The size and significance of local government in advanced capitalist democracies vary enormously, primarily because the functions performed by this level of government are extremely diverse. For instance, Caulfield (2002, p. 159) has observed that "Scandinavian local governments, for example, have carried the weight of responsibility for the welfare state, while at the other end of the spectrum in Australia and New Zealand local government has been restricted largely to property service functions." Given the limited range of functions carried out by municipal councils in New Zealand, it is thus not surprising that local government enjoys a comparatively limited role in the overall New Zealand economy.

Figure 6.1 illustrates the relatively small size of local government in New Zealand in revenue terms compared with other OECD countries over the period from 1980 to 1995. Figure 6.1 shows that, in general, federal countries (with the marked exception of Australia) have relatively large local government sectors compared with their unitary cousins. New Zealand has the smallest local government among unitary nations, with Japan, Luxembourg, Iceland, and France slightly ahead.

In their useful survey of the devolution of fiscal responsibilities between different tiers of government among OECD member countries, Joumard and Kongsrud (2003, pp. 7–9) have developed a helpful checklist for assessing fiscal relations across levels of government. The checklist can assist in evaluating New Zealand local government in a comparative perspective. Joumard and Kongsrud identified four major criteria. First, the assignment of expenditure responsibilities is an important index of the degree of decentralization. Significant dimensions of this criterion include the size of jurisdictions, the existence of overlapping responsibilities, and the existence of social transfers and redistributive activities. Second, the principles on which subnational government funding is based are paramount, in particular, taxation powers, tax competition, hypothecated intergovernmental grants, and equalization schemes. Third, macroeconomic management in a

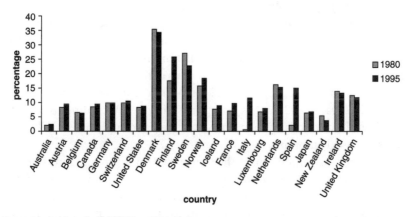

Source: Adapted from Caulfield 2002, p. 160, table 2.

Note: The large increase in total revenue to Italy and Spain between 1980 and 1995 is explained by the introduction of regional governments in these countries.

FIGURE 6.1 Local Government Total Revenue (Tax, Nontax, and Grants), 1980 and 1995, as a Proportion of GDP

decentralized setting, involving macroeconomic consistency, fiscal rules, and market discipline, requires careful scrutiny. Finally, the extent of information sharing and operational transparency—especially the clarity of definitions for subnational expenditure responsibilities and revenue-raising functions—is important.

We examine those dimensions of the Joumard and Kongsrud (2003) taxonomy that have a bearing on New Zealand municipal government. Given the comparative simplicity of local government in New Zealand, especially in terms of its range of functions and straightforward method of finance, many aspects of the Joumard and Kongsrud typology are not significant—for example, social transfers and redistributive activities, intergovernmental grants, and vertical and horizontal fiscal equalization schemes.

The extent of fiscal decentralization is difficult to demonstrate empirically for several reasons, not least of which is the fact that fiscal autonomy has various dimensions that occasionally conflict with one another and are thus not easy to assess. In addition, it is extremely difficult to find comparable data that can enable international comparisons. With these caveats in mind, table 6.4 does shed some numerical light on the problem.

From a perusal of table 6.4, it is immediately apparent that the data in the table confirm figure 6.1: New Zealand local government is quite small by international standards in terms of employment and revenue. Although the share of municipal government in overall New Zealand public expenditure is not shown, we know from table 6.2 that for the period from 1999 to 2003, in aggregate, councils ran operating surpluses. Moreover, from our earlier analysis, we know that with only approximately 10 percent of its financial requirements coming from central government, New Zealand local government is clearly close to self-funding, with a remarkably low degree of vertical fiscal imbalance by international standards (Joumard and Kongsrud 2003, p. 28, table 3). Moreover, recent analysis by Szalai and Tassonyi (2004, p. 502, table 4) supports this view. According to conventional wisdom in local public finance, these data imply a relatively high degree of fiscal autonomy.

Another way of looking at the same problem is provided in table 6.5, in which the data show various indicators of revenue-raising powers. In table 6.5, the nations included are ranked in accordance with a "summary indicator" that is determined as a product of the ratio of municipal government taxes to gross domestic product (GDP) and the degree of discretion in setting taxes. But because municipal taxation represents a small proportion of GDP in New Zealand, despite a score of 98.0 in the "Discretion to set taxes" column in table 6.5, New Zealand appears only

TABLE 6.4 Indicators of Fiscal Decentralization
(percent)

Country	Subnational government spending and employment				Subnational government revenues			
	Share in general government spending[a]		Employment as a share of total public employment		Share in general government revenues[b]		Attribution of tax revenues as percentage of total tax revenue[c]	
	1985[d]	2001[e]	1990[f]	2001[g]	1985[d]	2001[e]	1985	2001
Federal countries								
Australia	..	..	76.7	83.3	..	..	18.6	17.2
Austria[h]	28.4	28.5	62.6	62.3	24.6	21.4	23.8	18.9
Belgium	31.8	34.0	..	..	11.4	11.3	4.8	28.6
Canada[i]	54.5	56.5	84.7	86.0	50.4	49.9	45.4	44.1
Germany	37.6	36.1	87.6	88.5	31.9	32.4	30.8	29.2
Mexico	..	..	..	..	..	..	1.0	3.1
Switzerland	..	..	..	..	..	..	44.1	40.4
United States	32.6	40.0	81.8	85.5	37.6	40.4	32.7	31.7
Unitary countries								
Czech Republic	..	..	32.3	34.0	..	..	..	10.6
Denmark	53.7	57.8	..	..	32.3	34.6	28.4	33.8
Finland	30.6	35.5	74.7	77.8	24.8	24.7	22.4	22.4
France	16.1	18.6	..	45.8	11.6	13.1	8.7	9.3
Greece	4.0	5.0	..	87.8	3.7	3.7	1.3	1.0
Hungary	..	..	65.5	65.1	..	..	..	5.5
Iceland	..	..	.	..	..	..	18.6	24.3
Ireland[i]	30.2	29.5	13.2	11.3	32.3	34.6	2.3	1.9
Italy	25.6	29.7	..	20.6	10.7	17.6	2.3	12.2
Japan	46.0	40.7	..	..	26.8	26.0	26.0	25.9
Korea, Republic of[h]	..	..	32.3	34.8	..	..	..	17.8
Luxembourg	14.2	12.8	94.8	92.5	8.0	7.4	6.6	5.6
Netherlands	32.6	34.2	27.5	25.6	11.4	11.1	2.4	3.5
New Zealand	..	..	12.2	9.5	..	..	6.5	5.6
Norway[j]	34.6	38.8	..	..	22.5	20.3	17.7	16.3
Poland[h]	..	..	6.5	6.2	..	..	..	18.3
Portugal	10.3	12.8	..	..	7.6	8.3	3.5	6.5
Slovak Republic	..	..	..	..	..	..	..	3.8
Spain	25.0	32.2	47.1	63.6	17.0	20.3	11.2	16.5
Sweden	36.7	43.4	..	..	34.3	32.0	30.4	30.8
Turkey	..	..	84.2	85.5	..	..	10.2	13.1

(continued)

TABLE 6.4 Indicators of Fiscal Decentralization (*continued*)
(*percent*)

Country	Subnational government spending and employment				Subnational government revenues			
	Share in general government spending[a]		Employment as a share of total public employment		Share in general government revenues[b]		Attribution of tax revenues as percentage of total tax revenue[c]	
	1985[d]	2001[e]	1990[f]	2001[g]	1985[d]	2001[e]	1985	2001
United Kingdom	22.2	25.9	..	..	10.5	7.6	10.2	4.1
Average[k]	29.8	32.2	55.2	57.0	21.5	21.9	16.4	17.8

Source: Adapted from Joumard and Kongsrud 2003, p. 11, table 1.
Note: .. = negligible.
a. Excluding the transfers paid to other levels of government, according to national accounts data.
b. Excluding transfers received from other levels of government and including tax-sharing arrangements, according to national accounts data.
c. Including tax-sharing arrangements, according to revenue statistics data.
d. Or earliest year available: 1986 for Ireland; 1987 for the Netherlands and the United Kingdom; 1990 for Japan, Luxembourg, and Norway; 1991 for Germany; 1993 for Sweden; 1995 for Austria, Belgium, Denmark, Finland, Greece, Portugal, and Spain.
e. Or latest year available: 1996 for Ireland; 1997 for Canada; 1999 for Portugal; 2000 for Japan, Luxembourg, and the United Kingdom.
f. Or earliest year available: 1991 for Germany and New Zealand; 1994 for Poland; 1996 for the Netherlands; 1997 for the Czech Republic, Hungary, and Turkey.
g. Or latest year available: 1998 for Greece and Italy; 1999 for France; 2000 for Austria, Germany, the Netherlands, Poland, Turkey, and the United States.
h. Public sector employment data are registered in full-time equivalent format.
i. Data based on the System of National Accounts 1968 methodology.
j. The share in general government revenues is expressed as a percentage of mainland government revenues.
k. Simple average of federal and unitary countries. Under each heading, the average takes into account only countries for which data are available for both years.

ninth in the ranking of summary indicator of taxing powers. As shown, New Zealand local government has extensive discretion in setting rates: Drawing a comparison with the fiscal autonomy of Norwegian municipal government, Caulfield (2002, p. 157) has observed that "New Zealand's level of autonomy over that [tax] share is much greater because it has discretion over both the tax rate and base." It thus appears that local government in New Zealand enjoys a comparatively high degree of fiscal autonomy in terms of discretion with respect to striking a rate. It is worth recalling that property taxes constitute an overwhelming proportion of total local government tax in New Zealand.

TABLE 6.5 Subnational Government Taxing Powers in Selected OECD
Countries, 1995
(*percent*)

Country	Subnational government taxes relative to		Discretion to set taxes[a]	Summary indicator of taxing powers[b]
	Total taxes	GDP		
Sweden	32.6	15.5	100.0	15.5
Denmark	31.3	15.5	95.1	14.7
Switzerland	35.8	11.9	92.4	11.0
Finland	21.8	9.8	89.0	8.7
Belgium	27.9	12.4	57.9	7.2
Iceland	20.4	6.4	100.0	6.4
Japan	24.2	6.8	90.3	6.1
Spain	13.3	4.4	66.6	2.9
New Zealand	5.3	2.0	98.0	2.0
Germany	29.0	11.1	12.8	1.4
Poland	7.5	3.0	46.0	1.4
United Kingdom	3.9	1.4	100.0	1.4
Netherlands	2.7	1.1	100.0	1.1
Austria	20.9	8.7	9.5	0.8
Portugal	5.6	1.8	31.5	0.6
Czech Republic	12.9	5.2	10.0	0.5
Hungary	2.6	1.1	30.0	0.3
Norway	19.7	7.9	3.3	0.3
Mexico	3.3	0.6	11.2	0.1

Source: Adapted from Joumard and Kongsrud 2003, p. 13, table 2.
Note: The countries are ranked in descending order according to the value of the summary indicator of taxing
powers.
a. The figures show the percentage of a country's total taxes for which subnational governments hold full
   discretion over the tax rate, the tax base, or both the tax rate and the tax base. A value of 100 designates full
   discretion.
b. The summary indicator is the product of the ratio of subnational government taxes to GDP and the degree
   of discretion to set taxes. Thus, it measures subnational government taxes with full discretion as a percentage of GDP.

Macroeconomic management questions in local governance, which
form an important part of the Joumard and Kongsrud (2003) taxonomic
system, have not yet been addressed in this chapter. Fiscal discipline at
the local level represents an important macroeconomic consideration
because unexpected high local public expenditure can have adverse
external effects on the broader economy. In most OECD countries, this

problem is tackled either through cooperative federalism (for example, in Australia) or by means of fiscal rules (for example, in New Zealand). Table 6.6 places New Zealand in the context of other OECD nations with respect to fiscal discipline.

Various types of fiscal rules regimes can be used, including those that target the overall budget deficit, the operating deficit, a ceiling on subnational debt, and a ceiling on expenditure. As shown, New Zealand prevents local authorities from using operating budget deficits. Table 6.7 situates New Zealand local government within an international context.

TABLE 6.6 Strategies for Ensuring Fiscal Discipline

Administrative control	Centrally imposed rules	Formalized cooperation	No institutional coordination
France, Greece, Ireland, Japan, Republic of Korea, Luxembourg, Turkey, United Kingdom	Brazil, Finland, Hungary, Italy[a], New Zealand, Norway, Poland, Portugal, Slovak Republic, Sweden	Australia, Austria, Belgium, Denmark, Germany, Iceland, Netherlands, Spain	Canada[b], Czech Republic, Mexico, Switzerland[b], United States

Source: Adapted from Joumard and Kongsrud 2003, p. 43, table 6.
Note: This table emphasizes the main coordination strategy in place in different countries. However, the relationship among different government tiers is complex, and the division of countries in this table is, therefore, not clear cut. In practice, such controls result in limited fiscal autonomy at the subnational level.
a. A domestic stability pact has been imposed by the central government, but the enforcement of the pact is left to a cooperative institution.
b. Canada and Switzerland have loose and informal budget coordination mechanisms.

TABLE 6.7 Use of Rules and Sanctions in Selected Countries

Type of rule or sanction	Sanctions in case of noncompliance		
	No sanctions	Administrative sanctions	Financial sanctions
Deficit target[a]	Finland, Sweden	Belgium, Spain	Austria
Operating deficit target[b]	Italy, New Zealand, Portugal	Norway	Slovak Republic
Debt ceiling[c]	Hungary	Poland	Brazil, Portugal
Expenditure ceiling	Germany	Belgium	

Source: Adapted from Joumard and Kongsrud 2003, p. 44, table 7.
a. Usually takes the form of a balanced budget requirement.
b. May also take the form of a "golden rule."
c. Limits on debt service, debt-to-revenue ratio, or debt-to-GDP ratio.

TABLE 6.8 Fiscal Framework and Enforcement Mechanisms

Country	Fiscal framework	Enforcement mechanisms
New Zealand	*Fiscal rule:* Local authorities are required by law to set operating revenues at a level sufficient to cover operating expenses in any financial year (with a relatively narrow exception to run deficits). Local authorities are largely self-funded, and the central government has no formal role in reviewing or approving the budgets of local authorities. *Borrowing:* No restrictions on borrowing.	*Market discipline:* Subnational loans are not guaranteed by central government.

Source: Adapted from Joumard and Kongsrud 2003, pp. 50–57, annex table A1.

Even though central government does not regulate borrowing by New Zealand municipal councils, except by forbidding borrowing to cover operating deficits, lending activity is nevertheless controlled by market discipline because local authority debt is not guaranteed by the national exchequer. As shown earlier, this approach appears to have worked well in the case of New Zealand. The fiscal rules that the central government imposes on municipal councils in New Zealand are summarized in table 6.8.

Lessons for Developing Countries

In common with most other advanced English-speaking democracies, New Zealand local government has experienced bracing reforms over the past two decades. Although the nature of local government reform across Australia, Canada, the United Kingdom, and the United States has differed considerably in both its breadth and detail, a concern with enhancing the economic efficiency of municipal service delivery has formed the capstone of their various reform initiatives. Nevertheless, the New Zealand experience is particularly instructive because it followed on the heels of a radical restructuring of the entire New Zealand public sector, a transformation that not only preceded similar reforms elsewhere but also exceeded them in both its extent and its degree (Dollery and Wallis 2001).

Most writers on local government policy in New Zealand take the position that the passage of the Local Government Act 1989 marks its most significant historical watershed (see, for instance, Bush 2003; Palmer and Palmer 2004). The territorial and organizational restructuring that followed this legislation effectively modernized this sector and made it possible for policy makers to consider the option of devolving to local authorities the powers of general competence—an option that was eventually legislated for in the Local Government Act 2002.

Any lessons taken from the New Zealand experience for local government restructuring in developing countries should be considered against the background of this relatively recent modernization. What emerges from the historical evolution of New Zealand local governance is that from 1876 (when the two-tier, central-local government structure was first established in New Zealand) until 1989, local government was allowed to develop in a way that perpetuated its institutional weaknesses. Thus, although for a country of its size New Zealand has historically had a vast number of local authorities (with more than 700 authorities existing before the 1989 reforms), by comparison with most of the OECD area, excluding Australia, the functions of local government have been extremely limited. This situation is reflected in the fact that New Zealand's local authorities have never had primary responsibility for health services, income redistribution, justice, police, or education; in addition, until 2002, they had not even been given the legal power of general competence. The proliferation of small authorities and the ad hoc formation of special authorities created a dynamic in which the more authorities there were, the more their overlapping functional boundaries led to weakness and the stronger central government became as a consequence.

The question of municipal reform did periodically rise to prominence on the policy agenda, particularly in the form of restructuring through council mergers, but supporters of the status quo were invariably able to mount sufficient resistance to block this first step to modernizing local government. This resistance was effective not only because it reflected the pressures of local parochialism but also because the functions of local government were so limited relative to central government that little was to be gained from a more efficient and rational municipal structure. Accordingly, despite the emergence of reasonably broad bipartisan support for local government amalgamation after the formation of the Local Government Commission in 1946, neither of the two major political parties was able and willing to take the risk of pushing through necessary reforms.

This position was transformed with the election of a reformist Labour Government in 1984. The amalgamation of small municipal councils into larger local government units not only was featured in its election manifesto but also appeared to be the pet reform initiative of Michael Bassett, its minister of local government, and Brian Elwood, who was appointed in 1985 to chair the Local Government Commission. In an insightful article, Bassett (1996) provided his own account of how these two "policy entrepreneurs" were able to couple municipal amalgamation with their government's drive to establish a contractualist system of public management at all levels of government in New Zealand and to succeed, where their predecessors had failed, in overcoming resistance to these structural reforms. According to Bassett (1996), the reform process was akin to a military campaign in which speed, control of the "commanding heights" of the policy process, and a refusal to be deflected from the achievement of clear objectives were of the essence. Such blitzkrieg tactics have been severely criticized for their tendency to circumvent and undermine public trust in the democratic policy process in New Zealand. However, both Bassett and Elwood appear to have adopted the view that the ends justified the means if the reforms could be designed to balance democratization of process and the efficient and effective use of limited resources.

From the perspective of its architects, the objectives of the municipal reform process were relatively straightforward. Bassett sought "technically stronger, functionally more efficient and politically more accountable local authorities with whom the central government could discuss meaningful devolution of functions to the local level." Moreover, he argued that "it was my goal to move to the next stage which I saw as enactment of a general power of competence for local government" because "my vision was, and still is, that local government should be real government; that there should be as few restrictions on powers as possible, and that councils should be driven by the principles of sound business management and act transparently and accountably." In addition, the "contracting out of services, and the sale of business ventures would have my support where these actions met proper criteria" (Bassett 1996, p. 34).

The way in which Bassett and Elwood sought to reconcile the potentially conflicting values between local democracy and municipal efficiency by engaging the local government policy subsystem on a quest for greater accountability has been a source of some debate. For example, McKinlay (1998) evaluated the reform process from the perspective of "what was ordered" and "what has been delivered." He also examined the way in which the reform policy was advanced through additional reporting requirements imposed by the Local Government Amendment Act 1996 that sought to make more transparent those longer-term council decisions in the areas of financing and service delivery. The reforms implemented between 1989 and 1996 can be viewed as a process that eventually produced an entirely new structure for local authorities in New Zealand. The most salient aspects of this new structure are the areas of governance, management, organization, service delivery, consultation, finance, and human resources.

McDermott and Forgie (1999) provided a detailed empirical analysis of the effect of these structural reforms on the real value, relative size, and functional composition of New Zealand local government spending as well as on the democratic functions. The statistical material produced by McDermott and Forgie (1999) seems to suggest a trend toward greater activism in the 1990s as local authorities reallocated spending from a services to property approach to a services to the people approach, while substantially absorbing the costs of complying with the accountability requirements of the 1989 reforms and the increased statutory responsibilities for environmental regulation imposed by the Resource Management Act 1991, without significantly increasing their spending or the burden on ratepayers. Although McDermott and Forgie (1999) view these trends as an achievement, those same trends have also been seen as a source of concern by a minimalist advocacy coalition, which largely took its lead from the New Zealand Business Roundtable (NZBR). The NZBR, a self-selected lobby group that includes in its membership most of New Zealand's leading chief executives, is alarmed that the growing activism of local authorities could place more publicly funded services outside the control of the center and diminish the capacity for activist councils to meet the demand for "traditional" local public goods.

The findings by McDermott and Forgie (1999) about shifts in the real value, relative size, and functional composition of New Zealand local government spending are shown in tables 6.9, 6.10, and 6.11. These findings are representative of the empirical background against which both minimalists and activists have sought to evaluate the effect of the 1989 reforms. Table 6.9 indicates that although public sector reforms appear to have induced a downward (albeit modest) trend in the rate of increase of central government expenditure, the same cannot be said of local government. Spending by local government increased by 2.7 percent in real terms over the 1990s, after falling 0.9 percent in the period immediately preceding the reform of this sector. Table 6.10 nonetheless shows that the effect of these trends on the relative size of local government has been negligible. Local government's share of GDP rose 0.4 percent between 1978 and 1984 and remained stable at approximately 2.4 percent thereafter.

TABLE 6.9 Average Percentage Shift in Final Expenditure, 1978–97

Source	1978–84	1985–90	1991–97
Central government	3.0	1.5	–0.11
Local government	6.1	–0.9	2.70
Households	1.9	1.9	2.40

Source: Adapted from McDermott and Forgie 1999.

TABLE 6.10 Percentage Changes in Final Expenditure in Relation to GDP, 1978–97

Source	1978	1984	1990	1997
Central government	15.5	16.4	17.2	15.0
Local government	2.0	2.4	2.3	2.4
Household consumption	67.0	65.9	71.1	73.6
Saving	14.2	14.2	7.2	7.5
Nonprofit services	1.0	0.9	1.2	1.5
GDP[a]	99.7	99.8	99.0	100.0

Source: Adapted from McDermott and Forgie 1999.
a. Because of rounding, individual figures may not add up to 100.

TABLE 6.11 Patterns of Functional Change, Lower North Island, 1993/94–1997

Functions	1993–94		1997		Shifts from 1993/94 to 1997	
	NZ$ million	Percentage	NZ$ million	Percentage	NZ$ million	Percentage
Democracy	19.0	3.3	20.9	3.6	1.9	10.0
Regulation	49.9	8.7	52.6	9.0	2.7	5.4
Services to property	339.9	59.7	315.5	53.8	–24.4	–6.7
Services to community	161.7	28.3	196.7	33.6	35.0	21.6
Total	570.5	100.0	585.7	100.0	15.2	30.3

Source: Adapted from McDermott and Forgie 1999.

However, these aggregate trends conceal significant changes in the functional composition of expenditure, shown in table 6.11. Although table 6.11 is based on McDermott and Forgie's (1999) analysis of the annual reports of 15 councils covering both urban and rural areas in the Lower North Island over the period from 1993 to 1997, it is representative of a nationwide trend that both minimalists and activists have highlighted. The increases in the costs of democracy and expenditure on regulation reflect not only the additional reporting, monitoring, and consultation that were imposed on councils but also their greater responsibility for environmental regulation. However, the most dramatic expansion in spending has been on services to the community, which has more than offset the reduction in spending on property services, thus confirming the proposition that any potential for contraction of local government has been offset by a realignment of functions.

From a minimalist perspective, the welcome emphasis that activists such as McDermott and Forgie (1999) place on these trends is itself a source of concern. These writers view as an achievement the fact that local authorities have been able to absorb the costs of complying with the accountability requirements of the 1989 reforms and the increased statutory responsibilities for environmental regulation imposed by the Resource Management Act 1991, all without significantly increasing their spending or the burden on ratepayers. However, the NZBR position is that this achievement is simply not good enough. Central government departments also underwent a radical restructuring after 1989 and had to cope with the burden of complying with the demands of what Schick (1996, p. 13) termed a "hard-edged contractualism." However, the fact that local government spending tended to creep upward during the period from 1991 to 1997 (a period in which tight fiscal discipline reversed the upward drift of central government spending) may be attributable, at least in part, to the fact that local authorities were under less pressure to seek efficiency gains to offset additional compliance costs because they continued to have the discretion to pass those costs on in the form of rate increases.

In an analogous fashion, minimalists similarly view the trend toward a functional realignment of local government spending in a way that is diametrically opposed to that of activists. On the one hand, McDermott and Forgie (1999) suggest that the effect of the 1989 reforms should be positively evaluated in terms of the way that the reforms enhanced the capacity of local authorities to take on more functions and thereby to play a more activist role in the social and economic development of their communities rather than be evaluated in terms of any overall contraction in the size of this sector. On the other hand, the NZBR has become increasingly concerned that this trend could place more publicly funded services outside the control of the central government and, consequently, could diminish the capacity for activist councils to meet the demand for traditional local public goods. The NZBR has also argued that some of those urban councils that "continue to engage in a wide range of activities that should be left to the private sector or central government" may have "neglected their traditional activities, such as roading, sewage disposal, and drainage, to such an extent that inadequate services are limiting growth and development" (Kerr 1999, p. 2). Through such arguments, the NZBR may have cultivated the climate of mistrust in local government that shaped recent proposals for the reform of road and water service delivery.

The minimalist desire for smaller local government that focuses on its "core business" has been presented by Roger Kerr (1999). He essentially proposed that local government policy should be shaped by the residuality principle—namely, "that local government should be selected only where the benefits of such an option exceed all other institutional arrangements" (Kerr 1999, p. 3). Kerr conceded that local authorities may have a comparative institutional advantage in "administering necessary local regulations" (Kerr 1999, p. 4) and in funding (but not typically providing) genuinely local public goods, such as library services and rubbish collection, whose benefits do not extend significantly beyond a particular community. Nevertheless, he argued that even when councils possess superior information on the value that their communities place on such goods, relatively weak accountability arrangements may not give them sufficient incentive to use that knowledge to the benefit of their communities.

An alternative perspective is presented by Reid (1999), who expressed the concern that, during the 1990s, a process of devolution occurred in an ad hoc manner in the absence of any overarching policy framework to organize and structure central-local governance relations. Reid has proposed that the devolution of government functions to the local level should be governed by the subsidiarity principle that "no organization should be bigger than necessary and nothing should be done by a larger and higher unit that can be done by a lower and smaller unit" (1999, p. 166). Reid (1999) goes on to argue that this principle could be used to formulate a checklist of the key criteria for determining the location of accountability, not only among different spheres of government but also between governments and communities. Thus, although this principle can be contrasted with the residuality principle in that it implies a presumption for, rather than against, the devolution of responsibilities to local government, its application would require an empirical assessment of the capability of different levels of government to undertake particular activities. The granting of general powers of competence to local authorities through the Local Government Act of

2002 would seem to represent a significant advance in the activist quest for principled devolution (Reid 2003).

How can these developments in the restructuring of municipal governance in New Zealand be generalized in a way to suggest lessons for developing countries? First, from the perspective of political economy, the scholarly literature indicates that the New Zealand local government reform process described in this chapter should be counted as one of the areas in which the reformers were highly successful, by both historical and international standards, in overcoming resistance to a radical restructuring of this sector. The reformers appear to have accepted that resistance to restructuring of this magnitude could be expected to subside after it was undertaken only if those reforms established the conditions for a postreform consensus on the core objective according to which the reforms were to be evaluated. The completion of the restructuring process would then remove the ex ante uncertainty about the identity of winners and losers that Rodrik (1996) has argued provides much of the political support for groups opposing structural reform. It would also reconfigure the policy networks surrounding local governments so that they could be closed as a channel for postreform resistance. By this stage, decision makers in the restructured local authorities would be more reluctant to reverse the process because they would have already incurred the "sunk costs" of complying with the reforming legislation. In addition, they might have begun to experience unforeseen benefits from reform, such as an increased capacity for community governance, which could spring from efforts to comply with the restructuring and managerial disciplines imposed by this legislation.

According to Bassett (1996), policy makers appear to have appreciated that this anticipated decline in resistance may not have materialized if the restructuring had advanced the value of efficiency in local governance at the expense of the value of strengthening local democracy in the sense of making it more responsive to the preferences of local citizens. An advocacy coalition structure could then have emerged in which resistance to the ascendancy of an "efficiency coalition" would have coalesced within a coalition committed to strengthening local democracy. In considering this possibility, Jenkins-Smith and Sabatier (1994, p. 194) have argued that "significant perturbations external to the subsystem (e.g., changes in socioeconomic conditions, system-wide governing coalitions or policy outputs from other subsystems)" could alter the distributions of resources among these rival coalitions and give the local democracy coalition the opportunity to effect a significant change in (or even reverse) the direction of local government policy.

To prevent the future emergence of this type of advocacy coalition framework, Bassett (1996) seems to have attempted to design the municipal reform program to reconcile the conflicting values of efficiency and democracy by engaging the restructured local authorities on a quest for greater accountability. Thus, accountability was established as the core objective of the policy subsystem surrounding local government so reform in this area could unfold in the coherent direction that Schick attributed to the New Zealand public sector reform process at all levels where "accountability has not been an afterthought; it was designed into the system at the outset, and as gaps in accountability have been identified, additional requirements have been imposed" (Schick 1996, p. 73).

It could be argued that the Local Government Amendment Act 1996 is a tribute to the success of the reformers in establishing a consensus on the principles that should guide local government policy development because it represented a logical extension of the concept of accountability contained in the Local Government Act 1989. By the same token, it could also be argued conversely that the 1996 act advanced the quest for greater accountability to the point where it called attention to the issue of central-local government trust, an issue that had much greater potential to divide this policy subsystem along the competing minimalist-activist lines set out above.

At least to some degree, this tendency seems to have been latent, because of a lack of clarity in the understanding of "government failure" that different elements in the 1989 reforming coalition held. On the one hand, the policy entrepreneurs advocating the 1989 reforms appear to have viewed them as the crucial first step in the process of modernizing local government by increasing its capacity "to deal with complex issues and meet local expectations" (Reid 1999, p. 168). On the other hand, the New Zealand Treasury and its highly influential private sector allies in the NZBR, who operated as gatekeepers in seeking to maintain the systemwide coherence of the New Zealand reform process, were essentially economic rationalists who allowed the proposals to advance because they saw the proposals to be consistent with a reform model that sought to minimize the scope for agency failure and fiscal irresponsibility at all levels of New Zealand government. Thus, beneath the surface of the postreform consensus on accountability, divergent views on the comparative institutional advantage of the restructured local authorities have developed that seem to have divided the local government policy subsystem into minimalist and activist advocacy coalitions.

Three features of the advocacy coalition framework proposed by Jenkins-Smith and Sabatier (1994) appear to be relevant to the current debate on the future direction of local government policy in New Zealand. First, Jenkins-Smith and Sabatier (1994) contend that the main controversies in a policy subsystem should involve disputes about the core beliefs of opposing coalitions. There are some indications that this involvement is occurring with respect to the issue of how much trust central government should place in local authorities. This issue cuts to the heart of the different core beliefs about the comparative institutional advantage of local government held by the minimalists, as epitomized by Roger Kerr (1999), and those held by the activists, as represented by Mike Reid (1999, 2003), and it shows the potential these beliefs have to divide the policy subsystem into rival minimalist and activist advocacy coalitions. Second, the divergent ways in which minimalists and activists have evaluated the local government expenditure trends in the 1990s, as set out by McDermott and Forgie (1999), seem consistent with the view that such coalitions will use substantive policy information to buttress their position in an advocacy fashion. Third, the abrupt changes in local government policy direction that have followed the most recent changes in government in New Zealand are in line with the prediction that changes in government can produce this type of shift where they "alter the resources and opportunities of various coalitions" (Jenkins-Smith and Sabatier 1994, p. 193).

The breakdown of the two-party coalition that had formed after the first election under mixed member proportional representation rules in 1996 gave the minority National Cabinet the opportunity to shake off the reform fatigue that had characterized New Zealand governments since 1993 and to embark on some bold reform initiatives along the minimalist lines advocated by the NZBR. In 1998, two of these initiatives—the government recommendations for road reform, known as Better Transport, Better Roads, and the announcement of a comprehensive water review by the minister of commerce—appeared to threaten community involvement in two areas that had traditionally been considered the core business of local authorities. The signal these proposals sent to local authorities was that those authorities were not trusted sufficiently to provide even their core services in an efficient manner and that a National Cabinet and its Treasury advisers had joined the NZBR in the drive to find institutional alternatives to their ownership and management of these services.

These proposals constituted a significant departure from the core objective to make local democracy more effective by making it more accountable, an objective that had formed the basis of the post-1989 consensus on local government policy. Activists within Local Government New Zealand were able to find a common cause with its other members in lobbying to modify these proposals and thus allow local authorities to retain their stake in the governance of road and water services. At issue was the extent of trust that the central government was prepared to place in local councils to manage competing interests, preserve citizen rights of access to basic services, and determine future ownership and service delivery arrangements in respect of assets that play a fundamental role in promoting efficient and cohesive communities.

The issue of central-local trust therefore appears to have replaced the issue of accountability as the primary focus of the local government policy debate. Although a consensus developed on the desirability of strengthening accountability, the debate over road and water reforms has produced a policy subsystem that is more sharply divided. The NZBR, the Treasury, the Manufacturers Federation, and the "New Right" politicians all appear to be lined up against Local Government New Zealand in its efforts to preserve local autonomy and build trust-based relations with the center. Nevertheless, the balance of power appears to be shifting toward Local Government New Zealand. By aligning itself with the social capital movement, it has been able to gain a sympathetic hearing from those government agencies and left-of-center politicians who have sought to "bring back balance to policy development" (Robinson 1997, p. 7) through taking into account the effect of policies on social capital and social cohesion. This support became evident after the election of a Labour-Alliance coalition in 1999, when the new government moved quickly to fulfill its preelection commitment to rebuild relations of trust by initiating a regular forum "to identify policy issues requiring debate and further work and to develop a long-term coherent strategy for local government as a whole" and by indicating that the Better Transport, Better Roads proposal is "well and truly dead" (Hutchings 2000, pp. 11–12). This shift in policy direction culminated in the Local Government Act 2002, which endorsed the activist call for the devolution of authority to local authorities by, at long last, recognizing that they had a power of general competence in their communities. The legislation also acknowledged the increasing role local authorities have come to play in community development by establishing mechanisms according to which they could be held accountable for their performance of that role.

Accordingly, a central lesson for developing countries can be drawn from the political economy of New Zealand local government reform and the evolution of local government policy in New Zealand after the radical restructuring set in motion by the Local Government Act of 1989. That lesson suggests that effective consolidation may be more difficult to achieve than effective implementation. Although the resistance to the municipal reforms subsided significantly once the restructuring process was completed, sources of conflict that were latent within the reforming coalition have surfaced, and the quest to reconcile efficiency and democratic values by making local government more accountable appears to have exhausted itself. Those areas of conflict, which relate to diverging core beliefs on the comparative institutional advantage of local government, have come to reflect the ideological divisions between parties to the left and right of center. They may therefore have the potential to cause more abrupt shifts in local government policy direction after changes in the composition of governing coalitions than would occur if a coherence of policy development were maintained by the effective consolidation of core reform principles.

A second broad lesson that can be drawn for developing countries from the radical New Zealand experience of public sector reform has been discussed inter alia by Wallis and Dollery (2001) and Schick (1998). For example, looking at New Zealand public sector reform in general, rather than local government reform in particular, Wallis and Dollery have argued that "while the New Zealand model may offer a coherent and comprehensive package of contractual solutions to pervasive problems of government failure, the logic of its hard-edged contractualism may hinder the development of social capital required to enhance the [developing] state's capacity in areas where a bottom-up approach to policy implementation is required" (Wallis and Dollery 2001, p. 259). Instead, they support Schick's view that developing nations should follow "a logical sequence of steps that diminish the scope of informality while building managerial capacity, confidence and experience" (Schick 1998, p. 129). In particular, in developing countries, "politicians and officials must concentrate on the basic process of public management" rather than esoteric models of managerial change (Schick 1998, p. 130). Bureaucrats must thus "be able to control inputs before they can control outputs; they must be able to account for cash before they are asked to account for cost; they must abide by uniform rules before they are authorized to make their own rules; they must operate in integrated, centralized departments before being authorized to go it alone in autonomous agencies" (Schick 1998, p. 131). In short, developing countries should focus first on achieving sound public administration and building up the requisite administrative capacity before embarking on more sophisticated methods of delivering local goods and services along the lines of the New Zealand model of local government. Thus, although important lessons from the New Zealand experience of local government reform exist for local governance in developing nations, especially with respect to the political economy of a reform process and the difficulties involved in consolidating a reform program after it is in place, actual public administration should not adopt the technical characteristics of the New Zealand model until the fundamental building blocks of efficacious municipal administration are entrenched.

Notes

1. Names and boundary maps for all New Zealand councils are provided by Local Government New Zealand (2004a).
2. This information is far too voluminous to be reproduced here. It can be found at http://www.measures.net.nz. Full particulars on the sources, nature, and quality of the data can also be found there.
3. Total gross debt as of June 30, 2003, for each of the 74 TLAs can be found at http://www.measures.net.nz, together with definitions of the measures used to compute the data.

References

Bailey, Stephen. 1999. *Local Government Economics: Principles and Practice.* London: Macmillan.

Bassett, Michael. 1996. "The Context of Local Government Reform: The New Zealand Perspective." In *An Agenda for Local Government,* ed. Philip McDermott, Vickie Forgie, and Robert Howell, 29–38. Local Government Studies Occasional Paper. Massey University, Palmerston North, New Zealand.

Bush, Graham. 1995. *Local Government and Politics in New Zealand.* Auckland, New Zealand: Auckland University Press.

————. 2003. "Local Government." In *New Zealand Government and Politics,* 3rd ed., ed. Raymond Miller, 161–70. Auckland, New Zealand: Oxford University Press.

Caulfield, Janice. 2002. "Local Government Finance in OECD Countries." In *Local Government at the Millennium,* ed. Janice Caulfield and Helge O. Larsen, 153–68. Berlin: Leske and Budrich.

————. 2003. "Local Government: Reform in International Perspective." In *Reshaping Australian Local Government: Finance, Governance, and Reform,* ed. Brian E. Dollery, Neil A. Marshall, and Andrew C. Worthington, 11–34. Sydney, Australia: University of New South Wales Press.

Dollery, Brian E. 2002. "A Century of Vertical Fiscal Imbalance in Australian Federalism." *History of Economics Review* 36: 26–43.

————. 2003. "Local Government Failure." In *Reshaping Australian Local Government: Finance, Governance, and Reform,* ed. Brian E. Dollery, Neil A. Marshall, and Andrew C. Worthington, 212–28. Sydney, Australia: University of New South Wales Press.

Dollery, Brian E., and Joe L. Wallis. 2001. *Political Economy of Local Government: Leadership, Reform, and Market Failure.* Cheltenham, U.K.: Edward Elgar.

Drage, Jean. 2002. "New Zealand's Local Government: What of the Future?" In *Local Government at the Millennium,* ed. Janice Caulfield and Helge O. Larsen, 93–110. Berlin: Leske and Budrich.

Hayward, Janine. 2003. "Introduction." In *Local Government and the Treaty of Waitangi,* ed. Janine Hayward, xi–xvi. Melbourne, Australia: Oxford University Press.

Howell, Robert. 1995. "Governance and Management: The New Zealand Experience." In *An Agenda for Local Government,* ed. Philip McDermott, Vickie Forgie, and Robert Howell, 77–82. Local Government Studies Occasional Paper. Massey University, Palmerston North, New Zealand.

Hutchings, John. 2000. "Creating Solutions to Transport Concerns: The New Zealand Experience." Paper presented to the 2000 National Rural Roads Congress, Moree, New South Wales, New Zealand, March 5–8.

Jenkins-Smith, Hank C., and Paul A. Sabatier. 1994. "Evaluating the Advocacy Coalition Framework." *Journal of Public Policy* 14 (2): 175–203.

Joumard, Isabelle, and Per Mathis Kongsrud. 2003. "Fiscal Relations across Government Levels." Economics Department Working Paper 375, Organisation for Economic Co-operation and Development, Paris.

Kerr, Roger. 1999. *Toward a More Efficient and Democratic Local Government.* Hamilton, New Zealand: Business Network.

Kerr, Suzi, Andrew Aitken, and Arthur Grimes. 2004. "Land Taxes and Revenue Needs as Communities Grow and Decline: Evidence from New Zealand." Motu Working Paper 04-01, report to the Lincoln Institute of Land Policy, Wellington.

Local Government New Zealand. 2004a. *Council Websites and Boundary Maps.* http://www.lgnz.co.nz/lg-sector/maps.

———. 2004b. *Local Government New Zealand Measures Reports—2004.* http://www.measures.net.nz.

McDermott, Philip, and Vickie Forgie. 1999. "Trends in Local Government: Efficiency, Functions, and Democracy." *Political Science* 50 (2): 223–41.

McKinlay, Peter. 1998. *Local Government Reform: What Was Ordered and What Has Been Delivered.* Wellington: Local Government New Zealand.

Palmer, Geoffrey, and Matthew Palmer. 2004. *Bridled Power: New Zealand's Constitution and Government,* 4th ed. Melbourne, Australia: Oxford University Press.

Reid, Mike. 1999. "The Central-Local Government Relationship: The Need for a Framework." *Political Science* 50 (2): 164–81.

———. 2003. *Policy Effectiveness and the New Zealand Local Government Act.* Wellington: Local Government New Zealand.

Robinson, David, ed. 1997. *Social Capital and Policy Development.* Wellington: Institute of Policy Studies.

Rodrik, Dani. 1996. "Understanding Economic Policy Reform." *Journal of Economic Literature* 34 (1): 9–41.

Schick, Allen. 1996. *The Spirit of Reform: Managing the New Zealand State Sector at a Time of Change.* Wellington: State Services Commission.

———. 1998. "Why Most Developing Countries Should Try New Zealand's Reforms." *World Bank Research Observer* 13 (1): 123–31.

Statistics New Zealand. 2002. *New Zealand Official Yearbook 2002.* Wellington: Statistics New Zealand.

———. 2004. *Local Authority Statistics.* Wellington: Statistics New Zealand.

Szalai, Ákos, and Álmos T. Tassonyi. 2004. "Value-Based Property Taxation: Options for Hungary." *Environment and Planning C: Government and Policy* 22: 495–521.

Wallis, Joe L., and Brian E. Dollery. 2001. "Government Failure, Social Capital and the Appropriateness of the New Zealand Model for Public Sector Reform in Developing Countries." *World Development* 29 (2): 245–63.

Worthington, Andrew C., and Brian E. Dollery. 2001. "Diversity in Australian Local Government: The Case against the Imposition of National Uniform Standards." *International Review of Public Administration* 6 (1): 49–58.

7

Local Government Organization and Finance: *Nordic Countries*

JØRGEN LOTZ

The Nordic countries are Denmark, Finland, Iceland, Norway, and Sweden. Their total population is only about 24 million; the largest country is Sweden with nearly 9 million inhabitants (see table 7.1). The people of these countries share cultural values and even understand one another's languages, except for Finland, which has somewhat different roots.

The political systems are based on proportional representative democracy and comprise many parties as well as the kind of coalition or even minority governments that are often associated with weak expenditure control,[1] leaving, at times, considerable political power to local politicians and their associations. The Nordics believe in highly egalitarian policies and tolerate tax ratios close to 50 percent of gross domestic product (GDP) to pay for personal welfare services such as education, health, social services, and care for elderly people, free of charge to all. Nevertheless, their public finances are among the healthiest in the Organisation for Economic Co-operation and Development (OECD), with surpluses on the general government accounts.

The average GDP is about 20 percent higher than the European area average, mostly because of a high employment rate rather than high productivity. Also, the employment rate for women is high,

223

224   Jørgen Lotz

TABLE 7.1 Average Population of Local Authorities in Nordic Countries, January 1, 2000

Authority	Average population				
	Denmark[a]	Finland	Iceland	Norway	Sweden
Municipalities	19,600	11,400	2,200	10,300	30,700
Counties	333,100	None	None	235,700	422,000
Nation	5,330,000	5,146,000	278,700	4,478,500	8,861,000

Source: Based on Mønnesland 2001 and national sources.
a. In Denmark, a reform being implemented for 2007 will replace the counties with five regions and will result in the voluntary amalgamation of 271 municipalities into only 98. The average size of the counties will be 1,082,200; the average size of the municipalities will be 56,500.

being related to the extensive coverage of institutions for care of children and elderly people.[2]

The Nordic countries have introduced unsurpassed high degrees of decentralization of their (large) public sectors compared with decentralization in other OECD countries (see table 7.2). Local government expenditure is close to 20 percent of GDP compared with an average of less than 10 percent for the other OECD countries, most of the difference being explained by spending on welfare services, including some social transfers. Nordic local revenues are double those of non-Nordic countries, the difference being equivalent to the difference in revenue from local income taxes.

The high degree of decentralization generally enjoys wide support in the populations. It is a common belief that the Nordic public sectors are less

TABLE 7.2 Measures of Decentralization, Nordic Countries Compared with Other OECD Countries, Recent Years

Measure	Average OECD non-Nordic countries	Average Nordic countries
Local government expenditure (as % GDP)	9.2	19.1
Local welfare expenditure (as % GDP)	4.2	12.3
Local current revenue (as % GDP)	9.0	19.7
Local current revenue (as % general government revenues)	26.2	42.3
Local income tax revenue (as % GDP)	1.3	10.6

Source: Based on IMF 2002 and OECD 2001.

bureaucratic and are more user friendly and efficient than the public sectors in less decentralized countries. Surveys suggest that the Nordic populations are more satisfied with their public sectors than people in other countries are with theirs (Finansministeriet 1998).

The Nordic experience demonstrates that large, decentralized public sectors are not incompatible with prosperity and citizen satisfaction. But the idea of welfare gains from decentralization in the Tiebout-Musgrave-Oates tradition is not particularly relevant.[3] Decentralization in the Nordic countries has quite a different meaning from that in the standard literature, mainly as a consequence of the decentralization of redistributing functions, the low mobility of households, and the objective to offer similar high-quality public services to all citizens.

This chapter discusses a number of aspects of the Nordic decentralization compared with the systems of other countries. Considered first are the legal and organizational frameworks and the development of the Nordic systems, as well as the size and structure of the local sector. Next, the discussion focuses on the decentralization of expenditure and on the decentralization of revenues—in particular, issues related to the powerful local own-source taxation rights and the Nordic local income tax. The chapter also explores issues relating to borrowing and to budget constraints, as well as the role of general, specific, and discretionary grants.[4] Last, the discussion centers on the horizontal imbalances and equalization. The chapter ends with a summary and conclusions.

Throughout the chapter runs the theme of concern about control—control not only to secure a hard budget constraint but also, perhaps even more, to secure the satisfaction of national needs without losing the advantages of decentralization. These concerns vary and do not arise at the same time in all countries. For example, Danish people have concerns about how to prevent local governments from raising tax rates to unsustainable levels in a globalized world. Swedish and Finnish people are concerned about how to maintain an intertemporal balance and how to avoid increased local deficits that contribute to macroeconomic overheating. And all Nordic people share concern about how to ensure that local governments deliver high-quality services that are accessible to all citizens at a low cost.

Had this chapter been written 20 years ago, the description of the concerns for the Nordic governments would have been very different. At that time, the challenge was to improve the regulatory framework and liberalize local governments from overly bureaucratic rules. Efficiency and savings through improved regulation were key words.

But times have changed. The difficult challenge for politicians of today in the Nordic countries is quite different—to find the best methods of controls in a workable compromise between decentralization and national priorities.

Legal and Organizational Frameworks: The Development of Nordic Decentralization

Two forces have played and are playing a role in shaping the systems of decentralized public sectors in the Nordic countries.[5] One is concern about administrative efficiency. The other is to encourage and strengthen democracy and spread the political power more broadly.

The local government legislation in Denmark and Sweden originates from oligarchic types of local administration a few centuries ago. At the time, administrative conditions were poor. Effective central rule was impossible because lines of communication were time-consuming and the quality of the administration was poor. Thus, even the absolute monarchs needed some kind of local administration, primarily through agents appointed by the king or by parsons.

Political readiness to share power more broadly also seems to have been in play. Contemporary Swedish historians argue that the king needed the alliance with the parsons and peasants of the local governments to counterbalance the power of the nobility (Wetterberg 1997). And powerful and enlightened advisers to the Nordic kings understood the importance of the revolutionary developments in central Europe.

The result was a process of democratization of the local administrations beginning in the mid-19th century. The motives behind this process seem to have been both efficiency and democracy. The central government needed local expertise and human resources. And early in the 20th century, contemporary ideas of democracy came to play a role in promoting local government.

But democracy came at a price. Obviously, as long as local government councils were a mixture of elected and appointed members, central governments had significant instruments of control. The counties—having in their early life both control and approval functions over the municipalities—were headed by centrally appointed civil servants, and the administrative chiefs in the cities also were appointed by the king. The appointed people came from positions in the central administration; the local appointment was normally the final step of their career. Even up to quite recent times, in some cases, chief local executives were centrally appointed.

In general, the role of government-appointed civil servants has now been reduced to handling appeals on the legality of local acts. The counties generally have no controlling functions in relation to municipalities, and their chief executives are now elected. The control problem did not become easier.

Legislation on local government functions distinguishes between what is here called *local communal affairs* and *local delegated affairs*. Because the difference between these terms is a legal distinction, it needs to be precise. What in economic terms is called a *local public good* would tend to fall in the category of local communal affairs. In contrast, it would be difficult to classify a national public good as anything but a local delegated affair.

Local Communal Affairs

In Norway and Sweden, local governments have not only the right to decide on all matters relating to their own local communal problems but also the right to finance expenditures related to such matters. For example, in Sweden, local communal problems were understood to be those concerning more than 75 percent of the local population. Today, the legal conditions in Sweden are modified somewhat: a local government in Sweden (as in Norway) may now take up any function of a local communal nature when it is not by law made the responsibility of another public agency and when it is not commercial. A Norwegian commission report (NOU 1990) describes this policy as being extremely laissez-faire, but despite this criticism, local activity remained unimportant until the 21st century.

Denmark has taken a more centralized legal approach. Danish local governments were, until recent times, allowed only to take up functions specifically delegated to them by law.[6] However, this difference has not resulted in significant differences in the size and functions of local government in the three countries.

Thus, considering the Nordic countries in general, when local activity increased through the past century, it was often local governments—the bigger ones in particular—that took up new joint local functions. Subsequently, these new local functions were made mandatory by central legislation after the local experiment had been evaluated.

Local Delegated Affairs

Most local expenditure in the Nordic countries of today is for delegated (or mandated) functions. These functions are described in special legislation, quite often in detail, not only with respect to the outcome to be produced but also, in some cases, with respect to the methods of production.

The legislation in any specific country is drafted by and presented to the parliament by the sector ministries. In the 1950s and 1960s, the ministries responsible for the mandated functions were greatly concerned about how to supervise and control local governments. The eagerness to control was and is perhaps most marked in Norway, where, until recently, the mandated sectors for a municipality had their own local earmarked grants, and the municipalities for each sector had to balance the respective expenditure against their earmarked revenues. In all the Nordic countries, these efforts resulted in much bureaucracy.

During the 1970s, the existing systems of controls of local elected bodies were increasingly criticized. Many examples of bureaucratic, elaborate, and complicated decision making were cited. For example, a Danish newspaper could report that the construction of a public roadside toilet required the approval of more than 20 authorities.

This development was part of a world trend, in line with Ronald Reagan's and Margaret Thatcher's policies of deregulation in the United States and United Kingdom. The trust in planning and in big government was no longer there. Instead, the institutions were asked to produce a desired outcome in the way they found best, and they were given a budget to accomplish those outcomes. The control became ex post facto and was related to whether the outcome had been forthcoming and to how effectively and efficiently the outcome had been achieved.

Already in the 1970s, steps had been taken to eliminate what was called "double administration." In the 1980s, Denmark and Sweden organized the "free commune" experiments, resulting in a number of simplifications of legislation. Local governments today rarely find reasons to complain about regulation's being an obstacle to efficiency.

But the purpose of these reforms was not to give up the central government's right to design the outcome of the delegated functions. It was to get a more efficient, flexible public sector—a point that was perhaps a bit overlooked in the frenzy of reform and deregulation during the 1970s and 1980s. Parliaments in the Nordic countries rarely sought to decentralize the outcome of public functions. The goal of decentralization was, first of all, to get centrally delegated public services delivered more effectively than would have been the case with direct central delivery.

The Control Question

Several arguments have been made (see, for example, Lotz 1991) about why some central control of local government activity is called for:

- Local governments tend to act in a countercyclical way.
- Local government expansion crowds out capital or real resources.
- Local borrowing is inflationary.
- Local income tax increases result in wage pressure and disincentives, in reduced private savings, and in reduced labor supply.

Hence, Nordic countries had to find ways to ensure that local decisions would conform both to national priorities and to macroeconomic objectives. Many instruments could be used to ensure that local priorities would conform to national priorities, including legislation, specific grants, discretionary grants, and rules for borrowing. However, with respect to macroeconomic control, the central government could not use the same tools for local government activity as it used to influence private demand (tax and credit policies), because public decision making is not as swift and strong as private reactions to economic incentives. Other ways had to be found.

The basic instrument for macroeconomic control in Norway has, since 1911, been a capping of local tax rates. Iceland has set an extremely narrow interval for local tax rates. In Finland, the main instruments of controls are the block grant system and a system of negotiations between key ministers and the local government association. In Sweden, control became a concern in the 1990s when a tax freeze and, later, fines on local tax increases were tried; both have now been replaced with rules for balancing local government budgets.

Denmark and, in a less formal way, the other Nordic countries have annual negotiations between the chairmanship of the local government associations and senior ministers of the government—in other words, between the local government associations and the national government. In Denmark, the negotiations are concluded with an agreement, and this approach has been the prime instrument of Danish control. The agreement obliges the national government to seek parliamentary approval of an agreed amount of grants, and it obliges the local government associations to recommend that their members respect the agreed tax rates and level of activity for the following year. But the value of a system built on agreements with the associations depends on whether their members follow the agreed recommendations. Some observers have found that, in Denmark, compliance has not been the case and that local governments have not followed the agreements made by their associations well enough (OECD 2003a).

The local government associations in the Nordic countries play an important role in advising on national legislation related to delegated functions and in communicating macroeconomic signals from the central government to the local governments. It is generally believed that there are national benefits in having strong local government associations. In Denmark, these associations became powerfully influential after they united into two associations, one for all municipalities and another for all counties. These united associations are now presenting the views of local authorities in communications and negotiations with the central government and its agencies. In Sweden, local government associations play the same role; they are now consolidating counties and municipalities into one association to improve their influence, but the Swedish associations perhaps have interfered less in national policy making than their Danish counterparts. The associations in the other Nordic countries are strong and influential, though perhaps less so than in Denmark and Sweden.

The central government side of organizing local government matters frequently changes when new governments take office. Most often, the ministry of interior (MOI) in the various countries is responsible for the legislation relating to the organization of local governments, and it is the responsibility of the ministry of finance (MOF) within those countries to ensure that local policies are in accordance with central priorities and macroeconomic objectives. In Norway, the formal ministerial responsibility for grants is with the MOI, whereas the macroeconomic control of local government activity is shared between the MOI and the MOF. In Denmark and Sweden, control used to be the responsibility of the MOI. But in the early 1990s, the responsibility for control in Denmark was transferred to the MOF, and in Sweden, the MOI was abolished in 1996 and the legal questions were transferred to the Ministry of Legal Affairs (in 2003, they also were moved to the MOF). In Denmark, legal questions, borrowing, and distribution of grants are still the responsibility of the MOI.

Have the control efforts been successful? Lotz (1991) compared the policy objectives with actual local government behavior during the 1980s in Denmark, the Netherlands, Norway, Sweden, and the United Kingdom and found that only the Danish model of negotiation had delivered results. Jens Blom-Hansen (1997) obtained the same result, repeating this exercise for Denmark, Norway, and Sweden and including the years up to 1997. But since the mid-1990s, central government dissatisfaction has been growing in Denmark—as in Norway—with local government performance.

Size and Structure of Local Governments: Amalgamations and the Alternatives

The population size of the local jurisdictions limits which functions they are able to perform. In all Nordic countries, changes in local government structure require legislation, and local participation in the decision is assumed (Council of Europe 1995). Local jurisdictions in the Nordic countries are relatively large after a strong wave of amalgamations in the second half of the 20th century that were initiated by migration from rural areas to the cities and that resulted in small municipalities.

But now, discussions on the optimal size of local jurisdictions have again surfaced in the Nordic countries, not only in Finland and Norway with the smallest units but also in the other countries. The structure of the local government, the working of the middle tier (box 7.1), and the handling of functions by the smallest municipalities have again come under discussion. The coming years will probably see changes in the Nordic local government structures.

But amalgamations are not without costs. The past waves of amalgamations had been compulsory after voluntary attempts had failed, and the political costs of compulsory amalgamations are high. Ongoing research in Denmark and Finland (Moisio and Uusitalo 2003) will show that when small and big municipalities are amalgamated, increased local total spending is likely to result, despite savings on administrative expenditure. Early research in Denmark (Mouritzen 1991) had suggested more satisfaction with local government in small municipalities than in large ones; however, later examinations tend to show that the difference is, rather, between the satisfaction of the populations in rural and in urban areas (Finansministeriet 1997; Lolle 2001).

Wetterberg (1997) has argued that a decrease to fewer local jurisdictions would weaken the democratic role of local government because fewer local jurisdictions lead to fewer elected council members, which suggests that fewer people then will be schooled in practical politics. Pettersson-Lidbom and Wiklund (2002) found that the larger the local council is, the smaller expenditures tend to be, which could be relevant if larger jurisdictions lead to larger councils.[7]

The urge for amalgamations of small jurisdictions results in particular from the idea that capability depends on size and from the idea that such amalgamations lead to economies of scale. In relation to the idea that capability depends on size, it is argued that the small jurisdictions are unable to handle more complicated functions, thus preventing decentralization of functions to the most efficient level. It is also argued that the smallest municipalities cannot attract suitable local councilors or qualified staff members for many of their functions, including administering taxes, protecting the environment, or addressing complicated social problems.

BOX 7.1 The Middle Tier of Local Government

A regional tier of government, as found in federal countries or large unitary countries such as France, Italy, Spain, and the United Kingdom, generally does not exist in the Nordic countries. In 1994, Finland, normally described as a one-tier country, created regional councils to carry out regional plan functions and to promote local employment opportunities, but these councils are central government agencies, and their budgets are small. Iceland is too small for a middle tier.

But Denmark, Norway, and Sweden have powerful local elected county councils (see table 7.1). Denmark's and Sweden's councils have own-source taxation rights, can run hospitals, and oversee intermediate education and specialized social policy. The councils' role in running the hospitals, however, has recently come under critical discussion. Norway has transferred the hospitals to new regional state authorities. In Denmark, the 14 counties will as of 2007 be replaced with five regions, which will be responsible for the supply of health services. Most of the other functions will be transferred to the state or to the new, larger municipalities. The regions will have elected councils, but—unlike the present counties—they will have no taxation rights.

The intermediate levels in the Nordic countries differ in some respects from those found elsewhere. In the Nordic model, the idea behind having an intermediate level is to have local units large enough to handle functions for a larger population size than those at the municipal level. The units of the intermediate level are not above the municipalities but parallel to them and with, in principle though not always in practice, separate and different responsibilities.

This model differs from systems in those countries where the intermediate levels have as a main function the oversight and control of local authorities, including—in some cases—having elements of ministerial regional administration.

Source: Author.

The other idea is that amalgamations may lead to economies of scale for local jurisdictions, as suggested by some empirical studies (Mau Pedersen and Møller 2001). But experts recognized that although economies of scale may be theoretically viable, they may not always be possible to achieve through amalgamations (for example, when small size is attributed to sparse population or minor island municipalities). As previously mentioned, the evidence seems to suggest, rather, that amalgamations lead to increased spending. Furthermore, cross-section studies of economies of scale often lack clear hypotheses and suffer from data problems.

As an alternative to amalgamation, an approach wherein several local governments cooperate in joint production is also being developed. Finland is the extreme example of this new approach, which has no middle tier and in which Finnish municipalities or associations of municipalities are running hospitals. Many fear that such municipal joint production will result in a loss of accountability. Therefore, the producing institutions are in some cases made independent of the local governments; consider, for example, the so-called purchaser-producer split in Sweden and Denmark. In addition, countries are introducing individual free choice of supplier, entitlement legislation for welfare services, and voucher systems. Large savings are realized from tendering functions to the private sector.

Observers have argued that in these developments are embodied threats to the whole idea of decentralizing these services. For Denmark, Finansministeriet (1996a) presented several scenarios showing how the increasing use of market mechanisms may result in the decreasing role of local governments as political units. In addition, Lotz (1998) argued (a) that free choice means speeding up mobility and risks creating tax-haven municipalities in which the rich can get high service for low taxes and (b) that free choice, in combination with the observed trend for party politics to lose popular support, might speed up the disappearance of political local units and increase emphasis on commercial suppliers. For Sweden, Söderström (2002) has argued that social security causes big enough equalization problems between jurisdictions that the financing of it needs to be transferred from the local to the national government. In Norway, von Hagen and Rattsø (2002) argue that the new trend toward entitlements to public services, the demand for equal service in all authorities, and the right of free choice for individuals to choose suppliers could result in municipalities fading out as suppliers of welfare services and their functions again becoming basically local communal affairs.

Those types of concerns are not yet expressed from any political side except possibly in Norway. But the national parliaments have begun to take an interest in the consequences of size for the competence of all local governments to produce similar services, and attempts have been made to provide incentives for voluntary amalgamations. Finland has already had a system of financial incentives for 15 years without any result; the incentives were increased as of 2001, which resulted in an increase in the number of voluntary amalgamations. Iceland has been through a long process of amalgamation, but still 40 percent of the municipalities have fewer than 200 inhabitants. Denmark has seen some voluntary amalgamations in recent years, and the government has introduced changes in the equalization scheme to further this process.

On the possible advantages of having a middle-tier authority, there has been much criticism in the press of the hospitals and their waiting time for treatment. Because hospitals are the dominant function of the middle tiers, this criticism has been linked to the management of the middle-tier authorities. Critics therefore argue either for amalgamation of middle-tier authorities or for their abolishment all together. In Norway, hospitals have been nationalized. In Denmark, a reform being implemented for 2007 will replace the 14 counties with five regions and has resulted in the voluntary amalgamation of 271 municipalities into only 98. In Sweden, the government decided in the 1990s to amalgamate five counties into two.

Decentralizing Expenditure

Local government expenditures in the Nordic countries are nearly 20 percent of GDP, compared with less than 10 percent in other OECD countries (table 7.2), and their local governments are major employers. Local government employment as a percentage of total national employment ranged in 1999 from 12 percent in Iceland to 26 percent in Sweden. The figures for Denmark, Finland, and Norway were 25 percent, 21 percent, and 24 percent, respectively (Mønnesland 2001).

Because the Nordic countries have decentralized the delivery of nearly all welfare services to local authorities, municipalities and counties have virtually no functions of a truly local nature. But they have much freedom in the ways that they produce these services. They are responsible for local planning, for determining the location of public infrastructure and the number of schools and hospitals, for deciding between institutional and home care for elderly people, and so forth. They also are responsible for personnel matters and can hire and fire employees. Wages are set in national negotiations between the local government associations and the unions, but local negotiations are becoming increasingly important.

The local authorities now provide mainly delegated functions, mostly services with redistributing functions such as no-cost schools, poverty assistance, and care and treatment of the sick. In addition, they play a role in providing cash transfers.

This development was speeded up by the creation of the modern welfare system in the 20th century, which resulted in a high level of local expenditure on welfare services, including a local share in transfers such as sickness benefits, housing assistance, disability pensions, and social assistance (see table 7.3)—all supported by conditional grants. As already said, observers have for some years expressed concerns about whether this level of expenditure can continue.

Central governments today have become quite concerned about the quality of the local sector services.[8] There may be differences in their zeal to control, and those differences are extremely difficult to quantify. In Norway, the trust that municipalities can handle the challenges of today is perhaps lower than in the other countries, and though municipalities are responsible for most basic services to citizens, national laws more often than not define minimum quality standards (see, for example, OECD 2002b on Finland).

Decentralizing Revenues

Another distinction of the systems of the Nordic countries compared with those of most other countries is the use of own-source taxes. In Nordic countries, each municipality is allowed to set its own tax rate. Furthermore, the major local tax is the personal income tax, which yields very high local tax revenues compared with own-source taxes in other countries (see table 7.2).

This section first discusses the experiences and problems of macroeconomic controls of own-source local taxes. The discussion then compares the Nordic structure of local taxes with the local tax structures of other countries and describes the Nordic local personal income tax. Next is a discussion of

TABLE 7.3 Relative Importance of Welfare Services in Local Government Budgets

Location	Local government expenditure (% GDP)	Category of local government expenditure (% total)			
		Education	Health	Social security	Total welfare
Non-Nordic countries (average)	8.8	20.8	11.2	12.2	44.3
Nordic countries (average)	20.2	21.2	16.2	30.2	67.5

Source: IMF 2002.

the risk that tax sharing may become a more prominent element in financing Nordic local governments. The section ends with a short description of the use of fees and charges.

Local Own-Source Taxation: Accountability or Irresponsibility?

Local governments in the Nordic countries have in general much higher own-source tax revenues than are seen in other countries. Only scant systematic information is available on the extent to which countries allow their local governments to collect own-source taxes. The OECD (1999) presented figures for 1995 suggesting that 10 out of 18 countries allowed local governments more than 85 percent of their tax revenues as local taxes. However, related to GDP, only five countries (Japan and four Nordic countries) had more than 5 percent own-source local tax revenues. In conclusion, own-source local taxation appears to be a Nordic specialty that is important elsewhere only in Japan (and to some degree Switzerland).

Local governments in the Nordic countries fiercely defend their right to collect own-source taxes. They argue that their own-source taxation rights result in accountability and make the behavior of the local population and local councils more responsible. Own-source taxation means that local residents must suffer higher taxes if they want better services and that taxes will also rise if a local government is inefficient and wasteful. Modest service standards and good management are rewarded by low local taxes.

Seen from the central government point of view, an advantage of local own-source taxation is that, to some extent, it deprives the local councils of the possibility of blaming responsibility for failing to deliver local services on lack of money from the central government. The combination of small vertical imbalances not financed ex ante and own-source local taxation has been used as a recipe for better efficiency, an issue that is taken up again later in this chapter.

Does an international comparison suggest that own-source local taxation is associated with big government? It is undeniable that the countries with own-source local taxation and highly developed welfare services are also the highest taxed countries. But the group of OECD high-tax welfare states also includes countries with limited, if any, local taxation power (Austria, France, and Norway). And Switzerland is an example of a decentralized country with own-source local taxation and a small public sector. No clear conclusion can therefore be drawn as to whether decentralizing taxation powers increases the level of taxation.

But doubts have been raised. It has become fashionable to talk of globalization and international tax competition, and concern is expressed that local governments are driving up the income tax because they ignore the negative externalities in terms of reduced labor supply and growth potential. For own-source local taxation to promote accountability, local governments must function responsibly. Can the Nordic model deliver on this need for tightly disciplined budget constraint?

Borge and Rattsø (1995) have examined the response of local governments to changes in demography for Norwegian municipalities. They conclude that local governments in areas where age groups are in decline are able to resist reallocations and therefore gain in terms of spending per capita. The Danish MOF (Finansministeriet 1996b) found similar asymmetric local reactions among Danish municipalities. These results raise the question whether own-source taxation can be relied on in times of future demographic changes with a growing proportion of elderly people.

It also has been argued that local governments do not raise taxes because they wish to do so but because the pressure for higher expenditure becomes greater than the desire to prevent tax increases. The central government governance plays a role here. If the MOF and the prime minister's office cannot or will not control the behavior of the sector ministers for health, education, social affairs, or environmental protection, who are pressuring local authorities to spend more, then the result is a shift in local government preferences in favor of tax increases (Lotz 2001).

Norway, as already mentioned, many years ago introduced a cap on the local income tax rate, and today, all local governments in Norway apply the maximum rate (OECD 2002c). The situation is somewhat similar in Iceland (Mønnesland 2001). In Norway, a government commission proposed a set of reforms, including introduction of local tax discretion for all municipalities in setting a broad property tax, but this reform proposal failed because of the unpopularity of the property tax (Rattsø 2003).

Heavy threats of sanctions may have, at least temporarily, stabilized local tax rates in Denmark—but at a price of stifling the very variation in tax changes that is the whole rationale behind having a local own-source tax system (OECD 2003a). An interesting solution has been proposed to introduce a system of tradable permits to increase taxes (Det Økonomiske Råd 2002; OECD 2003a), but thus far it has failed to gain support, because it was considered a bit too radical. Moreover, any steps to stop tax increases may not succeed unless ministers for health and social affairs stop pressing for better service.

Sweden imposed a local tax freeze in the early 1990s. Then, in 1997–99, it introduced a fine on local tax increases of 50 percent of the extra revenue over the following three years. That strategy effectively stopped local tax rate changes.[9] The scheme, however, was declared unconstitutional by the constitutional court and was repealed. Since then, local governments in Sweden have been tax averse and are at present more concerned with balancing their budgets and borrowing than with adjusting the local tax rate. Nevertheless, 2003 saw ominous local tax increases in Sweden.

Among the Nordic countries, tax rate setting in Finland has been called "puzzling" (OECD 2003b). The difference between the highest and lowest tax rates has been declining in both Denmark and Sweden in recent years; this difference is now less than 5 percentage points in Sweden and 6 percentage points in Denmark. But even less difference is found in Finland. Despite similar freedom in rate setting, the vast majority of Finnish municipalities set their income tax rates between 18 and 19 percent.[10] The OECD (2003b) explains this action as a result of a tacit agreement not to use the personal income tax regime to compete for taxpayers.

In conclusion, in Denmark, the government has felt dissatisfied the past 10 years about its macroeconomic control of the local government sector. In Sweden, several years of a tax freeze in the early 1990s seemingly halted Swedish local tax increases, but recent experience suggests that the "Danish disease" may spread to Sweden. And can Finland avoid contagion in the long run?

Which Taxes Are Decentralized?

We still await empirical research that could help to clarify why countries choose considerably different tax structures and why convergence over time is exceedingly slow.[11] The same clarification is needed with respect to why different tax structures are chosen at the local level.

Local tax structures are products of national history, culture, and tradition. Those cultural differences are clearly identified in table 7.4.

English-speaking countries have a tradition of enacting local tax structures that are dominated by property taxes. Experts generally agree that property taxes are the easiest to assign to subnational governments—especially to local jurisdictions. Thus, these taxes should play an important role in countries where subnational governments work well (Tanzi 2001). But property taxes seem to have limits as a revenue source; OECD data over a longer period show that in no country has the revenue from property taxes exceeded 3 percent of GDP.[12]

The local tax structures of the unitary countries of central and southern Europe have been characterized by the importance of "other taxes."

TABLE 7.4 Local Tax Structures, 1994
(*nonweighted averages, percent*)

Type of tax (tax-sharing receipts included)	English-speaking countries[a]	Nordic countries[b]	Unitary countries[c]
Income tax	1	91	18
Property tax	92	7	39
Other taxes	7	2	43
Total	100	100	100

Source: Based on OECD 2002e.
a. Australia, Canada, Ireland, New Zealand, the United Kingdom, and the United States.
b. Denmark, Finland, Norway, and Sweden.
c. France, Italy, Portugal, and Spain.

Those other taxes may include composite base taxes, which are now disappearing. For example, business taxes such as the *taxe professionelle* in France and the *Gewerbesteuer* in Germany originally included payroll, turnover, and rental values of building and equipment, but in recent years the tax base has narrowed.

Two taxes, the property tax and the income tax, stand out in practical experience as having interesting possibilities for serving as local taxes, but few countries have adapted their tax systems to make these their local tax instruments. Even when advantages such as the neutrality of the local property tax or the buoyancy of the local income tax are recognized, reforms to change from one major tax source to another are rare.[13] Introduction of local taxes is politically sensitive; new taxes have been difficult to introduce, and once introduced, they are difficult to replace with other local tax sources.

The Nordic Local Income Tax System

The Nordic countries allow local governments to use the income tax as an own-source local tax. The Nordic local income tax is a "piggyback" system; the local government annually votes a flat tax rate to be applied to the taxable income assessed for national income tax purposes. The local flat rate is added to the national (progressive) rates.

Personal income tax

The personal income tax revenue belongs to the jurisdiction where a taxpayer resides and not to the jurisdiction where the taxpayer works, because local expenditure, which is mainly for welfare services, primarily benefits the family. Sharing revenue between the jurisdiction of residence and that of employment has been tried but was given up for administrative reasons.

Corporate income tax

In general, the Nordic local income tax applies only to personal income. It originally included company income, but companies began moving their headquarters to jurisdictions with lower tax rates; therefore, the local corporate income tax was changed to become a shared tax. That change created other problems, not with the taxpayers but with the local authorities fighting legal battles over the right to revenue from companies with offices in many municipalities (banks, for example). Consequently, the local tax on company income was abandoned in Norway and Sweden.

Denmark and Finland still struggle with tax-sharing arrangements that they find difficult to abolish, because the revenue flows disproportionately to bigger cities that have high spending and considerable political influence. Finland, however, has recently cut the local share and compensated for the local revenue loss through block grants, making the argument mainly that the action better protects local governments from cyclical shocks.

In 2003, the Norwegian government decided to reestablish a tax-sharing system for company taxation. The argument used was that it would create incentives for the municipalities to attract business. Two municipalities—one of them being the capital, Oslo—will receive 40 percent of the revenue, and changes in the equalization system have been proposed to compensate the other municipalities, which will lose money in the switch back to a company tax-sharing system. The Norwegian government fully realizes the complications of the system; it will not attempt to distribute the revenue where the profit is created but will legislate distribution based on the municipal distribution of employment in each company.

The revenues from company taxation fluctuate widely from year to year, which argues against using corporate income tax as a local revenue source. Finland is highly aware of the budget instability stemming from fluctuations in corporate income tax revenues. Denmark pays the revenue share to local governments with a three-year lag so that the fluctuations will be foreseeable in the local budget process.

Tax administration and collection

Tax administration is, in all the Nordic countries except Denmark, a central government function. But even in Denmark things are changing: the income assessments of all companies have been centralized, and small Danish local authorities increasingly form joint tax administrations with other authorities. A particular moral hazard arises when equalization is high and assessments are local. The Danish government found a technical solution,[14] but it may not be one that others can copy. Overall, the lesson is to not decentralize the assessments.

The costs of local tax administration are small because the tax piggybacks the existing central government income tax. The only extra requirement in that approach is that the residence of all taxpayers must be established.

Tax collection is accomplished through employer withholding. The employers, in turn, transfer the revenue either to the local authority (in the case of Norway) or to the central government (in the case of Denmark and Sweden). In Denmark and Sweden, the amounts transferred in monthly rates from the central government to each local authority are not the same amounts as those that are collected for that year. For the sake of local predictability of financing, each local authority receives the revenue voted in its budget. In Sweden, local authorities must budget the income tax revenue for the year by applying central government forecasts for income developments[15] (but in subsequent years, there are adjustments to reflect actual revenues). The crucial feature is that the contemporaneousness of the economic cycle and local revenues is broken in both countries, and the local governments become protected against unforeseen cyclical swings in revenue.[16] Thus, under all circumstances, they receive the revenue they have budgeted to finance their expenditure. In Denmark, adjustments occur in subsequent years but are announced ahead so that they enter the local budgets and cause no unexpected revenue shocks.

The situation is different in Norway, where the revenue is transferred by employers to the local authority, which in turn forwards to the central government its share of the revenue, leaving the local finances subject to the cyclical swings in revenue. Proposals were made in Norway to change to the system of the other countries, but local authorities managed to prevent parliamentary approval.

Tax sharing

Tax sharing, well known in continental (particularly German-speaking) Europe, has not become a major source of local revenue in the Nordic countries. Exceptions mentioned above are the capping of the Norwegian income tax and the Danish and Finnish sharing of corporate income tax revenues. The lesson to be learned is that if an own-source local tax is desired, then rate setting should be freely determined. Any intervals or caps could cause the tax system to change over time into a tax-sharing system.

Nevertheless, it is conceivable that tax sharing will be introduced in the Nordic countries in the future. Although the politically powerful local authorities strongly support systems based on own-source taxation, that situation could change. For example, we questioned earlier whether it is possible for central governments to control the growth of local income tax rates. If this issue becomes more serious, then capping may result, and that change may easily become a first step toward tax sharing. Capping may begin with a tax freeze like that in Sweden in the early 1990s, but in the long run, a tax freeze needs to be based on uniform tax rates, which subsequently will result in a tax-sharing system.

Fees and charges

Nordic countries vary considerably in the ways that they use local fees and charges, except in one key way: in all the countries, costs of waste and wastewater treatment are borne fully by the polluters. Another common feature is the strict rule forbidding local authorities to engage in any activity posing competition to private business,[17] though loan guarantees to local commercial activities exist and are often cause for trouble (see Rattsø 2003).

As a percentage of total local government revenues, fees and charges ranged in 1999 from 5 percent in Iceland to 25 percent in Finland. The figures for Denmark, Norway, and Sweden were 21 percent, 14 percent, and 22 percent, respectively. However, comparisons of municipal revenues in terms of their fees and charges tell little about differences in the fees and charges being paid by users. In many cases, utilities—electricity, gas, water, and sewerage—have been transferred to independent enterprises, and their accounts are no longer included in the local budgets. Furthermore, figures for fees and charges include revenue not paid by users but by other local authorities for use of hospital beds, accommodation in old-age homes, and so forth.

In Denmark and Finland, separate accounts must be maintained for municipal utilities, and the tradition is that the prices must equal the costs; that is, neither surplus nor subsidization is allowed, though some softening of this rule has been seen for energy in a first step toward future privatization. In Norway, the legislation demands that the prices for utilities must be below costs, though for waste and wastewater, prices must cover the full costs.

Fees for welfare services are for equity reasons often regulated by law, except in Iceland, where municipalities are free to collect fees for services. In Denmark, Norway, and Sweden, maximum fees have been legislated for child care and old-age care; in Sweden, the argument for child care fees has been to increase female participation in the labor market. There are also, except in Denmark, minor fees for primary health care and hospital stays, and there are copayment systems for pharmaceuticals in all countries.

Borrowing

Theoretical arguments assert that, in the right setting, creditors, homeowners, and the local electorate could provide a good incentive framework for subnational decisions (Rodden, Eskelund, and Litvack 2003). Although the conditions for that possibility seem to be met in the Nordic setup, the main rule for borrowing in the Nordic countries is the traditional "golden rule" restriction, a balanced budget rule implying that current revenues in local governments must finance current spending, including debt servicing. Investments are to a large extent financed by loans. The financing of investment is spread over time, and the design is assumed to stimulate intertemporal efficiency.

But, Rodden, Eskelund, and Litvack (2003) ask, why establish regulations for local governments with respect to borrowing? Originally, regulations were introduced in times when local governments were less trusted and respected than they are now. Over the years, there have been cases of local governments getting into trouble because of excessive borrowing. It is part of Nordic legal tradition that a municipality cannot go bankrupt; hence, bailouts have been needed, demonstrating that a risk exists. The idea of regulating local borrowing in keeping with the implied golden rule has met little opposition and has thus become a nonissue (except in Denmark, which will be discussed later). Another reason to maintain regulation has been that loan-financed expenditure loosens fiscal policy outside the control of the national government.

But the bailout recourse cannot be described as a major softening of the budget constraint. The conditions set for help in terms of savings and budget consolidations are seen as humiliating for the municipal councilors and have considerable preventive effect (see also Rattsø 2003). Under those circumstances, the capital markets have no reason not to lend to local governments in trouble, and there is hardly any market penalty for irresponsible municipal behavior.

Despite the golden rule framework, the risk-averse Nordic local governments often choose to finance investments from their savings, and local investments are not financed 100 percent by loans. In Norway, for example, loan financing has been, on average, 40 to 50 percent of local investments in recent years. In Finland, loan financing has been only about 30 percent of local investments. This level of loan financing means that there is a hidden reserve for extra spending that could in theory materialize one day and become a soft budget constraint. However, not enough variation in local behavior has been observed for this possibility to be a problem in practice.

Since World War II, Norway has seen only a few examples of local governments experiencing serious economic imbalances. In case of slippage, the local governments would have two years to restore a balanced budget. If they were to fail, they would come under the supervision of the central government, which would have to approve their budgets and borrowing.

During the 1970s, much concern arose in Denmark about the macroeconomic destabilization caused by the high rates of growth in local government spending. Because of the high growth rates in that period, the government annually reduced the percentage of investments that were allowed to be financed through loans; by 1980, the percentage was zero, and no municipal borrowing was allowed. Loans to finance investments in utilities, however, are allowed—the reason being that their debt servicing is borne by the consumers, not the taxpayers. Such loans need no prior approval. This area of automatic access to borrowing has, over the years, been expanded through the political process to include other important investments, such as energy savings, slum clearance, ferry connections to small islands, and homes for elderly people.

Mau Pedersen (2002) of the Danish Ministry of Interior—who has participated in the annual negotiations with local government for a number of years—describes some interesting consequences of this policy. One is that tightening or loosening the restrictions on borrowing enters the central government's annual negotiations with the local government associations—a practice he describes as being less complicated and much faster to implement than a change in grants, which would require parliamentary approval. He also notes that permission to borrow has the advantage over grants because it does not reduce the surplus on the central government accounts. However, the European Monetary Union (EMU) debt question—and on this question Denmark has ambitious plans—sets limits for this policy because EMU debt includes not only local but also central government debt. Mau Pedersen also mentions how loan restrictions have been loosened to stimulate activities—at a cost to the fiscal stance.

Mau Pedersen (2002) also expresses concern over the use of the pool of funding made available annually from which the MOI dispenses discretionary loans in response to applications from local authorities. This pool was meant to help small municipalities that were finding it difficult to even out investments over the years, but it is now being used to reach general agreement with the local associations (and this way actually) softening budget constraints.

Finally, Mau Pedersen (2002) notes that the prohibition on borrowing for municipal investments has resulted in municipalities exploring all kinds of sale-and-lease-back arrangements. These arrangements have required detailed and complicated regulation and constant surveillance.

In Finland, municipalities are supposed to maintain a medium-term balance between current receipts and disbursements. Among the municipalities, borrowing to finance building projects is common, whereas borrowing to cover running expenses is rare. Finland requires no prior approval of loans.

In Iceland, municipalities are free to borrow, and approval is not needed. If a municipality is unable to pay its debts, it can be put under the direct administration of the state.

In Sweden, too, municipalities are free to borrow. The current concern there is about how to improve the budget balances so that the need for borrowing can be reduced. The policy has been changing. From 1979 to 1991, the rule was that the budget should be balanced, but this rule was found to be too rigid, and in 1991, it was replaced by a requirement that local governments should follow responsible financial policies. However, in 1997, a new rule was introduced to balance the budget. To be implemented by local governments in 2000 at the latest, the new rule was more clearly defined than the old one and was built on an objective of intergenerational balance (Pettersson-Lidbom and Wiklund 2002). From 1997 to 1999, a fine on tax increases was in operation, squeezing local finances and perhaps adding to the budget-balancing problems that led to reintroduction of a balanced-budget rule. Time will show whether the real problem for Sweden is local government debt or whether it is that the Swedish local tax rates will resume increasing, adding to a tax ratio that is already the highest in the OECD.

The Role of General, Specific, and Discretionary Grants

Hardly any country in the world has a central government that does not pay grants to the local governments. Central governments never allow local governments sufficient taxation powers to finance the full expenditure assigned to them.

This section discusses the grants needed to finance vertical imbalances. A statistical overview provides the background for the subsequent discussion of the Nordic use of grants in regulating local government activity. The section ends with a discussion of specific and discretionary grants as instruments for control of local priorities.

Grant Policy in the Nordic Countries

When one considers grants as a percentage of GDP, only a small difference is evident between the Nordic countries and other countries (see table 7.5). But total local expenditure is much higher in the Nordic countries (see table 7.2), and in view of those data, the Nordic vertical imbalances appear more modest.

An interesting question is why there are vertical imbalances and grants in countries such as Denmark, Finland, and Sweden, where local governments have the taxation power to pay for themselves. In the early 1990s, Danish counties argued for the elimination of grants; they offered to raise county tax rates if the central government would use its budget savings to lower the national tax rates, but the central government flatly refused to accept the offer. Only one explanation seems plausible: grants are instruments of central control that the central governments cannot afford to lose.

One difference between Nordic grant policies and those of many other countries is a mechanism for annual regulation of grants. In the Nordic countries, central governments are obliged to compensate local governments for any costs imposed on them by new regulations or legislation passed by the national parliaments. Furthermore, general grants are adjusted each year to finance the difference between needs and expected tax revenue. In principle, this adjustment feature should help stabilize foreseen financial conditions over the cycle, enabling local governments, in principle, to deliver, without tax increases, the services deemed necessary by the central government.

In practical political life, however, grants often have had a tendency to increase when local tax revenues are booming. In negotiations, local governments have pressured the central government for lavish compensation for any new legislation or for demographic changes causing extra expenditure for local government. Conversely, central governments in Nordic countries have tried to reduce the grants, referring to presumed productivity

TABLE 7.5 Grants to Local Governments, 1999

Location	Grants (as % GDP)	Total current local revenue (as % GDP)	Grants (as % total revenue)
Non-Nordic countries (average)	4.1	9.0	46.0
Nordic countries (average)	5.7	19.7	29.0

Source: Based on IMF 2002.

gains in the local sector, and have focused on small vertical imbalances before the local budgets are made.

Asymmetric information makes it difficult for central authorities to know where the balance is; thus, the Nordic central governments tend to be quite strict about productivity demands. But if their strictness goes too far, it may easily result in unwanted tax increases or deficit financing and accumulation of local debt.

The OECD (2002b) notes no formal relationship between taxes and grants in Finland. In particular, it notes that Finland has no automatic mechanism leading to higher grants in periods of declining tax revenues. But perhaps the concern in Denmark, Finland, and Sweden is, rather, how to avoid higher grants when local tax revenues are booming.

In conclusion, the Nordic model uses grants as instruments to increase the local predictability of funding and to protect local services such as schools as well as health and social services against stabilization policies. Nevertheless, recent experiences of economic crises in Finland and Sweden have shown that pro-cyclical cuts in grants cannot be totally avoided. General grants are not the only parameter entering the annual negotiations, however. Specific and discretionary grants, as well as borrowing, play a role.

Specific Grants

The 1980s and 1990s brought a wave of reforms in the OECD countries to replace specific grants with general grants on a large scale.[18] The reforms were made for several reasons. High reimbursement rates were pushing up spending and had become a drain on the central government finances, often because local discretion had been underestimated. In addition, specific grants required controls, auditing, and much bureaucracy. Furthermore, it was argued that specific grants result in inefficient decision making and reduce local responsibility. But in some countries, specific grants have been used all the time for certain purposes and are not negligible, though internationally, comparable data on grants are not available.

Most Nordic specific grants are conditional, and auditors determine controls ex post facto. Where local discretion is low, grants are often conditional, but to compensate for the lack of central information and to test the strength of local priorities, some local cofinancing is often used. In Denmark, such conditional specific grants are used for local expenditure for mandated transfers (that is, to early retirement, social cash benefits, and so forth) because these expenditures are thought to be outside the control of local authorities. But this approach is now being rethought in Denmark, where the reimbursement rates have recently been reduced to give clearer incentives for local authorities to initiate applications for aid instead of requesting permanent transfers.[19]

Specific grants needing pre-approval—typically for investment, equipment, or projects—have been rare, but they seem to be getting increasing attention. In Finland, specific grants are used for investment purposes, but anecdotal evidence suggests that the conditions are often so tight and cumbersome that the local authorities prefer loans to grant financing.

As stated earlier, in recent years, profuse discretionary grants have been introduced, some of them needing pre-approval for specific projects, not only in the health sector but also for education, child care, and care of elderly people. The OECD (2002b) notes that Finland has no formal relationship between taxes and grants and has no automatic mechanism leading to higher grants in periods of declining tax revenues; however, Denmark, Finland, and Sweden are possibly more concerned about how to prevent higher grants when the local tax revenues are booming. Much effort is currently being made to make the so-called flypaper effect work, so that money will "stick where it hits" and so that specific grants will be transformed into local services and not into private wealth of the local citizens.

Discretionary Grants

Thus far, this chapter has discussed the role of grants whose allocation is determined by criteria in the law. But in the intensive attempts by the central government to control the quality of local services, discretionary grants are also used—though in some cases the discretionary element may be thinly veiled in somewhat unclear criteria listed in the law.

The use of discretionary grants has been a visible recent trend in Denmark. But the role of discretionary grants is also under discussion in Finland and Norway. The OECD recently argued that "a potentially significant source of budgetary abuse by municipalities lies in the moral hazard created by the use of discretionary central government support to those municipalities in financial difficulties" (2003b).

Norway is a case in point. Discretionary grants are small and during the 1970s, were shown to favor municipalities with high debt service costs, which led to strengthening the supervision of local borrowing (Rattsø 2003). As already noted, all Norwegian local governments hold tax rates exactly at the cap for fear that they will be punished by the central government in the allocation of discretionary grants if they reduce the tax rate below the cap. That reaction is strange because equalization in Norway is not based on potential but on actual tax revenues. The discretionary grant systems reduce incentives to improve the cost-efficiency of local spending programs and to cut local taxes.

Horizontal Imbalances and Equalization

The Nordic countries, with their ambitious egalitarian objectives of individual equity and their far-reaching decentralization of welfare services and the local income tax rates, have quite strong reasons for local government equalization. First, the variation in expenditure needs among local governments is large. Expenditure on social assistance is highest in urban areas. Education and child care spending is highest in areas where young families and their children live. Spending on old-age care and institutions for elderly people is highest in areas where the younger adults have left and elderly people are in the majority. Similar differences also exist under central government delivery of social assistance, but they become more visible when the functions are decentralized. The goal to obtain uniformity of service levels requires countries to equalize those differences in costs.

The second reason for local government equalization is much more important in terms of resources to be transferred: there are large differences in local tax bases per inhabitant because taxable incomes and property values differ among local governments. Equalization is needed to prevent local governments in low-income areas from levying income tax rates higher than those levied by local governments with high-income areas. Equalization also helps to prevent the formation of tax havens, where rich people enjoy high service and low tax rates.

Differences among municipalities are largest with respect to the tax base per capita. In Denmark, the poorest municipality has a tax base that is 24 percent below the national average, and the richest has a tax base 100 percent above the average. The same asymmetrical distribution is found in other Nordic countries. Differences in expenditure needs per capita are smaller; in Denmark, the highest need per capita is 14 percent above the national average, and the lowest is 14 percent below.

In the Nordic countries, equalization of differences both in expenditure needs and in tax capacity is implemented, in principle, without central government grants. Instead, equalization is based on the so-called solidarity, or "Robin Hood," model (as found in Germany). In that model, the resources needed to support poor local governments are taken from wealthier ones. The method has the potential to create more complete equalization than equalization that is based on grants given to the poorest local governments, a system that in many countries leaves rich governments untouched. In contrast, the solidarity model also draws rich localities into the equalization system.[20] The OECD (2002b) is concerned that this model poses a risk for rich local governments: with weak equalization, a boom in tax revenues may give rise to spending that may be more difficult to prune in leaner times, and poor governments may run deficits.

The design of the grants systems involves the same basic elements in all Nordic countries. In Denmark, for example, general grants are distributed according to the local share of the tax base; in Sweden, distribution is done according to the local share of the population. A third option now being considered in Denmark is distributing general grants according to the relative share of local expenditure needs. Obviously, the different models call for differences in the equalization design, but they do not necessarily lead to different equalization results (see Lotz 1997 for a more formal presentation of these relationships).

In terms of revenue, table 7.6 shows a generalized comparison of the strength of the equalization systems in the Nordic countries. Although all the Nordic countries use the solidarity equalization model, some (for example, Finland and Norway) tend to protect the rich local governments from the full force of the solidarity equalization. Nevertheless, the rich pay something in all the Nordic countries, and Sweden now has reached a level of equalization believed unrealistic in many countries.[21]

A problem with such powerful equalization systems arises when equalization is based on accounts from an earlier year. If an economic crisis leads to a loss of tax revenue in one year, the equalization payment to compensate for that loss may not come into play until several years later.

Sweden has solved the problem by basing local tax revenues and equalization transfers on known income from two years before, inflated by a national percentage to the expected level of the year. Denmark has not been able to find support for introducing a common updating factor for the known tax base of a previous year but has solved the problem by introducing a system of self-assessed "instant equalization" through which equalization payments are based on the same budget figures as the revenue is. The OECD (2003b) recommends that Finland introduce a similar system to solve problems caused there by lack of synchronization in the timing of revenues and equalization payments.

Equalization is based on the taxable income per person as a measure of potential tax revenue. Norway is an exception and equalizes differences in the actual tax revenue (this way giving an incentive to cut taxes, though without result).

Political criticism from certain quarters in the Nordic countries claims that a high degree of equalization removes the incentive for local governments

TABLE 7.6 Subsidies, Contributions, and Brackets for the Solidarity
Equalization Schemes for Revenue

Country	Amount of subsidy or contribution (% municipal potential tax revenue)	Highest bracket (% national average income tax base)
Subsidies received by poor municipalities		
Denmark[a]	85	90[b]
	45	90–100[b]
Finland	100	90
Norway	90	110
Sweden	95	100
Contributions paid by rich municipalities		
Denmark	85	100[b]
Finland	40	90
Norway	50	134[c]
Sweden	96	100

Source: Mønnesland 2001; OECD 2002c, 2003b.
a. The rates describe the system as of 2006. The first row describes the poorest municipalities (average tax base
   below 90 percent of national average) and the metropolitan municipalities (nearly all above national
   average tax base). The second row describes the rates for the remaining one-third of municipalities, with a
   tax base close to the national average.
b. Approximation; 10 (out of 215) nonmetropolitan municipalities above the national average tax base per
   inhabitant face the low 45 percent equalization, and 8 (out of 60) metropolitan municipalities below the
   national average face the high 85 percent equalization.
c. 2004 data.

to develop their own tax base. The Norwegian government used this argument in 2003 to reintroduce sharing of the corporate income tax, a system
abandoned in 1999. Rattsø states that, for Norway, tax base equalization limits the "incentives for industrial growth" (2003).

Söderström (1994) has thoroughly analyzed this argument. Local politicians want to be reelected, he says, and the best way to secure reelection is to
attract business and employment. This incentive is much more powerful
than whether new business activity fills the coffers of the local government.[22]
The OECD (2003b) argues that a great number of factors influencing location decisions are largely beyond municipal control and that, therefore, they
cannot be used to defend the low equalization rate for wealthy local governments in Finland.

Another favorite criticism is that the system of local government equalization is too complicated. Equalization systems need to be complicated for
several reasons. The category of expenditure needs is a difficult variable to

quantify. Equalization is politically difficult to handle because the losers complain that they had to give so much and the winners complain that they did not get enough. Complicated compromises have to be made, very often by compensating for "needs" of a petty nature, and similar changes are being added over the years.

In conclusion, equalization is complicated and criticized, but it is necessary when important functions are decentralized. It is understandable why the solidarity model of equalization has gained political support in so few countries outside the Nordic group. The alternative method, equalization financed by grants from the central government to needy local governments, by some fiscal illusion seems to make everybody happy, because all get something and nobody appears to pay.[23]

The Calculation of Expenditure Needs

It is a basic requirement in the Nordic countries, as elsewhere, that the equalization system—like the grant system—should not distort local behavior in any undesirable way but should leave the local authorities free to find the locally most efficient ways to deliver the services. The need for any one local authority must be described in reference to its potential—not its actual—number of clients. Performance-related criteria such as kilometers of local roads or number of accommodations at local high schools could not be used in a neutral way.

For example, the measure of local expenditure needs for old-age care is not the number of elderly people staying at an old-age home; it is the number of people in an age group that, according to the national statistics, are most likely to need institutional care. And this measure does not stop at demographic indicators; it also should take into account the share of elderly people living alone if, empirically, they are shown to need extra care.

The problems involved in finding acceptable objective criteria for measuring expenditure needs are formidable, and measures of expenditure needs that are based on objective criteria tend to be complicated. Because so many functions have been decentralized in the Nordic countries, the number of factors to be considered has become large. How complicated the Nordic measures of needs have become is demonstrated in table 7.7, which shows the criteria used in the Danish, Norwegian, and Swedish measures of expenditure needs.

Three factors explain the variation in expenditure levels among local governments: differences in expenditure needs, differences in service levels, and differences in efficiency. The selection of each of these criteria and its

TABLE 7.7 Criteria Used in Calculating Municipal Expenditure Needs in Denmark, Norway, and Sweden

Denmark, 2003	Norway, 2000	Sweden, 2000
Age-related criteria	**Age-related criteria**	**Child care criteria**
Number in these	Number in these	1–9 years of age
age groups:	age groups:	Employment frequency
0–6 years	0–5 years	Income level
7–17 years	6–15 years	Population density
7–16 years ±3 years	16–66 years	
17–19 years	67–79 years	**Primary school criteria**
20–24 years	80–89 years	7–15 years of age
25–39 years	90+ years	Share of foreign
40–64 years		language pupils
65–74 years	**Other criteria**	Population density
75–84 years	Number of divorced	Size of schools
85+ years	people, 16–59 years	Travel time for pupils
	Mortality rate	
Social index criteria	Number of single people,	**Secondary school criteria**
Number of children with	67+ years	16–18 years of age
a single parent	Number of immigrants	Study specialty
Number of rental apartments	Predicted travel time (a	Population density
for elderly people	number of measures	Distance
Number of unemployed,	measuring population	
20–59 years	density)	**Care for elderly criteria**
Number of immigrants	Number of psychiatric	Number of elderly
from certain countries	cases, 16+ years	Marriage status
Number of inhabitants	Number of psychiatric	Former employment
living in deprived	cases, 0–16 years,	Foreign background
neighborhoods out-	Number of unemployed,	Population density
side metropolitan	15–69 years	Distance
Copenhagen		
		Other criteria
		Share of immigrants
		Unemployment level
		Number of single parents
		Number of low-income
		families
		Soil quality
		Winter climate
		Heating costs in public
		buildings
		Declining population
		Share of workers
		commuting out of
		municipality

Source: Data for Denmark from Indenrigs- og Sundhedsministeriet 2002; data for Norway and Sweden from Mønnesland 2001 and the Norwegian MOI.

weight in calculating expenditure needs is, in a tradition developed in Denmark and the United Kingdom during the 1970s, based on empirical studies of its significance when regressed against the variation in local expenditure per capita.

The regression analyses used to describe expenditure needs based on objective factors, all highly significant, explain a little more than half of the variation in local expenditures. Some Swedish observers—Schwartz and Weinberg (2000) and Söderström (2002)—have been critical, believing, despite the high levels of significance, that this level of explanation is not enough. In Denmark, the use of regression analysis is generally accepted. Mau Pedersen of the Danish MOI writes, "We find it possible to identify objective criteria and implement them in an objective way. However, we cannot avoid some value judgements in the process" (Mau Pedersen and Kabelmann 1999). Rattsø (2003) holds that the Norwegian measure of expenditure needs overcompensates small municipalities and delays amalgamations into larger municipalities. In addition, Rattsø finds that local authorities will push criteria that benefit them, and thus, rule-based expenditure needs become discretionary over time.

Is it easier politically to defend a small number of criteria than to defend a large number? The question is difficult to answer. The number of criteria in Sweden is much larger than in Denmark. That difference could be explained by the much wider geographic variation in living conditions in Sweden than in Denmark. Nevertheless, Norway's geographic situation is similar to Sweden's, yet Norway has to some degree been better able to resist demands for adding more criteria. So perhaps the answer is that the number of criteria reflects differences in egalitarian zeal.

Summary and Conclusions

A theme running through this presentation of the systems of decentralization in the Nordic countries is the difficult challenge of finding the best methods of controls for a workable compromise between decentralization and national priorities. Had this chapter been written 20 years ago, the concerns of the Nordic governments would have been described much differently. At that time, the challenges were to improve the regulatory framework, to free local governments from overly bureaucratic rules, and to let the market play a bigger role.

But conditions have changed over a short span of years, and we do not quite understand why. Has the work for better regulation run its course? Are there no more problems to solve? Or are parliaments interfering more with the decentralized welfare services because the European Union has taken over much of what they were doing before?[24] Has the growing international tax competition made high tax rates more risky? Have the rules for budget deficits of the European Union contributed to making parliaments more concerned about the local government sector finances? Or has the new technology in transportation and communications changed preferences away from local differences and toward nationally shared preferences?[25]

Tanzi (1999) compares these swings in ideology with those of a pendulum. He describes how, peaking in the 1980s and early 1990s, "a frontal attack on the thinking of earlier years has made many people wary and more sceptical about the expanded role of the government and [has] set the stage for greater reliance on the market." Tanzi fears "that the pendulum might swing too far, from the view that assigned the solution to most problems to the state to one that identifies the state as the problem" (Tanzi 1999). The recent Nordic experience suggests that his worry is unfounded; the pendulum may already have begun its swing the other way, in favor of the state.

Two forces have in the past played a role in shaping the decentralized public sectors in the Nordic countries. One has been the need to improve administrative efficiency in the public sector; the other has been the readiness to strengthen democracy and to spread political power more broadly. It would not be possible to say that one of these forces is more important than the other; both have found fertile soil in the small and homogeneous Nordic countries.

The result has been that the Nordic countries have decentralized not only all welfare services but also a good deal of the social transfer expenditures to be made by local governments. These functions have become the main local government functions; the traditional "local public goods" play a limited role today. Decentralization has probably improved efficiency in the delivery of welfare services, but the process to decentralize functions related to national redistribution has not been without problems.

Today, however, as ever more sophisticated functions are decentralized, and with the introduction of individual free choice of producer, the issues of not only whether a bigger size is needed to improve the administrative and technical capabilities of the local authorities but also whether municipalities are able to handle these developments at all have surfaced again. The most pressing need now is to be better able to control how the national aspiration for service quality is realized. On this subject, the leading Nordic scholar in local finances, Jørn Rattsø, concluded that Nordic local governments look quite different from what is described in economic theory (Rattsø 1998). Nordic local governments provide redistribution services, the populations they serve are homogeneous and with low mobility, and the political emphasis on equality has motivated central government controls restricting local decision making. Consequently, many Scandinavian colleagues have complained that the international literature on fiscal federalism has not been helpful in describing their reality (Lotz 1998). When local governments primarily supply redistribution services, the perspective changes, and we tend to see local government delivery of welfare services more as an administrative convenience rather than an action based on economic principles.[26]

A common Nordic governing feature is the existence of strong local government associations. Because of them and the established tradition that they do not take positions on questions of national policies, current negotiations between the local and the central governments have contributed to better governance and legislation in the public sector. For more than 20 years in Denmark, the various levels of government have negotiated formal annual agreements that set targets for tax rates and expenditure; recently, those agreements have focused increasingly on setting national standards for local services.

The reason local governments have been able to perform these complicated functions is the amalgamation reforms in the last half of the 20th century, which were caused by the migration that depopulated the rural areas and increased the size of local governments, at least in Sweden and Denmark, to a level deemed necessary for performing those functions. As said, new challenges may, in the coming years, result in new waves of amalgamations—or perhaps even removal of welfare functions from the local level.

An important difference between the Nordic countries and other countries is the use of local own-source income taxes, with each municipality setting its own rates and raising extremely high local tax revenues. The examination of the Nordic income tax system uncovers a number of surprising results:

- The local income tax yields revenue of up to 16 percent of GDP.
- The variation in local income tax rates, though declining over recent years, is significant—in some cases more than 5 percentage points.
- Tax havens are less likely because of the strong equalization systems.
- Tax-induced migration seems not to be a problem, perhaps because tax differences are capitalized in property prices.
- Local taxation of companies raises difficult administrative problems.
- Local revenue stability has been improved by cutting the link between the cycle and local authority tax revenue.

But recently, criticism of the local income tax has been voiced. In particular, critics have claimed that growing income tax rates hurt labor supply and competitiveness in an increasingly global world. Only Norway and Iceland among the Nordic countries have introduced tax capping on a permanent basis; in both cases, the practice has led to systems with tax-sharing qualities. But the public tolerance of municipal diversity has in recent years faded somewhat, and other Nordic countries may move in the direction of Norway and Iceland. Parliaments are not yet likely to enact such legislation. The local income tax has become synonymous with independent local government. However, the pendulum may swing again, as so often before, and reverse the antidecentralization mood. Other methods of creating control without capping—for example, tradable permits to increase tax—have been proposed but have not entered the thinking of the governments.

A problem also exists inside the central governments. If the MOF is unable to prevent the sector ministers from pressing local authorities to improve services, then the local choice between tax reductions or service improvements becomes distorted, and accountability suffers.

Reasonably hard budget constraints are in place, and the Nordic general government finances are in excellent shape. But in Sweden, discussions have resulted in tightening up the rules for budget balance. In general, the golden rule is followed, and borrowing is allowed to finance investment but not current spending. Denmark, however, has rather unusual rules for local borrowing: Danish local authorities are not allowed to borrow—except for investments in utilities, where the debt charges are borne by the users, not the taxpayers. However, this strict restriction causes numerous problems of avoidance and control.

The relative size of general grants to local authorities in the Nordic countries is not much different from the size of such grants in other OECD countries. But the way in which they are regulated after annual consultations with the local government associations may differ. First, the grants are adjusted to compensate for any effect of changes in central laws and regulations on local spending. Second, in principle, the grants work countercyclically, attempting to stabilize the local government finances over the cycle.

Specific and discretionary grants, as well as loan conditions, have become instruments for central governments to influence local priorities— and, in some cases, to buy local support for the policy of the government. Concern is being voiced about moral hazard when discretionary instruments are used in this way.

Nordic local government equalization is, as may be expected, quite strong. Sweden has the strongest system of them all; 95 percent of differences are equalized so the rich municipalities keep barely 5 percent of their excess over the average municipality revenue. A special feature is the use of the "Robin Hood" model of equalization by which the resources needed to pay the poor municipalities are collected from the rich ones. In principle, no grants from the central government are needed for equalization, though in practice, asymmetric treatment protecting rich municipalities often calls for some supplementary element of grants. Another distinctive feature involves the detailed criteria used for comparing expenditure needs, which reflects the complicated welfare functions delegated to local governments.

What are the key issues in the Nordic decentralization experience? This chapter has highlighted three:

- The Nordic countries have decade by decade been influenced by the same swing of the pendulum between liberalism and control that has affected other OECD countries. After decades of liberalization and talk about market mechanisms, the first decade of the 21st century is turning more in the direction of better control of local government.
- The high degree of decentralization, understood as local delivery of personal welfare services, enjoys popular support in most cases. Surveys suggest that the Nordic populations are more satisfied with their public sector than those in other countries. The Nordic people tend to believe that decentralized public sectors are less bureaucratic, more user friendly, and more efficient than the public sectors in less decentralized countries. But some observers think that the recent trend in the Nordic countries toward individual choice and entitlements to services may turn out to be too difficult for a local level of government to handle.
- Finally, local governments have, in some cases, been raising taxes a bit more than the central government wants—perhaps because local governments are inherently less skilled than national governments in exercising financial discipline or perhaps because they are closer to the real preferences of the population?[27]

Having examined the systems of decentralization in a number of countries, Rodden and Eskelund (2003) place these issues in a comparative context, saying, "Credibility and incentives change over time, and it follows that decentralisation can deepen over time, reflecting greater trust and respect as it evolves. This deepening is also more likely to take place at higher levels of income, education, and institutional capacity, and as the rule of law, independence of the judiciary, and mechanisms for democratic participation are strengthened." Decentralization in the Nordic countries is an example of this kind of development, and the Nordic experience demonstrates that a public sector that is both large and decentralized is not incompatible with prosperity and citizen satisfaction.

Notes

1. See Rattsø (2003) for a discussion of the budget effects of the Nordic-style political system. See also Annett (2002) for a recent survey of the literature on the influence on fiscal outcomes of political and institutional factors.
2. For some empirical evidence on this relationship, see OECD (2002a).
3. For reference on the European break with the American school, see Rattsø (2002).
4. For definitions of grants, this chapter uses the Economic Commission for Europe definitions (Council of Europe 1985), recently used also by the OECD. *General grants* are grants not earmarked for any specific purposes; if the criteria for distribution are not specified in the law, general grants are called *general discretionary grants*. *Specific grants* can be used only for specific purposes; the criteria for the use and distribution are formalized in law. If specific grants do not require prior approval, they are called *conditional specific grants,* and the control is ex ante. When the criteria for distribution are not specified in the law, the grants are called *discretionary specific grants.*
5. This section is based in part on NOU (1990) and SOU (1996).
6. This delegation was to some degree formulated in a kind of common law concept called *kommunalfuldmagten* (the local authority).
7. Interestingly, the number of inhabitants represented by an elected representative is much higher in Denmark (1,084), and that representative has the most visible problems of controlling local spending compared with representatives in Finland (representing 394 inhabitants), Norway (representing 515 inhabitants), and Sweden (representing 667 inhabitants) (Council of Europe 1995).
8. A few examples can be given to explain better what is going on today. In Norway, the Ministry of Social Affairs and the local government association have entered into a binding agreement on the quality of the care for elderly people, and the government has introduced minimum standards for the housing of homeless people. They have published plans to use grants as incentives for child care and care for elderly people (resulting in a strategic game in which municipalities hold back on these functions, waiting for the government to introduce the grants). Denmark and Sweden have legislated free choice among service providers, and Denmark also allows services supplied by another municipality than that of residence. And in a number of recent changes in Sweden, (a) Sweden has restricted municipal freedom, (b) municipalities have been obliged to offer preschool classes to all 4- to 6-year-old children, (c) municipalities have been prevented from selling their public housing stock, and (d) Sweden has legislated the maximum charges for child care and care for elderly people. But compared with the arrangements in Denmark, the OECD (2002d) finds the Swedish arrangements much simpler, more clearly defined, and less contentious. For Denmark, the OECD (2002a) has recently noted that legal regulation is perceived to have increased in scope and detail.

9. During the tax freeze, tax increases were implemented by two municipalities that were excluded from the fine because they were heavily hit by a simultaneous change in equalization, and another five to six small municipalities increased taxes and paid the fine. There were also a few tax reductions. For comparison, in a normal year, about 30 percent of all Danish municipalities tend to make changes in their tax rates.

10. The range from the lowest to the highest tax rate in Finland, however, was similar to that in Sweden and Denmark. For 2000, tax rates ranged between 15 percent and 20 percent (OECD 2002b).

11. Messere (1998, 88) notes that "between 1965 and 1985, country divergences increased considerably." But "over recent years, this isolationist trend has been largely, but by no means entirely, reversed, most likely as a consequence of the increasing globalisation of national economies, international tax competition, and the influence of the European Union."

12. In the Nordic countries, property tax rates vary from nothing in Sweden to 1.2 percent in Iceland. For countries wanting to decentralize high levels of expenditure, as in the Nordic countries, the use of the property tax would result in large vertical imbalances to be covered otherwise, and relatively small differences in expenditure would result in relatively large differences in the property tax rates.

13. Messere (1998, 26) observes that "majority opinion has converged on a number of issues," including that "subordinate levels of unitary countries are best financed by a mixture of local income and property tax, with some, but not too much, discretion at the subordinate level of government to vary rates and base."

14. The solution is to base equalization on the self-assessed incomes so that subsequent changes resulting from municipal reassessments are not equalized. This solution is possible because "self-assessed" incomes are determined by the central authorities on the basis of central registration of nearly all transactions relevant for tax purposes.

15. A similar rule was proposed in Denmark, but the Danish parliament failed to reach agreement and ended with an undesirable compromise that permitted local authorities a choice between using their own estimate or following the central forecast (and obtaining a government guarantee for the revenue budget).

16. They are protected from foreseeable cyclical changes by the annual regulation of the grants to local authorities (see the section that follows).

17. This rule does not mean that the central governments respect a clear separation between public and private sector activity. Finland and Sweden are among the European countries with the largest government shares in market companies (CEEP 2000).

18. See note 3 for definitions of grants.

19. Hence, a profound change is currently taking place. Increasingly, the government compensates for increases in spending on welfare services because this spending is covered by the guarantee to compensate for costs from new legislation. On the mandated transfers, which were previously financed by conditional grants, the degree of compensation is being reduced.

20. This exact argument, to "catch" the rich local governments, has been made in Sweden for strengthening equalization (see SOU 1994).

21. As to the equalization of differences in expenditure needs (resources that are transferred are much less important), Norway and Sweden have a 100 percent equalization, Denmark has a 45 percent equalization, and Finland has different models for

each sector (Mønnesland 2001). The effects of the model in these countries, of course, depend on the formulation of the needs and on the use of discretionary weights in the formula.

22. But later, Söderström (2002) expressed concern about the equalization system (discussed later), and he has argued that the needed equalization transfers will become unsustainable when aging begins to influence the local budgets.

23. Of course, the redistributing grants have to be financed by the more or less progressive taxes of the central government, and this financing also moves resources from the rich local governments to the poor ones.

24. This line of argument is opposite to—and in the Nordic context more realistic than—the arguments by Tanzi (1998), asserting that globalization will reduce the importance of national governments, thus leaving an even more important role for the municipal level.

25. Groes and Petersen (2001) have argued that the variation in local tax rates and in local preferences declines as globalization develops.

26. See also Rattsø (2002), who broadens this diagnosis to be not only a Nordic view but also a European one.

27. The latter provocative point was made by Ernesto Stein (1998), commenting on the empirical evidence from his large cross-section analysis that decentralization tends to be associated with higher government expenditure.

References

Annett, Anthony. 2002. "Politics, Government Size, and Fiscal Adjustment in Industrial Countries." IMF Working Paper WP/02/162, International Monetary Fund, Washington, DC.

Blom-Hansen, Jens. 1997. "Macroeconomic Controls of Local Governments in Scandinavia." In *Studier i statens styring af den kommunale sektors økonomi*. Århus, Denmark: Politica.

Borge, Lars-Erik, and Jørn Rattsø. 1995. "Demographic Shift, Relative Costs, and the Allocation of Local Public Consumption in Norway." *Regional Science and Urban Economics* 25: 705–26.

CEEP (European Centre of Enterprises with Public Participation and of Enterprises of General Economic Interest). 2000. *CEEP Statistical Review 2000*. Brussels: CEEP.

Council of Europe. 1985. *Policies with Regard to Grants to Local Authorities*. Strasbourg, France: Council of Europe.

———. 1995. *The Size of Municipalities, Efficiency and Citizens Participation*. Local and Regional Authorities in Europe Series 56. Strasbourg, France: Council of Europe.

Det Økonomiske Råd. 2002. *Dansk Økonomi, Efterår 2002*. Copenhagen: Det Økonomiske Råd.

Finansministeriet. 1996a. *Budgetredegørelse '96*. Copenhagen: Finansministeriet.

———. 1996b. *Kommunal budgetredegørelse*. Copenhagen: Finansministeriet.

———. 1997. *Budgetredegørelse '97*. Copenhagen: Finansministeriet.

———. 1998. *Borgerne og den offentlige sektor*. Copenhagen: Finansministeriet.

IMF (International Monetary Fund). 2002. *Government Finance Statistics Yearbook*. Washington, DC: IMF.

Indenrigs- og Sundhedsministeriet. 2002. *Kommunal udligning og generelle tilskud 2003.* Copenhagen: Indenrigs- og Sundhedsministeriet.

Lolle, Henrik. 2001. "Kommunestørrelse og borgertilfredshed." In *Det fremtidige kommunestyre,* ed. Rolf Norstrand and Nils Groes, 201–16. Copenhagen: AKF Forlaget.

Lotz, Jørgen. 1991. "Controlling Local Government Expenditures." In *Public Finance with Several Levels of Government,* ed. Rémy Prud'homme, 249–62. The Hague/Koenigstein: Foundation Journal Public Finance.

———. 1997. "Denmark and Other Scandinavian Countries: Equalization and Grants." In *Financing Decentralized Expenditures,* ed. Ehtisham Ahmad, 184–212. Cheltenham, U.K.: Edward Elgar.

———. 1998. "Forholdet mellem stat og kommuner: Teori og praksis." *Nationaløkonomisk Tidsskrift* 136: 224–42.

———. 2001. "Styrer staten kommunernes valg af skat og service?" In *Det fremtidige kommunestyre,* ed. Rolf Norstrand and Nils Groes, 275–84. Copenhagen: AKF Forlaget.

Mau Pedersen, Niels Jørgen. 2002. "Local Government and Debt Financing in Denmark." In *Local Public Finance in Europe,* ed. Bernard Dafflon, 93–114. Cheltenham, U.K.: Edward Elgar.

Mau Pedersen, Niels Jørgen, and Thomas Kabelmann. 1999. "Measuring Social Expenditure Needs—Is It Possible to Be Objective?" Paper presented at the International Institute of Public Finance 55th Congress, Moscow, August 23–26.

Mau Pedersen, Niels Jørgen, and Inge Lene Møller. 2001. "Economies of Scale in Local Governments: Theoretical and Empirical Investigations of Danish Municipalities." Paper presented at the International Institute of Public Finance Conference, Linz, Austria.

Messere, Ken, ed. 1998. *The Tax Systems in Industrialized Countries.* Oxford, U.K.: Oxford University Press.

Moisio, Antti, and Roope Uusitalo. 2003. *Tukimus kuntien ydhistymisten menovaikutuksista.* Helsinki: Ministry of Interior.

Mønnesland, Jan. 2001. "Kommunale Inntektssystemer i Norden." Working Paper NIBR 2-2001. Norsk Institutt for By- og Regionforskning, Oslo.

Mouritzen, Poul Erik. 1991. *Den politiske cyclus.* Århus, Denmark: Politica.

NOU (Norges Offentlige Utredninger). 1990. "Forslag til ny lov om kommuner og fylkeskommuner." NOU 1990:13, Norges Offentlige Utredninger, Oslo.

OECD (Organisation for Economic Co-operation and Development). 1999. "Taxing Powers of State and Local Government." Tax Policy Studies 1, OECD, Paris.

———. 2001. *Revenue Statistics, 2001.* Paris: OECD.

———. 2002a. *Economic Survey of Denmark, 2002.* Paris: OECD.

———. 2002b. *Economic Survey of Finland, 2002.* Paris: OECD.

———. 2002c. *Economic Survey of Norway, 2002.* Paris: OECD.

———. 2002d. *Economic Survey of Sweden, 2002.* Paris: OECD.

———. 2002e. *Revenue Statistics, 2002.* Paris: OECD.

———. 2003a. *Economic Survey of Denmark, 2003.* Paris: OECD.

———. 2003b. *Economic Survey of Finland, 2003.* Paris: OECD.

Pettersson-Lidbom, Per, and Fredrik Wiklund. 2002. "Att hålla balansen: En ESO-rapport om kommuner och budgetdisciplin." Ds 2002:18, Expergruppen för Studier i Offentlig Ekonomi, Stockholm.

Rattsø, Jørn. 1998. "Introduction." In *Fiscal Federalism and State-Local Finance,* ed. Jørn Rattsø, xi–xiv. Cheltenham, U.K.: Edward Elgar.

———. 2002. "Fiscal Controls in Europe: A Summary." In *Local Public Finance in Europe,* ed. Bernard Dafflon, 277–90. Cheltenham, U.K.: Edward Elgar.

———. 2003. "Vertical Imbalance and Fiscal Behavior in a Welfare State: Norway." In *Fiscal Decentralization and the Challenge of Hard Budget Constraint,* ed. Jonathan Rodden. Cambridge, MA: MIT Press.

Rodden, Jonathan, and Gunnar S. Eskeland. 2003. "Lessons and Conclusions." In *Fiscal Decentralization and the Challenge of Hard Budget Constraint,* ed. Jonathan Rodden. Cambridge, MA: MIT Press.

Rodden, Jonathan, Gunnar S. Eskeland, and Jennie Litvack. 2003. "Introduction and Overview." In *Fiscal Decentralization and the Challenge of Hard Budget Constraint,* ed. Jonathan Rodden. Cambridge, MA: MIT Press.

Schwartz, Brita, and Susanne Weinberg. 2000. *Serviceproduktion och kostnader, att söka orsaker till kommunala skillnader.* Stockholm: Ekonomisk Forskningsinsitutet, Handelshögskolan.

Söderström, Lars. 1994. "Utjämning och kommunala incitament." Appendix 8 of *Betänkande från beredningen för statsbidrag och utjämning i kommunsektorn,* SOU 1994:144, Statens Offentliga Utredningar, Stockholm.

———. 2002. "Hotet mot kommunerna." Ds 2002:7, Expergruppen för Studier i Offentlig Ekonomi, Stockholm. [Working paper.]

SOU (Statens Offentliga Utredningar). 1994. "Ütjämning av kostnader och intäkter i kommuner och landsting." In *Betänkande från beredningen för statsbidrag och utjämning i kommunsektorn* SOU 1994:144, Statens Offentliga Utredningar, Stockholm.

———. 1996. Den kommunala självstyrelsen och grundlagen. SOU 1996:129, Statens Offentliga Utredningar, Stockholm.

Stein, Ernesto. 1998. "Fiscal Decentralisation and Government Size in Latin America." In *Democracy, Decentralisation, and Deficits in Latin America,* ed. Kiichiro Fukasaku and Ricardo Hausmann, 95–120. Paris: OECD Development Centre.

Tanzi, Vito. 1998. "The Demise of the Nation State?" IMF Working Paper WP/98/120, International Monetary Fund, Washington, DC.

———. 1999. "The Changing Role of the State in the Economy." In *Fiscal Decentralisation in Emerging Economies,* ed. Kiichiro Fukasaku and Luiz De Mello Jr. Paris: OECD Development Centre.

———. 2001. "Pitfalls on the Road to Fiscal Decentralization." Working Paper 19, Carnegie Endowment for International Peace, Washington, DC.

von Hagen, Terje P., and Jørn Rattsø. 2002. "Trenger vi kommunene." *Aftenposten,* July 1.

Wetterberg, Gunnar. 1997. *Kommunerne.* Stockholm: SNS Förlag.

8

Local Government Organization and Finance: *United Kingdom*

DAVID KING

This chapter surveys the organization and finance of local government in the United Kingdom. It discusses the system of local government and then looks at local government spending. Later sections discuss local government revenues, describing in turn taxes and charges, fiscal transfers, and borrowing. The chapter then looks very briefly at local administration, gives an overall assessment, and finally suggests some lessons for developing countries from the U.K. experience.

First, however, it is important to explain exactly what is meant by the United Kingdom.

The Component Countries of the United Kingdom

The U.K. parliament, which is located in Westminster, London, governs the entire United Kingdom, which comprises four separate countries. Three of these countries—England, Scotland, and Wales—form what is known as Great Britain. The fourth country is Northern Ireland. As table 8.1 shows, England has more than 80 percent of the total population.

I am very grateful to Matthew Pashley for his tireless help in assembling the data for this chapter. The main draft of this chapter was prepared in January 2004.

TABLE 8.1   Population of the United Kingdom, by Country, 2002

Country	Population	Percentage of United Kingdom
England	49,558,800	83.673
Scotland	5,054,800	8.534
Wales	2,918,700	4.928
Great Britain	57,532,300	97.136
Northern Ireland	1,696,600	2.864
United Kingdom	59,228,900	100.000

Source: Data from Office for National Statistics Web site (http://www.statistics.gov), accessed October 23, 2003.

Wales effectively joined England in 1284, although the act confirming the union dates only from 1536. Scotland joined England and Wales in 1707, so it is only from then that the Westminster government has covered the whole of Great Britain. The United Kingdom itself came into existence only in 1800, when the whole of Ireland joined Great Britain. However, southern and central Ireland seceded in 1922 to form the Irish Republic, so the United Kingdom now comprises Great Britain and Northern Ireland.

Local government has always varied slightly among the four countries. The most different is Northern Ireland, where, during the sectarian troubles of recent years, the central government has assumed many of the responsibilities that were formerly entrusted to local authorities. The future role of local government there is a matter for the new Northern Ireland assembly, for which elections took place in both 1998 and 2003, but which has been suspended since 2001. Owing to past differences and future uncertainty, this chapter ignores Northern Ireland and instead considers only Great Britain—chiefly England, which is by far the largest country—but it notes a few differences in Scotland and Wales.

A Comment on Recent Reforms

Since the 1960s, U.K. central governments have adopted a rather cavalier approach to reforming the structure of local government, and they have undertaken a number of radical reforms. Also, especially since 1988, they have taken many steps toward reducing financial autonomy for local authorities. The result is that tax revenues in the United Kingdom are now among the most centralized in any country in the Organisation for Economic Cooperation and Development (OECD). To supporters of decentralization, perhaps the best that can be said on the financial side is that the current domestic property tax has some interesting novel features and that the system of equalization grants tries very hard to pursue equalization.

An Overview of the Current Local Government System

This section looks in turn at the history of local government,[1] its structure, its legal status, and its revenues and expenditures.

Origin and History of Local Governments

Local government in the United Kingdom really dates from 1130. Before that time, the kings of both England and Scotland, which were then independent, had divided their countries into counties. But these counties were not a form of local government. Instead, they were simply administrative areas of the central government, and each had a sheriff to implement central government policy. The sheriffs' main function was to secure law and order. This system of counties was later extended to Wales and Ireland.

The larger towns disliked being under the control of a sheriff, and in 1130, the English town of Lincoln, in the county of Lincolnshire, was allowed to opt out of the control of its county's sheriff by making a payment directly to the king (Stenton 1962, 173). Effectively, its county's sheriff became responsible for an area with a hole in it, for he had no jurisdiction in the town of Lincoln, which is in the middle of Lincolnshire. Soon, more towns paid to opt out of sheriff control, and they became the first local authorities. Their main functions were those that they took over from the sheriffs. In time, the ancient word *borough* was reserved for such towns. The chief advantage to kings in creating boroughs was to secure one-off payments, and many boroughs were created by kings who needed money for crusades.

Even in the parts of their counties for which sheriffs retained control, their power was later reduced by the creation of small parishes to do some minor functions. The role of parishes was extended greatly in 1601, when English and Welsh parishes became responsible for helping the poor. This change created a problem with the itinerant poor, who tended to migrate to the most generous areas. When parishes in Scotland later assumed this responsibility, the problem was avoided, for there poor people had to seek help from the areas where they were born.

By the late 19th century, relief for the poor had become a central responsibility. But by then government activity had greatly increased, with functions that included housing, education, waste collection and disposal, fire services, social services, and water and sewerage, as well as increasing responsibilities for roads. These new responsibilities were initially given to a plethora of elected bodies called *boards*, which were, in effect, single-service local authorities. The various boards had assorted boundaries that often overlapped.

The rationalization of the 1890s

The existence of these boards created a complex system of local government, and the central government rationalized the system in drastic reforms in the 1890s. The underlying goal of the reforms was to create a two-tier structure of local authorities. The old counties formed the upper tier and became genuine local authorities for the first time. The government respected all the ancient county boundaries, even though some counties were arguably too small. For example, Kinross in Scotland had only 8,000 people. A new set of generally much smaller and far more numerous authorities called *districts* formed the lower tier. The division of functions between the tiers was generally as shown in the first data column of table 8.2.

However, a complete reform of this two-tier basis would have abolished the independence of the boroughs. Thus, two amendments to the reform were adopted to show respect for them. First, the largest 90 or so boroughs were allowed to retain complete independence and to perform all local authority functions. Consequently, these boroughs continued to form holes in the areas served by the counties surrounding them. Second, many smaller boroughs were allowed to be independent of their surrounding districts and to perform the lower-tier functions themselves. Consequently, many districts also had one or more holes in the areas that they served.

From 1960 to 1996

By the 1960s, further reforms clearly were needed. One problem was that the holes created difficulties. For instance, all the boroughs were responsible for public housing and waste disposal, yet they often had little space in which to build new homes or dispose of waste. A second problem was that some areas were too small to provide services at a reasonable cost. As noted in the preceding section, one county had a population of only 8,000, and many districts had populations of fewer than 2,000. A third problem was that the counties were responsible for social services and thus had to help families with difficulties; the main difficulty facing many families, however, was having nowhere to live, and public housing was a responsibility of the districts.

TABLE 8.2 Main Functions of Local Authorities in Great Britain

Function	Most areas from 1890s to 1974[a]	London, 1965–86, and six English metropolitan areas, 1974–86[b]	Scotland, Wales, and most of England, 1974–96, and much of today[c]	London and six English metropolitan areas since 1986[d]	Scotland, Wales, and parts of England since 1996[e]
Education	Upper	Lower	Upper	Lower	Unitary
Secondary roads[f]	Upper	Upper	Upper	Lower	Unitary
Police	Upper	Upper	Upper	Joint board	Joint board
Fire	Upper	Upper	Upper	Joint board	Joint board
Social services	Upper	Lower	Upper	Lower	Unitary
Tertiary roads[f]	Lower	Lower	Lower	Lower	Unitary
Housing	Lower	Lower	Lower	Lower	Unitary
Waste collection	Lower	Lower	Lower	Lower	Unitary
Waste disposal	Lower	Upper	Upper	Joint board	Unitary
Water supply	Lower	n.a.	n.a.	n.a.	n.a.
Sewerage and sewage disposal	Lower	n.a.	n.a.	n.a.	n.a.

Source: Author's compilation.

Note: n.a. = not applicable.

a. About 90 large boroughs had separate authorities responsible for all functions. The central government provided police in the London area. The division between the upper and local tiers varied slightly in parts of Scotland. From 1965, new arrangements were made for London (see second data column).

b. The central government continued to provide police in the London area. The six metropolitan areas were all in England and lay around Birmingham, Leeds, Liverpool, Manchester, Newcastle, and Sheffield. Water and sewerage were provided by the upper tier throughout England and Wales until 1974 when they were taken over by the central government. They have since been privatized.

c. This column has never applied to the London area or to the six metropolitan areas of England (see second and fourth data columns) or to three groups of Scottish islands, where services were entrusted to three unitary authorities. Joint boards now supply police services. Water and sewerage in England and Wales were taken over by the central government in 1974 and later privatized. Water and sewerage were local (upper-tier) functions in Scotland until 1996 when they were given to independent authorities. See also fifth data column.

d. The central government continued to provide police in London until 2000. Then, a new upper-tier authority for London was reestablished, called the Greater London Authority.

e. This column does not apply to those parts of England that retain two tiers (for which see third data column) or to London and the six English metropolitan areas (for which see fourth data column).

f. The central government handles primary roads that are of national importance.

Reforms took place gradually.[2] The first reform was in London in 1965.[3] There a different two-tier structure was established on almost entirely new boundaries: (a) one upper-tier authority, Greater London, which was formed by merging the then counties of London and Middlesex and adding parts of the surrounding counties and (b) 33 lower-tier authorities. There were no holes in the authorities of either tier. The authorities were all of adequate size for their functions. And as shown in the second data column of table 8.2, housing and social services were each entrusted to the same tier, namely, the lower tier, whose authorities have populations of 150,000 or more. Thus, the London reform met all the main objections to the system of the 1890s.

Elsewhere, reforms were done in the 1970s on three other systems[4]:

- Six large metropolitan areas in England were given two-tier systems identical to that in the London area, as shown in the second data column of table 8.2.
- In almost all other areas, local government was given two tiers, with a division of responsibilities that was similar to what had gone before, as shown in the third data column of table 8.2. The new authorities were still called counties and districts, except that the upper-tier authorities in Scotland were called regions. However, most of the boundaries were new because the new authorities comprised much larger populations, ranging up to nearly 3 million for the region of Strathclyde in Scotland. A further feature of the reforms was that the boundaries were drawn up to ensure that the areas covered by any authority had no holes.
- Finally, a few Scottish islands were given single-tier authorities, or unitary authorities, that were responsible for all local authority functions, as noted in the footnote to the third data column in table 8.2.

Two main problems became evident with the new authorities in the nonmetropolitan areas. First, social services and housing were still split between the tiers. Second, the authorities were extremely large. In creating the new and larger authorities, the government believed that it had enabled economies of scale in the delivery of local services, and its main goal was to ensure that all authorities could fully capture these economies. For example, one view was that education authorities had to contain at least 200,000 to 250,000 people. At the same time, no consideration was given to the possibility that large authorities would be less able to cater to varying preferences, so no one worried about having local authorities with well more than 250,000 people. In fact, outside London and the six metropolitan areas, education was provided by upper-tier authorities that had an average size of some 750,000 people.

Further reforms were considered in the 1980s to tackle these problems in the nonmetropolitan areas. However, the only actual reform in the 1980s was the abolition of the upper tier in London and the six metropolitan areas. There is little doubt that the government undertook this step because it felt that the upper-tier metropolitan authorities were spending too much and were of the wrong political persuasion. The abolition meant that some previously upper-tier functions were handed down to the lower tier, while others were entrusted to joint boards—that is, special single-function bodies run by representatives from each of the lower-tier authorities. The current arrangements in these areas are shown in the fourth data column of table 8.2.

The 1996 and 2000 reforms

By the 1990s, the government felt that it should have another look at the two-tier structure of local government outside London and the six metropolitan areas. The government's ideal solution would have been a uniform arrangement of unitary local authorities that would, in principle, be responsible for all functions.[5] Unitary authorities were created throughout Scotland and Wales, where the government imposed wholesale reforms. In England, the government adopted a more piecemeal approach and created unitary authorities only in some places. Ironically, some of those English unitary authorities now create a hole in the area that is serviced by a surrounding upper-tier county. In all three countries, areas served by unitary authorities have joint boards for some functions, as shown in the fifth data column of table 8.2.

The government used four arguments for establishing unitary authorities where feasible. First, it believed that having just one tier would reduce administration costs and reduce confusion. Second, it felt that some of the extremely large authorities that had been set up in the 1970s were too large to be considered local. Third, it asserted that the new concept of local authorities contracting out some of their services to private providers would lessen the need for large authorities that could exploit possible economies of scale, which had been the case in the 1970s. Fourth, it felt that the public had not accepted some new local authorities; the most obvious example was Humberside in England, which had been created out of parts of two ancient counties, Lincolnshire and Yorkshire, on opposite sides of a wide river.

The most recent reform came in 2000, when an upper-tier authority, called the Greater London Authority, was re-created in London. As indicated in the footnote to the fourth data column of table 8.2, this authority is chiefly responsible for the police, which previously had always been a central government responsibility in London, and for fire services. But, arguably, the authority's most notable achievement has been the introduction of congestion charging, whereby all vehicles using central London roads during the daytime have to pay a daily charge.

TABLE 8.3 Local Authorities in Great Britain, 2001

Area	Total population	Number of authorities	Mean population of authorities
Greater London Authority	7,188,000	1	7,188,000
London districts	7,188,000	33	218,000
Metropolitan districts	10,822,000	36	301,000
English unitary authorities	8,181,000	46	178,000
English two-tier areas: upper tier	22,991,000	34	676,000
English two-tier areas: lower tier	22,991,000	239	96,000
Scottish unitary authorities	5,064,000	32	158,000
Welsh unitary authorities	2,903,000	22	132,000

Sources: Data from http://www.statistics.gov.uk/STATBASE/Expodata/Spreadsheets/D6545.xls and http://www.gro-scotland.gov.uk/grosweb/grosweb.nsf/pages/01-populations.

Local authorities in 2004

The end result of all this evolution is now a variety of authorities. Their different types and average 2001 populations are shown in table 8.3.

The reforms of the 1970s and 1990s show that drastic reforms are possible. However, the resulting structure is not necessarily ideal. As noted, holes still exist, and in many places, social services and housing are still each provided by different tiers. Also, as noted later, it is arguable that joint boards are not wholly satisfactory.

The Legal Status of Local Authorities

The legal status of local authorities is most affected by three factors: ultra vires, dissolution, and autonomy. These factors are explained here.

Ultra vires

In many countries, local authorities have a fairly general degree of competence, being able to undertake anything that is not specifically prohibited. The opposite applies in the United Kingdom.[6] There local authorities are not allowed to undertake any activity unless they can point to a specific piece of legislation that entitles them to undertake it. If they were to undertake any other activity, then they would be acting *ultra vires* (that is, beyond what is permitted by law).

However, the principle of ultra vires does not mean that local authorities have no choice in what activities to perform. Instead, the law requires them to undertake some mandatory activities, such as educating all children of school age, except those whose parents arrange private education, and it permits them to undertake other discretionary activities, such as those related to leisure facilities. Many of the broad functions shown in table 8.2 comprise a mix of mandatory and discretionary activities. Thus, it is mandatory for a local authority to have a fire service that will put out fires, but it is discretionary for it to ask its fire service to rescue people trapped in cars after accidents or, indeed, to rescue cats which have climbed trees that they cannot climb down.

A further extension of local activity arose in 1998, when local authorities were given the powers to undertake any activity that promoted well-being. Of note, however, is that they were not given any extra resources at that time.

Dissolution

With respect to dissolution, it is clear from the earlier overview of the U.K. countries that local authorities are created by the central government and can equally be uncreated by that government. In addition, the government has the power to remove from local authority control any schools that it deems to be failing.

Autonomy

Local autonomy is circumscribed in several ways. First, as noted above, it is circumscribed by the principle of ultra vires. Second, again as noted above, it is circumscribed by the array of mandatory activities, some of which are specifically stated by the government to be a matter of "delivering national objectives locally" (ODPM 2003c, 17). Third, it is circumscribed by local authorities' limited ability to control their revenues (which is explored in later sections). But three further issues also influence local autonomy: the Audit Commission, ring-fenced grants, and capping. These issues are further described here.

THE AUDIT COMMISSION. In England and Wales, local authorities are subject to the scrutiny of the Audit Commission. This body answers to the Office of the Deputy Prime Minister, and it is concerned with the central government's health care bodies and criminal justice agencies as well as local authorities. The Audit Commission is far more than a mere auditor of accounts. It has long inspected local authority services, and it has also produced reports about best practices. More recently, it has measured local services on a basis of best value performance indicators.

In many ways, this scrutiny is an advantage to local government because individual authorities can learn lessons from others. And, indeed, the commission has the laudable goal of helping local councils improve local services for their communities. But arguably, a possible danger is that this nonelected commission will end up effectively telling local authorities how to run their services. Indeed, one can imagine a future time when the commission not only decides exactly what services should be provided and how but also encourages uniformity in place of the diversity that lies at the heart of the rationale for decentralization.

Certainly, the commission's powers continue to grow. For instance, it introduced a new Comprehensive Performance Assessment in 2002/2003. This assessment involves the commission in monitoring how each authority delivers its key services—for example, education, social care, and housing— and considering how well each council is run, because that evaluation will affect how well each authority delivers its services in the future. Under this system, each authority is graded on each of its key services, on its use of resources, and on the council's ability. In addition, it receives an overall grade of poor, weak, fair, good, or excellent.[7]

RING-FENCED GRANTS. A further constraint on local authorities is the use of specific grants, which are known in the United Kingdom as *ring-fenced grants*. Since 1997, when the present Labour Government took office, these grants have risen from 5 percent of government grants in England to 12 percent. Manifestly, this increase reduces local autonomy.

CAPPING. U.K. governments have long wished to control local authority spending, chiefly citing the need to do so for macroeconomic purposes. The actual need for this control is, to say the least, subject to debate, and indeed, it has recently been argued that countries whose subnational authorities have the greatest financial freedom also tend to be the countries with the best macroeconomic performance (see, for example, King and Ma 1999a, 1999b).

Until the 1980s, government efforts to influence local authority spending relied chiefly on the fact that the government provided a large share of local revenues through grants. Consequently, it could encourage squeezes or expansions in local spending by reducing or increasing the overall level of grants. However, changes in grants could be offset by changes in local tax rates, and in the 1980s, the Conservative Government took a more hands-on degree of expenditure control, chiefly through capping. Capping was essentially a way of limiting increases in spending by individual local authorities. It applied before the local government financial year started on April 1. By then, each local authority had to propose a budget, and if that budget breached the government's capping rules, then the government could require the budget to be revised.

The exact way in which capping was used evolved over time, but the arrangements for 1994/95 provide a fair example. The capping rules related to two pieces of information: (a) the extent to which an authority proposed in 1994/95 to spend more than it spent in 1993/94 and (b) the sum that the government felt the authority would need to spend in 1994/95 if it were to provide its services at a reasonable level. (This calculation is made each year for grant purposes, as discussed later in the section on working out individual authorities' needs for individual services.)

Essentially, if an authority proposed to spend less in 1994/95 than the government deemed it needed to spend, then it would be permitted to adopt that budget. This condition would be the case no matter how much the budget might exceed the level of the previous year. Clearly, the government would have difficulty applying any sanctions to an authority that was intending to spend less than the government thought it needed to spend. It may be added that the longer capping was in force, the fewer authorities budgeted to spend less than was needed.

In contrast, if the authority planned to increase its budget to a level above what the government thought it needed to spend, then the authority would have to ensure that its budget did not breach any of the criteria that could lead to it being capped. In 1994/95, there were four criteria for sanctions (ACC 1994):

- An authority could not increase its budget by more than 1.75 percent if doing so would take it to, or leave it at, a level above what the government determined it needed to spend.
- An authority could not increase its budget by more than 1.25 percent if doing so would take it to, or leave it at, a level more than 5 percent above what the government determined it needed to spend.
- An authority could not increase its budget by more than 0.75 percent if doing so would take it to, or leave it at, a level more than 10 percent above what the government determined it needed to spend.
- An authority could not have a budget at a level more than 12.5 percent above what the government determined it needed to spend, except in a few specifically defined circumstances.

The legal and administrative arrangements behind capping were quite complex, and in principle, an authority could go ahead with an excess budget and set the requisite tax rate. But it would then be investigated by the government and would almost certainly have to make a retrospective and administratively cumbersome reduction to its budget and tax rate. So, in practice, almost all authorities proposed budgets that were within the rules.

The present Labour Government has claimed that its 1998 measures have abolished what it calls this "crude and universal" capping system (ODPM 1999, 1). Nevertheless, it is difficult to argue that capping has wholly disappeared. Authorities are subject to spending reviews and can still have their budgets limited. Also, a recent upsurge in local tax rates has led the government to threaten to reintroduce capping. Indeed, although the government has promised complete freedom over budgets to authorities that are deemed to be excellent, this promise is currently under threat.

Composition of Revenue and Expenditures

This section provides a broad overview of the composition of revenue and expenditures. The data in this section apply to England for 2000/01, and are presented in three tables. More details are given in the sections that follow.

Expenditure and revenue by accounts

Local authority accounts can be divided in two ways. First is a division between the so-called revenue account, which is a current account, and the capital account. Second, each authority's revenue account is further divided into accounts for trading services, housing, and general services. Trading services are those where most of the revenue arises from fees and charges, such as industrial estates used by businesses, markets, some toll roads and bridges, some ferries, civic halls, and some theaters. The housing account concerns the housing stock owned by local authorities. General services are those financed chiefly by taxes and grants.

Since 1989, housing accounts have been ring-fenced, which means that rents on local authority properties cannot be subsidized from general local authority funds and that rents cannot be raised to reduce the level of local taxes. In addition, the accounts have limits about the extent to which local authorities can transfer funds between general service accounts and trading accounts.

Table 8.4 outlines local authority expenditure and revenue on these various accounts for English local authorities in 2001/02. Their total expenditure and revenue was UK£97.974 billion, which was more than 10 percent of England's gross domestic product (GDP). About 90 percent of the expenditure was on the revenue account, and the other 10 percent was on the capital account. It will be seen that more than 40 percent of revenue comes in

TABLE 8.4 Summary of Gross Local Authority Expenditure and Income, England, 2001/02

Expenditure	Amount (UK£ million)	Percentage of total expenditure	Revenue	Amount (UK£ million)	Percentage of total revenue
Revenue account			**Revenue account**		
General services			*General services*		
Employees	41,297	42.2	Business taxes	15,144	15.5
Running expenses	39,635	40.5	Domestic taxes[b]	13,359	13.7
Minus subsidies to			General grants	21,095	21.6
other accounts	−890[a]	−0.9	Specific grants	18,793	19.2
			Charges	8,165	8.3
			Other income	5,099	5.2
Housing account			*Housing account*		
Management and			Rents[c]	2,925	3.0
repairs and			Grants	4,053	4.1
so forth[c]	4,088	4.2	Other income	412	0.4
Trading services			*Trading services*		
Employees	140	0.1	Sales	858	0.9
Running expenses	566	0.6	Other income	140	0.1
Interest payments	2,922	3.0	*Interest receipts*	917	0.9
Total revenue expenditure[b]	**87,760**	**89.7**	**Total revenue income**	**90,960**	**93.0**
Capital account			**Capital account**		
General services	6,412	6.6	Central government		
Housing	3,110	3.2	grants	2,027	2.1
Trading services	219	0.2	Other grants and		
			so forth	757	0.8
			Capital receipts	3,579	3.7
			Net borrowing	−197	−0.2
			Minus investments	−797	−0.8
			Other	428	0.4
Total capital expenditure	**9,741**	**10.0**	**Total capital income**	**5,797**	**5.9**
Minor adjustments	293	0.3	Accruals adjustment	1,037	1.1
Total expenditure	**97,794**	**100.0**	**Total income**	**97,794**	**100.0**

Source: ODPM 2003c, table 1.6b.

a. This expenditure is excluded here because it is included in other items below.

b. The expenditure side of the account omits payments by local authorities of the means-tested council tax benefit that is paid to poor local payers of the domestic council tax; instead, the revenue figure for domestic tax receipts shows receipts of these taxes net of this benefit.

c. The expenditure side of the account omits payments by local authorities of the means-tested rent rebates that are paid to poor tenants of local authority housing; instead, the revenue figure for these rents shows rent receipts net of these rebates.

TABLE 8.5 Local Authority Expenditure by Service, England, 2001/02

Service	Amount (UK£ million)	Percentage of total expenditure
Education	30,903	31.6
Social services	15,110	15.5
Police	8,711	8.9
Fire	1,827	1.9
Housing revenue account	7,099	7.3
Other housing	7,198	7.4
Transport	6,437	6.6
Other services	17,182	17.6
Nonapportionable (for example, interest payments)	3,326	3.4
Total expenditure	97,794	100.0

Source: ODPM 2003c, table 1.6c.

the form of grants. And although table 8.4 shows about 29 percent coming from taxes, the business taxes are scarcely local taxes, as explained in a later section on the uniform business rate.

Expenditure by service

Table 8.4 shows that the total expenditure of English local authorities in 2001/02 was UK£97.794 billion. Table 8.5 shows how that total was divided among the main local authority services. Education and social services account for almost half the total. The expenditure labeled "other housing" that is not part of the housing revenue account mostly comprises a means-tested cash benefit that is known as the *housing benefit* and is paid to low-income tenants of both public and privately owned housing. A more detailed breakdown of spending by service, but for a later year and on a slightly different basis, is given in a later section.

Organizing Local Government

As already indicated in table 8.2, much of England has two main tiers of local government. These tiers are usually called *counties* and *districts,* but in London they are the Greater London Authority and the London boroughs. However, parts of England, along with Scotland and Wales, have one main tier of unitary authorities. The one-tier areas have joint boards for police and fire services. Indeed, even in the two-tier areas, police are now typically provided by joint boards. In addition, many areas have a further tier of authorities with minor functions, which operate below the unitary authorities and the districts. This tier is known in England and Wales as *parish* or *town councils* and in Scotland as *community councils*. A later section discusses these councils in more depth.

Organizing the main councils

All the main tiers have elected representatives who are variously known as *councilors* or *members*. The former term is used here. Each council is divided into wards. In many cases, each ward elects a single councilor, but in some cases, each ward may elect two or three councilors. In general, the more important authorities have about 10,000 electors per councilor, whereas the less important authorities may have as few as 2,500. Given that there are two tiers in many places, the total number of councilors in England is about 20,000. The independent Boundary Commission draws up the ward boundaries.

If a ward has only one councilor, each elector may make only one choice, but if a ward has two or three councilors, each elector can vote for two or three. The winner or winners are those who get the most votes. Elections always take place in May, except when there is a by-election to replace a councilor who dies or for some reason chooses to stand down. In many authorities, an entire council is elected every four years. In other cases, one-third of the council is elected every year, with the wards having elections in turns. No one who is employed by a council may stand for election to its council. And senior local government employees are not allowed to stand for election to any council. The elected council appoints its chief official and, in turn, the other principal officials.

However, some experimental new voting arrangements are now being introduced, as indicated in the following list. The stimulus for change has been falling voter turnouts, which in England are now nearer 30 percent than the 40 percent or so that applied until the 1990s. Arguably, however, low turnouts are not a result of any deficiency in the present voting arrangements; rather, turnouts are low because local authorities have so little freedom that the results of local elections do not seem all that important.

- The Greater London Authority, where all wards have single members, is pioneering a modified voting system that asks people to indicate their first and second choices, and second choices will be taken into account.
- Some London boroughs propose to allow people to vote for not only a party but also a councilor. Then, in addition to the councilors elected by wards, a few more will be chosen on the basis of the party votes to try to get the party balance closer to that desired by voters.

■ Some local authorities are exploring the use of arrangements such as all-electronic ballots, all-postal ballots, and early voting.

■ Traditionally, the elected councilors themselves elected one of their number to be leader of the council, often called a *mayor*. However, a few authorities are experimenting with having directly elected mayors, who therefore need not be previously elected as councilors. The most notable example of such an authority is the Greater London Authority.

The joint boards

Electors do not directly elect representatives to sit on joint boards. Instead, the local authorities choose from their own elected members those who will represent them on the joint boards. However, the situations of fire and police boards are slightly different.

All members of a fire board are chosen by the councilors of the authorities whose area they cover, and they are chosen to reflect the political balance of those authorities. The board meets only a few times a year, but it appoints the senior officers and is ultimately responsible for the fire service. It also decides what tax revenue the fire board will raise.

The United Kingdom's view of police as a local authority service is unusual, but then, it is generally viewed as an unusual local service. The joint board will have some members who are chosen by the councilors of the authorities it represents, reflecting their political balance. But it will also have some members who represent local magistrates and some who are independent, all being approved by the central government. However, local authority members are always in a slight majority, so seemingly they are in ultimate control. In fact, their powers are limited because once they have appointed the chief police officer, who is called the *chief constable,* this officer has operational independence from the board—and hence from local authorities—and indeed from the central government. The advantage of this arrangement is that it ensures that policing is not subject to any political intervention. The disadvantage is that operational independence can be guaranteed only by making it extremely difficult for a board to fire an unsatisfactory chief constable, so firings almost never happen. The police board also appoints all senior police officers, proposes and comments on strategies, oversees the budget, and decides how much tax the police authority will raise.

The parish and town councils

The whole of England is divided into more than 10,000 parishes, which range from small settlements of about 50 people to small towns of 25,000.

Outside London, the great majority of these parishes have decided to have a parish council (sometimes called a town council). There are analogous parish councils in Wales and community councils in Scotland. These councils are perhaps best seen as a means for local people to voice their concerns to the main authorities. But the councils are allowed to spend small sums on local amenities, so they are also allowed—except in Scotland—to levy a tax in addition to the taxes of the main tier or tiers above. The government is currently considering strengthening parish councils, perhaps increasing their tax powers and perhaps allowing the larger ones to take over some functions from the tier above. At present, the parish councils in Wales have the most power of all the similar councils throughout Great Britain.

Local Government Expenditure Responsibilities

The main services provided by local authorities are as follows:

- **Education.** Local authorities provide the primary and secondary schools that most children attend, although a few children go to private schools. Local authorities also provide some schools for children younger than five years, and they subsidize many other schools. In addition, local authorities provide special education for children with various serious problems, and they provide some adult education. However, they have never had responsibility for universities. Until 1989, local authorities did provide colleges called *polytechnics;* however, the central government took over these polytechnics in 1989 and later gave them university status. Similarly, until 1993, local authorities provided other colleges of further education; these, too, were then taken over by the central government.
- **Social services.** Local authorities provide homes for homeless children, and they organize foster care and adoption. They provide various types of support for adults younger than retirement age who have physical, learning, or mental disabilities. In addition, they provide residential homes for elderly people who cannot live in their own homes, some financial support for elderly people who choose to live in privately owned residential homes, and assistance to elderly people who manage to live in their own homes.
- **Protective services.** Local authorities run fire services; fire prevention advice and enforcement; emergency planning for disasters such as floods, chemical emissions, and terrorist attacks; and police services. But, as explained in the earlier section on joint boards, their role in policing is

limited. Local authorities also provide magistrates courts, which are the lowest courts and are used for minor offenses.

■ **Housing.** From the 1920s to the 1980s, local authorities provided a large proportion of the housing stock, typically letting the housing at subsidized rents. Today, these authorities have little property left, but they are responsible for ensuring that everyone has a home, so they have to accommodate anyone who might otherwise be homeless. They also give cash benefits to poor people who rent private or public accommodations, although this service is virtually an agency service provided on behalf of the central government. In addition, they give some subsidies to people who improve their own homes.

■ **Transportation.** Local authorities provide and maintain secondary and tertiary roads, and they handle traffic and parking regulations on these roads. Motorways and other primary roads of national importance are the responsibility of the central government. Local authorities also offer some subsidies to privately owned public transportation concerns, notably by compensating them for concessionary fares to older people and other groups.

■ **Cultural services.** Local authorities operate most public libraries. They also have some responsibilities for historic buildings, and they provide some art galleries and museums. In addition, they provide many sports halls, swimming pools, and playing fields as well as some parks and other open spaces. Finally, they promote tourism, chiefly with tourist information offices.

■ **Planning.** Local authorities decide where new developments will take place, and they handle applications for development, which they have the power to accept or reject, subject to an appeal to the central government.

■ **Environment.** Local authorities are responsible for street cleaning, waste collection, and waste disposal. They also coordinate many other environmental services, including the provision of public conveniences, food safety, housing standards, control of noise and other types of pollution, and some cemeteries and crematoria. Some people are still buried in graveyards owned by churches, but these are increasingly becoming full.

In addition to these main services, local authorities perform many other minor services, such as registering births, marriages, deaths, and electors.

The Central Government's Role in Local Government Services

It is difficult to claim that local authorities have complete control over many of their activities. Local authorities are created by central governments, and although the case for local government is arguably to allow services to vary in accordance with local wishes, central governments impose numerous rules and regulations. Indeed, one could say that local authorities now provide most of their services in a national framework, with some room for marginal discretion.

A good example is education. Here, the central government determines the age at which children must start school and the lowest age at which they may leave the education system. Also, especially in England, it enforces a national curriculum within schools, and it funds children at sixth-form level in a way that effectively bypasses local authorities, even though local authorities provide the schools. The government can make it difficult for local authorities to operate selective schools, although it is now becoming a little more open to this idea. Moreover, central governments have acted to give schools some independence from the local authorities that provide them (a) by requiring all governing bodies to have representatives of parents and of the local authority and (b) by requiring local authorities to give much management and financial independence to schools.

Another example is the fire service. Here, the central government has regulations about recruitment, training, promotion policies, and pensions, and it has regulations about fire appliances and the number that must be available in an authority.

Nevertheless, even though the influence of the central government is notable, local authorities generally provide different services from those provided by the central government. Thus, although the central government provides motorways and primary roads, and although it also provides much of the funding for universities, it does not provide secondary or tertiary roads, nor does it provide primary or secondary schools.

Expenditure Responsibilities

From the spending figures given in table 8.4, it can be deduced that in 2001/02, local authorities in England spent UK£80.042 billion from the revenue account for general services. Table 8.6 gives a detailed breakdown of their spending on those services. However, note that the figures in table 8.6 differ from those in table 8.4 in two respects. First, the figures in table 8.6 concern 2003/04. Second, the figures in table 8.6 are net spending figures, which means that they exclude revenue from fees and charges and from many specific grants. These deductions create a much lower total figure of UK£64.31 billion, even though the table concerns a later year.

TABLE 8.6 Net Revenue Expenditure by Local Authorities, England, 2003/04

Service	Amount (UK£ million)	Percentage of total expenditure
Education		
Under-five education	824	1.3
Primary education	10,251	15.9
Secondary education	10,376	16.1
Special education	1,072	1.7
Education services provided by local authority central offices	3,964	6.2
Other education	904	1.4
Total education	**27,390**	**42.6**
Social services		
Children and family services	3,241	5.0
Adults younger than 65 with physical, learning, or mental disabilities	3,453	5.4
Older people's services	5,192	8.1
Other social services	791	1.2
Total social services	**12,677**	**19.7**
Protective services		
Fire services	1,714	2.7
Police services	8,257	12.8
Magistrates courts and so forth	374	0.6
Total protective services	**10,345**	**16.1**
Housing (except housing revenue account)	848	1.3
Transportation		
Roads and bridges	1,698	2.6
Public transportation	1,486	2.3
Other transportation	−13	0.0
Total transportation	**3,172**	**4.9**
Cultural services		
Libraries	745	1.2
Culture and heritage	432	0.7
Sport and recreation	575	0.9
Parks and open places	642	1.0
Tourism	102	0.2
Total cultural services	**2,496**	**3.9**

(continued)

TABLE 8.6   *(continued)*

Service	Amount (UK£ million)	Percentage of total expenditure
Planning	1,236	1.9
Environment		
Street cleaning	454	0.7
Waste collection	754	1.2
Waste disposal	1,057	1.6
Other environment	840	1.3
Total environment	3,105	4.8
Local authority central offices (chiefly administration and so forth)	2,404	3.7
Other services	637	1.0
Total	64,310	100.0

Source: ODPM 2003a, table 3.

Local Government Own-Source Taxes and Charges

A brief history of local taxation, including a look at rates and the poll tax, will provide helpful context for understanding local government own-source taxes and charges. From at least the 13th century until the 1980s, the sole local government tax in Great Britain was a property tax called *rates*.[8] This tax was levied on the occupants of both domestic properties and non-domestic properties at tax rates known as *poundages*. Each local authority set its poundage, which then applied to domestic and nondomestic properties, although sometimes the government paid grants to reduce the poundage on domestic properties. The tax base was the annual, or rental, value of the property concerned. Revaluations were meant to occur every five years, but frequently they were deferred. For example, in England and Wales, a revaluation was done in 1973, but not in 1978, nor in 1983, and not even in 1988. The next revaluation actually took effect in 1990, but in that year, rates on domestic properties were abandoned, so the much-delayed revaluation applied only to nondomestic property.

By the 1980s, rates accounted for roughly half of local current spending, not including fees and charges, and grants accounted for the other half.

The half covered by rates included almost equally rates on domestic properties and rates on nondomestic properties.

In 1989 in Scotland and in 1990 in England and Wales, the government effectively centralized the rates on nondomestic properties. It simultaneously replaced the rates on domestic properties with a poll tax (see Gibson 1990; HMSO 1986; and King 1990). Consequently, domestic rates survive only in Northern Ireland. Most likely, a major reason for replacing domestic rates was the fact that in any forthcoming—and much-delayed—revaluation, the tax base would be substantially redistributed among different areas, which would be highly unpopular in areas where local tax bills would rise. (It might be thought that in areas where the tax base would rise, local taxpayers would have lower poundages, but the equalization grant scheme attempts to ensure that tax rates in all areas are equal for similar spending levels.) Officially, however, the case for replacing domestic rates rested on four other arguments:

1. The domestic rates burden was notably high in areas with high property values, chiefly London and southeast England.
2. Domestic rates were seen as inequitable. The classic example given was of a single pensioner living next door to a family with two working parents and two grown-up working children. If these two households had similar homes, they would pay identical rates, despite having inordinately different incomes.
3. Many people never saw a local rates demand because this document was sent to only one person in each household. Hence, critics argued that other voters in the household might be encouraged to vote for extravagant services.
4. It was argued that local authorities provided services for people, not homes, and that people in expensive homes did not necessarily receive more costly services.

Although all these arguments could be used against the domestic rates, it was chiefly the philosophy behind the fourth argument that led to the decision to introduce a poll tax. The poll tax was a flat rate tax on adults, with local authorities setting the tax per head in their areas. However, not everyone really paid the same amount because means-tested transfer payments were paid to about 30 percent of adults on low incomes to help them pay some or most of the tax. Thus, the poll tax was effectively an income tax on poor people, in that it was related to income, but it was a true poll tax for everyone else.

The poll tax was very unpopular, chiefly because poor people—or at least those not quite poor enough to receive help—paid as much for local services as rich people. This argument was perhaps less robust than it seemed because the poll tax covered only about 25 percent of local spending, the other 75 percent being financed by grants. These grants were, in turn, financed by central taxes, which, taken as a whole, are undoubtedly levied more on rich people than on poor people. Nevertheless, the popular perception remained, even when the level of the poll tax was later reduced to approximately 15 percent of current local spending, after an increase in the level of grants. Ultimately, public pressure forced the poll tax to be replaced in 1992, except, of course, in Northern Ireland, where domestic rates still survive.

Council Tax

In England, Wales, and Scotland, the poll tax was replaced in 1992 by a tax known as the *council tax*. The council tax is a property tax on the occupants of domestic properties, but it differs from the old domestic rates and from other conventional property taxes in several ways.

First, depending on each home's capital value in relation to the mean value of homes, each home is placed in one of eight bands, called bands A to H. The first three columns of table 8.7 show how properties are allocated among the eight bands in England. Scotland and Wales use similar procedures, but the bands there relate to the lower mean values of homes in those countries. Because properties are put only into bands, valuing them is simpler than when each property needs to be given an allegedly precise value. Few appeals were made when the valuations were first done, perhaps because any attraction of paying less tax by being in a lower band is partly offset by the disadvantage of making it harder to sell the property for a price above what its official band implies. The central government makes the valuations.

A second difference is that, within any authority, the council tax bill sent to each home in each band is the same. So in England, for example, the bill sent to a home worth UK£161,000 is the same as the bill sent to a home worth UK£319,000 because they are each in band G. The bill is sent out by a billing authority, which can be a London borough, a district, or a unitary authority, but the bill includes the taxes or "precepts" set by counties, joint boards, and parishes as well as the billing authority's own tax. The billing authority also collects the tax. Usually more than 97 percent is collected.

Third, local authorities set the rate of council tax in their own areas for properties in band D. If there is more than one tier, each tier sets its own rate.

TABLE 8.7 Council Tax Bands and Tax Bill Ratios for English Local Authorities

Band	Range of property values[a] (% mean)	Range of property values at the time of revaluation[a] (UK£)	Tax bills (as a ratio of the bill for a property in band D)	Tax bills (as a fraction of the bill for a property in band D)
A	Under 50	Under 40,000	0.67	6/9
B	50–65	40,000–52,000	0.78	7/9
C	65–85	52,000–68,000	0.89	8/9
D	85–110	68,000–88,000	1.00	9/9
E	110–150	88,000–120,000	1.22	11/9
F	150–200	120,000–160,000	1.44	13/9
G	200–400	160,000–320,000	1.67	15/9
H	More than 400	More than 320,000	2.00	18/9

Source: ODPM 2003c, table 2.2c.
a. The band of each property actually depends on the value it had at the time of revaluation.

Once an authority has set the tax rate for band D properties, it must follow a formula to work out the tax rate for properties in other bands. This formula is reflected in the figures in the fourth column of table 8.7. For example, if an authority sends a bill of UK£1,000 for each Band D property, then it must send a bill of 0.67 × UK£1,000, or £670, to each band A property, and it must send a bill of 2 × UK£1,000, or UK£2,000, to each band H property. The percentage figures in the fourth column of table 8.7 have a certain rationale, which can be seen most easily by expressing them as fractions, as in the fifth column of table 8.7. Note that the bills for each band do not rise in proportion to the values in that band. For example, properties in band G are worth about four or more times as much as those in band B, but their tax bill is little more than twice as much. And indeed, the bill for the most costly house in band H is only three times the bill for the humblest home in band A. This limited range of payments has received criticism, and the government is currently considering creating extra bands.

Fourth, some properties are entitled to a discount on the sum that is usually due on their tax band. A 25 percent discount is allowed on properties where (a) only one adult resides or (b) more than one adult resides but only one adult is not a student. Approximately 34 percent of properties receive this discount. Another group of properties are entitled to a 50 percent discount. This much smaller group accounts for only 3 percent of properties, and the discount applies to homes that are no one's main dwelling. This situation occurs chiefly with homes that are empty (strictly, they must have been empty for more than six months) and with second homes. Starting from 2004/05, local authorities have been allowed to reduce this discount to anywhere between 10 and 50 percent.

Fifth, 3 percent of properties are wholly exempt. These properties fall into a range of categories, but perhaps the most noteworthy are homes occupied wholly by students. The categories include the following:

- An empty home subject to repair and alteration (up to 12 months' exemption)
- A home left unoccupied by someone who is a student, who is in prison, who is in the hospital or a care home, who has moved to give care to someone else, or who has died
- Any other empty home, for up to 6 months (after which it gets the 50 percent discount mentioned above)
- Student halls of residence
- Homes where all the adults are students, are school or college leavers, or are mentally impaired
- A home lived in only by people younger than 18
- A home where at least one resident is a diplomat.

The various features of the council tax mean that it goes some way toward meeting some of the objections to domestic rates. For example, the amount of money that can be raised from the occupants of high-value properties is limited, because people in the highest-value properties (band H) pay only three times as much as people in the lowest-value properties (band A). This limit reflects the objection to domestic rates that people in high-value homes paid very substantially more for local services than people in low-value homes. Also, the council tax ensures that the single adult in one house pays a little less than the household next door with two working parents and two working grown-up children.

A curious feature of the council tax is that it does not provide for regular revaluations. The argument is that if there were a revaluation based around a new mean, most properties would have the same value relative to the new mean as they had relative to the old one, so they would end up in the same band. Nevertheless, relative property values in different areas do change over time, and this fact is not captured by the tax. Accordingly, the present government has given some thought to the idea of having a revaluation to affect the tax bills sent out in 2007.

Uniform Business Rate

Local authorities do receive some tax revenue from businesses, but they do not do so by using a directly set local business tax. Instead, the central government requires local authorities to collect nondomestic rates at a uniform, centrally set rate. The government then redistributes the total nondomestic rate yield so that each area receives the same amount per capita. In an area with two or more tiers, the government decides how the tiers will share the amount allocated to that area.

Although these uniform business rate receipts show up as tax revenues in table 8.4, they are really more appropriately thought of as a central tax that is collected on an agency basis by billing authorities, then transferred by them to the central government, and then finally given back to local authorities on an equal per capita basis as a form of general grant. The case for seeing them as a central tax is strengthened by the fact that the base (which is the annual value), the valuations, and the uniform poundage are all determined centrally, with only the collection being handled locally. However, the present government has considered allowing individual authorities some discretion over the revenue from this tax (see DETR 1998). One idea is for local authorities to be able to levy a small additional tax on businesses in certain areas, called *business improvement districts,* and use the yield to benefit businesses in those districts (see ODPM 2001, para. 7.41). Run-down business areas are the most likely locations.

Perhaps one advantage of having separate property taxes on businesses and homes is that the government is happy to conduct revaluations of business properties every five years. Revaluations were made in 1990, 1995, 2000, and 2005.

The coverage of the uniform business rate actually extends beyond businesses to cover virtually all nondomestic property, including public buildings, pipelines, and advertising hoardings such as billboards and signs. However, churches and embassies are exempt, as are agricultural land and buildings. Certain types of property are given mandatory relief. The main examples are (a) charities, which receive 80 percent relief; (b) village shops, public houses, petrol filling stations, and food shops in isolated areas, which receive 50 percent relief; and (c) empty properties, which receive 50 or 100 percent relief. Additional relief, called *transitional relief,* is allowed following a revaluation to properties facing a steep increase, and it is generally financed by cutting the fall in tax payments of properties that are facing a steep fall. All these reliefs, except the last, merely reduce the total amount that is available to be redistributed among local authorities.

However, local authorities are allowed, at their own expense, to offer further discretionary reliefs. For instance, they can increase the relief on charities to 100 percent and give up to 100 percent relief to other nonprofit organizations such as sports clubs, and they can offer relief to any business ratepayers facing hardship. This last relief was widely used during the 2001 outbreak of foot-and-mouth disease.

The government is proposing further mandatory reliefs. One will apply to all small businesses. The relief will be 50 percent for those whose assessed annual value is UK£3,000, and it will then taper to 0 percent for those whose value is UK£8,000. There will also be some mandatory reliefs for small non-profit organizations and for small shops in deprived urban areas.

Charges

Table 8.4 shows that in 2001/02, English local authorities financed only UK£8.165 billion, or 3 percent, of their revenue spending on general services from charges. The source used for that table gives some details showing how almost all of these charges—about UK£8.137 billion—were divided among the major services headings. Table 8.8 shows this distribution and indicates some of the main charges in each group.

For many years, governments have spoken enthusiastically about local authorities raising more money from charges, but little extra use has in fact been made. However, the present government is making a start by saying that local authorities can charge for discretionary services unless they are specifically prohibited (ODPM 2001, para. 8.12), which is a change from their being unable to charge unless they are specifically permitted to do so.

Intergovernmental Fiscal Transfers

Table 8.4 shows that in 2000/01, English local authorities received UK£21.095 billion in the form of general grants and UK£18.793 billion in the form of specific grants. These two types of grants are discussed in this section. Note, however, the earlier discussion, which argued that the UK£15.144 received from the uniform business rate can also be seen as a type of general grant.

Specific Grants

The specific grants that were paid to English local authorities in 2001/02 were paid under many different programs. Some of these programs were

TABLE 8.8 English Local Authority Charge Revenues, 2001/02

Service	Charge revenue (UK£ million)	Examples
Education	1,718	Vocational courses at adult colleges
		Cookery and woodwork items taken home by school pupils
		School meals
Social services	2,258	Residential care for the elderly
		Meals-on-wheels delivered to the elderly
		Day nurseries for children
Protective services	265	Police attendance at major sporting events
		Police escorts for large loads on the roads
		Charges for certain nonemergency fire services
Roads and transportation	1,040	Parking fees
		Some toll roads and bridges
Cultural services	551	Entrance fees to museums, galleries, and sports centers
		Photocopying fees in libraries
Planning and environment	1,297	Crematoria charges
		Public conveniences
		Planning applications
		Nondomestic waste collection and disposal
Other	1,008	
Total	**8,137**	

Source: Revenue figures from ODPM 2003c, table 1.6b; examples from Bailey 1999.

handled by the Office of the Deputy Prime Minister, which oversees local government, and some were handled by other government departments in pursuit of some of their goals. However, almost 80 percent of the total amount paid in the form of specific grants is accounted for by the eight programs shown in table 8.9.

The first two grants in the table refer to two programs of means-tested transfer payments that are distributed by local authorities. One program provides support—sometimes up to 100 percent—to poor tenants in making rent payments. The other provides help—again sometimes up to 100 percent—to poor taxpayers with their council tax payments. In essence, local authorities can be seen as operating these programs on an agency basis for the central government, because all the rules, conditions, and levels are determined centrally. One might expect that, being an agency

TABLE 8.9 Main Specific Grants to English Local Authorities, 2001/02

Grant	Amount (UK£ million)
Mandatory rent allowance	5,183
Council tax benefit grant	1,937
Police grant	3,798
Education standards fund	1,558
School standards grant	583
Teachers pay reform	547
Asylum seekers grant	541
Greater London Authority transport grant	596
Other	4,050
Total	18,793

Source: ODPM 2003c, table C2b.

service, the local authority would recoup 100 percent of what it distributes through specific grants. However, that type of arrangement would give local authorities no incentive to check the validity of statements made by claimants, and essentially for this reason, the grants meet only 95 percent of their costs.

The police grant reflects the fact noted earlier in that police boards are not totally under local authority control and that, in turn, police services are not seen as a conventional local authority service. The police grant is paid by the Home Office—or Ministry of the Interior—on the basis of a complex formula that refers to the needs of each police force to handle crimes, calls from the public, traffic control, public order management, community policing and patrols, and payments for pensions.

The education standards grant is really a raft of more than 40 grants covering school improvement, social inclusion, schools facing challenging circumstances, teaching assistants, teacher training, and curriculum developments. In many cases, the grants are matching grants that meet 48 percent of relevant expenditure. However, the schools' standard grant is paid directly to each local authority school as a lump sum that depends on the school's size. The teacher's pay reform grant is provided to help local authorities introduce performance pay for teachers.

The asylum seekers grant is paid to local authorities that face costs incurred by asylum seekers while their claims are being processed. Finally, the Greater London Authority transport grant is paid in response to the particular needs of public transportation in London. It was introduced with the Greater London Authority in 2000.

The General Revenue Support Grant

General grants to English local authorities are paid on an equalization grant scheme known as the revenue support grant (RSG).[9] Scotland and Wales have closely related schemes. The operation of the RSG has four steps:

1. For each authority, the government works out how much money it thinks the authority would need to spend to provide its services at levels that the central government deems reasonable, after allowing for receipts of all specific grants and charges.
2. For each authority, the government works out the amount that it could raise from the council tax if it set a reasonable rate for band D properties (and so, in turn, for each other band).
3. For each authority, the government works out how much money each authority will receive through its distribution of the proceeds of the uniform business rate.
4. For each authority, the government deducts the amounts found in steps 2 and 3 from the amount found in step 1, and then it pays a grant equal to the difference.

The result of this procedure is that any two authorities that provide their services at the levels deemed reasonable by the central government could set the same council tax rates.

Formula spending shares

The most controversial part of the RSG calculation is the determination of the amount that the government thinks each local authority needs to spend. These amounts are called formula spending shares (FSSs). The methods by which FSSs are calculated are laid down by the central government (ODPM 2003b). The government actually presents these FSS estimates as measures of relative need rather than of absolute need, but given the way in which the estimates are incorporated into the grant formula, they play the role of estimates of true need.

The procedures for determining FSS figures have five steps:

1. The government works out the total amount of tax plus grant financed expenditure that it thinks would be appropriate for local authorities to spend, consistent with its own macroeconomic policies.
2. The government decides how much of this total should be allocated to each of the main areas of local authority spending. It actually divides this spending into seven broad groups of services.

3. The government works out how much of the spending on each of these groups is likely to be accounted for by specific grants. The remaining amount of approved spending in each group is called a *control total*.
4. The government apportions each control total among individual local authorities.
5. Finally, the government looks at each individual authority. It adds up the amounts of each control total that it allocated to calculate that authority's individual total FSS. As noted earlier, the government then deducts the amount that the local authority could reasonably raise in council tax, plus the amount it will get from the uniform business rate, to arrive at its RSG payment.

The control totals for 2003/04

Table 8.10 shows the control totals that were used in England in 2003/04. The seven broad groups were education; social services; police; fire; highway maintenance; environmental, protective, and cultural services; and capital

TABLE 8.10 Control Totals for Service Groups for English Local Authorities, 2003/04

Item	Amount (UK£ million)	Percentage of total
Education	25,013.9	43.20
Primary education (children 5–11)	8,242.2	14.23
Secondary education (children 11–16)	8,835.3	15.26
Under-five education	2,600.6	4.49
High-cost pupils	2,304.5	3.98
Local education authority central functions	2,418.3	4.18
Other education	613.0	1.06
Social services	11,171.0	19.29
Social services for children	3,038.4	5.25
Social services for older people	4,893.2	8.45
Social services for younger adults	3,239.4	5.59
Police	4,152.0	7.17
Fire	1,777.6	3.07
Highway maintenance	1,954.2	3.37
Environmental, protective, and cultural services	11,570.4	19.98
Capital financing	2,269.3	3.92
Total	57,908.4	100.00

Source: ODPM 2003b.

financing. The control totals for the first two groups are each divided into a few subgroups, as shown in the table.

The government is responsible for allocating the UK£57.908 billion among the various control totals. Some arguing among the government's ministers is inevitable. For instance, the minister of transport will want a large allocation to highway maintenance, the education minister will want a high allocation to education, and the social services minister will want a high allocation to social services. These arguments may seem surprising:

■ It may seem odd that central government ministers care about what local authorities do. However, the central government believes that it has an overall responsibility (a belief that is reasonable because most local revenues are secured from the government), and ministers want voters to approve of services that relate to their ministries.

■ The amounts are used only to calculate FSSs and, in turn, grants; they in no way force local authorities actually to spend those amounts on various services. However, the amounts do set a sort of benchmark, so an increase in the allocation—for example, to police at the expense of roads—could well lead to some actual redistribution of local spending to police from roads.

Implications of altering the control totals

The allocation among control totals has an important implication. If funds were reallocated from roads to police, then the total grants paid to authorities with relatively low needs for roads and relatively high needs for police would rise, while the total grants paid to authorities with relatively high needs for roads and relatively low needs for police would fall. So, by changing the allocation, the government can alter the total grant paid to various authorities.

If the government wishes to favor a particular sort of authority, it may be able to do so by making an appropriate change in the allocation. It is widely thought that the government does manipulate things in this way. Undoubtedly, some manipulation goes on, but probably less manipulation occurs than is generally thought, because changes that help some authorities that the government wishes to help will usually also hurt some other authorities that it also wishes to help. Nevertheless, in general, Conservative Governments tend to help rural authorities more, whereas Labour Governments tend to help urban authorities more.

Dividing control totals among authorities: Problems with regression

The government's biggest task is to allocate each of the control totals among individual local authorities. In the 1970s, much use was made of regression in this process. For instance, it was possible to regress actual past local spending on education against a large number of factors to derive an equation that, to some extent, explained the level of spending by individual authorities on education. Analysts could then use this equation to estimate the amount that each authority might reasonably need to spend, though these amounts would have to be scaled to ensure that they added up to the control total for education.

However, regression analysis done with many of the independent variables fell from favor. The problem with regression analysis is that there might be, say, six authorities, each with a high level of immigrant children. These six authorities know that if they were to raise their education spending levels sharply, regression analysis would show that high numbers of immigrant children were associated with high education spending. In turn, these authorities would find that next year's grant formula would classify them as having a high need to spend and would give them high grants.

Regression does still play some part in the procedures. However, it is typically used only in a base year to gain insight into the relative importance of a few key factors. The next section examines each of the control totals to show how present methods work.[10]

Working Out Individual Authorities' Needs to Spend on Individual Services

The formulas for working out the needs of each local authority to spend on each service block and subblock are quite complex. This section seeks only to give a flavor of them, but it gives a fair bit of detail for education because that category is the most important part of local expenditure. In each service block, one factor that affects an authority's need to spend is the level of labor costs in its area. However, this factor is ignored until the final part of this section, which deals with area cost adjustments.

Primary education

The control total for primary education in 2003/04 was UK£8,242.2 million, as shown in table 8.10. At the heart of the allocation of this sum among individual authorities—and, indeed, at the heart of the allocation of several other control totals—lies the concept of a "client group." Essentially, the client group for primary education is the number of primary school pupils attending an authority's schools. The number of pupils must be recorded sometime before the financial year begins because the grant payments have to be worked out in advance. In 2003/04, the FSS allowed a basic amount of UK£2,004.65 for each of these children.

However, the cost of providing a similar level of education in two authorities with equal numbers of school pupils might be different. There are several reasons for this difference. One is that some pupils have additional educational needs. For example, about 2 percent of children have to be educated in special schools—perhaps because they have mental or physical disabilities—and the cost of their education is about four times that of ordinary children. Moreover, within typical schools, provision must also be made for children with special needs, such as the need for remedial teaching. In addition, some children need to be seen by psychologists and other specialists. Some local authorities have far more need for these forms of additional spending than other authorities do.

It would not be appropriate to use the actual number of pupils being given special attention when calculating grants because authorities will have different policies. So, instead, analysts rely on estimates. Three factors are allowed for. First, an extra UK£520 is allowed for each pupil from a home where English is not the first language. Second, an extra UK£1,001 is allowed for each pupil whose parents are not working and are reliant on social security benefits. Third, an extra UK£312 is allowed for each pupil whose parents are working in low-paid jobs that entitle them to central government transfers.

However, the allowance for extra needs is not quite as generous as the previous paragraph implies, because planners assume that if the sum required in an authority is less than UK£158.92 per pupil overall, then the authority could finance the extra needs from the basic sum per pupil without special help. So the actual extra sum allowed by the FSS is either the sum required –UK£158.92 per pupil or zero, whichever is greater.

Another reason costs might vary among authorities is that some authorities have sparse populations. Those authorities' main problem is that they typically have to run small schools in isolated areas, so they end up with far more teachers in relation to population. FSSs allow for these costs chiefly by allowing an extra UK£577.50 for every pupil who lives in a *supersparse* electoral ward—that is, a ward with one-half or fewer residents per hectare. In addition, planners allow an extra UK£165 for every pupil living in a *sparse* ward—that is, a ward having more than one-half but not more than four people per hectare.

Secondary education and under-five education

The FSS for secondary education is similar to that for primary education, though with some slightly different parameters. The main difference is that the basic amount per pupil is UK£2,656.92. Note that this amount covers only children up to about 16. For older children, schools receive funds from the central government—through a centrally established body called the Learning and Skills Council—rather than from local authorities. So local authorities themselves have no need for money with respect to these older pupils. No allowance is made for population sparsity with secondary education because the assumption is that secondary pupils will, if necessary, travel long distances to a large school.

The FSS for under-five education is also broadly similar to that for primary education. For each four-year-old pupil, the basic amount is UK£2,546.58. For each three-year-old pupil, the basic allocation is half the amount for four-year-olds because the assumption is that three-year-olds attend school for half a day whereas four-year-olds attend for a full day. Again, no allowance is made for population sparsity.

Other main components of education

The high-cost pupils subblock is intended to cover the extra costs of pupils whose attainment levels are four or more years below what is normal for their age. For each high-cost pupil, the FSS allows an extra UK£6,800.86. The government could ask authorities how many children they have who fit this category, but the concern is that each authority might have "different statementing policies" (ODPM 2002, 5). Consequently, the government estimates the number. Its estimate is a flat 1 percent of children in every area, plus 7 percent of children whose parents are unemployed and rely on central government transfers, plus 21 percent of children who were born with a weight below 2,500 grams.

The subblock for local education authority central functions concerns activities that are handled directly by the central offices of local authorities. The formula is complex, but it can be approximated as a payment of UK£212.84 for every school pupil. Extra amounts are allocated for pupils with extra needs and for population sparsity. Sparsity is relevant here because one function handled by the central offices of local authorities is transporting children to and from school.

Social services for children

Children's services include providing residential homes for homeless children, foster parents, social work support, and special services for children with mental and physical disabilities. Children are defined as being younger than 18, and the government provides a basic allowance of UK£92.60 per child. The idea is that when all of this funding is actually devoted to the relatively few children in need, the amount should go a long way toward meeting the relevant costs.

However, it is accepted that the proportion of children in need will be higher in areas where many children can be seen as deprived. Five factors are allowed for here: an extra UK£267.71 is allowed for each child living in flats; an extra UK£2,066.05 is allowed for each child with a limiting, long-term illness; an extra UK£384.30 is allowed for each child whose parents are unemployed and rely on state transfers; an extra UK£743.71 is allowed for each child in a one-adult household; and a further allowance is provided that increases the amount allowed for areas with a high-density population. However, the FSS is not quite as generous as these figures imply because the assumption is that if the sum required in an authority is less than UK£106.97 per child overall, the authority could finance the extra needs from the basic sum per child without special help. So the actual extra sum allowed by FSS is either the sum required −UK£106.97 per child or zero, whichever is greater. Finally, however, a further adjustment is provided to favor areas where many people were either born outside the United Kingdom or born outside a few other specified countries.

Social services for adults

Adults are divided into "older" adults, age 65 and older, and "younger" adults, age 18 to 64. A basic amount of UK£337.77 is allocated for each older adult. The amount is increased if the proportions of those who are older than 74 or older than 84 exceed stated levels. Further allowances are provided, which depend on the number of pensioners in the following categories: those who live in rented accommodations; those who have long-term, limiting illnesses; those who rely almost wholly on central government benefits; those who live alone; those who need attendance in their homes; those who have disabilities; those who do not live as a couple; and those who are not the head of a household. Finally, there is extra help for areas with sparse populations.

For younger adults, the basic amount is just UK£73.84 each. Further allowances are provided for those who rely on central government benefits, for those with no family, and for those living in public sector rented flats.

Police

The police FSS depends chiefly on two measures of an authority's population. It allows UK£28.70 for each permanent resident and UK£35.53 for each person in its daytime population, which is its resident population plus estimates of the numbers of commuters, U.K. visitors, and foreign visitors. Extra allowances are made for areas with highly dense or notably sparse populations. In addition, allowances are provided for each kilometer of motorway and for each kilometer of road subject to speed limits below the national maximum of 70 miles per hour, where the density of population is highest.

Further allowances are added for deprived areas. Deprivation is measured in a complex way that refers to factors such as the number of households that reside in rented property; that reside in terraced property (that is, rowhouses); that consist of a single-parent family; that have more than one person to a room; that include only one person age 16 or over; that include unemployed adults who rely on central government benefits; or that include long-term unemployed adults. Finally, there is an allowance for police forces with specified security commitments, perhaps to guard properties occupied by members of the royal family and high-profile politicians.

Fire services

The key component in the fire FSS is the resident population, with UK£17.50 allowed for each person. Authorities with coastlines receive additional funds, chiefly because they could less easily rely on help from adjacent authorities at moments when their resources might be fully stretched. Similarly, areas with high-risk properties such as chemical plants received additional allowances. Further help is also provided for areas with deprivation, which is measured in relation to several factors that include the number of children with unemployed parents who rely on central government benefits, the number of homes that are not detached residences, the number of people in rented accommodations, and the number of pupils absent from school for whatever reason. Other factors include the number of properties that need fire certificates—to certify that they have installed necessary fire escapes and firefighting equipment.

Highway maintenance

As noted earlier, the central government maintains the most important roads. Local authorities maintain only roads of lesser importance. The chief factor for calculating the FSS for highway maintenance is the length of roads of different types. Essentially, an authority is given a "weighted road length," which is double the length of roads in areas with speed limits below the national maximum of 70 miles per hour (because these roads are in the most densely populated areas) plus the length of other roads. An allowance of UK£406.33 is made for every kilometer of weighted road lengths.

Three further major allowances are calculated. First is an addition that depends on traffic flows over the roads, with special help for traffic in the form of vehicles carrying heavy goods (the help depends on usage by vehicles that can carry heavy goods, irrespective of whether they are loaded).

Second is an addition that depends on the daytime population (which is defined slightly differently from the definition used for police). Third is an allowance that depends on the average number of days when an area has snow to clear and the average number of days when cold weather requires its roads to be gritted.

Environmental, protective, and cultural services

This spending block for environmental, protective, and cultural services covers a wide range of services—indeed everything not specifically covered by the other blocks. Also, the services concerned are typically divided between tiers in two-tier areas. As a result of these factors, the formula is quite complex. In essence, though, the formula is related to the resident population, the daytime population, the population density, and the number of people claiming central government benefits. Additional allowances are made for areas responsible for flood protection, coastal defense, and national parks.

Capital financing

Because FSSs refer only to current expenditure, it might seem odd that there is a control total for capital financing. However, local authorities finance some of their capital spending by borrowing, and this final control total refers chiefly to the repayment of their past loans and the interest payments on those loans. The allocation procedures are complex, but broadly, the FSSs seek to cover the amount of repayment and interest that local authorities must pay on their debts, provided that they borrow only such amounts as the government approves and also that they repay old debts at a rate of 4 percent per year.

Area cost adjustments

One further point about FSSs must be noted. In addition to all the factors noted so far, the government seeks to compensate authorities where labor costs are high. So, for each authority in a high labor cost area, the FSS for each service group (other than capital financing) is increased. The extent to which FSSs are increased for a high-cost authority varies a little from service group to service group because some groups involve proportionately more labor costs than others. For instance, labor costs are calculated to account for a larger proportion of police services than other services, so policing attracts the highest area cost adjustments.

Labor costs tend to be highest in London and other parts of southeast England, so areas there get the highest area cost adjustments. The overall result of these adjustments is that authorities in inner London have FSSs that are 20 to 35 percent higher than they would otherwise be, whereas authorities near London have FSSs that are typically 5 to 15 percent higher than they would otherwise be. Some other authorities also get small increases.

This labor cost factor may seem reasonable, but it has an unsatisfactory effect. Labor costs are high in southeast England chiefly because workers there want compensation for high-cost housing, which results from a high density of population. If local authorities there received no extra FSSs and hence received no extra grants for their high labor costs, their local tax rates would be higher. That situation would encourage people to move, which, in turn, would reduce housing costs and thus help to ease labor costs. Instead, the payment of higher grants simply perpetuates the problem and, indeed, probably aggravates it. Also, these adjustments reduce the extent to which the richest areas of the country transfer money to other areas by means of the public sector.

Local Government Borrowing and Other Capital Revenues

Table 8.4 shows that in 2001/02, English local authorities spent UK£9.741 billion on capital expenditure. This figure is, of course, chiefly accounted for by spending on buildings, land, vehicles, plant, and machinery. For accounting purposes, other expenditures that are not strictly capital expenditures are included along with this UK£9.741 billion to take the total spending that has to be financed to UK£10.028 billion. The sources of finance for this amount are shown in table 8.11.

TABLE 8.11 Funding Sources for Capital Spending by English Local Authorities, 2001/02

Source	Amount (UK£ million)	Percentage of total
Credit approvals	2,551	25.4
Central government grants	2,027	20.2
Other grants and contributions	757	7.5
Use of usable capital receipts	1,975	19.7
Revenue finance	2,330	23.2
Other sources	387	3.9
Total	**10,028**	**100.0**

Source: ODPM 2003c, table 4.2a.

The first source, credit approvals, relates to loans. The total revenue of UK£2.551 billion may seem surprising given the figure of –UK£197 million shown in table 8.4. However, the table 8.4 figure shows the amount borrowed minus the amount repaid, whereas table 8.11 shows only the amount borrowed. Loans are discussed further in the next section. First, however, because loans fund only about a quarter of the capital expenditure, it is worth saying a few words about some of the other sources.

Central government grants are given only for specific projects—usually projects concerned with transportation, housing, or regeneration. The relevant central government departments finance such grants. Of course, the government gives local authorities additional support for capital projects beyond that shown in table 8.11 because the capital spending element of the revenue support grant helps authorities service debt.

Local authorities also receive occasional grants or contributions from sources other than the central government. Examples include grants from the National Lottery and contributions made by the private sector for access roads or traffic management schemes. In addition, some grants come from nondepartmental public bodies such as the Countryside Commission and the Sports Council.

Capital receipts are revenues raised by selling assets and revenues received as repayments of grants and loans that have been made by local authorities themselves. In the past 25 years, a large proportion of these receipts have come from the sale of local authority homes to their occupants. However, only part of these receipts may be used to fund new capital spending. It is mainly for this reason that the figure in table 8.11 for the capital receipts that are so used (UK£1.975 billion) is so much less than the total revenue from these receipts (UK£3.579 billion), as shown in table 8.4. This source of finance might seem to work to the advantage of local authorities with many assets to sell, but in fact, the government has a fair idea which these authorities are, and it is likely to impose an offsetting reduction in the extent to which they can borrow.

Credit Approvals

For more than 100 years, local authorities have needed central government permission to borrow. From 1990 until recently, their borrowing in England was regulated by limiting the extent to which they could spend funds on loan-financed projects. To use funds in this way, a local authority had to point to a relevant credit approval. Each local authority was given two types of credit approval. One type was a *basic credit approval*. A local authority received a basic credit approval each year and could spend it on any capital project, although it had to be spent within the year. The other type was a *supplementary credit approval,* which was normally linked to a specific project. Supplementary credit approvals could be spent over a two-year period.

Beginning in 2004, however, the system in England was reformed. Instead of having credits, local authorities are now required to set "prudential limits" to their borrowing, and they are free to borrow within those limits. Local authorities are not allowed to exceed the limits, and the government can overrule the limits if it thinks that they are excessive.

At first sight, this reform may seem to increase local freedom greatly. But local authorities have to take their future revenue position into account, and given the difficulty of meeting their revenue expenditure, even ignoring the servicing of debt, any prudential limit will clearly be very tight. Prudential limits also have to take account of existing debt levels and the level of reserves held. Moreover, the government sets a national borrowing limit for all local authorities taken together, and if the total self-declared figures for prudent borrowing exceed that limit, then local authorities must trim their plans.

Once local authorities do borrow, they can enter the capital markets and borrow from banks or other financial intermediaries, and they can also issue bonds and other financial claims. Occasionally, they borrow from abroad. However, they borrow most of their money from a body called the Public Works Loan Board, which, by acting on behalf of all of them, is typically able to secure better terms.

The Private Finance Initiative

Table 8.11 implied that local authorities could acquire new assets for their use only by using one of the sources of funding listed there to purchase a new asset. Since 1996, however, local authorities have been able to take a quite different route called the Private Finance Initiative (PFI). In 2001/02, this initiative financed an additional UK£634 million worth of extra assets for local government use, beyond those covered by the funds and spending shown in table 8.11.

The following example will help to explain how the PFI works. Consider a local authority that wants a new school. Traditionally, it would borrow or find the funds in another way and build the school, which would then be its property. Under the PFI, it arranges for a private consortium to raise the funds as well as to build and manage the school. But it has a contract with the consortium that runs over a period of many years, and under the contract, it will be allowed to pay an annual fee to use the school.

The idea for the PFI came about because it was felt that controlling inflation meant controlling the money stock, which in turn meant controlling public sector borrowing. The PFI introduced a way for the public sector to secure the use of extra assets without borrowing, and the PFI is also used by the central government. The PFI is not an unmixed blessing, however, because the authority loses some control over the design of the assets that it will use.

Local authorities are limited in the extent to which they can use the PFI. The government determines the total value of PFI projects that can be undertaken in a given year, and it allocates this total among government departments. The departments, in turn, determine how much will be available to local authorities. Individual local authorities apply for PFI credits for individual projects.

Local Government Administration

Local civil servants are hired by the elected councilors. The councilors can set their terms of employment. However, many local authorities belong voluntarily to a national agreement that sets forth a broad framework for pay, conditions, and employment relations. A recent report (Local Government Pay Commission 2003) looked into local government conditions, and broadly, it asserts that the agreement will continue. Of course, the government can make its preferences clear, and one issue that it is currently emphasizing—and that it included in its evidence to the commission—is the need for more performance-related pay.

Local government employees comprise many categories, including teachers, police officers, and fire service officers, for whom local authorities essentially agree on national pay scales with trades unions. But there is scope for higher rates of pay in areas such as southeast England.

An Overall Assessment

In the author's view, the general effect of the reforms on local government in recent years has been to weaken it and to make it less accountable to local voters. Indeed, it is difficult to think of any act in the past 20 years that has significantly strengthened local government. The falling turnouts in local elections lend support to this view. This alleged weakening had been caused by both the structural changes and the financial changes.

The Effect of the Structural Changes

Three major structural reforms of local government were conducted in the past century. Of course, circumstances change over time, and certainly the problems of areas with holes in them and of social services and housing being entrusted to different tiers needed attention, even if these problems still exist in places. However, one could argue that a reason for these frequent changes is that governments have not formed a clear philosophy of local government's purpose. Its primary purpose must surely be to provide services in accordance with variations in local wishes. That purpose is not necessarily consistent with the holes that arose in the 1890s, or with the large authorities that arose in the 1970s, or even with the rather untidy arrangements that exist today. Those reforms seem to have been led primarily by perceptions of what could be supplied rather than what was being demanded.

Another problem is that the recent, relatively frequent changes to local government structure have reduced people's understanding of how local government works. Of course, if the present structure is left alone long enough, then this problem will diminish. But past experience suggests that central governments will be unlikely to adopt a hands-off approach.

A further structural issue is the existence of joint boards whose democratic credentials are perhaps a little unclear. At the very least, these boards are not directly accountable to the electorates in the areas they serve. That indirect accountability surely weakens their authority. The need for at least one board in every area with unitary authorities must call into question the wisdom of having a single tier in those areas.

The Effect of the Financial Changes

On the financial side, local authorities have been weakened because their revenues from genuine local taxes have fallen. In the 1980s, a time when local authorities directly levied domestic rates and nondomestic rates, those revenues were approximately 50 percent of local spending financed by taxes and grants. Table 8.4 shows that the only genuine local tax now levied—the domestic council tax—meets only about 20 percent of local spending financed by taxes and grants, if we view the business property tax as a grant. This low percentage has several problems.

First, because central governments finance a high proportion of local spending, they argue plausibly that they deserve a large share in its control. But allowing that large share makes local authorities generally accountable to the central government.

Second, because the only locally set tax accounts for such a small percentage of revenue, small increases in spending lead to disproportionately large increases in tax rates. Indeed, tax rates can rise several percentage points without any discernible change in services, and local authorities merely blame the government for inadequate grants. Indeed, in early 2004, the substantial increases in local taxes were blamed on the government, so central politicians said they would look for new sources of local revenue. Meanwhile, local politicians largely escaped the blame. For reasons such as these, central politicians introduced capping—and since 2003 have threatened to reintroduce it—but that move clearly constrains local accountability.

Another way of looking at this issue is to consider "gearing." Say a local authority spends UK£X million and raises UK£$0.5X$ million from its own taxes. Then suppose it wants to raise its general grant plus tax financed spending by only 10 percent to UK£$1.1X$ million. It will have to raise the entire remainder from taxes, so its tax rates must rise by a fifth, or 20 percent, to get a tax revenue of UK£$0.6X$ million. For a typical English authority, the taxes would raise only UK£$0.3X$ million, so a 33 percent rise in tax rates would be needed to raise the extra UK£$0.1X$ million. And for some authorities, taxes raise less than UK£$0.2X$ million, so tax rates would have to be raised by more than 50 percent to secure a mere 10 percent rise in spending.

As a result of the gearing problem, central governments must try to get the general RSG payments to individual authorities done correctly. This responsibility has led to the complicated system of needs assessment. A problem with needs assessment is that relatively minor tweaks to the system can have big effects on some authorities and their tax rates.

How can local revenues be strengthened? It might seem that a large increase in the council tax would solve the problem. But property taxes are poorly related to ability to pay, and international experience suggests that it is hard to make a domestic property tax account for more than 2 percent of GDP. So with local spending more than 10 percent of GDP, another tax is needed, and indeed, only a local income tax has the potential to bridge a large part of the gap between spending and the existing tax. The present government is undertaking a balance of funding review, which might in principle lead to an increase in the level of local taxation. But few people would expect anything beyond a very small increase.

Nevertheless, the United Kingdom's system of local finance does have two attractive features. First, the council tax does attempt to address some of the criticisms of traditional property taxes. It does so by not making payments proportional to property values and by offering an array of discounts and exemptions.

Second, the United Kingdom has one of the few systems that attempt full equalization, and indeed, it has done so for many years. Anything less than full equalization creates an incentive for people to move from areas with low resources and higher needs to areas with high resources and low needs, with no gain from the economy as a whole. As just indicated, the formula could be much simpler if it were allowed to be less precise, which would be feasible if grants were relatively less important.

However, by allowing for different wage costs in different parts of the country, the grant system seems to result in transfers from low-wage areas to high-wage areas. Moreover, it deters people from moving from high-wage areas to low-wage areas, which would benefit the economy by cutting the cost of local services.

Lessons for Developing Countries

The discussion in this chapter—quite a lot of these issues arose earlier—points to some interesting lessons for developing countries that are embarking on reforms to their system of local government:

- It is important to have a clear philosophy when reforming local government. Are local authorities intended to be locally elected bodies that reflect local wishes, or are they meant to be primarily agents of the central government? The United Kingdom has moved steadily away from the first approach toward the second, and governments nevertheless seem surprised by low turnouts at local elections. If governments really want near uniformity, then perhaps a better strategy would be not to establish local government at all because it might end up being largely a charade.
- There are no doubt times when the structure of local government needs some change. But the case can be made for not reforming the structure of local government if it can feasibly be left alone. Also, if people have developed loyalties to an existing structure, then it may be difficult for them to transfer their loyalties to another.
- Large authorities may enjoy economies of scale (though little evidence supports this notion), and they may enjoy economies of scope, perhaps being large enough to have large museums or large parks. But their reduced ability to cater to varying preferences is a disadvantage.
- Establishing authorities with holes in them, where other authorities undertake services, can cause problems.
- Problems can arise if related services—such as social services and housing—are entrusted to different tiers.

- Joint boards seem to have some special problems, and perhaps having more tiers of genuine local authorities is better. One problem with the boards is that their members are not directly elected by voters. In turn, the members are unlikely to face direct accountability to voters if spending is considered too high or if services are poor. Also, the boards have little scope for weighing the merits of more or less spending on their services vis-à-vis other services.

- If a country wants some genuine local authority discretion, it should give local authorities enough tax-raising power that dependence on grants— a major excuse for central interference—is modest. Further problems with limited local taxes are that small spending increases lead to large increases in tax rates and that a complex system of needs assessment is required to try to accurately measure needs. If grants accounted for, say, only 25 percent of spending, then only modest tax rate increases would be needed to offset any shortcomings in the assessments. Little evidence suggests that countries with decentralized taxes have problems operating successful macroeconomic policies, and some evidence suggests the opposite.

- U.K. experience suggests that local domestic property taxes are hard-pressed to raise more than 2 percent of GDP. Their poor relationship with ability to pay and their visibility make higher yields politically unacceptable. If a country's state of development permits it, a local income tax is the best way of raising large local revenues.

- The United Kingdom's property tax has some interesting features. One of these is simply putting properties into bands rather than valuing each one. This approach might particularly appeal to developing countries in which qualified assessors are scarce. Also, it reduces appeals because there is no point appealing against alleged errors unless they result in the property being in a band that is considered too high. And it makes valuations simple and revaluations necessary less often.

- The United Kingdom's council tax offers an interesting array of exemptions and discounts, particularly the 25 percent discount for one-adult homes.

- The United Kingdom's system of needs assessment is complex, but it is an example of complete equalization. And the formulas have some interesting features. Nevertheless, one has to question equalizing differences in labor costs because that approach may result in the grant system implicitly transferring funds from poor, low-wage cost areas to rich, high-wage areas.

- The concept of the Private Finance Initiative may appeal to countries in which private firms find it easier to borrow than governments or in which governments are concerned about high public sector borrowing.

Notes

1. For a brief history of local government from early times until the latest reforms, see Watt (1996, 21–38).
2. For a review of the English reforms, see Redcliffe-Maud and Wood (1974).
3. Before making this reform, the government had established a commission to study local government in London; see Herbert (1960).
4. Before making these reforms, the government had established one commission to study local government in England (see Redcliffe-Maud 1969) and another commission to study local government in Scotland (see Wheatley 1969).
5. For insights into government thinking, see, for example, DoE (1991) and Scottish Office (1992).
6. This section draws heavily on Watt (1996, 32–33).
7. For more information, see http://www.audit-commission.gov.uk/cpa/.
8. For a short history of rates, see Foster, Jackman, and Perlman (1980, 152–71).
9. For an overview of the RSG, see King (1990).
10. The discussion here is based on ODPM (2003b).

References

ACC (Association of County Councils). 1994. *Revenue Support Grant 1994/95, England.* London: ACC.

Bailey, Stephen J. 1999. *Local Government Economics: Principles and Practice.* London: Macmillan.

DETR (Department of the Environment, Transport, and the Regions). 1998. *Modernising Local Government: Business Rates.* London: DETR.

DoE (Department of the Environment). 1991. *Local Government Review: Shaping the New Councils: A Consultation Paper.* London: DoE.

Foster, Christopher D., Richard A. Jackman, and Morris Perlman. 1980. *Local Government Finance in a Unitary State.* London: Allen & Unwin.

Gibson, John. 1990. *The Politics and Economics of the Poll Tax: Mrs. Thatcher's Downfall.* West Midlands, U.K.: EMAS.

Herbert, Edwin, chairman. 1960. "Royal Commission on Local Government in London 1957–60." Report Cmnd. 1164, Her Majesty's Stationery Office, London.

HMSO (Her Majesty's Stationery Office). 1986. "Paying for Local Government." Report Cmnd. 9714, HMSO, London.

King, David. 1990. "Accountability and Equity in British Local Finance: The Poll Tax." In *Decentralization, Local Governments and Markets,* ed. Robert J. Bennett, 143–56. Oxford, U.K.: Clarendon Press.

King, David, and Yue Ma. 1999a. "Central Government Control over Local Authority Expenditure: The Overseas Experience." *Public Money and Management* 19: 3, 23–28.

———. 1999b. "Decentralisation and Macroeconomic Performance." *Applied Economics Letters* 7: 11–14.

Local Government Pay Commission. 2003. *Report of the Local Government Pay Commission.* http://www.lgpay.org.uk/Documents/lgpayreportoct03.pdf.

ODPM (Office of the Deputy Prime Minister). 1999. *Local Leadership Local Choice.* http://www.odpm.gov.uk/index.asp?id=1135553.

———. 2001. *White Paper—Strong Local Leadership: Quality Public Services*. London: ODPM.

———. 2002. *Formula Grant Distribution System—Methodology*. London: ODPM. http://www.local.detr.gov.uk/finance/0304/method.pdf.

———. 2003a. "Local Authority Revenue Expenditure and Financing England 2003–04 Budget." Statistical release, July, ODPM, London. http://www.local.odpm.gov.uk/finance/capital/natstats/natstats3.pdf.

———. 2003b. *Local Government Finance in England: The Local Government Finance Report (England) 2003/2004*. London: ODPM.

———. 2003c. *Local Government Financial Statistics England, No. 14, 2003*. London: ODPM.

Redcliffe-Maud, Lord, chairman. 1969. "Royal Commission on Local Government in England 1966–69." Report Cmnd. 4040, Her Majesty's Stationery Office, London.

Redcliffe-Maud, Lord, and Bruce Wood. 1974. *English Local Government Reformed*. Oxford, U.K.: Oxford University Press.

Scottish Office. 1992. "The Structure of Local Government in Scotland: Shaping the New Councils." Consultation paper, Scottish Office, Edinburgh.

Stenton, Doris May. 1962. *The Pelican History of England: English Society in the Early Middle Ages*. Middlesex, U.K.: Penguin.

Watt, Peter A. 1996. *Local Government Principles and Practice: A Text for Risk Managers*. London: Witherby.

Wheatley, Lord, chairman. 1969. "Royal Commission on Local Government in Scotland 1966–69." Report Cmnd. 4150, Her Majesty's Stationery Office, London.

9

Local Government Organization and Finance: *United States*

LARRY SCHROEDER

Subnational governments in the United States are highly devolved both organizationally and fiscally; they are also extremely diverse and complex both organizationally and fiscally. Consequently, this relatively brief chapter cannot do justice to the tremendous differences found across states within the United States with respect to how local governments are organized, what services they provide, and how they are financed. Instead, the intent here is to provide a broad overview, with enough examples of exceptions to the generalizations to give some glimpse of the subject's complexities.

The structure of government in the United States is federal, consisting of the federal (central) government, 50 state governments, and numerous local governments. Unlike some federal countries such as India, the constitution of the United States does not explicitly list the responsibilities of the federal and state governments. In fact, the U.S. constitution (10th amendment) explicitly states: "The powers not delegated to the United States by the Constitution, nor prohibited by it to the states, are reserved to the states respectively, or to the people."

The 10th amendment means that individual states retain considerable powers. Among these is the power to establish local governments (because the federal constitution makes no mention of local governments). Thus, the organizational structure of subnational governments, their functional responsibilities, and their revenue powers differ across states (and, in many instances, even within states).

The first section of this chapter focuses on the general pattern of local government organization, and the second section discusses the expenditure responsibilities. The third, fourth, and fifth sections focus on subnational government current revenues—their own-source revenues, shared taxes, and transfers. The sixth and seventh sections discuss, respectively, the borrowing powers of state and local governments and public employment patterns. The eighth section focuses on the mechanisms that generally hold local governments accountable, and the final section attempts to derive a set of lessons that developing countries, especially, can draw from this review.

Organization of Subnational Governments

According to the U.S. Census Bureau, more than 87,000 governmental units were operating in the country as of June 30, 2002.[1] In addition to the federal (central) government and the 50 state governments, the Census Bureau recognizes five basic types of local government units. Three of these—counties, municipalities, and townships—are general-purpose governments in that they are intended to provide an array of public services. Two additional types of limited-purpose local governments are also recognized—school district governments and "special district" local governments. The purpose of this section is to provide a general overview of these various governmental units and to explain how they are linked and generally how they are governed. However, because these units vary tremendously, it is not possible to give detailed descriptions of each.[2]

Primary Types of Local Governments

With few exceptions, states are fully subdivided into counties, and the number of counties per state varies greatly, from 254 in Texas to fewer than 20 in some states. Likewise, the number of residents of counties range from fewer than 100 in one Texas county to more than 9.5 million in Los Angeles County, California.[3] Counties generally perform a number of different public services and rely on taxes, user charges, and intergovernmental transfers for revenues.

Municipalities probably are closest to what individuals think of as local government. But the term *municipality,* as defined by the U.S. Census Bureau, encompasses a wide range of localized government—from large cities to small towns and villages with relatively few residents. Municipalities may be located within a single county, but in some instances, they cross county (and, in a few instances, state) borders. The numbers of municipal governments also vary considerably across the states, with Illinois, Pennsylvania, and Texas each having more than 1,000 such entities and Hawaii and Rhode Island having 1 and 8 municipalities, respectively. Populations living outside municipalities receive public services either from the county or from the third type of general-purpose local government, the township, found in 20 states, primarily in the Northeast and Midwest. (In 9 of the 20 states, these entities are called *towns.*)

The history of towns and counties in the 13 original states is particularly interesting (and parallels what one observes in developing countries today). In the northeastern states, counties were essentially established as administrative units of the state government; in those states, the town became the primary unit of popular local government. In fact, the town meeting of the New England states, which all residents of the town are expected to attend and participate in, is still considered the epitome of participatory local government. In the original southern states of the late 18th century, counties not only performed administrative functions but also were considered the principal local government. Interestingly, even today local services are primarily provided by counties in the southern states, whereas in the northeastern states, municipalities (including the township) play a primary role.

In the Midwest, townships were formed coincidentally with the mapping of the area; therefore, they were not linked specifically to a local economy or even natural boundaries. Instead, cartographers were instructed to create townships often containing 36 square miles—6 miles on each side.

Primary and secondary schooling in the United States is, in most instances, provided by single-purpose school district governments rather than by general-purpose counties or municipalities. A school district is governed by its own independent board consisting of locally elected individuals. This board too has the power to impose certain taxes, receive intergovernmental transfers, and incur debt for the sole purpose of educating the youth residing in the boundaries of the district. However, not all primary and secondary education is provided by independent school districts. In some areas, local school services are the responsibility of a county or municipality. For example, Maryland and Connecticut have no independent school districts, and Virginia has only one; in Hawaii, primary and secondary education is provided directly by the state. In other states, some of the school districts are independent local governments, whereas in other jurisdictions, schooling is provided by a municipality or county.

The final type of limited-purpose local government is known as the *special district government*. These districts are authorized under the laws of individual states to provide a single or limited number of services. At the same time, they have sufficient administrative and fiscal autonomy to act independently from other local governments. Some, but not all, have the authority to levy taxes, and most have the ability to incur debt. Examples of the sorts of public services performed by these special districts include fire protection, water supply, sewage services, and drainage and flood control as well as capital-intensive services such as airports. Because state statutes govern the formation of special districts, the number of such districts differs substantially from state to state. In 2002, Illinois had more than 3,100 special districts, and California was the home to more than 2,800. In contrast, several states had only a few—Alaska (14), Hawaii (15), and Louisiana (45). McCabe (2000) and Stephens and Wikstrom (1998) provide further discussions of the roles of special districts.

As is the case in many other countries, the capital region of the United States is treated differently from all other state and local governments. The District of Columbia, or Washington, D.C., is officially neither a state nor a municipality.[4] Instead, it takes on the functions of both a state and a city (although for statistical purposes, the Census Bureau considers the District of Columbia a municipality).

Numbers of Local Governments

Table 9.1 shows the numbers of each of these types of local government for 2002 as well as for 1992 and 1962. The number of counties declined slightly from 1992 until 2002, primarily because Massachusetts abolished several counties during the late 1990s and transferred responsibility for the functions they had been performing to the state government. The number of municipalities has grown slightly over the past 40 years, whereas the number of townships has declined.

As shown in table 9.1, the primary reason the total number of local governments declined during the 30-year period from 1962 to 1992 is the decrease in the number of school districts. Many small school districts, particularly those in rural areas of the country, were consolidated into fewer, larger districts. This trend has continued through the

TABLE 9.1 Quantity of Local Governments in the United States, 1962, 1992, and 2002

Type of local government	1962	1992	2002
Counties	3,043	3,043	3,034
Municipalities	17,997	19,279	19,429
Townships[a]	17,144	16,656	16,504
School districts	34,678	14,422	13,506
Special districts	18,323	31,555	35,052
Total	91,185	84,955	87,525

Source: U.S. Census Bureau 2002.
a. Called "towns" in 11 states.

past 10 years. At the same time, the number of special districts has increased rapidly, and they now represent approximately 40 percent of all local governments.

Several conclusions can be drawn from this brief review of the structure of local governments in the United States. First, the obviously complex structure is made more so by the fact that each state has the autonomy to choose the way how it wishes to define local government. Second, although the country is geographically large, with a population in excess of 290 million, its more than 87,000 local governments is a large number (about 1 local government for every 3,333 people). Finally, the data in table 9.1 reveal an important fact about local government in the United States: it is far from static.

Observers recognize both advantages and disadvantages of this type of system. On the negative side is the fact that the large number of local jurisdictions, which commonly overlap, can create considerable confusion among voters and taxpayers. One individual may be a resident of a county, a town, a municipality, a school district, and one or more special districts. The individual will be expected to render taxes to each of these local governments and to participate in elections to choose the elected leaders of each. Simply learning to whom one should go to resolve local public service concerns can entail considerable transaction costs.

The large number of local governments can also lead to wasteful duplication of efforts and greater coordination costs. Furthermore, because some costs are fixed, particularly those associated with administrative overhead, the costs of local government can be increased by having large numbers of small jurisdictions.

On the positive side, the multiplicity of local governments is in keeping with the underlying rationale for decentralization. With multiple small jurisdictions, the particular needs or demands for public services by individuals within a relatively homogeneous neighborhood are more likely to be met than if public services are provided uniformly across a larger geographic area. Likewise, the transaction cost of voicing concerns about the quality or quantity of services is lower if officials are nearby. Finally, the threat of mobility (that is, exit) to an alternative locality that is providing a more desirable set of services and tax prices is greater where there is increased variability in these combinations. All those factors can lead to increased efficiency in the provision of local public services.

The heavy reliance on independent school districts and the large number of special districts help differentiate local governments in the United States from those in most other countries. Local control over education has a long history in the United States. Even though there may be substantial spillover effects from primary and secondary education (particularly when students educated locally move to other areas), local constituents commonly oppose efforts to permit states or the national government to "interfere" in education decisions. Nevertheless, because states often provide a substantial portion of the revenues available to local schools, states have used this funding to leverage greater control over what locally elected school boards are permitted to do. This control has included rules governing the curriculum, sizes of classes, and minimum requirements for graduation, as well as subtle and not-so-subtle pressures on schools to consolidate.

Equally interesting is the role of special districts in the United States. Good conceptual arguments favor the establishment of these entities for at least some public services. For example, the spatial boundaries associated with draining water from an area are unlikely to coincide with the boundaries of political jurisdictions such as counties or municipalities; instead, drainage follows laws of hydrology. Thus, forming a governmental district concerned solely with drainage is likely to yield better outcomes than if the task requires coordination of a number of independent, multipurpose local governments.

Similarly, the scale and service areas of certain capital-intensive public services such as airports or hospitals often exceed a single municipality or county. Financing these services through debt that all users of the area must pay off may be considered more equitable and efficient than having a single multipurpose local jurisdiction, or a combination of those jurisdictions, exclusively provide the service. The ability of special districts to issue debt is often argued to be one of the major factors explaining the rapid growth in these governments, particularly over the past 20 years (see Leigland 1994). Because many states have imposed constraints on the powers of counties and municipalities to tax, spend, and issue debt (which will be discussed later), those local governments may then create special districts to skirt those state-imposed limits.

Finally, the fact that a special district is intended to provide a single or limited number of services can, in principle, lead to improved management and more efficient production of the service. However, again, inefficient duplication of administrative overhead services could offset those potential gains.

Elected Officials

Except for many special districts, the various types of local governments outlined above are all governed by elected officials. But again, there are differences in the structures of those elected bodies. Municipalities generally can have three types of governing structures: mayor-council, council-manager, and commission. Note that each of these structures may be in place in different municipalities within a single state; in other words, there is no single prescribed format.

Under a *mayor-council* government, one individual is chosen by the entire electorate to serve as the chief executive of the municipality. Under this format, the mayor holds considerable power because he or she is generally able to choose heads of departments and oversees the drafting of the annual budget, which ultimately must be approved by a majority of the council.[5] The council in a mayor-council municipality also consists entirely of elected representatives. In some municipalities (particularly smaller ones), all council members are elected by all eligible voters; in other jurisdictions, the members of the council are chosen on the basis of geographic areas within the municipality. In yet other municipalities, some members of the council are chosen from districts and others are elected at large. District-based voting is generally viewed as being more able to ensure that minority groups living in particular areas of a jurisdiction will be represented on the council.

During the early 1900s, a reform or progressive movement within the United States took place in some cities to overcome the corrupt practices of certain strong mayors. Rather than choose a mayor from the general population to serve as the chief executive and administrative officer, cities opted to hire a trained professional administrator to serve as the city manager at the pleasure of the council. Thus, under a *council-manager* form of government, the voters elect the council, and the council, in turn, hires a city manager to administer the municipality. Although the council still has the power to approve the budget, the manager prepares the budget. The manager also has the power to choose department heads and oversee the production of services within the jurisdiction. Cities with a council-manager form of government still have a mayor; however, his or her responsibilities are primarily ceremonial with no special executive powers.

A third organizational structure is called the *commission* form of local government. Under this format, commissioners are elected (at large from throughout the jurisdiction). Individual commissioners then take on responsibilities for particular municipal services—for example, police, finance, and so forth. This form of local government is not particularly common among municipalities; however, many counties are currently governed in this manner.

The elected council and mayor positions may or may not be considered full-time jobs. Generally, elected officials in smaller municipalities maintain their regular employment and serve in their official capacity only on a part-time basis. For large cities (other than those with a council-manager form of government), the position of mayor is generally a full-time task (with compensation reflecting that fact). Large cities, even with a strong mayor-council format, often also hire a professional manager to serve as the chief administrative officer to oversee the day-to-day operations of the city. These administrators do not, however, have powers equivalent to city managers under the council-manager format, because the chief administrative officer serves at the pleasure of the mayor.

The governing form of counties and towns also differs. The majority of counties and towns, however, include a relatively small number of elected officials (generally serving on a part-time basis). As already noted, counties are commonly governed by elected commissioners. Some counties, however, have adopted a format similar to the mayor-council form of government, with both an elected executive (similar to a mayor) and an elected council.

Independent school districts are generally governed by a board of individuals voted into office by the residents of the district. The board is expected to make general policy decisions for the school district, with a professional educator hired to serve as the chief administrative officer (superintendent) of the school district.

Special districts may or may not have popularly elected boards of decision makers. The specific method depends on the state-level legislation that authorizes formation of districts. Foster (1997) notes that most (but not necessarily all) districts with taxing powers provide for an elected board, whereas districts for which revenues are derived primarily from the sale of services more commonly appoint a board. These types of appointments are generally made by the county (or counties) or municipalities that overlap the district's service area.

State Limits on Local Autonomy

As previously mentioned, the state of Massachusetts has within the past decade initiated policies to abolish certain county governments and take over their functions. This situation is, however, an exception in state-local intergovernmental relations in the United States. In part, the action in Massachusetts stems from the fact that, historically, town and municipal governments have been expected to play the primary role in the providing of local public services, with county governments playing a relatively unimportant role.

There are, however, still differences across states in the degree to which states limit the actions of local governments (many of these will be considered in more detail in the sections that follow).[6] The one institutional feature related to states' control over local governments that is sufficiently unique to merit discussion here is the concept of home rule.

In 1868, Chief Justice John Forrest Dillon of the Iowa Supreme Court wrote a judicial decision that held the following:

> Municipal corporations owe their origins to and derive their power and rights wholly from the [state] legislature. It breathes into them the breath without which they cannot exist. As it creates, so it may destroy. If it may destroy, it may abridge and control. (*City of Clinton v. Cedar Rapids and Missouri River Railroad Co.*, 24 Iowa 455, 1868)

This finding, which was upheld by the United States Supreme Court and subsequently became known as *Dillon's Rule*, meant that local governments' powers were totally constrained by the state governments and that they could undertake actions only if the state permitted those actions.[7]

Partially in response to Dillon's Rule, many states adopted another principle of state-local relations, beginning with Missouri in 1875. This principle, known as *home rule*, states that a local government within the state may exercise any power, unless the state has explicitly denied it. Thus, under Dillon's Rule, local governments can carry out functions and powers only if the states permit them to do so; under home rule, the local jurisdiction can undertake functions and powers unless prohibited by the state.

Commonly, home rule status is provided to larger municipal governments in a state; for example, the original Missouri constitutional provision for home rule was limited to cities with populations greater than 100,000 (only St. Louis qualified). Other states' constitutions give home rule status to all local governments (sometimes including counties) with populations exceeding a certain number but also permit localities to use referenda of eligible voters in the municipality, regardless of its size, to opt for home rule status. At present, 45 states have some type of provision for home rule. Provisions such as these can, therefore, greatly strengthen the decentralized power of local government.

Although nearly all states have provisions for home rule, the states can and do limit revenue powers. Another limit to total local control over what services are rendered is the use of expenditure mandates by both the federal and many state governments. Mandates are rules issued by these higher levels of government that require local governments to perform certain services. Although some states compensate local governments for the costs of carrying out mandated activities, many do not—or do so only partially. This situation results in less fiscal autonomy for the affected local governments. (The federal government also imposes mandates on both state and local governments.)

Services and Expenditures of Subnational Governments

State and local governments in the United States play relatively important roles in total expenditures. Preliminary estimates for 2003 show that government consumption expenditures and gross investment by all levels of government amounted to 18.7 percent of gross domestic product; of that spending, more than three-fifths (63.1 percent) was carried out by subnational governments.

Because the constitution of the United States provides no definitive list of public service responsibilities for subnational governments to perform and because there are considerable differences in the structure of local governments across states, it is not surprising to find that the spending patterns of state and local governments differ substantially from state to state. In this section, we first consider aggregate levels of spending by state and local governments combined and the mix of state-level vis-à-vis local-level expenditures across states. We then turn to analysis of patterns of spending on different types of subnational public services.

Expenditures by State and Local Governments

Analysis of the relative size of subnational government spending in the United States requires that the state and local sectors be aggregated, because the various states rely differentially on local governments to provide particular services. State and local government spending is carried out for a variety of purposes. Aggregate spending includes direct expenditures on public services, transfer payments to eligible individuals, interest on debt, and capital expenditures. Each of these subcomponents can be influenced by specific conditions affecting a state at a particular point in time. For example, capital spending is notoriously "lumpy"; during a particular year, a state might spend a large amount relative to its ordinary levels. Transfer payments depend greatly on the specific economic conditions facing households at a particular time, and interest on debt depends on past borrowing behavior and interest rates. For those reasons, we analyze (a) aggregate spending at the state and local levels (but in per capita terms) and (b) only expenditures for current operations that exclude transfer payments, interest on debt, and capital expenditures.

Table 9.2 shows the total direct expenditures for the five states (including the District of Columbia) spending the most in per capita terms and the five states spending the least in 2000.[8] There is, obviously, considerable diversity in the levels of spending across the 50 states and the District of Columbia, with per capita spending ranging from about US$4,500 in Arkansas to three times that amount in Alaska.[9] Although some of the interstate variation can be attributed to differences in income levels across states, this factor does not explain all the variability. As shown in table 9.2, the coefficient of variation in per capita direct expenditures in fiscal year 2000 was 24.7 percent, whereas the coefficient of variation in per capita incomes across the states in 2000 was substantially smaller at only 16.5 percent.

Shown in the right-hand columns of table 9.2 is the percentage of total direct state and local expenditures that are made by the local governments in the state (here local governments include all types—namely, counties, municipalities, townships, school districts, and special districts). Although, on average, about one-half of all state and local expenditures are made by local governments, the percentages range from only 21.8 percent in Hawaii to 66.2 percent in Nevada.

When capital expenditures, transfer payments, and interest payments are excluded from the data and only direct expenditures on current operations are measured, rather similar findings emerge—although, interestingly, different states show up among the top and bottom five in each category.

TABLE 9.2 Levels of State plus Local Expenditures, Fiscal Year 2000, and Relative Reliance on Local Governments

Direct expenditures[a]			
Per capita total state and local direct expenditures (US$)		**Local government direct expenditures (as % total)**	
Mean	6,220	Mean	50.9
Median	5,891	Median	52.1
Coefficient of variation	24.7%	Coefficient of variation	17.8%
Highest five states (US$)		**Highest five states[b] (%)**	
Alaska	13,583	Nevada	66.2
District of Columbia	11,410	California	64.0
New York	9,023	Florida	63.1
Wyoming	7,578	Arizona	62.0
Minnesota	7,201	New York	61.7
Lowest five states (US$)		**Lowest five states (%)**	
Missouri	4,996	Rhode Island	38.0
South Dakota	4,981	West Virginia	38.0
Idaho	4,949	Delaware	34.9
Oklahoma	4,614	Alaska	34.4
Arkansas	4,480	Hawaii	21.8
Expenditures for current operations			
Per capita current operations expenditures (US$)		**Local government current operations (as % total)**	
Mean	4,635	Mean	54.3
Median	4,405	Median	55.8
Coefficient of variation	23.7%	Coefficient of variation	16.5%
Highest five states (US$)		**Highest five states[b] (%)**	
Alaska	9,615	Nevada	68.8
District of Columbia	8,897	New York	65.0
New York	6,443	California	65.0
Wyoming	5,466	Florida	64.1
Minnesota	5,268	Arizona	63.5

(*continued*)

TABLE 9.2 (*continued*)

Lowest five states (US$)		Lowest five states (%)	
Texas	3,793	Kentucky	43.3
Missouri	3,752	Vermont	42.8
Arkansas	3,648	Delaware	39.0
South Dakota	3,626	Alaska	33.8
Oklahoma	3,421	Hawaii	22.3

Source: U.S. Census Bureau 2003b.
a. Direct expenditures include spending on current operations, capital expenditures, interest on debt, and
   transfer payments to individuals, but they exclude transfers to governments.
b. The District of Columbia is excluded from these entries because it simultaneously carries out both state and
   local government functions even though it is considered a local government by the Census Bureau.

There is still considerable variation in spending levels and in the reliance on local governments to carry out that spending.

Spending by Function

Here we first briefly review the types of services that are generally provided at the subnational level and then illustrate differences in spending patterns across states.

Education—primary, secondary, and tertiary—is primarily a state-local function in the United States, with primary and secondary schooling generally being the responsibility of local governments and higher education being the responsibility of state governments. Closely linked to education is the provision of public libraries, which is generally a municipal responsibility.

A particularly important function, but one whose responsibility is split among the federal, state, and local governments in the United States, is the provision of public welfare services. As recently as the early 20th century, providing for the indigent was considered a local responsibility. However, with the development of major antipoverty programs, the federal government became increasingly involved. At present, many public welfare programs are governed by federal statutes, with eligible families and individuals deemed "entitled" to participate in the programs; however, both the administration of these programs and a portion of their costs are the responsibility of state and local governments. Some states take on the entire responsibility of funding the state-local share of welfare programs, whereas in a few states, the state-local share of the costs is split between the state and local (generally county) governments.

The health sector is also split between state and local governments (commonly also financed in part by federal government transfers). Most states administer state-level hospitals (particularly teaching hospitals associated with institutions of higher learning), but municipalities and counties (as well as regional-level special districts) also sometimes provide hospital services.

Public safety, including fire services and various types of police protection, is also split between the state and local governments. Fire protection is provided by both municipalities and towns and, in some instances, by special fire protection districts. Police services include state crime investigation units, highway police, and localized police services. Although local governments provide jails and prisons, larger facilities and those associated with longer prison sentences are the responsibility of state governments.

Transportation service responsibilities are also split among all levels of government. For example, major highways (including the interstate highway system) involve shared responsibility between the federal and state levels of government, with capital costs being shared between the two levels and maintenance costs primarily being the responsibility of the states. All levels of subnational governments may provide nonfederal highways and roads. For example, a local area may include a state highway, county roads, and township roads (primarily in rural areas), as well as municipal roads and streets. Special public authorities may also be created to provide toll-financed roads. Airports are commonly a function of a municipal or county government or, in some instances, a special district. Local transit (buses and rapid transit) is generally provided by a municipality or by a specially created transit authority (which, in some instances, even extends across state boundaries).

States as well as counties and municipalities commonly provide for parks and recreation, with larger parks being the domain of states and neighborhood parks being provided by municipalities. Other natural resource services, such as forests, are more commonly the responsibility of state governments.

Municipal governments, townships, and special districts are commonly responsible for providing local public utilities, particularly sewage, solid waste, and water services. And although in the United States electricity and gas are most commonly provided through privately owned companies, some local governments are also involved in those services.

Housing, too, is primarily a private sector activity. However, some housing is provided by the public sector, with local governments generally taking the lead role (although financing is primarily from the federal government).

Table 9.3 provides some perspective on the relative importance of these various subnational government activities. Shown in the table, for the nation as a whole, are (a) the percentage of total (noncapital) expenditures across these various activities and (b) the percentage of the state-local totals that are provided by local governments. Thus, the first entry in the table illustrates that, of all state plus local government expenditures in fiscal year 2000, 9.23 percent was spent on higher education and that, for all higher education expenditures by state and local governments that year, local governments accounted for only about 16 percent of the total.

The table reveals that education is, among the categories of spending shown, the largest component of state and local government spending. Approximately one-fourth of all dollars spent by state and local governments are for elementary and secondary education, with higher education constituting another 9.23 percent of total spending. Public welfare expenditures are about 18 percent of total expenditures. Highways (including streets and roads) do not constitute a substantial portion of total expenditures; however, for this category and for other capital-intensive sectors such as sewage, water, and other utilities, the data may be misleading, because the entries in the table exclude capital spending.

The proportion of these expenditures that are made by local governments is generally in line with the comments above. Local governments are the predominant providers of primary and secondary education, libraries, and police and fire protection, as well as ordinary local utilities such as water, sewerage, and solid waste disposal, and they occasionally provide electricity and gas.

The entries in table 9.3 are for the nation as a whole. If a state-by-state analysis were shown, then rather substantial differences would again become evident among at least some of these categories of expenditures. For example, although nearly all states rely totally on local governments to provide primary and secondary education, Hawaii is an exception; in Hawaii, education is totally provided by the state government. Probably the best example of differences across states with respect to the role of state versus local governments is in the area of public welfare. Nine states (Alaska, Arkansas, Delaware, Massachusetts, Rhode Island, South Carolina, Vermont, Washington, and West Virginia) rely on local governments to provide less than 1 percent of total public welfare spending. In contrast, local governments in California, New York, Virginia, and Wisconsin directly finance more than 20 percent of that service.

TABLE 9.3 Total State and Local Government Expenditures by Functional Area, All States plus the District of Columbia, Fiscal Year 2000

Expenditure function	State and local functional expenditures (as % total)	Local expenditures (as % functional total)
Education services		
Education		
Higher education	9.23	16.14
Elementary and secondary	24.80	99.11
Libraries	0.55	95.33
Social services and income maintenance		
Public welfare	18.08	14.86
Hospitals	5.59	57.13
Health	3.98	46.71
Transportation		
Highways	3.48	54.80
Other transportation[a]	1.36	87.80
Public safety		
Police protection	4.40	84.89
Fire protection	1.79	100.00
Correction	3.49	32.19
Protective inspection and regulation	0.71	36.57
Environment and housing		
Natural resources	1.23	22.94
Parks and recreation	1.40	83.42
Housing and community development	2.06	88.11
Sewerage	1.39	96.93
Solid waste management	1.22	86.41
Governmental administration		
Administration	6.33	57.75
Water supply	2.77	99.01
Electric power	3.08	92.56
Gas supply	0.29	99.85
Transit	2.47	76.77
Liquor stores	0.28	16.59

Source: U.S. Census Bureau 2003b.
a. Includes airports, sea and inland ports, parking, and subsidies to transit systems.

The results of devolution are no more apparent than when comparing spending by functional area across states. The theory of decentralization holds that one should find substantial differences in how subnational governments allocate their budgets, depending on the relative demands for public services. Table 9.4 provides some perspective on this concept,

TABLE 9.4 Allocation and Per Capita Expenditures by Major Functional Expenditure Categories, State and Local Governments, Fiscal Year 2000

Function	Mean	Median	Minimum	Maximum	Coefficient of variation
Total state and local spending in state (%)					
Higher education	10.14	10.57	1.45	15.51	22.90
Elementary and secondary education	24.86	25.74	14.88	34.50	14.10
Public welfare	18.16	17.75	7.52	27.73	22.51
Hospitals	5.44	4.66	0.10	14.71	64.00
Health	3.76	3.39	1.40	7.37	33.41
Highways	4.29	3.94	0.26	8.49	40.38
Police protection	4.08	3.90	2.37	6.63	22.11
Fire protection	1.66	1.64	0.50	3.32	35.78
Correction	3.25	3.19	1.41	5.87	28.65
Parks and recreation	1.45	1.32	0.60	3.59	41.91
Housing and community development	1.90	1.81	0.43	4.80	46.22
Governmental administration	6.61	6.47	4.04	10.19	20.33
Water supply	2.60	2.34	1.01	8.08	50.74
Per capita state and local spending in state (US$)					
Higher education	456	454	275	661	22.76
Elementary and secondary education	1,117	1,099	810	1,865	18.44
Public welfare	811	804	257	1,538	28.26
Hospitals	240	219	5	702	65.97
Health	167	148	71	337	37.24
Highways	196	167	80	625	46.74
Police protection	180	171	95	301	25.61
Fire protection	73	69	24	145	36.60
Correction	143	136	59	282	31.45
Parks and recreation	64	58	30	146	39.95
Housing and community development	89	74	20	296	58.31
Governmental administration	298	283	195	804	32.48
Water supply	113	99	49	329	48.37

Source: U.S. Census Bureau 2003b.

showing for several major spending categories indicators of the extremes and variability across states of both the percentage of a state's total state and local government spending on a particular function (top panel) and the per capita amounts spent by state and local governments on each of those functions (lower panel). Thus, the first line of entries in the top panel shows that, on average, state and local government spending on higher education amounted to approximately 10 percent of their expenditures; one state allocated more than 15 percent of its spending to higher education, whereas for another the proportion was less than 2 percent. The lower panel provides some perspective on not only the average but also the variability in per capita spending by these functional areas. Expenditures on elementary and secondary education show the least relative variability (lowest coefficients of variation) under both measures; however, even for this sector, the dispersions are quite large: across the states, expenditures made on this function range from nearly 15 percent to more than 34 percent of total expenditures and expenditures per capita range from about US$800 to more than US$1,850. At the other extreme are wide disparities in allocations and spending per capita on hospitals and water supply.

This review reveals that there is a general correspondence between the assignment of service responsibilities and that which is suggested by economic theory. Services for which benefits are primarily local are commonly assigned to local governments. Larger-scale infrastructure and broader-based service levels are more commonly the responsibility of state governments. And, even though local governments may participate in providing public welfare programs, financial responsibility is commonly shared between the central and subnational jurisdictions.

Own-Source Revenues of Subnational Governments

State and local governments in the United States are required to raise a substantial portion of their resources using their own taxing and charging powers. For the nation as a whole, more than 70 percent of state general revenues are derived from their own sources; the proportion of own-source local government revenues is approximately 60 percent.

In keeping with the general theme, this section will illustrate that uses of these powers differ substantially from state to state. We first review in general the types of tax instruments used at the subnational level and then turn to a review of the extent to which these taxing powers are used.

Primary Own-Source Subnational Government Revenues

Three broad-based tax instruments are used in most, albeit not all, states to generate revenues for state and local governments. The property tax remains a primary revenue source for local governments—counties, townships, municipalities, and school districts. Most states also impose taxes on the personal income of individuals and net income of businesses; in some but not all cases, local governments may also be given the option to impose such taxes. General retail sales are also imposed in the majority of states; again, some states allow local governments the power to impose additional taxes on retail sales made within the jurisdiction. Generally, when localities are given "local option" powers, the "local taxes" are actually collected by the state, but the local proceeds are then transferred back to the locality in which they were collected.[10]

There are other subnational government tax bases beyond the three mentioned above. They include a variety of selective sales taxes on individual commodities—for example, motor fuel, tobacco, alcoholic beverages, and consumption of utility services such as telephones and electricity. Motor vehicle licenses are considered by the U.S. Bureau of the Census to be taxes, although they could also be considered to be a charge for the right to use the streets and highways of a state or locality.

In addition, state and local governments charge fees for the use of many public services. For example, states charge tuition to students attending state universities, and local governments charge for use of sewer systems and facilities such as hospitals. Finally, state and local governments earn other miscellaneous types of revenue, the most important of which is interest earned on cash balances deposited in interest-earning accounts.

Table 9.5 shows for all states the percentage of general revenues (excluding revenues raised in fiscal year 2000 by utilities such as public water systems, electric power utilities, and public transit systems) from these various sources. The data reveal that taxes constitute about three-fourths of all state own-source revenues and slightly more than 60 percent of local government own-source revenues. State governments depend heavily on the sales-based taxes (both general and selective sales taxes) and on income taxes levied on individuals and corporations. Income taxes constitute more than a quarter of total own-source revenues of states, and retail sales taxes contribute nearly as much. The entries in table 9.5 also illustrate that the local governments rely heavily on property taxes. Property taxes constitute about 44 percent of local government's own-source revenues and more than 70 percent of all local tax revenues. But states also rely on charges for services provided, especially on fees and charges associated with higher education. Local governments are also quite

TABLE 9.5 Own-Source Revenues of State and Local Governments,
Fiscal Year 2000
(as a percentage of total own-source revenues)

	Level of government		
Own source of revenues	Total state and local	State	Local
Taxes			
Property	19.94	1.55	44.19
General retail sales	17.22	24.56	7.54
Selective sales	7.54	10.94	3.06
Motor fuel	2.48	4.22	0.18
Alcoholic beverages	0.35	0.58	0.05
Tobacco products	0.69	1.18	0.04
Public utilities	1.43	1.30	1.60
Other selective sales	2.60	3.66	1.19
Individual income	16.94	27.39	3.17
Corporate income	2.89	4.58	0.66
Motor vehicle license	1.31	2.13	0.24
Other taxes	3.98	4.83	2.87
Total	**69.82**	**75.96**	**61.73**
User charges			
Education	5.25	7.03	2.90
Institutions of higher education	4.43	6.95	1.10
School lunch sales (gross)	0.44	0.00	1.01
Hospitals	4.37	2.62	6.69
Highways	0.59	0.66	0.51
Air transportation (airports)	0.89	0.12	1.90
Parking facilities	0.11	0.00	0.25
Sea and inland port facilities	0.20	0.10	0.34
Natural resources	0.24	0.25	0.22
Parks and recreation	0.50	0.16	0.95
Housing and community			
development	0.34	0.06	0.70
Sewerage	1.95	0.01	4.50
Solid waste management	0.82	0.05	1.83
Other charges	2.64	1.12	4.64
Total	**17.89**	**12.17**	**25.42**
Miscellaneous general revenue			
Interest earnings	5.64	4.93	6.58
Special assessments	0.31	0.01	0.69
Sale of property	0.16	0.07	0.29
Other general revenue	6.18	6.86	5.29
Total	**12.29**	**11.86**	**12.85**

Source: U.S. Census Bureau 2003b.
Note: Individual entries may not sum to the totals shown because of rounding.

dependent on user charges. (If utility revenues, particularly from water, were included here, the percentage reliance on local user charges would be even greater.)

Because the Census Bureau provides detailed revenue (and expenditure) data for the various types of local governments (defined earlier in this chapter) for only the years in which the census of government is taken, we cannot provide a breakdown of these local government revenue sources by type of local government for fiscal year 2000. However, through table 9.6, we can provide some perspective on the sources of revenue for the various types of local governments by showing the composition of revenues for counties, municipalities, and other local governments for fiscal year 1997. (The information in table 9.6 also provides a perspective on the relative importance of intergovernmental transfers, a topic discussed later.) The data in table 9.6 reveal that taxes other than the property tax are important only for counties and

TABLE 9.6 Composition of Revenues of Local Governments, 1997 *(as a percentage of total revenues)*

Types of revenues	Level of local government				
	Counties	Municipalities	Townships	School districts	Special districts
Own-source revenues					
Property taxes	24.7	20.7	55.6	31.2	8.9
General sales taxes	6.4	7.4	0	0	2
Selective sales taxes	1.5	4.9	0	0	0
Income taxes	1.2	6.2	0	0	0
Motor vehicle taxes	0.4	0.2	0	0	0
All other taxes	1.4	3.2	4.6	1.0	0.8
Total taxes	35.5	42.5	60.2	32.3	11.6
User charges	18.6	19.1	10.7	2.8	56.0
Miscellaneous own-source	8.4	10.1	6.2	3.5	8.3
Total own-source revenues	62.6	71.8	77.1	38.5	75.9
Intergovernmental transfers					
Federal	2.6	5.3	1.3	0.6	6.5
State	33.5	20.7	19.7	51.8	6.5
Other local governments	1.5	2.3	2.0	9.0	11.1
Total transfers	37.5	28.3	22.9	61.4	24.1

Source: U.S. Census Bureau 2000a.
Note: Individual entries may not sum to the totals shown because of rounding.

municipalities; townships and school districts must rely almost entirely on the property tax for own-source tax revenues. As already noted, special districts are particularly reliant on user charges for own-source revenues.

The previous section stressed the considerable differences in level of public expenditures made by the state and local governments within a state, as an indicator of the relative sizes of the public sector across states. A slightly different perspective on these differences can be obtained by observing the interstate differences in own-source revenues. It is particularly useful to observe differences in ratios of own-source revenues to personal incomes, because, unlike per capita spending differences, these ratios reflect differentials in the willingness and ability of the resident population to pay for state and local government services, and they ignore differences in the flows of transfers to the states from the federal government.[11]

The left-hand set of entries of table 9.7 shows that, on average, approximately 15 percent of state personal incomes are collected in the form of own-source revenues (taxes plus user charges). However, again, these ratios vary considerably (as reflected in the coefficient of variation of nearly

TABLE 9.7   State and Local Total Own-Source Revenues and Total Taxes, by State, Fiscal Year 2000

State and local own-source revenues (as % personal income)		State and local taxes (as % personal income)	
Mean	15.8	Mean	10.5
Median	15.1	Median	10.3
Coefficient of variation	24.9	Coefficient of variation	11.2
Highest five states (%)		**Highest five states (%)**	
Alaska	40.6	District of Columbia	14.1
New Mexico	19.3	New York	13.0
Wyoming	19.3	Maine	13.0
Delaware	17.9	Alaska	12.3
Maine	17.7	Wisconsin	12.2
Lowest five states (%)		**Lowest five states (%)**	
Massachusetts	13.2	Alabama	8.9
Missouri	13.2	Texas	8.9
Texas	13.1	South Dakota	8.9
Tennessee	12.3	Tennessee	8.3
New Hampshire	11.4	New Hampshire	7.9

Source: U.S. Census Bureau 2003b.

25 percent). Alaska contributes greatly to that variability with its measure of 40.6 percent. This extremely high ratio occurs because petroleum companies pay the state royalties for crude oil pumped from the state.

The right-hand columns of the table reveal that state and local taxes combined constitute approximately 10 percent of the revenue from personal incomes across the 50 states, but again, the ratios vary from only 7.9 percent in New Hampshire to more than 14 percent in the District of Columbia. Although the relative variability in these ratios (as measured by the coefficient of variation) is less than observed for per capita spending, the findings do support the proposition that states differ in the willingness of their residents to tax their own incomes. The differences between the percentages of revenues only from taxes and all revenues reflect different policy choices with respect to the application of user fees.

Individual Revenue Sources

The three major revenue sources of state and local governments in the United States are property taxes, retail sales taxes, and income-based taxes. Here we highlight some of the major components (and differences) in the base and rates used by subnational governments in the country.[12]

Property taxes

As suggested in tables 9.5 and 9.6, property taxes are the principal tax revenue source for local governments. State statutes specify the major features of the tax within the state, but local governments generally control the administration of the tax. Each state's statutes can differ with respect to the rules governing the tax, including what property is included in the tax base, the tax rates that can be applied and features associated with the payment of the tax (for example, whether the entire tax is due on a certain date or whether payments can be spread across time).

Property taxes in the United States are levied against the capital value of the property (or some proportion thereof); however, states differ with respect to the types of properties included in the base. Although real property (land and buildings) is always included in the base, some states also include the value of inventories held by business, the value of their machinery and equipment, and the value of individuals' personal property such as automobiles. Some states have included the value of intangible personal property—stocks, bonds, and so forth that are owned by individuals—although given the difficulties of discovering such ownership, the tendency has been to remove that category of property from the defined property tax base.[13]

As in most countries around the world, properties such as hospitals, private schools and universities, and not-for-profit organizations are excluded from the local property tax base. Property of state and local governments and property of the federal government are not taxable by local governments in the United States. The federal government owns nearly 29 percent of the land area of the United States in the form of national parks, national forests, grazing lands, and so forth (U.S. Census Bureau 2000b). Because local governments cannot tax this land, it can substantially decrease the property tax revenues of counties. For that reason, the federal government finances a program, administered by the U.S. Bureau of Land Management, which makes payments in lieu of taxes (PILTs) to counties in which large amounts of federally managed land are located. In a similar vein, the federal government makes PILTs to school districts in which large numbers of children of federal government employees (for example, members of the armed forces) are enrolled.

Although the estimated market value of a property is to serve as the basis for assessments, some states define the taxable value of the property to be a fraction of its market value. Furthermore, these percentages differ in some states, depending on the type of property (for example, residential, commercial, or agricultural).

Assessment of property is generally a local government responsibility (an exception is Maryland, where it is a state government function).[14] According to one paper (Behrens 1998, 245), the country comprises about 13,500 assessing jurisdictions, and the assessment jurisdiction generally coincides with the county. One rather unique feature of the system in the United States is that in some states, local assessors are elected by the voters; in other states, local government officials appoint the assessor along with other heads of departments.

Even though local assessors have the task of deriving taxable values, state agencies in many states have oversight responsibilities; in fact, in some states, the state can change local assessments if they are deemed to be in error. Another task carried out by most of these agencies is equalization of property values. Individual assessment units may, despite statutory requirements to the contrary, assess properties at different fractions of their full market value. Equalization involves estimating what the assessed values of all properties would be if a constant proportion of full market value were used. This task is necessary for several reasons. One is linked to the structure of governments discussed previously. An individual parcel of property may be taxed by several local governments, all levying property taxes. But if a taxing jurisdiction—for example, a school district—overlaps two assessment districts that assess at different fractions of market values, equity in taxation requires that the assessed values of parcels in each assessing district be equalized to the same fraction of their underlying market values.

A second rationale for equalizing assessed values is linked to tax limits (discussed later). If total property tax levies cannot exceed some proportion of assessed values (as at least some tax rate limits are defined), the assessed values should be recalibrated to some set proportion of market value. Finally, many transfer program formulas (also discussed later) are linked to the size of the property tax base of a local government. Equitable treatment of different local governments therefore requires that these property tax bases be based on a common fraction of the market values of all properties.

The underlying structure of a local property tax is based on the statutes of the state; however, tax rates are generally determined exclusively by the taxing jurisdiction. Although in most states the same rate is applied to the assessed value of all properties in the taxing jurisdiction, the state of Pennsylvania allows localities to impose higher rates on the assessed value of land than on the assessed value of improvements.

Many states do, however, place upper limits on tax rates. In some instances, these limits are defined to be the ratio of the total tax levy to the (equalized) value of the tax base. More attention, however, has been paid recently to efforts by states to limit the amount of taxes by individuals through manipulation of the assessed values of individual properties. Probably best known among these efforts was the referendum that was passed by the voters of California in 1978 (Proposition 13), which broadly limited the growth in property taxes on individual parcels. Specifically, Proposition 13 stated the following:

- The property tax rate on any parcel cannot exceed 1 percent of its assessed value.
- The assessed value of all properties will be set back to their 1975–76 values.
- The assessed value of any property can increase at no more than 2 percent per year, *except when there is a change of ownership,* in which case the property is reassessed to its market value.

These provisions ensured that property tax revenues could not grow rapidly, because a maximum rate was established, and increases in the base were limited to only 2 percent regardless of market conditions. The third provision has also resulted in greatly different assessed values for otherwise similar properties. During the 1980s, many other states followed the example of California and imposed limits on the property taxing powers of local governments or imposed spending limits.

There are, however, other mechanisms by which governments have attempted to lower the property tax burden of selected property types. For example, in many states, the assessed values of houses occupied by their owners (as opposed to rental units) are lowered by a certain dollar amount simply because they are owner occupied; in some instances, the state then reimburses the local government for the revenues forgone, but in most cases, the local government must either raise property tax rates or find alternative revenues to replace the lost revenues. Particular groups—for example, low-income elderly people, veterans, and people with disabilities—are also sometimes targeted for exemptions. These exemption policies are generally part of legislation that affects all local governments (or a certain type of local government such as local school districts). Another type of exemption, which is generally granted at the discretion of a local government, is a tax exemption or abatement to specific businesses in hopes of encouraging economic development. As in the case of group-based exemptions, such tax incentives consequently involve either other property taxpayers having to pay higher taxes to offset the lost revenues or local governments needing to find alternative revenue sources (or needing to curtail spending).

One variant on this technique that has proved to be increasingly popular in many localities is the creation of tax increment financing (TIF) districts (Johnson 1999). Economic development activities are undertaken by a local government within a specified geographic area (the TIF district), and the expenditures are financed through borrowing. Then, because it is anticipated that the value of properties within the district will increase as a result of the additional public investment, the tax revenues generated from the increments in property values are used to repay the debt. The underlying idea here is that the properties that benefit from the investments will directly pay for them. Of course, this strategy also requires that properties outside the district bear the cost of other general services that are normally financed from property taxes.

In summary, property taxes remain the mainstay of local government finance in the United States. And these local governments retain considerable control not only over the determination of the size of the base of the tax but also, more important, over the rates that are imposed. However, over time, the dislike of property taxes has prompted many states (either directly through referenda of voters or by statutes passed by state-level politicians) to limit property tax revenues. It is therefore not surprising to find that local governments have been increasingly relying on other broad-based taxes to finance local government spending. Both local income taxes and local retail sales taxes have been used to help fill that revenue gap.[15]

Retail sales taxes

Table 9.5 reveals that the retail sales tax is both the second most important tax source for state governments and the second most important source of taxes for local governments. As in the case of the property tax, the tasks to define the statutory base and to administer the tax are left up to the states. The tax base is the sales price of goods and services purchased by consumers; however, determining which goods and services are taxable is up to the individual state. Among the goods that are exempt from the sales tax in some states are food for consumption at home (food purchased in restaurants is generally not exempt), prescription drugs, and certain items of clothing. Other states tax these items but at lower rates.[16]

Services are not as uniformly taxed across states as are goods for consumption. For example, some states apply the sales tax to repair services, others tax only the materials used in repair, and still others make no attempt to tax such services (although in states with income taxes, the income earned by the individual carrying out the repair is taxed). Most states, however, do not impose sales tax on services rendered by professionals such as lawyers, accountants, engineers, and doctors (see Federation of Tax Administrators 1997).

Statewide retail sales tax rates in 2003 ranged from zero (in Alaska, Delaware, Montana, New Hampshire, and Oregon) to 7 percent (in Mississippi, Rhode Island, and Tennessee). Both Mississippi and Rhode Island exempt food and prescription drugs; however, Tennessee taxes food for home consumption at a reduced rate of 6 percent.

Of the 50 states, 32 provide sales tax revenues to local governments. However, in two of the states—California and Virginia—the tax is imposed throughout the state with no local option for setting tax rates; consequently, these states essentially have tax-sharing arrangements (see later discussion) rather than truly local taxes. A sales tax can be considered a local tax if local political leaders have the option of whether to impose it (even if they do not have the power to define what goods and services are taxed).

Local governments do not directly administer the local sales tax even though they decide whether such a tax is to be collected. Instead, the state taxing authority receives the total state and local sales tax revenues collected by retail establishments (in some but not all states, the retailer is compensated for the additional expense incurred in collecting the tax). The state agency then remits the local portion of the sales tax collections to the locality in which the taxes were originally collected. The maximum local option sales tax rates in 2003 varied from 0.25 percent in Mississippi to 6 percent in Alabama.

Income taxes

The largest source of tax revenue for states is income taxes. Most states levy this type of tax; however, seven states—Alaska, Florida, Nevada, South Dakota, Texas, Washington, and Wyoming—impose no income taxes. (Two others— New Hampshire and Tennessee—impose income taxes only on interest and dividend income.) As with other revenues, states determine the state tax structure as they see fit, which therefore leads to substantial differences across the states. States do, however, generally design their tax structures so taxpayers who file federal income tax returns can use the same information when filing state income taxes.[17] (In the United States, individuals are responsible for filing annual income tax returns even if most of their taxes have been withheld by their employers.)

Direct and meaningful comparisons of income tax rates across states are not possible simply because taxable income is defined differently across states; for example, although many states make only small adjustments to taxable income as defined by the Internal Revenue Service of the federal government, some states, such as Indiana, impose income tax on *adjusted gross income,* that is, annual income of an individual before adjusting it further for deductions. All but five states that impose personal income taxes use progressive rate structures with zero rates imposed up to a certain level of taxable income and higher rates at higher income levels. But because the income brackets differ across states, it is not feasible to directly compare rates.

Probably the simplest tax structure is that of Rhode Island; that state's income tax is simply 25 percent of the federal income tax liability. Other states have considerably more complex structures with numerous income brackets (for example, both Missouri and Montana use 10 different income brackets). Some states allow a taxpayer to deduct income taxes paid to the federal government; most do not.

In 11 states, local governments (or at least some local governments) within the state are given the option of imposing additional local taxes on incomes. These states are Delaware, Indiana, Iowa, Kentucky, Maryland, Michigan, Missouri, New Jersey, New York, Ohio, and Pennsylvania. Again, administration of these local income taxes is generally carried out by the state tax agency, with the revenues from the local portion of the tax remitted to the local government. However, in Missouri, the only two cities permitted to impose local income taxes are St. Louis and Kansas City, and the cities collect the tax. These taxes are based on only the earnings of individuals residing or working in these cities.

Missouri is not alone in permitting only some local governments the option of imposing income taxes. For example, in New York, only the cities of New York and Yonkers have that option. Cities in Michigan have the option of imposing income taxes on city residents along with earnings taxes on nonresidents. In Maryland, all counties have the power to impose a local income tax. The same is true in Indiana; however, Indiana counties can choose from among three types of local income tax.

Rates of local income taxes are generally low and quite simple. For example, in Maryland, the flat rates across counties vary from 1.25 to 3.10 percent of taxable income. In Indiana, the maximum rate is only 1.25 percent, and in Michigan, the maximum rates (outside Detroit) are 1 percent on residents and corporations and 0.5 percent on nonresident earnings. The city of Detroit has, however, been given the option of levying higher rates— up to 2.65 percent on residents, 2 percent on corporations, and 1.325 percent on nonresidents. The local income tax rate structures are not, however, always simple and low. For example, in the city of New York, tax rates are progressive, with a maximum marginal rate of 4.25 percent on incomes above US$150,000 for married couples filing joint returns (and on incomes above US$100,000 for individuals).

Other state and local own-source revenues

Property, retail sales, and income taxes constitute the primary revenues of state and local governments. Of course, the list is hardly exhaustive. Localities in most states, but particularly in areas with high numbers of tourists, commonly impose taxes on guests of hotels and motels. Another potentially important tax at the local level is imposed on sales of homes or on mortgage loans taken to pay for the homes. Utilities such as telephones provide substantial revenues in some localities. Finally, most states in the United States now sponsor some form of gambling.

Not included in the previous discussion were the various taxes imposed on purchases of specific goods such as petroleum products (principally gasoline and diesel fuel for trucks and automobiles), tobacco products, and alcohol products. Although the structures of these excise taxes do not differ greatly across states, their rates can differ substantially. Perhaps the best example of this variation is the cigarette tax. As of January 2004, the tax on a single pack of cigarettes in New Jersey was US$2.05, whereas the same tax in Kentucky (a tobacco-producing state) was US$0.03. Local governments in six states are permitted to impose an additional tax on cigarettes sold within their jurisdictions. Although these local taxes are generally less than US$0.15 per pack, the city of New York currently imposes an additional US$1.50 on top of the US$1.50 state cigarette tax.[18] Huge differentials such as those in New York create strong incentives to form illicit businesses that purchase large quantities of cigarettes from low-tax states and sell them illegally in high-tax jurisdictions. The potential for not only legal tax avoidance in the face of substantial differentials in tax rates across localities but also the likelihood of illegal tax evasion constitutes an important constraint on local own-source revenue autonomy in any devolved system.

Shared Taxes

Sharing of tax revenues among levels of government in the United States is less prominent than in many developing countries. For example, in the United State, the federal government does not significantly share federal taxes with state and local governments.[19] However, in certain instances, state governments determine the structure and rates of a tax, with the shares based either on a formula or on the basis of the location from which the tax was collected. They then share the revenues with local governments. However, there is essentially no uniformity in how the technique is applied across states.

Probably the most common revenue base for tax sharing is tax associated with the use of motor vehicles—motor fuel taxes and licenses. As noted earlier, county and municipal governments are expected to provide local streets and roads; at the same time, local administration of motor vehicle taxes, particularly fuel taxes, can be costly, and if differential rates are charged across jurisdictions, motorists can easily avoid paying such taxes by purchasing fuel in neighboring jurisdictions with lower rates. Thus, though states impose motor fuel taxes, many divide a portion of the revenues with local governments responsible for local roads.

It is not feasible to list the complete sharing arrangements of motor fuel taxes here; however, a description of how one state allocates the revenues may be instructive.[20] In the state of Kansas, 40.5 percent of fuel tax revenues are allocated to cities and counties; of that amount, 57 percent is allocated to cities and 43 percent to counties. The city portion is distributed among cities on the basis of their population; the county allocation mechanism is more complex. Each county receives a flat amount of US$5,000; of the remainder, 44.06 percent is distributed on the basis of registration fees collected in each county, 44.06 percent is distributed on the basis of average daily vehicle miles traveled (exclusive of travel on interstate highways), and the remaining 11.88 percent is distributed on the basis of the total miles of road in each county. The state further specifies that at least one-fourth of the amounts to counties must be allocated to roads and bridges on which school buses and mail carriers travel.

Most states allocate funds among counties and municipalities using some ratio (although the ratios that are used may be as much the outcome of political bargaining as a conclusion based on scientific principles). Like Kansas, many other states also use formulas to allocate the funds among the various counties or municipalities; others, however, appear to use discretionary methods to determine the share going to an individual jurisdiction.

A wide variety of other state tax revenues are shared with local governments. Some states distribute a portion of broad-based taxes such as the income tax. For example, the state of Illinois shares 10 percent of income tax revenues with local governments, basing the distribution on population. Likewise, the state of Arizona distributes 15 percent of income tax revenues with cities and towns in the state. Again, population is used to allocate the funds among the various municipalities. The state of Tennessee also uses population to allocate shared retail sales tax revenues with municipalities within the state; approximately 5 percent of total sales tax revenues are shared. Using population size as a factor in distributing the funds rather than sharing the tax on the basis of where it is collected obviously results in tax revenues being redistributed from areas with high levels of economic activity to less prosperous areas.

State excise taxes in addition to taxes based on motor vehicles are also shared with local governments in some states. For example, in Tennessee, taxes on alcohol (alcoholic beverage tax, beer excise tax, and wholesale beer tax) are shared with counties and municipalities. Different formulas for distributing the funds are used for each of the taxes. An alcoholic beverage tax is distributed to counties on the basis of area (25 percent) and population (75 percent). Counties that have a population greater than 250,000 and include a city with a population greater than 150,000 are to pass on 30 percent of the county's allocation to the city. A beer excise tax is distributed to both counties and cities (10.05 percent of total collections to each type of local government); the city portion is allocated on the basis of population, whereas the county portion is divided equally across all counties. Finally, 96.5 percent of wholesale beer tax collections are distributed on the basis of where the retailers making wholesale purchases are located; that is, if 4 percent of all wholesale beer purchases were made by retailers located in the city of Memphis, the city would receive 4 percent of the total. Tennessee distributes some other shared taxes on the basis of where the taxes were collected. For example, one-half of gross receipts tax revenues that are collected on mixed (alcoholic) drink sales are returned to the locality in which the business establishment is located; also, one-third of severance taxes on mined coal, pumped crude oil, and natural gas are returned to the counties in which the operations occur (Tennessee Advisory Commission on Intergovernmental Relations 2000).

Intergovernmental Transfers

Intergovernmental transfers—both from the federal to state and local governments and from state to local governments—include a vast array of programs about which this short chapter can provide only general insights. In this section, we will first consider the importance of fiscal transfers from the federal government to state and local governments and then provide a brief overview of the nature of these transfer mechanisms.

As shown in table 9.8, transfers from the federal government in 2000 constituted approximately one-fourth of state government general revenues in the United States. Local governments were not heavily dependent on direct grants from the federal government; however, more than one-third of local government general revenues were derived from transfers from the states. (The low level of federal transfers to local governments is somewhat misleading, because some grants pass through state government treasuries but are ultimately spent at the local level; for statistical purposes, such federal grants are considered to be made to state governments.)

Reliance on transfers is, however, not uniform across the states. For example, Alaska, with its large amount of revenues from petroleum royalties, relies relatively less on federal transfers (16.3 percent of general revenues) than most states, whereas 37.5 percent of Tennessee's general revenues in 2000 were from federal grants. Likewise, local governments rely to varying degrees on transfers from both the federal and state governments. As shown in table 9.6, the reliance on transfers differs greatly by type of local government, with school districts generally depending heavily on such

TABLE 9.8 Intergovernmental Transfers, Fiscal Year 2000
(as a percentage of general revenues of state and local governments)

	Level of government		
Source of transfers	State and local	State	Local
Federal government	18.9	26.3	3.7
State government			35.7

Source: U.S. Census Bureau 2003b.

transfers. In Vermont, more than one-half of the general revenues for all local governments combined derived from transfers from the state government. In Hawaii, however, only 10 percent of general local government revenues were from transfers, which reflects the fact that the state of Hawaii provides primary and secondary education directly rather than through local school districts.

Federal Grants to States

The federal government currently administers approximately 660 programs designed to transfer funds to state and local governments (U.S. Census Bureau 2003a). In no case, however, are these funds allocated as fully general-purpose transfers, and no transfer program is designed purely to equalize fiscal capacities of subnational governments. Instead, the transfers to state governments are of three basic types: nonmatching categorical transfers, open-ended matching grants, and closed-ended matching grants. (Open-ended transfers have no ceiling associated with total expenditures, whereas closed-ended transfers are limited in size.)[21]

The most important types of transfer programs are designed to provide direct or indirect assistance to low-income individuals and families, support for education, and support for roads and highways. At present, the largest federal program providing aid to state governments is the Medical Assistance Program (Medicaid), which pays for medical care for low-income families and individuals. The program is interesting in several respects. First, it is considered a federal government "entitlement" program in that any family or individual who qualifies is entitled to receive the assistance. Although Medicaid is authorized under a federal government statute, the law specifies that each state organizes and administers its own program. Second, Medicaid is financed by both the federal and subnational governments. The federal government provides a transfer to the state to help finance Medicaid, but because it is an entitlement program, the grant can be considered an open-ended transfer, so as needs arise in a state, the federal transfer also increases. Third, the matching rates differ across the states. States with lower median incomes derive a larger share of the costs from the federal transfer. In 2004, for example, the matching rates varied from 50 percent federal-state shares in higher-income states to approximately a 77 percent–23 percent federal-state share in Mississippi (a state that has a large proportion of poor families). Finally, because each state can design the program as it sees fit, some states have opted to require local governments (generally counties) to bear a portion of the total costs of the program. For example, the state of

New York (which receives US$0.50 for each dollar spent on Medicaid in the state) requires county governments to pay one-half of the state-local share of the cost.

One important feature of the system currently used by the federal government to transfer funds to state and local governments is the use of block grants. These grants are a hybrid of a categorical and general-purpose transfer in that a sum of money is transferred to a state, which then can decide how to allocate the funds within a specified sector. Thus, like a general-purpose transfer, a block grant provides the recipient government some autonomy with respect to how the funds are to be used; however, the granting government also has the discretion of determining the size of the allocations across sectors, not unlike a categorical transfer.

Certain transfer programs are allocated solely on the basis of a formula. An important one is the program to distribute funds supporting the construction of roads and highways. (The federal aid to highways restricts the use of funds to construction and reconstruction of roads and requires state and local governments to support their maintenance.) With states differing greatly in terms of their area and population, it is not surprising that a distribution formula is also quite complex (and the result of considerable political debate). The current formula, therefore, includes the length of highways in a state (relative to the total in the nation), the number of vehicle miles traveled in the state, the amount of diesel fuel used on highways in a state, and the length of roads relative to the state's population.

State Transfers to Local Governments

The mechanisms used for fiscal transfers from the 50 state governments to their large number of local governments really cannot be called a system because there is little that is systematic about them. Each state handles its assistance to various local governments differently. The mechanisms include formula-based allocations (using a wide variety of formulas) for general-purpose or sector-specific spending along with categorical transfers (with and without matching requirements).

The one area of transfers from state to local governments that probably receives the greatest amount of attention in most states is state aid for education. This tenable possibility is not surprising given the numbers shown in table 9.6, where it was noted that, on average, school districts throughout the country rely heavily on transfer revenues and that those transfers constitute a substantial share of total state government spending. But attention to the role of the states in financing education has been affected by another branch of government in many of the states—the judiciary. Since 1973, many state courts have recognized that not all localities have equal abilities to finance primary and secondary education, mainly because the principal revenue instrument used to finance education at the local level is the property tax. Some localities have very low property tax bases, which limit how much can be spent on education, whereas other areas have relatively large property tax bases and can therefore afford to spend considerably more on education without much concern for the number of children. The result is substantial interdistrict differentials in the quality of education within a state as measured by expenditures per student, and courts in many states have found such inequities to be unconstitutional on the grounds of equal protection under the law. As of 2003, lawsuits pertaining to this issue had been filed in 43 of the 50 states; in 25 of the states, the courts have mandated that state legislatures take steps to ensure that *all* school districts in a state receive adequate funding.

States use at least five types of transfer mechanisms to provide revenues for the operating costs of local education services (Blanchard and Duncombe 1999). The first type of transfer mechanism is a flat grant that transfers equal per pupil revenues to each school district without regard to the district's revenue capacity or its relative need because of cost differentials or more-costly-to-educate pupils, such as those in special education programs. In 1990, only two states used this type of mechanism. The second type is the most common mechanism. Known as a *foundation program*, 38 states applied it in 1990. The state determines (a) a minimum (foundation) amount of spending necessary to educate students in the state and (b) a "fair" property tax rate. A grant is then provided that fills any gap between what would be necessary to educate the district's students and the amount of taxes the district could raise locally if it were to apply the state's fair property tax rate. The third type of mechanism, a percentage- or power-equalizing program, was used in six states in 1990. Under this mechanism, the state government matches some percentage of local spending on education with a rate that is inversely related to a school district's tax capacity. Although conceptually such grants could be open ended, states generally place a maximum on the amount of aid that a district can receive. The fourth type of transfer mechanism, a guaranteed tax base or tax yield program, was used in only two states in 1990. Under this approach, quite similar to the percentage-equalizing program, the state guarantees that a district will obtain a certain amount of total revenues (own-source plus transfer) for a given level of tax effort. Thus, a locality that has low tax capacity but puts forth considerable effort at mobilizing resources from that capacity will receive larger amounts of financial assistance than a district that exerts lower levels of effort. The fifth mechanism, practiced in the states of Hawaii and Washington, does not involve transfers, because the states fully finance local education.

In addition to the programs financing current operating costs of schooling, most states also provide a variety of categorical assistance to school districts. They may, for example, support transportation of students or vocational education. Likewise, many states provide grants for construction of new facilities (with or without matching requirements).

In summary, despite the relatively high level of fiscal autonomy given to many local governments in the United States, it is far from the case that local governments are fully responsible for mobilizing locally all the resources necessary to provide local public services. At the same time, the transfer programs that are in place are seldom designed to permit local governments to spend whatever they wish without any fiscal discipline imposed on them. It is for that reason that the bulk of all transfer programs either require some local (or state-level) matching funds or include some measure of the fiscal capacity and effort put forth by the recipient in taxing that capacity.

Borrowing by Subnational Governments

With only a few exceptions, both state and local governments in the United States are permitted to borrow money. In fact, in 2000, aggregate debt of state and local governments amounted to more than US$5,000 per person. In this section, we discuss the various types of debt instruments used by subnational governments, the purposes for which those borrowed funds are used, and some of the institutional features associated with public sector borrowing, including the rules that limit the ability of local governments to incur debt.

Constitutionally or by statute, most subnational governments are prohibited from incurring current budget deficits. Nevertheless, most state and local governments are allowed to issue long-term debt for the purpose of investment in capital infrastructure such as roads, water and sewer systems, or drainage projects. Likewise, because the flows of taxes do not necessarily coincide with current spending needs, subnational governments sometimes can and do borrow to meet short-term budget needs.

Rather than rely directly on banks or specialized institutions designed specifically to lend to subnational governments, state and local governments in the United States participate directly in the capital market by issuing bonds. These bonds are purchased by financial institutions and private companies as well as by individuals. Because they are marketed in competition with other debt instruments issued by corporations and the central government, the interest paid by state and local governments must be sufficiently high to be attractive to these buyers.

One aspect of the capital market in the United States that does give subnational governments a competitive advantage over other borrowers is that the federal income tax does not apply to interest earned by holders of such bonds. For this reason, the interest rates paid by state and local governments are below those paid by other bond issuers.

State and local government bonds (generally called *municipal bonds* regardless of the nature of the issuing government) can be either short term or long term, although the latter dominates the municipal bond market. The bond maturity is as long as 30 years; there is, however, an active secondary market in these debt instruments so that current bond holders can always sell their bonds.[22] Short-term "notes" constitute borrowing that must be paid off in less than one year; they are commonly issued to cover short-term shortfalls in cash flow in anticipation of revenues that will accrue in the near term.

Two types of bonds are issued by state and local governments—*full-faith and credit bonds* and *nonguaranteed bonds*. Under the former, the issuing government pledges that tax revenues will be used to pay the interest and principal on the bond; short-term credit is nearly always in the form of full-faith and credit debt. The source of funds to pay off nonguaranteed bonds is the revenue associated with the capital project being financed; as a result, these debt instruments are often called *revenue bonds*. Because the risk to bond holders is greater for revenue bonds than for full-faith and credit obligations, the interest rates that state and local governments must pay are generally greater (even though the interest is still not taxed by the federal government).

Two types of limits are placed on the ability of subnational governments to incur debt. One is statutory. Nearly all states put limits on the amount of full-faith and credit bonds or notes that a local government can issue. The limits are commonly linked to the property tax base of a locality because property taxes constitute the primary own-source tax revenue for most local governments. Likewise, the constitutions of some states limit the amounts of debt that can be guaranteed from the tax base. Another rule in some states that limits issuance of full-faith and credit debt is the requirement that any long-term debt issue must be approved by a majority (or, in some cases, a supermajority) of voters because, ultimately, it is the voter-taxpayer who will be required to pay back the debt. Finally, in response to the observation that some state and local governments were taking advantage of the nontaxable status of interest from municipal debt by borrowing and relending to private entities, the federal government in 1986 established rules that limited these uses of municipal debt.

The capital market constitutes another constraint on state and local governments' issuance of debt. If the market perceives that a subnational government entity is issuing an unreasonably large amount of debt that makes repayment less likely, then the interest that the borrowing government will have to pay will rise, making it a less desirable undertaking. There is, however, obviously considerable lack of information in the financial markets concerning the ability of a local government to repay its debt. At least two types of institutions have developed in response to that information asymmetry. One type is the private bond rating institution such as Standard & Poor's, Moody's Investors Service, and Fitch Investors Service. Before the issuance of municipal debt, the borrowing government can use the services of these firms to study the economic and fiscal health of the local government and issue ratings that are then used by potential buyers of the bonds. Lower ratings caused by poor economic or fiscal conditions (including an already high level of debt) will result in higher interest rates for the borrowing government to pay. A second market-oriented institution that is used to decrease information asymmetry is the bond guarantee. Bond guarantees come in several forms. Private firms have been established that issue municipal bond insurance (the insurance premium of which is paid by the government issuing the bond). A purchaser of an insured bond is guaranteed that even if the local government is not capable of paying the interest and principal, the insurance company will. Private banks also sometimes issue a letter of credit that pledges the bank's resources to repay lenders to the state or local government. Finally, some states have established state-credit guarantees for debt issued by local governments. The strength of those guarantees, of course, ultimately depends on the ability of the state to pay back creditors and, as a result, may be viewed as less reliable than if the guarantee comes from a well-financed private firm.

Administration of Subnational Governments

In 1997, approximately 20 million individuals were employed by all levels of government in the United States. Of these individuals, state and local governments employed about 84 percent. At the subnational level, local government employment dominates employment at the state level. This domination, of course, reflects the fact that local government services, particularly education and health, are labor-intensive compared with the services provided by the federal and state governments. The federal government, for example, relies on contracts with private firms to produce items associated with services such as national defense and space exploration.

The rules that govern federal government employment do not, in general, apply to subnational governments. In other words, there is no single civil service in the United States. Instead, public sector employment is governed by individual states. States have their own civil service systems for state employees, with rules governing their hiring and firing.

Some states (but not all) also mandate that counties and municipalities within the state adopt merit-based employment practices. In addition, states commonly prescribe certain minimum requirements for employment within specific sectors (for example, education), including, in some instances, rules with respect to additional in-service training. Nevertheless, local governments retain considerable autonomy in managing employees.

One additional factor that can limit that autonomy is collective bargaining. Federal law applies to collective bargaining by federal employees but is silent on other public employee unionization. Each state has its own set of laws and regulations. At present, about one-half of the states have extended collective bargaining rights to all state and local government employees; another 15 states provide for limited collective bargaining by some state or local government workers. Even when they permit collective bargaining, most states limit the right of public employees to strike.

Accountability of Local Governments

A variety of mechanisms create incentives for local government accountability in the United States, and they generally work reasonably well. These mechanisms include both "voice" and "exit" actions on the part of citizen taxpayers as well as oversight by state governments and, to a lesser degree, the federal government.

As discussed earlier, all local governments (other than most special districts) have popularly elected public officials serving in executive and legislative decision-making positions. Local government elections are generally held on two- or four-year cycles. Some states and localities have limits concerning the number of terms an elected representative may serve; however, those limits are far from universal. Thus, it is quite possible for the public to voice its approval or disapproval directly through the ballot box. However, it is also the case that turnout of eligible voters in many local elections is light, unless there is a local issue that draws a strong level of interest.

As already mentioned, many states and localities require that voters approve, in some instances with a supermajority, long-term borrowing using full-faith and credit bonds. In addition, a few states require some budgets to be approved annually by the electorate. For example, in New York State, budgets for local independent school districts must be voter approved.

Civil society has, traditionally, been quite strong in the United States. Local organizations, including neighborhood groups, chambers of commerce, and other special interest groups, let locally elected officials know of their needs and wants and pay attention to decisions made by local government leaders. Likewise, local media generally keep the electorate informed of the actions of local governments.

This information exchange is particularly vibrant during the budget-setting process. Once budgets have been drafted for a local government, they are published in local media outlets, and the public is invited to comment on the proposed budget in open hearings before it is enacted into law. Thus, several possible avenues are available for local citizens to voice their approval or disapproval of the actions of local government officials.

The large number of local governments in the United States also influences accountability. Because many local governments represent relatively small numbers of residents, it is quite likely that the elected local leaders are well known by their constituency. This familiarity can, in turn, increase the effectiveness of the voiced comments made to the leaders. But it also increases the likelihood that "exit" or the threat thereof will be effective at encouraging accountable actions by local officials. The United States is a mobile population. For example, the U.S. Census Bureau estimates that approximately 15 percent of the population changed residences between March 2002 and March 2003. Of the movers, nearly 58 percent (nearly 9 percent of the total population) moved within their county of residence; however, given the large number of school districts, townships, and municipalities, it is quite possible that a reasonably large proportion of those movers crossed some sort of local government boundary. Other movers crossed county boundaries, including 20 percent of migrants who moved to another state.

Even though the level and quantity of public services, as well as their tax price, are unlikely to be the most important determinant of mobility, the fact that individuals do or may move can encourage local officials to be concerned about keeping or creating local public services, as well as taxes and charges, that are attractive. (For example, parents of school-age children are often especially concerned about the quality of public schooling available to their children and take that into consideration when they move.) Furthermore, although the data above pertain to individuals, business firms also can and do move, which, in turn, can affect local tax bases. These possibilities for emigration of businesses and households place considerable pressure on local political leaders to provide services at the lowest possible cost.

Several mechanisms enhance (if not ensure) financial accountability. One is the use of internal auditors, whose task is to enhance the efficient operation of local governments. As of the early 1990s, most states authorized or mandated that city and county accounts be audited by state authorities. Likewise, the federal government has audit powers that it imposes on state and local governments that receive federal transfers. Many local governments (at least larger ones) also contract with private accounting firms to perform financial audits of their books. All these efforts are made more feasible by the mandating of generally accepted accounting practices as determined by the Governmental Accounting Standards Board. Influential professional groups, such as the National Association of Local Government Auditors, which provides information and training for local government personnel, and the Government Financial Officers Association, also exist. Finally, when local governments borrow money through the capital market, the bond rating agencies include an analysis of the financial management practices of local governments.[23]

One final institution that creates incentives for local government accountability is the justice system. State and local governments in the United States not only have the power to sue but also can be sued for illegal or improper behavior. Citizens can and do use the court system to receive compensation for failure of local governments to perform services as mandated in the law. Even the threat of such lawsuits can increase pressures on local governments to be accountable.

In summary, there is a relatively long list of mechanisms that help to increase the likelihood that local governments will be accountable to local residents and will not waste resources. At the same time, one cannot be overly sanguine that local governments are always fully accountable to local constituents or do not engage in wasteful or even corrupt practices. Every year, one can read of instances in which local mayors, state governors, and other elected officials at the state and local levels have been indicted for some form of criminal activity. Fortunately, the fact that those events still make headlines suggests that such behavior is the exception rather than the rule; nevertheless, it also shows that perfection has not been attained.

Lessons for Developing Countries

The subnational government structure and the financial practices of these units in the United States provide lessons, both positive and negative, for developing countries. The fact that there are so many governments has both advantages and disadvantages. First, as has been documented in this chapter, there is tremendous diversity across local governments in the country; people are much more likely to find spending-taxing combinations to suit their preferences through mobility than through complete uniformity. Second, the relatively small size of many local governments with locally elected officials makes it much more likely that voices of the constituents will be heard. And the reliance on single-purpose districts can have the dual advantage of specialization and boundaries that are more in line with service areas than would be true in multiple-service local governments.

But the very large number of local governments with different sets of responsibilities (a) increases the transaction costs of learning which entity is responsible for a particular local service and (b) makes it more likely that certain service needs will remain unfilled because of the difficulties and costs of coordination. Furthermore, the multiplicity of taxing units with widely different tax structures can increase the costs of complying with local taxes, particularly for businesses with operations in multiple jurisdictions. Similarly, the uncertainties concerning which local government is responsible for a service make it harder for taxpaying voters to link service levels and quality with the tax prices they are required to pay. Finally, the freedom to design tax structures gives states and (to some extent) localities greater freedom to choose taxes that burden primarily nonresidents rather than local voters, which can lead to inefficiently high local government spending (because the voters influencing service levels are not bearing the costs of those services).

It is the case, however, that state and local governments in the United States do face hard budget constraints. A locality facing budget shortfalls cannot automatically expect that the state government will bail it out with budget-balancing transfers. This reality, together with the fact that a substantial portion of local spending must be financed from own-source taxes and charges, creates stronger incentives for accountability and efficient delivery of services. Of course, as is generally the case, local political leaders would still greatly prefer receiving transfers to taxing their own constituents; even in a wealthy county, people do not like to pay taxes. For that reason, state capitols are often crowded with locally elected officials hoping to convince state legislatures to provide them with additional fiscal transfers.

Fiscal transfer systems are critical. Although there are still instances of politically motivated special grants and transfers to specific localities, the bulk of most state-to-local transfer systems rely heavily on formula-based transfers and on cost-sharing, specific-purpose grants made in a transparent environment.

Perhaps the most important lesson for developing countries lies within the broad range of practices. By studying the highly diverse arrangements used to provide public services across the various states, policy makers may find a particular arrangement that would be most fitting for their country.

Notes

1. The U.S. Census Bureau, an office in the Department of Commerce, undertakes a "census of governments" every five years (those years ending in 2 and 7). Although the 2002 Census of Governments had been completed, much of the detailed financial data had not yet been released when this chapter was prepared; therefore, we relied on both the 2002 and the 1997 data for this discussion. See the U.S. Census Bureau Web site, http://www.census.gov.
2. For an overview of local government in the United States, including its historical development, see Miller (2002) or Ostrom, Bish, and Ostrom (1988).
3. Even the term *county* is not used consistently throughout the United States. In the state of Louisiana, this type of local government is called a *parish*, and in Alaska, the term *borough* is used.
4. Because the District of Columbia is not a state, it has no elected representatives with voting powers in either the House of Representatives or the Senate of the United States. Committees of both houses of Congress oversee the actions of the locally elected officials who govern the District of Columbia.
5. A variant on this approach in which the mayor has the authority to appoint department heads is a form of mayor-council arrangement sometimes called a *weak mayor-council* form. Under this approach, heads of major departments—for example, tax collection, police, tax assessment—are chosen directly by the electorate. Thus, the mayor is considerably less powerful. Colonial era towns of New England generally followed this format.
6. Although a bit dated, the Advisory Commission on Intergovernmental Relations compilation (ACIR 1993) of each state's laws with respect to the structure and administration of local government provides a good indication of the substantial differences in governmental structures across states. Unfortunately, the U.S. Congress decided to stop funding the ACIR in 1995. Before that, it had been the primary single source of information on intergovernmental relations in the United States.
7. It is, in fact, common in the United States for the judicial branch of government, at both the federal and state levels, to reach decisions that have significant effects on local governments. There have even been instances in which a court has taken over the administration of a local government service. See, for example, O'Leary and Wise (1991, 2003).

8. Note that even the designation of fiscal years differs not only across different states but also by different types of subnational government. Many states have July 1–June 30 fiscal years, but there are important exceptions; for example, in New York, the state's fiscal year is April 1–March 31. Likewise, local governments may have fiscal years that coincide with calendar years or that may start and end at other times. The data in the tables here refer to fiscal years that concluded at any point during 2000.

9. Alaska is a very special case, primarily because of its revenue structure, as discussed later.

10. Even though the taxes are administered by the state government, they are considered local taxes if the local government has the power to decide whether they should be levied and, in some instances, what rates to impose. This perspective differs from that for shared taxes. Shared taxes are levied by the higher level of government, which then shares the proceeds with local governments. In this way, shared taxes are effectively equivalent to fiscal transfers, because the policy decision is made by the higher level of government.

11. Of course, differences still occur in the degree to which a state exports its tax burdens to nonresidents; these differences are not reflected in the ratios.

12. For more specific information on these state and local taxes in the United States, see the chapters by Cornia and Wheeler (1999), Fisher (1999), Mikesell (1999), and Wallace and Edwards (1999) that are found in Hildreth and Richardson (1999).

13. These and other features of the statutory base of property taxes in the United States (circa 1991) are found in U.S. Census Bureau (1994).

14. States usually assess the value of utilities and railroads, however, in part because of the more technical nature of the process, but also to ensure that local jurisdictions do not attempt to greatly overassess these properties.

15. Other revenue instruments have also been used, of course. Particularly important among those instruments are charges imposed on the users of certain local government services.

16. Information on the basic structures of state-level taxes, including current rates, can be found at the Web site of the Federation of Tax Administrators (http://www.taxadmin.org/).

17. The federal government's Internal Revenue Service and state tax collections agencies share information to improve compliance with both federal and state income taxes.

18. The local excise tax on cigarettes in New York State is limited to the city of New York. The statute authorizing the city to impose such a tax is like most similar statutes in that it does not explicitly name the city of New York but, rather, allows any New York municipality with a population greater than 1 million to impose this type of tax. Of course, the state has only one municipality with that large a population.

19. In 1973, the federal government introduced a revenue-sharing program that transferred funds to all state and general-purpose local governments, but the program was discontinued in 1987.

20. A full list of the methods used by each state in distributing the proceeds of the motor fuel tax can be found on the U.S. Federal Highway Administration Web site (http://www.fhwa.dot.gov/ohim/hwytaxes/2001/tab6_toc.htm).

21. For a recent analysis of federal government transfer programs, see Gamkhar (2002).

22. Current prices of municipal bonds, like other similar debt instruments, fluctuate with current interest rates—increasing if interest rates fall and decreasing if interest rates rise.

23. See Finkler (2001) for a detailed discussion of local government financial management, including discussions of financial reporting requirements faced by local governments.

References

ACIR (Advisory Commission on Intergovernmental Relations). 1993. *State Laws Governing Local Government Structure and Administration.* Washington, DC: ACIR.

Behrens, John O. 1998. "Levels and Dispersion of Assessment Ratios in Taxable Property Values and the Courts." In *Proceedings of the Ninety First Annual Conference of the National Tax Association,* 241–45. Washington, DC: National Tax Association.

Blanchard, Lloyd A., and William. D. Duncombe. 1999. "Tax Policy and Public School Finance." In *Handbook on Taxation,* ed. W. Bartley Hildreth and James A. Richardson, 345–400. New York: Marcel Dekker.

Cornia, Gary C., and Gloria E. Wheeler. 1999. "The Personal Property Tax." In *Handbook on Taxation,* ed. W. Bartley Hildreth and James A. Richardson, 119–48. New York: Marcel Dekker.

Federation of Tax Administrators. 1997. *State Sales Taxation of Services—1996 Update.* Washington, DC: Federation of Tax Administrators.

Finkler, Steven. 2001. *Financial Management for Public, Health, and Not-for-Profit Organizations.* Upper Saddle River, NJ: Prentice Hall.

Fisher, Glenn W. 1999. "The Real Property Tax." In *Handbook on Taxation,* ed. W. Bartley Hildreth and James A. Richardson, 91–118. New York: Marcel Dekker.

Foster, Kathryn A. 1997. *The Political Economy of Special-Purpose Government.* Washington, DC: Georgetown University Press.

Gamkhar, Shama. 2002. *Federal Intergovernmental Grants and the States.* Northampton, MA: Edward Elgar.

Hildreth, W. Bartley, and James A. Richardson, ed. 1999. *Handbook on Taxation.* New York: Marcel Dekker.

Johnson, Craig. 1999. "Tax Increment Debt Finance: An Analysis of the Mainstreaming of a Fringe Sector." *Public Budgeting and Finance* 19 (1): 47–67.

Leigland, James. 1994. "Public Authorities and Their Use by State and Local Governments." *Journal of Public Administration Research and Theory* 4 (4): 521–44.

McCabe, Barbara C. 2000. "Special-District Formation among the States." *State and Local Government Review* 32 (2): 121–31.

Mikesell, John. 1999. "Sales Taxes." In *Handbook on Taxation,* ed. W. Bartley Hildreth and James A. Richardson, 71–90. New York: Marcel Dekker.

Miller, David Y. 2002. *The Regional Governing of Metropolitan America.* Boulder, CO: Westview Press.

O'Leary, Rosemary, and Charles Wise. 1991. "Public Managers, Judges, and Legislators: Redefining the 'New Partnership.'" *Public Administration Review* 51 (4): 316–27.

———. 2003. "Breaking Up Is Hard to Do: The Dissolution of Judicial-Administrative Partnerships." *Public Administration Review* 63 (2): 177–91.

Ostrom, Vincent, Robert Bish, and Elinor Ostrom. 1988. *Local Government in the United States*. San Francisco: Institute for Contemporary Studies.

Stephens, Ross G., and Nelson Wikstrom. 1998. "Trends in Special Districts." *State and Local Government Review* 30 (2): 129–38.

Tennessee Advisory Commission on Intergovernmental Relations. 2000. *State Shared Taxes in Tennessee*. Nashville: Tennessee Advisory Commission on Intergovernmental Relations.

U.S. Census Bureau. 1994. *1992 Census of Governments, Vol. 2, Taxable Property Values, No. 1, Assessed Valuations for Local General Property Taxation*. Washington, DC: U.S. Government Printing Office. http://www.census.gov/prod/2/gov/gc/gc92_2_1.pdf

———. 2000a. *1997 Census of Governments, Vol. 4, No. 1, Public Education Finances; No. 2, Finances of Special District Governments; No. 3, Finances of County Governments; No. 5, Finances of Municipal and Township Governments*. Washington, DC: U.S. Government Printing Office. http://www.census.gov/govs/www/cog.html.

———. 2000b. *Statistical Abstract of the United States, 2000*. Washington, DC: U.S. Government Printing Office.

———. 2002. *2002 Census of Governments, Vol. 1, No. 1, Government Organization*. Washington, DC: U.S. Government Printing Office. http://www.census.gov/prod/2003pubs/gc021x1.pdf

———. 2003a. *Federal Aid to States for Fiscal Year 2002*. Washington, DC: U.S. Government Printing Office.

———. 2003b. *Government Finances 1999–2000*. Washington, DC: U.S. Government Printing Office.

Wallace, Sally, and Barbara Edwards. 1999. "Personal Income Tax." In *Handbook on Taxation*, ed. W. Bartley Hildreth and James. A. Richardson, 149–90. New York: Marcel Dekker.

Index

horizontal imbalances, 249–52
income tax system, 239–43
independent agents, orders of
    government as, 253–54
legal framework, decentralization,
    226–30, 260n
local own-source taxation, 236–38
local tax structures, 239t
middle tier, local government, 232b
organizational framework,
    decentralization, 226–30, 260n
personal income tax, 239–40
property tax, 239, 260n
solidarity equalization schemes, 251t
structure of local governments,
    230–34, 260n
subsidies, 251t
tax administration, collection, 240–41,
    261n
tax sharing, 241–42
taxes, decentralized, 238–39, 260n
vertical imbalances, 260n
welfare services, importance of, 235t
Nordic model, local governance, central-
    local relations, 21–22
North American model, local
    governance, central-local relations,
    26
North Rhine-Westphalia, 136
Northern Ireland. See United Kingdom
Norway, 205, 207, 251, 254

Oita, 173
Okayama, 173
Okinawa, 174
Operating revenues for local authorities,
    composition of, 32f
Osaka, 173

Parks
    Germany, 119
    local government role, 8
    United Kingdom, 284
    United States, 328–29, 332
Penalties, Canada, 51
Permits, Canada, 51
Personal income tax, Germany, 118

Physical disabilities, individuals with,
    United Kingdom, 284
Poland, 205, 207
Police protection, 8
    Germany, 119
    local government role, 8
    United Kingdom, 269, 278, 293, 295
    United States, 328–29
Port facilities, United States, 332
Portugal, 205, 207
Primary agents of citizens, local
    government as, 20
Property registration tax, France, 93, 99
Property sale, United States, 332
Property tax
    Canada, 50–51, 63, 65
    France, 93, 97–98
    Germany, 118, 126, 144n–145n
    Japan, 157–58
    Nordic countries, 239
    United States, 333
Protective inspection, United States, 328
Protective services
    Canada, 46, 48, 55, 58
    United Kingdom, 284, 292, 295
Public choice, 10–11
Public health, local government role, 8
Public institutions, France, 108
Public management, 9–10

Quasi-public institutions, France, 108

Railways, Germany, 119
Recreation
    Canada, 46, 48, 55, 58
    United Kingdom, 284
    United States, 328–29, 332
Refuse collection, local government role, 8
Refuse disposal, local government role, 8
Regional planning
    Canada, 46, 55, 58
    development, Canada, 48
    local government role, 8
Rent allowance, United Kingdom, 293
Rentals, Canada, 51
Resource conversation, Canada, 48
Responsibilities of local governments, 5–20